THE SABBATH IN THE CLASSICAL KABBALAH

THE LITTMAN LIBRARY OF
JEWISH CIVILIZATION

Dedicated to the memory of
LOUIS THOMAS SIDNEY LITTMAN
who founded the Littman Library for the love of God
and as an act of charity in memory of his father
JOSEPH AARON LITTMAN
יהא זכרם ברוך

'Get wisdom, get understanding:
Forsake her not and she shall preserve thee'
PROV. 4:5

The Littman Library of Jewish Civilization is a registered UK charity
Registered charity no. 1000784

The Sabbath in the Classical Kabbalah

ELLIOT K. GINSBURG

Oxford · Portland, Oregon
The Littman Library of Jewish Civilization

The Littman Library of Jewish Civilization

Chief Executive Officer: Ludo Craddock
Managing Editor: Connie Webber

PO Box 645, Oxford OX2 0UJ, UK
www.littman.co.uk

Published in the United States and Canada by
The Littman Library of Jewish Civilization
c/o ISBS, 920 NE 58th Avenue, Suite 300
Portland, Oregon 97213-3786

First published 1989 by the State University of New York Press, Albany
First published in paperback 2008
First digital on-demand edition 2008

A catalogue record for this book is available from the British Library

The Library of Congress catalogued the hardback edition as follows:

Ginsburg, Elliot Kiba.
The Sabbath in the classical Kabbalah
(SUNY series in Judaica)
Bibliography: p. Includes index.
1. Sabbath. 2. Cabala—History. 3. Judaism—Customs and practices.
4. Jewish art and symbolism. I. Title II. Series.
BM685.G49 1989 296.4'1 87–26764

ISBN 978–1–904113–43–0

Printed in Great Britain by Lightning Source UK, Milton Keynes,
and in the United States by Lightning Source US, La Vergne, Tennessee

This book has been printed digitally and produced in a
standard specification in order to ensure its continuing availability.

Contents

Preface

All . . . life should be a pilgrimage to the seventh day.

A. J. Heschel, *The Sabbath:* 89

It would be no exaggeration to call the Sabbath the day of the Kabbalah. On the Sabbath, the light of the upper world bursts into the profane world in which man lives during the six days of the week. The light of the Sabbath endures into the ensuing week, growing gradually dimmer, to be relieved in the middle of the week by the rising light of the next Sabbath. It is the day on which a special pneuma, the Sabbath-soul, enters into the believer, enabling him to participate in the right way in this day, which shares more than any other day in the secrets of the pneumatic world.

G. Scholem, *On the Kabbalah and its Symbolism:* 139

The nature of ritual and mythological symbols has been a major topic of discussion in the fields of religion, folklore, and anthropology in recent years. Within the study of Judaism new attention has been drawn to the tradition of the Kabbalists, the Jewish mystics of the later Middle Ages, who have been well-known for their creativity in symbol-making and exegesis. Their radical re-reading of the earlier Jewish tradition has been called a model of mythopoeic revision, a revision rooted in a world-view that stressed the interrelation of all worlds and levels of being.

This study is concerned with the Kabbalistic re-reading of the Sabbath over the course of its classical period, from the late twelfth to the early sixteenth centuries. The historical significance of the topic, broadly speaking, rests on three factors: the centrality of the Sabbath within classical Judaism, the centrality of the Sabbath within the Kabbalistic mythos, and the Kabbalists' influence on the popular understanding of Shabbat in later Judaism.

The Sabbath has been one of the most significant and beloved institutions of Jewish life since late antiquity. The importance of the Sabbath is attested by the sheer number of legal dicta, imaginative works, songs, and rituals which pertain to the day. In its Rabbinic formulation, Sabbath-observance was both a hallmark of Jewish social identity, a sine qua non for membership in the Covenant Community, and a sacramental institution with salvific import. The classical Kabbalists were heirs to and revisors of the multiform Rabbinic legacy. Over a period of several centuries, they developed a rich body of ritual and myth that articulated a fresh vision—a mythopoeic revision—of the holy day. Several examples of this include the reformulation of the Sabbath as a mystical marriage ceremony; the Sabbath as a spiritual Axis around which Time and Cosmos are organized; and the Sabbath as a festival of spiritual transformation marked by the devotee's assimilation of the aforementioned Sabbath-soul. Owing largely to the efforts of the Safed Kabbalists and their subsequent popularizers, this mystical understanding of the Sabbath was transmitted to, and assimilated by, virtually every Jewish community.

Despite the acknowledged historical import of the Kabbalistic Sabbath and the richness of its literary sources, there has been relatively little scholarly study of its classical (pre-Safed) dimensions.[1] It is just this formative period that will concern us here. Throughout the study, I shall analyze the historical development of the mystical Sabbath in its various tradition strands, assess its relation to earlier understandings of Shabbat, and construct a theoretical framework for the interpretation of its dense myth-ritual structure. The format of the study is as follows:

The Introductory chapter consists of an historical overview of classical Kabbalah and an outline of its symbolic universe (with special emphasis on the sefirotic system). Its express purpose is to introduce the non-specialist to the varieties of Kabbalistic expression and to provide an historical framework in which the Sabbath material may be assessed.

Chapter 1 (The Symbolism of the Kabbalistic Sabbath) opens with a conceptual overview of the pre-Kabbalistic Sabbath and the major aspects of its Kabbalistic re-reading. The remainder of the chapter is devoted to historical and phenomenological analyses of the key mythic motifs which underlie Sabbath-observance and which lend it special resonance. Among the motifs studied are the Sabbath as source of cosmic blessing, the Sabbath as perfected Time, the drama of divine restoration (as reflected in the myth of *hieros gamos*), and the drama of human transformation (as articulated in the motif of the Sabbath-soul). These multi-faceted motifs all bespeak the profound renewal which the Kabbalists experienced on the day.

Chapters 2 through 4 are focused on the Kabbalistic reinterpretation of Sabbath-ritual, which served as the primary means for dramatizing and effecting the Sabbath-mythos. Chapter 2, "Aspects of Meaning in Kabbalistic Ritual," is devoted to a theoretical discussion of the function and meaning of Kabbalistic ritual and the problematics of its interpretation. The extended typology provided in this chapter paves the way for the close study of several particularly dramatic rituals located on the Sabbath's margins: the rituals of preparation (discussed in chapter 3) and the rituals of separation (analyzed in chapter 4).

Finally, two brief appendices deal with specialized issues in the interpretation of Kabbalistic symbolism and ritual, again focusing on the case of Shabbat.

It should be noted that this book is part of a two-volume study of the mystical Sabbath prior to the Safed Renaissance. While *The Sabbath in the Classical Kabbalah* is a synthetic study drawn from a wide range of sources, its companion volume is a translation of and critical commentary to a single text, entitled *Sod ha-Shabbat* (The Mystery of the Sabbath), from the *Tola^cat Ya^caqov* of R. Meir ibn Gabbai (1507). His is a summary exposition, inclusive yet succinct, perhaps the finest systematic treatment of the Sabbath in classical Kabbalah. It is hoped that the reader of the present work will be inspired to encounter Meir ibn Gabbai's words, to enter the *PaRDeS* that is his book.

Note

1. The only extended study of the Sabbath in the classical Kabbalah is that of I. Tishby [*Mishnat ha-Zohar* 2:487–507]. He concentrates almost solely on the *Zohar* and its ancillary sources (late thirteenth-early fourteenth century) briefly alluding to such earlier authorities as the *Bahir* and Naḥmanides. E. Gottlieb's article in the *Encyclopedia Judaica* ("Sabbath: in Kabbalah") is exceedingly brief and devotes but three paragraphs to the classical tradition. Two other works of note, A. Green's "Sabbath as Temple" and A. J. Heschel's poetic evocation, *The Sabbath*, discuss several classical sources, but do so primarily in relation to other concerns. G. Scholem touches on the Zoharic Shabbat in *On the Kabbalah and its Symbolism*: 139–40, but is concerned primarily with its Safed celebration.

Acknowledgements

It is a pleasure to be able to acknowledge a debt of gratitude to the many people who have contributed to this work, who have challenged and encouraged me, and brought me to this season.

An earlier version of the present study, here substantially revised, was a doctoral dissertation under the direction of Arthur Green. Art has been a teacher and friend for many years; it is difficult to express how much I have learned from him. He introduced me to the field of Kabbalah and its symbolic universe and helped me refine my skills in textual interpretation. I thank Art for his painstaking and insightful reading of this work, for warmly but firmly pushing me to clarify my ideas, for his numerous helpful suggestions. He has given valiantly of his time, thought, and effort; I am ever grateful.

Two other members of my dissertation committee, Anne Matter and Laurence Silberstein, contributed a good deal as well. I have gained much from Larry's methodological acumen and from his friendship over the years. Anne has encouraged me throughout and has added a specially valuable perspective as a scholar of medieval Christian spirituality.

Several colleagues have been especially helpful in the recent stages of writing. Dr. Elliot Wolfson has shared his numerous insights into *Sefer ha-Rimmon* and Professors Moshe Idel, Ze'ev Gries, and Mark Verman have called several important sources to to my attention. My good friends Jeffrey Dekro and Dr. Morris Faierstein also deserve a note of gratitude. I thank Jeffrey for introducing me to the *Tolaᶜat Yaᶜaqov*, a work that looms large in these pages, and for his comments in the early stages of writing. I have learned much from studying with him. I thank Moish for sharing his vast knowledge and for his special brand of humor, which both enlightened and helped put matters in perspective.

Most of this book was written at Oberlin College. I am grateful to my colleagues in the Department of Religion and the Judaic and Near Eastern Studies Program, and to the wonderful students there, as well. Together they helped create a thoroughly enjoyable and stimulating intellectual environment, ideally suited to productive work.

I also wish to thank the following institutions for use of rare manuscripts and first editions of key works: the Jewish Theological

Seminary of America, the Bibliothèque Nationale in Paris, the Schocken Institute in Jerusalem, and especially, the Institute of Microfilmed Hebrew Manuscripts and the Gershom Scholem Library, both housed at the Jewish National and University Library at the Hebrew University. To their staffs: *yavo'u kullam ᶜal ha-berakhah.*

The Memorial Foundation for Jewish Culture, by granting me a dissertation fellowship for 1981–83, enabled me to lay the groundwork for this study. Two generous research grants from Oberlin College in the summers of 1985 and 1986 permitted me to travel to research libraries, here and abroad. Finally, a fellowship from the National Endowment for the Humanities enabled me to complete this and several related studies, while the National Foundation for Jewish Culture supplied a subvention grant facilitating publication. I acknowledge their support with gratitude.

William Eastman, my publisher at SUNY Press, has been consistently supportive and understanding, and Judy Block and Marilyn Semerad, my editors at SUNY Press, precise and discerning. David Green, friend and editor, offered additional advice and Professor Luis Fernandez, dear friend and computer-*maven,* shared his time and expertise just when it was most needed.

Finally, five people have contributed to this study in unique ways. My parents, Rose and Bernard Ginsburg, kindled within me the desire to learn and taught me the virtues of perseverance. Their love and untold sacrifice have cheered and sustained me.

My two little boys, Jacob Uri and Noah Eitan, were born while this book was being written; they have been a constant source of surprise and delight, *ᶜerev va-voqer ve-ẓohorayim!*

My wife Terri has shared with me this labor from beginning to end. She has proof-read significant parts of this work and helped me with organization. But those not inconsiderable tasks are but a small measure of her contribution. Without her understanding, her patience and her love, this work would be unthinkable. Without her sense of humor and her wisdom, it would have been far less bearable.

This book is in many ways *mattenat bikkurim,* an offering of first fruits. It is in love and gratitude that I dedicate it to Terri, *'aḥoti khallah.*

Tam ve-nishlam, done and completed
7 October 1988
ᶜErev Shabbat Bere'shit 5749
Oberlin, Ohio

Illustrations

Abbreviations

AJS Review	*Association for Jewish Studies Review*
AQ	Meir ibn Gabbai, *ʿAvodat ha-Qodesh*
ARN	*'Avot de-Rabbi Natan*
BN	Bibliothèque Nationale (Paris)
D. Matt	Daniel Matt, ed. *Zohar: The Book of Enlightenment*
EJ	*Encyclopedia Judaica* (Jerusalem)
HUCA	*Hebrew Union College Annual*
IR	Zohar, *'Idra' Rabba'*
IZ	Zohar, *'Idra' Zuṭa'*
JAAR	*Journal of the American Academy of Religion*
JJS	*Journal of Jewish Studies*
JNUL	Jewish National and University Library (Jerusalem)
JTSA	Jewish Theological Seminary of America (New York)
KS	*Kiryat Sefer*
Legends	Louis Ginzberg, *Legends of the Jews,* 7 vols.
M.	*Mishnah*
Major Trends	Gershom Scholem, *Major Trends in Jewish Mysticism*
Meḥqarim	Efraim Gottlieb, *Meḥqarim be-Sifrut ha-Qabbalah*
Mekh.	*Mekhilta' de-Rabbi Ishmael*
MGWJ	*Monatsschrift fuer Geschichte und Wissenschaft des Judentums*
Mid. R	*Midrash Rabbah* (including Gen. R for *Genesis Rabbah;* Ex. R for *Exodus Rabbah;* etc.)
MN	Zohar, *Midrash ha-Neʿlam*
MV	*Maḥzor Viṭri*
MZ	I. Tishby with F. Lachover, *Mishnat ha-Zohar,* 2 vols.
OK	Ṭodros ha-Levi Abulafia, *'Oẓar ha-Kavod*
OKS	G. Scholem, *On the Kabbalah and its Symbolism*
OZ	David ben Judah he-Ḥasid, *'Or Zaruʿa*
Pirqei Yesod	G. Scholem, *Pirqei Yesod be-Havanat ha-Qabbalah u-Semaleha*

PR	Moses Cordovero, *Pardes Rimmonim*
PRE	*Pirqei de-Rabbi 'Eliʿezer*
PRK	*Pesiqta' de-Rav Kahana'*
R.	Rabbi
RM	*Raʿaya' Meheimna'*
ShA	Joseph Karo, *Shulḥan ʿArukh*
SHeLaH	Isaiah Horowitz, *Shenei Luḥot ha-Berit*
ST	Zohar, *Sitrei Torah*
STM	Joseph of Hamadan, *Sefer Ṭaʿamei ha-Miẓvot*
Tanḥ.	*Tanḥuma'*
TB	Babylonian Talmud *(Talmud Bavli)*
TJ	Palestinian Talmud *(Talmud Yerushalmi)*
Tos.	*Tosefot*
Ṭur	Jacob ben Asher, *'Arbaʿah Ṭurim*
TY	Meir ibn Gabbai, *Tolaʿat Yaʿaqov*
TZ	*Tiqqunei ha-Zohar*
TZḤ	*Tiqqunei Zohar Ḥadash*
Ursprung	G. Scholem, *Ursprung und Anfange der Kabbala*
Z	*Zohar*
ZḤ	*Zohar Ḥadash*

N.B.: *Sod ha-Shabbat* refers to my translation of and critical commentary to Meir ibn Gabbai's treatise on the mystical Sabbath; this treatise is part of the larger work, *Tolaʿat Yaʿaqov* (TY).

Note on Transliteration and Orthography

א	’	ל	l
בּ	b	מ	m
ב	v	נ	n
ג	g	ס	s
ד	d	ע	ᶜ
ה	h	פּ	p
ו	v	פ	f
ז	z	ק	q
ח	ḥ	צ	ẓ
ט	ṭ	ר	r
י	y, i	שׁ	sh
כּ	k	שׂ	s
כ	kh	ת	t

◌ָ ◌ַ ◌ֲ	a	◌ִ	i
◌ֵ ◌ֶ ◌ֱ ◌ְ	e	◌ֹ וֹ ◌ֳ	o
		◌ֻ וּ	u

◌ְ only *sheva’ na*ᶜ is transliterated

Dagesh ḥazaq (forte) is indicated by doubling of the letter, except for the letter שׁ. Certain Hebrew nouns frequently used in English are spelled in accord with common English usage, most notably, Kabbalah. Diacritical marks for the *’alef* and ᶜ*ayin* have been omitted from names set in roman type. The letter ו, generally transliterated as *v*, has been rendered as *w* in exceptional cases, e.g., when indicating the Tetragammaton, commonly notated in English as YHWH. Finally, in several instances the letter ב has been transliterated as a single *b*: שׁבת, e.g., has been rendered *shabat* to enable the non-Hebrew reader to more readily see the etymological connection between that term and שׁבת, i.e., *shabbat*.

INTRODUCTION

Classical Kabbalah, Its History and Symbolic Universe

In recent years our view of Judaism has been significantly transformed, in no small measure due to the rediscovery and reappraisal of the Kabbalistic tradition. The great historians of Judaism who wrote in the second half of the nineteenth century tended to ignore this mystical stream, or else treated it with a mixture of embarrassment and vitriolic scorn. Heinrich Graetz, arguably the greatest of these scholars, took the latter approach. To quote from one representative assessment:

> The secret science of the Kabbala . . . began [in the 13th Century] to foment discord . . . to ensnare the intelligence and lead astray the weak. What it lacked in intrinsic truth and power of conviction, it endeavored to supply by presumptuousness . . . . [The Kabbalists] obscured the mental light, with which men of intellect [i.e., the rationalist philosophers], from Saadiah to Maimonides, had illumined Judaism, and substituted for a refined religious belief, fantastic and even blasphemous chimeras. The intellectual degradation of the Jews in the following centuries is to a large extent their work. They led astray both their own times and posterity through designed or unintentional imposition, and the injuries which were inflicted on Judaism are felt even at the present day. (*History of the Jews,* Vol. 4, pp. 1, 3)[1]

As new arrivals in a Western society that demanded Jewish acculturation, many nineteenth century historians were concerned that Judaism be portrayed as a familiar rather than foreign tradition, at least in its purported essence. As children of the Enlightenment, they were also influenced by regnant rationalist ideologies and Hegelian notions of historical progress which underscored the continual refinement of religion. These factors contributed to the downgrading of those elements within Judaism—to wit, Kabbalah—which were perceived as exotic, irrational, or antiquarian.[2]

The renewed appreciation of Kabbalah is largely due to the pioneering work of Gershom Scholem and his Jerusalem school, along with insights afforded by the psychology and history of religion.

Freed from the burden of apologetics that visited earlier scholars, Scholem and his successors have portrayed Kabbalah in a far more sympathetic light, discovering in its sources a genuine and vital religious impulse. While maintaining an impressive methodological rigor, they have deciphered and brought to light sundry mystical texts, reconstructed the social and spiritual worlds of its adepts, and charted the impact of Kabbalah on Jewish life.[3] This vast labor has led to a reconsideration not only of the mystical stream within Judaism but a marked broadening of our notions of Judaism as a whole. Arthur Green, an historian of Jewish mysticism, has noted:

> All those definitions of Judaism so popular in the nineteenth and early twentieth centuries, whether by "essential spirit" [or] by a few "irreducible principles" . . . meet their match as they confront the great variety of evidence that research into Jewish mysticism has unearthed.[4]

So influential has this research been that it is virtually inconceivable to write on the history of later medieval and early modern Jewish spirituality without some understanding of the Kabbalah.

The purpose of this chapter is to introduce the non-specialist to some of the broad contours of Kabbalah's historical development and to the nature of its symbolic universe.[5] This presentation should provide a conceptual framework for the subsequent treatment of the Kabbalistic Sabbath—its historical dimensions and its myth-ritual structure.

Kabbalah is the traditional and most commonly used term for the variegated stream of Jewish mysticism and esoteric theosophical speculation, especially as it developed from the late twelfth century onwards. Kabbalah embraces a wide variety of literatures and concerns ranging from techniques of meditation to ritual magic, from esoteric exegesis of Scripture to theories of language and soul. The term itself simply means 'reception' or 'tradition,' connoting a teaching that is handed down by a religious authority. Long applied to sacred teachings in general, it was first associated with specifically mystical insights in the late 1100's; by 1300 it had become almost exclusively associated with such insights, functioning as a rubric for the Jewish mystical tradition as a whole.

The term *Kabbalah* is exemplary in two ways: first, it indicates the conservative self-perception of most Kabbalists. They saw themselves not as radical innovators, but as revitalizers seeking to penetrate to the hidden heart of the Tradition, to lay bare what had 'always' existed. Secondly, the term *Kabbalah* reflects the direct, oral nature of transmission from teacher to disciple that typified the sharing of esoteric knowledge, especially in the movement's earliest years.

Following the lead of Moshe Idel, we may distinguish between two broad modes of classical Kabbalah: a relatively small 'ecstatic' current which cultivated a spiritual path leading to *unio mystica* and a larger, more ramified tradition whose primary goal was theosophy and frequently, theurgy. (Theosophy denotes experiential knowledge of the hidden life of divinity, whereas theurgy signifies the attempt to act on and influence divinity, to restore its primordial wholeness.) The theosophical Kabbalists—as M. Idel calls them—generally stopped short of claiming the radical absorption in God expressed in ecstatic Kabbalah. Rather, they attested to a mystical communion wherein some distinction between devotee and divinity was maintained, however tenuously.

The chief transformative goals of ecstatic and theosophical Kabbalists may also be contrasted. The former aimed at radical self-transformation, viz., the assumption of a prophetic state, while the latter, as has been noted, tended to focus on the perfection of the divine. Moreover, the ecstatics stressed the contemplative efforts of the private individual and frequently used techniques from outside the realm of halakhic (legal) praxis, such as permutations of divine names and musical chants. By contrast, the mystical efforts of the theosophical Kabbalists generally unfolded in a more public (and traditionally validated) setting—while performing *miẓvot* (the religious commandments), learning Torah, and engaging in communal prayer. As we shall briefly see, the two streams also held distinctive views concerning the hermeneutical enterprise, differing in their exegetical approach to Scripture and in their theories of language.[6] Still, it must be noted that this typification is broadly drawn and some mixing of traditions and approaches did occur.

Like Medieval Jewish philosophy, Kabbalah may be characterized as an esoteric ideology, a self-conscious reflection on the meaning of Judaism; the likes of which was not found in Talmudic writing. In the face of criticism from within—the sectarian Karaite critique of Rabbinite hermeneutics and authority—and the external critique of Judaism by Islamic and Christian philosophers, many members of the Rabbinite religious elite were thrust beyond the relatively unself-conscious faith of their forebears. As the exoteric meaning of certain aspects of the Tradition was rendered problematic, emphasis was placed on uncovering its 'true,' i.e., esoteric, significance. Tradition was conserved and deepened through systematic reinterpretation. G. Scholem has argued that the rationalist philosophers tended to use allegory as a primary means of interpreting Torah, harmonizing its concrete language with the abstractions of Greek-influenced metaphysics. (By allegory Scholem means the representation of an expressible something by means of another expressible something.) Many ecstatic Kabbalists were influenced by this approach and developed allegorical exegeses of Scripture to express their unitive goals. By contrast, the theosophical Kabbalists were symbol-makers, finding in the Torah and sacred literature a dense weave of ciphers pointing to a multivalent, hidden, ultimately inexpressible reality.[7] This notion needs further refinement.

Theosophical Kabbalah may be considered a symbolically oriented form of mysticism with a decided contemplative-intellectualist cast.[8] Seeking to pierce beyond the constraints of ordinary cognition, its adepts developed a new symbolic language that served both as translation of and occasion for their experience of the divine mysteries that permeated the world. The power of this language, to the Kabbalists' mind, was that it was rooted in the divine reality itself, beyond the reach of ordinary language and philosophy. Of all their extensive symbol-making activity, the most important and distinctive concerned those ciphers which the adepts called *sefirot.* Arthur Green has explained:

> The [Kabbalists'] efforts centered around the ten *sefirot,* a series of symbol clusters that represented both the succeeding stages in the on-going self-revelation of the hidden Godhead and the steps the adept might take (for their structure permeates all of reality, including the soul) in the attempt to return to him. By "symbol-clusters" we mean that a group of well-known objects or realities are placed together and represent the same stage in the divine world. That "rung," itself inexpressible, is then understood by association with the symbols that represent it. One such aspect of divinity, for example, is that which might best be referred to as "Understanding/Mother/Womb/Palace/Jubilee/End/Persimmon/Upper Garden/World-to-Come/Repentance/Joy." A few other terms could be added to the list. For convenience, this aspect of divinity is called by a single name *Binah* (understanding). The mystic was to contemplate the associations, seeing them both in the words of Scripture and in the happenings of human life. Such contemplation was to create a new attitude of mind, one in which the symbolic consciousness was to supplant ordinary thinking as the chief focus of the adept's mental life, leading him ever to rise higher, or penetrate more deeply, into a world of unending mystery. ("Mysticism and Religion": 70–71)

The Godhead described—or pointed to—by the sefirot is frequently one of dynamic movement and stunning complexity. As depicted in such classic works as the *Zohar,* it is a God of Becoming, rather than the static God of Being that typified Medieval rationalism. Aspects within the divine personality alternately emerge and are hidden, sparkle and flow, separate and couple, in a kind of complex internal choreography. What constitutes the special mythical structure of theosophical Kabbalah is that the infinite aspects under which God may be known are restricted to these ten fundamental categories, ten 'notes' through which the divine music may be transcribed and heard. The remarks on the sefirotic system will be amplified throughout this chapter, first in the historical discussion, and thereafter in more detailed, systematic fashion.

It should be noted that much of the influence enjoyed by the theosophical Kabbalists in the later Middle Ages stemmed from these symbol-making (and myth-making) talents. Unlike most philosophers and ecstatic Kabbalists, they were able to integrate their intellectual vision with the whole of the Judaic tradition, treating its texts and realia as dense multivocal symbols. They thereby succeeded in giving added sacramental significance to the pattern of religious praxis, the corpus of sacred teachings and lore, and the inner life of prayer.[9]

Although we shall have occasion to touch on ecstatic Kabbalah later in this chapter, the focus will be on theosophical Kabbalah, the mystical stream which most strongly influenced the understanding of Shabbat.

SECTION ONE: AN HISTORICAL OUTLINE OF CLASSICAL KABBALAH

Origins

The origins of Kabbalah constitute a complex puzzle that has not been fully solved by scholars. Although intriguing evidence has been uncovered suggesting a more venerable theosophic tradition, the dominant tendency has been to associate the beginnings of Kabbalah proper with the emergence of *Sefer ha-Bahir,* the *Book of Brightness,* in the intellectually charged Rabbinic culture of Languedoc (or western Provence), in the latter decades of the twelfth century. The *Bahir* is a lavishly mythic work, a pseudepigraphic *midrash* (exegesis of Hebrew Scripture) attributed to the late first century rabbi, Neḥuniah ben ha-Qanah. In its extant form it is of uneven literary quality: although it is suffused with powerful and often exalted religious imagery, from a stylistic perspective the book leaves much to be desired. All known versions are, in varying degrees, corrupt. Passages are often fragmentary and elliptical; certain sections which begin like conventional *midrashim* suddenly break off or eventuate in seeming gibberish. Scholem suggested that at least some of this confusion is intentional: in all likelihood, portions of the book have been censored to avoid charges of heresy.

The *Bahir* is clearly the work of several hands, reflecting different locales and periods. That is, some of the later strata reveal the influence of the Spanish Jewish neo-Platonist, Abraham Bar-Ḥiyya (early twelfth century); others, the esoteric concerns of contemporary German Ḥasidism (*Ḥasidut 'Ashkenaz*).[10] Many of the distinctive features of the *Bahir*—its unusual midrashic style, its theurgic and theological concerns—seem to derive from a more ancient Middle-Eastern setting, from certain magical and mystical texts of the Geonic period.[11] The more radical divine imagery employed through the bulk of the work raises the possibility of a Gnostic influence.[12] Unfortunately, a precise history of the book's compilation has eluded scholars to date.[13]

The themes treated in the *Bahir* run a relatively wide gamut, including mystical rationales for the miẓvot, mystical interpretations of prayer, esoteric symbolism of the Hebrew alphabet and Torah cantillation, and theosophical speculation on the mysteries of Creation and God's inner life. It is this theosophical concern that forms the heart of the book. For what is apparently the first time, sefirotic symbolism is employed in a distinctively Kabbalistic manner. The term *sefirot* had its origins in a much earlier form of Jewish speculation. For example, in the third to sixth century Palestinian cosgmogonic work, *Sefer Yeẓirah* (the "Book of Creation"), the sefirot had denoted the ten archetypal numbers, neo-Pythagorean principles, through which God helped order the world. In the *Bahir* however, the sefirot are conceived as potencies within the divine pleroma (*ha-male'*); they are stages of divine life as well as instruments through which God's power is revealed.

The three upper or most recondite sefirot are generally portrayed in intellectualist imagery—as thought, silence, logos, wisdom, Torah, and so forth—whereas the lower seven sefirot are more commonly symbolized in images drawn from botanical, moral, cosmological, and anthropomorphic terminology. That is, these sefirot are portrayed as trees, gardens, and fountains; as love, fear and righteousness; as water, fire, sky, and earth; as the head, arms, legs, phallus, and womb; and as a series of Biblical heroes: Abraham, Isaac, and David, to name a few. One of the most striking innovations is the inclusion of a distinctively feminine aspect within the Godhead, specifically associated with the tenth and last sefirah, perhaps best known under the name *Shekhinah* (divine immanence or Presence). *Shekhinah* assumes a kind of liminal role in the divine pleroma, alternately bound to and separated from the rest of the Godhead.[14]

The dynamic between the different sefirot is described in a wealth of images: for example, springs irrigate gardens; left and right sides align in a variety of balancing configurations. In a move seemingly unprecedented in Jewish sources, divinity is portrayed as an androgyne: divine wholeness is symbolized in the coupling of the masculine and feminine principles, the union of Daughter/Bride and King. Not only Israel but God is in need of restoration: redemption, in the *Bahir,* entails the overcoming of *Shekhinah*'s separation from the Godhead, Her continuous coupling with the masculine principle. To this end, the *Bahir* underscores the theurgic valence of human activity, emphasizing the notion that the inner life of divinity not only affects but is affected by human behavior. Sacred activity helps restore harmony on high.[15]

Although we do not know the identity of *Bahir's* redactors or its exact provenance, Scholem has argued that its teachings were preserved in the most orthodox of Rabbinic circles, the sophisticated school of R. Abraham ben David (hereafter RaBaD) of Posquieres, one of the leading halakhic authorities of his day. The intellectual-spiritual life of RaBaD's circle was extraordinarily vital, cross-fertilized by several major ideational currents. Its members practiced a highly developed form of halakhic discourse and were conversant with various trends in Jewish, Christian-Byzantine, and Arab neo-Platonism. Several members of this extended group were also engaged in an organized mode of pietism called *nezirut* whose fellows immersed themselves in the contemplative life on behalf of the rest of the community. Detached from active participation in society (though not from family life), these contemplatives may well have played a crucial role in the development of Kabbalah.[16]

The mystical activity in RaBaD's circle seems to have centered on theosophic contemplation of the mysteries of Creation (*Ma^caseh Bere'shit*) and on the development of various mystical interpretations of prayer. These text-centered endeavors were accompanied by instances of individual inspiration. Several sources reported a proliferation of heightened spiritual experiences, including *gilluyei 'Eliyahu* (revelations from Elijah), a time-honored way of referring to authentic inspiration. (Elijah was traditionally seen as the eternal witness, the messenger of religious consciousness throughout the ages, who both vouchsafes insights and serves as a representative of Rabbinic authority.)

As the nature of transmission was almost exclusively oral in the earliest years, only fragments of the RaBaD's own Kabbalistic teachings are extant. His son, Isaac the Blind (ca.1165–1235), is the first member of the circle whose Kabbalah emerges with any sense of clarity to modern scholars. By reputation he was a "master of prayer" and a pneumatic, reportedly able to discern the halo surrounding individuals and to tell the status of their souls. The literary evidence reveals that his mysticism was of a marked contemplative, intellectualist bent, evincing a neo-Platonic-philosophical rather than pictorial-mythic orientation. He was the first Kabbalist to speak of *'Ein Sof,* that hidden non-personal aspect of God, the indescribable Ground from which the sefirot emerge.[17] His sefirotic symbolism was largely conceptual and linguistic in nature, employing such terms as *Maḥshavah* (Thought), *Qol* (Sound), and *Dibbur* (Speech). The progressive emanation of the sefirot into the world was imaged as the process of articulation: the movement of divinity from Thought (the first sefirah) to Undifferentiated Sound to Speech (the final sefirah). In mystical prayer, Isaac taught, the adept retraces the process of emanation, from below to on high, as God's hidden inwardness is progressively approached. As the adept's thought ascends, it moves through the sefirotic realm rung by rung until it is finally absorbed in Divine Thought Itself.

Isaac the Blind's picture of the cosmos is one of organic unity. The sefirot are seen not only as intra-divine potencies[18] but as principles suffusing the lower worlds. A particular creation is bound to its sefirotic matrix through a quasi-magnetic force released through *ẓippiyah,* literally, 'gazing' or contemplation. As in neo-Platonism, all existence is said to come from divinity and to return to it. Isaac spoke of a continual two-way movement of egression and regression taking place in the universe: at every moment divine energy pulsates into the lower worlds and returns via contemplation; existence is forever returning to ontological unity and breaking forth into multiplicity.

Let us sum up. By 1200, Kabbalah could already be classified as *sefirotic* mysticism. Yet, the sefirotic symbolism of Isaac the Blind stands in stark contrast to that of the *Bahir*. The latter employs a boldly mythical, pictorial imagery whereas R. Isaac used largely abstract, speculative symbols. The dialectic between these two tendencies, between 'Gnostic' myth and neo-Platonic abstraction, was to play a considerable role in determining the face of Kabbalah in succeeding generations.[19]

Gerona Kabbalah

By 1200, Kabbalah had spread south of the Pyrenées to Catalonia and Aragon. Judah ben Yaqar, a Provençal-born rabbi and one of the earliest Kabbalists, was active in Barcelona after 1175. His commentary on the liturgy and benedictions (*Perush ha-Tefillot ve-ha-Berakhot*) contained a number of allusive sefirotic interpretations, some of which were explicated by later adepts.[20] A broader dissemination of Provençal traditions in the early thirteenth century was aided by two related factors:

(1) The familial and cultural ties long shared by Catalonian and Provençal Jewry. That is, Catalonian students regularly studied in the Provençal *yeshivot* of Narbonne, Lunel, and Posquieres, while residents of both regions spoke virtually the same language and shared a similar religious outlook.

(2) The regular movement of several Provençal-educated Kabbalists, among them R. Isaac's nephew, Asher ben David, between the two communities.

By the 1210's, Kabbalistic activity was centered in the then small Catalonian town of Gerona. Here Kabbalah became a full-fledged literary tradition, as disciples of Isaac the Blind published their master's teachings and wrote down their own *qabbalot* (traditions). The Gerona community included an astonishing array of mystical personalities, most of whom were in regular contact with each other. Among their number were poets (e.g., Meshullam ben Solomon da Pierra), sharp tongued polemicists who inveighed against the radically allegorizing tendencies of Jewish Averroists (e.g., Jacob bar Sheshet in *Meshiv Devarim Nekhoḥim*), mystics with a marked contemplative bent (e.g., Rabbis Ezra ben Solomon and Azriel) and moralist-pietists (like Jonah Gerondi).[21] Some of these men boldly claimed that the Kabbalistic teachings represented innovations, whereas others stressed the conservative nature of Kabbalah, according authoritative status only to units of received tradition (*qabbalot*). The most prominent figure—and the one who lent Kabbalah a sense of authority and prestige much as the RaBaD had done earlier—was Moses ben Naḥman (hereafter, RaMBaN: 1194–1270), a disciple of Judah ben Yaqar and the towering Rabbinic figure of his age. RaMBaN combined the active life with mystical contemplation, exoteric writing with esoteric teaching. Only a few of his written works deal extensively with Kabbalah, though he included mystical 'secrets' in his magisterial exoteric commentary on the Torah, often in a kind of code with the appended message, *ve-ha-mevin yavin:* the wise will understand. His circumspect locutions may well have served to arouse interest in the Kabbalah as much as to veil its precise meaning![22]

Like its personalities, the themes of Gerona Kabbalah were diverse, encompassing sefirotic theory, cosmogony, and speculations on the soul; contemplative prayer, mystical interpretation of the Torah and other sacred literature (e.g., the Talmudic legends), and mystical rationales for the miẓvot. In general, the Gerona literature reflects a synthesis of neo-Platonic-philosophical and 'Gnostic'-theosophical elements. Like R. Isaac's teachings, however, it has relatively little of the mythic imagery (and virtually none of the sexual symbolism) found in the *Bahir* and that later classic of the Spanish Kabbalah, the *Zohar*.

The publication of some of these Gerona teachings in book form triggered internal controversy. Until this point, Kabbalah had been a doubly esoteric movement, seeking to plumb the hidden depths of the Tradition while conveying these teachings in a fashion accessible only to initiates, in coded language and via oral transmission. Like their elitist counterparts, the philosophers, the Kabbalists felt no need to point out the problems of naive Judaism to the masses, and moreover, feared the consequences of Kabbalistic learning unmediated by a proper authority or guide. Although virtually all Gerona adepts wished to place some limits on the dissemination of Kabbalah, there were some who were willing to make certain teachings public. Isaac the Blind was alarmed by this trend and sent a sharply worded letter to Jonah Gerondi and RaMBaN, criticizing those who wished to make Kabbalah "public in the market places and streets." Fearing this would lead to misunderstanding and the perversion of the Tradition, he summoned his considerable authority and wrote:

> It was not my custom to [speak publicly] nor was it that of my father and his ancestors . . . They did not discuss this on the street . . . and I learned from their example.

> I hear that in Burgos they are speaking openly and in a confused way. From this it is clear that they have removed their hearts from the sublime and cut off the shoots [engaged in a heretical act].[23]

Although there are any number of Gerona Kabbalists worthy of explication,[24] discussion will be limited to R. Azriel, perhaps the most profound contemplative within the circle, and his view of mystical prayer. His comments revealed an intense inner life and a neo-Platonic turn of mind. For Azriel, prayer is the means whereby one returns the sacred Words to the divine Nothing (the uppermost sefirah) and so reaches the mystic threshold. The adept's experience corresponds to the ascending rungs on the sefirotic ladder. As in Isaac the Blind's schema, Speech gives way Thought and finally, to that which is beyond expression, the mystical Nihil. Prayer is also seen—for the first time in the Kabbalah—as the return of the human will to the divine Will or *Raẓon,* another name for the highest rung. As one cleaves to *Raẓon,* the human will is first annihilated and then renewed, filled with the power of divine Life. This dialectical moment is at the heart of the devotee's mystical tranformation.[25]

Kabbalistic prayer is also given a distinctly magical, theurgic valence, transforming not only the devotee but the Godhead. Prayer promotes the unification of the sefirotic antimonies, or in Azriel's terminology, *hashva'ah.*[26] He described this mysterious process:

> Unification is when the light disappears and darkness comes, and when the darkness disappears and the light sparkles. This indicates that the Lord is unified amidst all permutations.[27]

Evincing a kind of mystical experience describable only in the language of paradox, he explained that at the uppermost rung of divinity, the 'Is' is equivalent to the mystical Naught. All the polarities and multiplicities that characterize ordinary perception are overcome—"rendered indistinguishable"—as they reach their primal Source.[28]

Other Trends in Thirteenth Century Kabbalah

By the mid-thirteenth century, Kabbalah had spread beyond the northeast corner of Spain into Navarre and Castile. Gerona tradition maintained a strong influence through the teachings of RaMBaN and, thereafter, two of his disciples, R. Solomon ben Adret (RaSHBa) and Isaac ben Ṭodros. Alongside this stream, several other

Kabbalistic currents developed which, rather than synthesizing the mythic-Gnostic and philosophical strands in Kabbalah, emphasized one side or the other. Mention might be made of two highly independent Kabbalists who betrayed a rationalist influence while lessening the emphasis on sefirotic nomenclature. The first, Isaac ibn Latif, attempted to self-consciously synthesize Kabbalah, Maimonidean philosopy, and neo-Platonism, not only of the Christian Byzantine stripe (as in Gerona) but also the Arabic tradition. Ibn Latif saw philosophy as the necessary precursor to mystical activity, but wrote that intellectual understanding reaches only unto the 'Backside' of divinity. The divine countenance itself may only be disclosed in supra-intellectual ecstasy, where the human will stands before the Primal Will.[29]

A second Kabbalist, Abraham Abulafia (1240–92), was a highly creative adept, graced with charismatic powers and a propagandizing talent. An itinerant seeker, Abulafia was active not only in his native Castile, but in Catalonia, Palestine, Greece, Italy, and Sicily, where he apparently spent his final years. Abulafia was influenced by sources as diverse as the Gerona Kabbalah, Maimonidean notions of prophecy, the letter mysticism of *Ḥasidei 'Ashkenaz,* and, in all likelihood, Sufism.[30] His own Kabbalah was ecstatic rather than speculative-theosophical in nature and included a highly developed exegetical method, freer and more dynamic than the approaches favored in the Provençal and Gerona circles.

Abraham Abulafia's mystical theory is a striking mixture of rationalism and emotionalism. The adept seeks to "untie the knots" that chain the soul to material forms, so that it may merge with the cosmic stream of life. This goal is reached through several stages of meditation. Philosophical contemplation and meditation on the ten sefirot form the preliminary stages of this quest. But the heart of Abulafia's method is *Ḥokhmat ha-Ẓeruf,* a means of meditating on and associatively recombining the letters of the sacred Hebrew alphabet. In so doing, the soul is liberated from ordinary perceptions, so that at length, the devotee may simultaneously confront his True Self and behold the Divine. Unio mystica is thereby attained, "he and He becoming one entity."[31]

Abraham Abulafia's meditative technique may better be grasped by focusing on his approach to exegesis. As M. Idel has shown, the adept essentially 'deconstructs' the Biblical text, atomizing the weave of sentences and words into their elemental letters. Indeed, only through this obliteration of social language—the exoteric aspect of

Scripture—can the primal language of divine Names, the pure essence of Torah, be recovered. The adept variously chants, writes, silently meditates on the letter combinations, reconstituting Torah and uncovering its divine core. This radical linguistic transformation creates a parallel transformation of the adept's consciousness. As the ordinary cognition founded on social language is overcome, the mystic's mind is said to become receptive to higher knowing, the influx of divine inspiration. A prophetic state of consciousness is reached, one that, Abulafia suggested, replicates Sinaitic experience. Indeed, he made the radical claim that one can authoritatively interpret or recover Torah only while in such a prophetic state, imbued with a "divine intellect."[32]

In its goals, the ecstatic Kabbalah of Abraham Abulafia recalled (and audaciously extended) the Maimonidean doctrine of prophecy whereby the human and divine intellects temporarily merge. In its techniques, Abulafia's Kabbalah has been called a Judaized *Yoga*, replete as it is with breathing exercises, postures, and highly developed forms of recitation and meditation.

Abulafia was the rare Kabbalist who published his meditative techniques in detail and provided autobiographical information concerning his mystical experiences. This material, only portions of which are extant, is invaluable to the historian of religion, but did not sit well with many of the more esoterically inclined Kabbalists. Abulafia's propagandizing efforts, along with his Messianic activism (culminating in an abortive mission to the Pope), made him one of the more controversial and criticized figures in the annals of Jewish Mysticism. Nonetheless, Abraham Abulafia's teachings exerted an important influence on classical Kabbalah, especially among devotees of Near Eastern, Byzantine, and Italian origin.[33]

Alongside these philosophically influenced trends coursed a Castilian stream of Kabbalah that evinced a mythic-gnostic mind-set unfettered by philosphical conceptions. This circle, sometimes called *ha-ma*ᶜ*amiqim* (those who delve deeply) by contemporary authorities and "the Gnostic reaction" by Gershom Scholem, consisted primarily of the brothers Jacob and Isaac ben Jacob ha-Kohen of Soria and their pupil, Moses of Burgos.[34] The two brothers, who flourished in ca. 1260–80, travelled widely in Spain and Provence collecting sundry Kabbalistic and esoteric traditions, most of which are preserved as pseudepigrapha and which may readily be distinguished from the Gerona tradition. Whereas the latter tended to stress contemplative and theosophic (i.e., sefirotic) concerns, the Castilian circle focused on extra-sefirotic themes: on the angelic worlds and most strikingly, on the demonic realm and the accompanying problem of evil. Whereas the Gerona Kabbalists usually employed an abstract symbolic language, relegating myth to a secondary role, the Castilians wrote in an extravagantly mythic vein. Moreover, although not eschewing speculative concerns entirely, these Kabbalists contributed to the growth of the magical element in the tradition, preserving theurgic teachings not known in the Gerona circle.

In the *Bahir* and Gerona Kabbalah, the problem of evil had played a relatively minor role. In contrast to the neo-Platonic notion of evil as the absence of good, most early Kabbalists had concluded that evil was an ontologically real force, a valence of limitation and death, whose roots are in the Godhead itself. (Most commonly, evil was associated with the sefirah *Gevurah,* the power of judgment.) Within divinity, evil did not have a destructive capacity because it was balanced by its sefirotic antipode, the root of goodness and life, *Ḥesed.* But outside the divine realm, as unity gave way to differentiation and multiplicity, evil became substantiated as an independent force. In most Gerona sources, evil's power was thought to wax and wane in direct relation to human action.

The Castilian circle was more radical in its views. These Kabbalists granted evil the status of a counter-emanation. According to the dominant myth, evil emerged from God during the turbulence of Creation, soon taking on an independent existence over against Him. Evil is depicted in blatantly dualistic terms: as *Siṭra' 'Aḥra'* (the Other Side) and as *ha-'aẓilut ha-sema'lit* (the Emanation of the Left). In the writings of Moses of Burgos, this realm was arrayed as a complete system of ten counter-sefirot. From the onset of Creation, he wrote, these dark emanations have engaged in constant battle with the forces of holiness. Unlike the *Zohar,* which was strongly influenced by these mythological conceptions, the 'Castilian Gnostics' regularly indulged in lavish personifications of the powers in the evil domain, resorting on occasion to earlier demonological belief, and calling the potencies of the Emanation of the Left by proper names.[35] In giving mythic expression to the problems of evil—its reality and horror—these adepts touched on widespread human fears that the sophisticated medieval philosophers ignored. The entry of these demonological concerns into Jewish mysticism played no small role in the popular success Kabbalah later attained.

It should be noted that the Castilians' concern with the Emanation of the Left and the myriad angelic worlds did not preclude individual mystical or visionary experiences. The Kohen brothers' father, the elder R. Jacob, who founded this 'Gnostic' school, wrote *Sefer ha-'Orah* ("The Book of Light"). Based on visions "accorded him in heaven," it contains a striking wealth of mythic images and symbols not known in other sources.[36]

All in all, consideration of these Castilian writings—along with the teachings of Isaac ibn Latif and Abraham Abulafia—reveals the multifaceted nature of Kabbalah in the mid-to-late 13th Century. Gershom Scholem has written that they are striking examples of how "an entirely new Kabbalah could be created side by side with the earlier one and it is as if each one of them speaks on a different plane." (*Kabbalah:* 57)

But the lines of demarcation were not rigidly drawn. From the 1270's on, there were Castilian Kabbalists who integrated several of these mystical currents.[37] For example, R. Ṭodros ha-Levi Abulafia, spiritual leader of Castilian Jewry, synthesized the Gerona tradition with imagery pioneered in the Gnostic reaction. Joseph Giqatilia assimilated first the Kabbalah of Abraham Abulafia and then various theosophical trends. But the richest synthesis, and the fateful one from a historical point of view, was that accomplished by Moshe de Leon of Guadalajara, the author of the "Bible of Spanish Kabbalah," the *Zohar*.

The Zohar

The *Zohar*, the *Book of Splendor* or *Enlightenment*, represents a new departure in Kabbalistic literature both in terms of the range of material treated and the boldness of mythic imagination exhibited. The earlier Kabbalistic sources tended to consist of terse allusions and discrete interpretations, written in a kind of shorthand. With the *Zohar* there is, for the first time, a voluminous work, a broad canvas of symbolic interpretation and speculation covering the whole world of Judaism as it appeared to its author. The discussion tends to cluster about two poles: the life of the divine, reflected in symbols in the created world and in the Torah; and secondly, the situation of the Jew and his fate in this world and the world of souls.

In its inspired, sometimes rambling way—for the *Zohar*'s spirit is antithetical to systematization—Moshe de Leon discussed mystical experience and sefirotic theosophy, the inner meaning of Torah and the life of the miẓvot. Primitive and highly sophisticated elements interweave. Passages on chiromancy and physiognomy co-exist with philosophically influenced allegory, linguistic symbolism with demonology. The fullness of sacred history is plumbed for recondite meaning. The mysteries of Creation—the progressive unfolding of divinity—are probed time and again, seen in endless variation. Israel's saga, its origin and role in the cosmos, its Exile and ultimate Redemption are given dramatic expression. Moreover, veiled Messianic speculation and social criticism, angelology and theodicy, mystical psychology and anthropology—all find their place in the *Zohar*'s pages. Gershom Scholem has noted:

> The deepening and broadening of a symbolic view of Judaism was very daring in an age when the Kabbalists still preserved in some measure the esoteric character of their ideas. (*Kabbalah:* 58)

Much of the *Zohar*'s appeal stems from its author's seemingly boundless mythic imagination. First of all, Moshe de Leon gave the sefirotic universe added density and emotional resonance, transmuting the rather abstract, intellectualist imagery of Gerona Kabbalah into affective myth. Sefirotic symbols that served as static images in the earlier literature are transformed into dynamic events, developed dramas. In addition, new clusters of symbols born of de Leon's imaginative reading of textual sources, greatly expand the sefirotic lexicon, extending the webs of significance, lengthening the chains of association.[38]

A subtle shift in sefirotic focus may also be noted. Whereas many of the Gerona Kabbalists concentrated on the upper or intellectual sefirot, new emphasis is placed on the lower, more active sefirot, especially on *Shekhinah,* the divine Female. The expansion of the feminine element in divinity remains one of the most interesting facets of Zoharic Kabbalah from a psychological point of view and was surely a factor contributing to its later popularity.[39]

Although deeply conservative—in the sense that the authority of the Torah and miẓvot were affirmed and placed in a cosmic setting—Moshe de Leon did not shy away from exploring radical notions regarding God's inner workings. Perhaps the most striking passages are found in the *'Idrot* sections, where de Leon engaged in a rather shocking form of anthropomorphism. The mystic focuses on the divine Corpus, contemplating the hollows of God's skull with its myriad inner worlds, His white hairs and beard, His 'faces' (*parẓufin*) or symbolic configurations. Each of these aspects signify a particular shading within the divine personality. It is no wonder that *'Idra' Rabba'* begins with a pointed warning against taking these images literally.[40] By utilizing such imagery, Scholem suggests, the author was straining to find an adequate God-language, to provide an "accurate allusion to that which is held to be beyond all images".[41]

Another striking feature of Zoharic theosophy is its explict use of sexual and erotic imagery. The unfolding of the sefirotic world is often imaged in terms of procreation: the bringing forth of 'life' from the divine womb. More daring is the intermittent genital imagery, especially the phallic symbolism associated with the ninth sefirah *Yesod,* the conveyor of divine blessing to *Shekhinah* and the worlds below.[42] Sexual love is a motif that finds a central place in the *Zohar*'s pages; it is no exaggeration to say that Moshe de Leon discovered the mystery of sex within the Godhead Itself. Perhaps the most outstanding cipher for divine harmony and completion is *hieros gamos,* the sacred marriage and union of the divine Male, *Tif'eret,* and the divine Female, *Shekhinah*. Through this loving union, the divine antimonies are overcome, pristine androgyny recovered, and earthly blessing—the fruit of their coupling—brought forth.[43] As Scholem notes, it is as though a kind of pagan mythology—the stuff of pre-Biblical religion—"were resurrected in the heart of mystical Judaism." (*Major Trends:* 228)

The language of the *Zohar* played an important role in making many of these radical notions acceptable. As elaborated below, the book was written in a strange, deliberately archaic pseudo-Aramaic, and its solemn, impressive tones served to obscure many of the bold ideas expressed in it.[44]

The *Zohar* is not a book in the usual sense of the term, but in Gershom Scholem's words "a complete body of literature which has been united under an inclusive title." (*Kabbalah:* 213) Scholem has identified well over twenty discrete strata, some of which are extant only in fragmentary form. The earliest stratum, the philosophically influenced *Midrash ha-Nelam* ("The Concealed Midrash") dates from the 1270's while the bulk of the work was composed between the years 1280–86. There is evidence that the *'Idrot* sections of the *Zohar* were completed at a later date, some time after 1291.[45] Stylistically, the *Zohar* bears resemblance to two literary forms or genres. It is both a mystical 'novel' or story and a pseudepigraphic midrash. As story, the *Zohar* is focused on the mystical adventures of the second century Rabbi, Shimon bar Yoḥai and his circle of friends. Set in the Galilee, (though often reflecting the contours of the Castilian landscape), R. Shimon and the comrades wander through the countryside exchanging Kabbalistic insights.[46] Several other discrete plots are enfolded into the work. For example a section called *Rav Metivta'* relates the journey of the souls of R. Shimon bar Yoḥai and his pupils to Paradise and its celestial academy, whereas the two *'Idrot* recount the final moments of R. Shimon and his mystical union with the *Shekhinah*. A good deal of the charm of the *Zohar* may be attributed to its narrative richness, a quality often overlooked by modern scholars who have, for the most part, concentrated on the *Zohar*'s theosophy.[47]

The *Zohar* is also a sprawling mystical midrash on the Torah and three books of the Hagiographa: the *Song of Songs, Ruth* and *Lamentations*. Most of these homilies purport to be the work of R. Shimon bar Yoḥai and his companions and hence are written in a kind of Aramaic vernacular considered to be appropriate to the second century (though, as Gershom Scholem has shown the language repeatedly betrays its medieval Spanish roots). While some interpretations hone closely to the Torah text, many merely use the Torah as a springboard for the mystical imagination. As in the Gerona tradition, the Torah is conceived as a *corpus symbolicum*, a texture of divine names and sefirotic symbols whose infinite meaning can never be fully grasped, but only approximately interpreted, further mined. The Torah is said to have seventy faces, each of which shines forth with multiple meaning. The traditional exoteric meanings of the text are not so much denied as revealed to be the outward manifestation of a mysterious—usually sefirotic-theosophical—essence.[48]

One of Moshe de Leon's central motives in writing the *Zohar* was to promulgate his Kabbalistic vision of Tradition over against two widespread religious tendencies of his day which he felt flattened the rich universe of sacred meaning. On the one hand, he was highly critical of radical rationalists, especially those upper class dilettantes who used an Averroistic philosophy to justify the neglect of Tradition and who emptied the mizvot of sacramental significance by equating them with abstract ideas.[49] On the other hand, he roundly critiqued a literalist-traditionalist conception of Judaism. According to de Leon, those persons remaining at the outer, more exoteric levels could have no knowledge of either the divine mysteries or themselves. In his early Hebrew work, the *'Or Zaruʿa* ("Light Is Sown"), he wrote:

> I have seen some people [i.e., the literalists] called "wise." But they have not awoken from their slumber; they just remain where they

> are . . . . Indeed, they are far from searching for His glorious Reality. They have exchanged His Glory for the image of a bull eating grass. [cf. Ps. 106:20][50]

In one well-known *Zohar* passage, de Leon went so far as to assert that if the Torah really contained only those tales, genealogies, and political precepts which are capable of being understood literally, then far better books could be written, even in the present day.[51]

We have previously noted the unusual literary character of the *Zohar:* a pseudepigraphon written in an archaic form (Midrash) and in an archaic language (Aramaic). Moshe de Leon wrote his other Kabbalistic books in Hebrew. With the exception of several brief tracts on ethics and the eschatology of the soul, they were signed works, written in conventional styles.[52] Hence the question that scholars have been grappling with for over a century: Why did de Leon employ pseudepigraphy for his *magnum opus*?[53] Some students have put forward functional explanations, seeing in archaic Midrash a congenial medium of expression for de Leon or a means for better advancing his Kabbalistic views, shrouding them in ancient authority.[54] Others have offered psychological explanations, arguing that de Leon saw himself as the transmigration of R. Shimon bar Yoḥai's soul or viewed the ancient Rabbi as his archetype.[55] Be this as it may, the effect that the pseudepigraphic mask had on Moshe de Leon is clear. For all their sophistication and interest, his signed Hebrew works lack the inspired tone and the theosophical daring of the *Zohar*. Somehow, the pseudepigraphic venture has set free the author's imagination, allowed his poetic gifts to blossom. Daniel Matt has written:

> By surrendering his identity to Rabbi Shimon and company, by adopting a talmudic alter ego, Moses de Leon has been liberated. Released from the constraints of acknowledged authorship, he can record his own ecstasy and pathos. Immune from all criticism, he expounds mythological and mystical revelations in anthropomorphic and erotic imagery . . . The literary trick has worked its magic on the author . . .[56]

Despite its unique qualities the *Zohar* reached its preeminent position in Kabbalah only gradually. Moshe Leon died in 1305. In the final years of his life and the decades thereafter the *Zohar* was disseminated in piecemeal fashion alone, reaching a rather limited audience. Moreover, the work itself met with a cool reception in certain quarters. Several leading Kabbalists made guardedly negative pronouncements regarding the value of the work and were suspicious regarding its origin. As late as 1340, Joseph ibn Waqar, one of the few Kabbalists to write in Arabic, warned that the book "is full of mistakes" and cautioned his readers to "keep a safe distance from it."[57]

On the other hand, the *Zohar* made a profound impact on several leading Kabbalists of the late thirteenth and early fourteenth centuries, such as the renowned exegete R. Baḥyya ben Asher, R. David ben Judah he-Ḥasid, Joseph Giqatilia and Menaḥem Recanati. Still other Kabbalists imitated the *Zohar*'s pseudo-Aramaic midrashic style, evidence that they did not see the book as being of ancient origin though they regarded it most highly. The most famous *Zohar* imitations are the *Tiqqunei ha-Zohar* ("The Elaborations on the Zohar," hereafter, TZ) and the *Raᶜaya' Meheimna'* ("The Faithful Shepherd," RM), which were probably composed in the 1290's or early 1300's. The TZ is a mystical midrash on the first chapters of Genesis, while the RM discusses the mystical rationales for the miẓvot. Despite some linguistic and conceptual differences from the *Zohar*,[58] these two imitations were convincing enough that they were soon accepted as part of the *Zohar* itself and published accordingly. In actuality, they were the work of an unknown Kabbalist who was thoroughly familiar with Moshe de Leon's magnum opus and was possibly one of his disciples.[59]

By 1400, the *Zohar* had reached a position of unparalleled prominence in Spain and Italy. Moshe de Leon's name had by this time faded, and the *Zohar* was gradually accepted as the work of R. Shimon bar Yoḥai and his circle. Still, the *Zohar* was slow to reach Ashkenazi lands and the countries to the East. Only in the sixteenth century did the *Zohar* begin to gain global influence, aided by certain historical factors: the waning of rationalist philosophy, the resurgence of Kabbalah in Safed, the invention of the printing press, and the Messianic atmosphere that enveloped world Jewry after the traumatic Explusion from Spain. Increasingly, public study of the *Zohar* was granted salvific, eschatological significance; in preparation for Redemption some mystics proclaimed that the esoteric was now to be made public.

The *Zohar* reached the peak of its authority in the seventeenth and eighteenth centuries when it was accorded quasi-canonical status alongside the Bible and Talmud. Although its status was undercut in the West with the rise of the Enlightenment, the *Zohar* retained its general prominence in Eastern Europe well into the nineteenth century; among many Ḥasidic and Sephardic Jews its preeminence has continued unto the present day.[60]

Kabbalah from the Fourteenth Century until the Safed Renaissance

There will be a good deal less to say about Kabbalah in the fourteenth and fifteenth centuries, i.e., the end of the classical period. A very rich Kabbalah existed in the former century in particular, but few new paradigms were produced. The fourteenth century was a time of expansion as Kabbalah spread beyond the Iberian peninsula into Italy, Germany, North Africa, and points east. The school of the RaSHBa preserved many Catalonian traditions including some of the oral teachings attributed to R. Judah ben Yaqar and RaMBaN. The Palestinian-born Isaac ben Samuel of Acco combined interest in the unitive and revelatory mysticism of ecstatic Kabbalah with the sefirotic and symbolic concerns of Geronese and Zoharic theosophy.[61] Kabbalistic systematizers flourished as well, further developing sefirotic theory. The most important example of this trend was an early fourteenth century work entitled *Maᶜarekhet ha-'Elohut* ("The Structure of the Godhead,") written by an anonymous member of the Naḥmanidean school. Together with the *Zohar,* this work exerted a seminal influence on the Italian Kabbalah. A survey of the literature produced reveals sustained interest in Kabbalistic interpretations of Scripture and the Rabbinic *'aggadot* (legends) and increased interest in mystical rationales for the miẓvot. Several important manuals for contemplative prayer were composed in this period, as well.

There were also several notable attempts to combine philosophy, both Aristotelean and neo-Platonic, with Kabbalah. These synthetic efforts took place over a rather wide intellectual spectrum: some thinkers tended more towards philosophy, whereas others concentrated more heavily on the Kabbalistic side. In sundry ways these philosopher-Kabbalists sought to correlate the doctrine of the ten sefirot with the neo-Platonic conception of the Cosmic Soul and the Aristotelean theory of Separate Intelligences; some were moved to reread Maimonidean philosophy in a mystical vein.[62] Such undertakings gave credence to the popular tradition that the great sage converted to Kabbalah in his last days[63] and served notice of Kabbalah's growing prestige.

In contrast to these harmonistic endeavors were several Kabbalistic schools which either ignored the philosophical tradition or explicitly rejected it. The former tendency was manifest in the burgeoning meditative movements of the period. Some schools focused on the world of sefirot and the innumerable lights contained therein, whereas others, influenced by Abraham Abulafia, focused on the inner world of Sacred Names.[64] A more explicitly anti-philosophical tendency was manifest in two pseudepigraphic works of considerable originality. The first work, *Sefer ha-Peli'ah,* is a melding of Kabbalistic traditions on the book of Genesis, often cast in highly mythological symbolism; the second composition, *Sefer ha-Qanah,* concerns the inner meaning of the miẓvot. These two books are linked not only conceptually but by a shared literary structure, revolving around an imaginary family of ancient mystics—grandfather, father, and son—who discourse on the inner meaning of Torah. Internal evidence suggests that the *Peli'ah* and *Qanah* were written in the early fifteenth century in the environs of Byzantine Greece. Their author, a skilled Talmudist with a highly idiosyncratic orientation, attempted to prove that the *halakhah* (Jewish Law) has no literal meaning beyond its mystical-theurgic import. Clearly, this view left no room for either a literalist or a philosophical stance. Gershom Scholem has called these two works "the peak of Kabbalistic extremism."[65] The most impassioned anti-philosophical stance was taken by the Spanish Kabbalist, Shem Ṭov b. Shem Ṭov (ca. 1400). In his two systematic works, he excoriated rationalist philosophy, accusing it of undermining Israel's faith (which was sorely tested amid the persecutions of 1391 and the rising tide of anti-Semitism) and holding it partially responsible for the declining fortunes of Spanish Jewry.[66] Such anti-philosophical critiques became increasingly widespread and influential in the strife-torn decades preceding the Expulsion.

As the fourteenth century drew to a close, Kabbalah was exerting increasing influence upon exoteric Judaism, especially in Spain. Mystical rationales entered into halakhic literature while Kabbalistic traditions were incorporated into ethical texts and commentaries on prayer.[67] On another front, Kabbalistic symbolism was increasingly absorbed into the semi-rationalist philosophies of the day, e.g., in the writings of Ḥasdai Crescas, Joseph Albo and Shimon Duran. It might be said that Kabbalah—qua intellectual tradition—was becoming the property of the religious elite as a whole.

Kabbalistic creativity in Spain diminished considerably in the fifteenth century. The literary evidence reveals unabated activity, but the work produced was largely derivative in nature. Greater originality was exhibited in Italy and points east.[68]

Several scholars have recently called attention to the distinctive Kabbalah which took root in the Byzantine setting from the early fourteenth to early sixteenth centuries. A distinct strain of ecstatic (Abulafian) Kabbalah was preserved there, frequently combining with theosophic traditions. Examples of this synthesis include the writings of Isaiah ben Joseph of Greece (1320's) and the voluminous *'Even ha-Sappir* (1368–70) of Elnatan ben Moshe Kalkis of Constantinople. Moreover, it now seems likely that the esoteric doctrine of the *shemiṭṭot,* the cosmic cycles which govern time, reached its fullest articulation in Byzantium. In a recent unpublished lecture, Moshe Idel has argued that the anonymous *Sefer ha-Temunah* ("The Book of the Figure"), the classic source for *shemiṭṭah* theory, is of mid-14th century Byzantine provenance, and so too, such related works as *Sod ha-Shem* ("The Mystery of the Name") and *'Ilan ha-'Aẓilut* ("The Tree of Emanation").[69] As noted, scholars have now come to the conclusion that Byzantium was the birthplace of the *Qanah* and *Peli'ah;* the important anthology, *SHOSHaN Sodot* ("656 Mystical Secrets") completed in 1498 is of similar provenance.[70] In light of these developing claims, it could be argued that Byzantium became one of the most vital centers of Kabbalistic activity—rivalling Spain—in the two centuries preceding the Safed revival.

The historical watershed that signalled the end of the classical period of Kabbalah was the explusion of the Jews from Spain in 1492. The profound upheaval in the Jewish consciousness caused by this catastrophe gradually changed the face of Jewish Mysticism. First, as Jews focused increasingly on the dialectics of Exile and Redemption, Kabbalah became ever more intertwined with Messianism. That is to say, Kabbalah increasingly concentrated on the mystery of the end rather than the mystery of origins that so fascinated legions of classical Kabbalists.[71] Secondly, amidst the eschatological fever that gripped much of Jewry in the sixteenth and seventeenth centuries, Kabbalah gradually ceased to be the sole property of the religious elite. As noted, its central texts were given wider circulation and Kabbalistic study, more explicit salvific value. Moreover, mystically influenced rituals and lore became widely disseminated, profoundly affecting the world of popular piety.

For the purposes of this book, the end of classical Kabbalah has been correlated with the reflowering of mystical life in the Palestinian town of Safed starting in the 1530's. The teachings and new rituals developed there—and in particular the new theosophy developed by Isaac Luria—marked a new chapter in the history of Jewish mysticism, one beyond the parameters of this study.[72]

In closing we should note that the transitional period between the Expulsion and the Safed renaissance contained several Kabbalists of the first rank.[73] Mention will be made of only Meir ibn Gabbai, a Spanish-Turkish mystic firmly within the Zoharic tradition and one of the great synthesizers of classical Kabbalah as a whole. His *Tolaᶜat Yaᶜaqov* (TY), a mystical commentary on the liturgy and assorted rituals (1507), contains the most comprehensive and systematic treatment of the Sabbath in classical Kabbalah. We shall have much to say about this treatise in the later pages of this book.[74]

SECTION TWO: THE *SEFIROT* AND THEIR SYMBOLISM

Theosophical Kabbalah, as we have seen, is pre-eminently sefirotic mysticism, sefirotic contemplation. It is this symbolic language which both articulates and shapes the inner life of the mystic and which gives this Kabbalah its distinctive coloration. In this section the sefirot will be discussed in more systematic fashion: their structure and nomenclature will be analyzed and several modes of interpretation, suggested.

With the sefirot the Kabbalists have created a nuanced language to convey their experience of divinity: on the one hand, the sefirot represent the successive stages in divine self-revelation, the process of His flowering into the cosmos; on the other hand, they represent stages of the mystic's ascent into the divine pleroma, serving as a map of inner experience. The first notion is spoken of frequently in the literature, the latter only rarely, for most theosophical Kabbalists spoke of personal experience in veiled fashion alone.

These mystics frequently underscored the symbolic and (at least partially) subjective nature of the sefirot. That is, the sefirot function as approximate translations of an inexpressible reality, colored both by the limitations of the Kabbalist's perspective and the limitations of language. According to the treatise *Maᶜarekhet ha-'Elohut* "everything is from the perspective of those who receive," while the *Zohar* cautions that "all this is said only from our point of view, and it is all relative to our knowledge." (2:176a) However, as Gershom Scholem has noted:

> This did not prevent them from indulging in the most detailed descriptions, *as if they were speaking after all of an actual reality and objective occurences.* (*Kabbalah*: 105; emphasis mine)

Indeed, as we shall see in the succeeding chapters of this study, the sefirot frequently serve as divine archetypes which structure and impregnate the cosmos, including the lower worlds. They are thus experienced as the most genuinely 'real' of entities, losing whatever subjective quality they might have in moments of critical reflection. In sum, it might be said that the sefirot oscillate between serving as symbols of an inexpressible reality and constituting that reality itself.[75]

Structural Overview

Terminology. *Sefirot* is simply the best-known term referring to the ten primary aspects by which the Kabbalist grasped and ordered the divine world. As it is used in the *Bahir*, it is related to the Hebrew word *sappir* (sapphire) to which God's luminosity is likened. Other suggestive synonyms include rungs, crowns, logoi, lights, names, garments, worlds, springs, streams, hues, inner faces, and prisms. Together these aspects compose a *Gestalt*, a multi-leveled ecosystem or personality which Moshe de Leon termed *'alma' de-yiḥuda'*, the world of unity. It should be noted that each sefirah itself constitutes a world of immense richness and variation. Therefore, the number ten in no way limits the number of aspects within the divine Being.

***'Ein Sof* and the sefirot.** According to most Kabbalists, the Godhead in Itself, in Its absolute essence, lies beyond contemplative speculation or even ecstatic comprehension. Rather, divinity may only be contemplated with respect to His Creation, viz., in His sefirotic unfolding. Gershom Scholem has written: "The attitude of the Kabbalah towards God [in Himself] may be defined as a mystical agnosticism." (*Kabbalah*: 88) To express this hidden aspect of God the Kabbalists coined the term, *'Ein Sof*, the Infinite. Like the mysterious One of neo-Platonism, *'Ein Sof* is generally held to be beyond accurate symbolization and attribution. Indeed, It is an impersonal Reality which can only be spoken of hyperbolically, referred to as *mah she-'ein ha-maḥashavah masseget* (that which lies beyond comprehension); *ha-'or ha-mitᶜallem* (the concealed light); as *yitron* (superabundance, or in neo-Platonic terms, *hyperousia);* or simply as *mahut* (essence).[76] In contrast to the changing, multi-faceted sefirotic world described in most sources, *'Ein Sof* is ontologically simple, unmoved, in the words of Azriel of Gerona, "absolutely undifferentiated in a complete and changeless unity." (*Perush ᶜEser Sefirot*) This hidden divinity is also the ultimate Ground of Being, "the Root of All Roots"; however, the process by which It moves from concealment to the first glimmerings of revealment are beyond human ken, constituting a sublime mystery that can only be surmised.

In part, the distinction between *'Ein Sof* and the sefirot may be explained phenomenologically, with reference to the nature of mystical contemplation. That is, *'Ein Sof* reflects the mystery of divinity that is never fully fathomed, the concealment entailed in each moment of mystical disclosure; alternately, It may represent the annihilation of multiplicity and thingness that occurs at the peak of mystical experience.[77] The sefirot, by contrast, represent divinity as It is more commonly encountered by the devotee. Here God's nature is in varying degrees manifest, open to contemplation, and approximate symbolization. It is as if the utter silence to which *'Ein Sof* is consigned has given way to inchoate speech; divinity's impersonal nature to that which might be called "personality." This unfolding is vividly captured in the *Zohar*. At the sefirotic level of manifestation, divinity feels, responds, loves, fears, articulates, couples, and attains androgynous wholeness. Here divinity sends forth light, flows like a river, gushes like a spring. The conceptually pure—and hence unknowable—God of *'Ein Sof* gives way to the devotee's overwhelming desire to commune with Him, to sing of Him, to "taste and know that the Lord is good." (ff. Ps. 34:9)

In distinguishing between these two moments or perspectives—God in His hidden essence and God as He is disclosed—the Kabbalists made creative use of two disparate theological languages. Even as *'Ein Sof* reflects the neo-Platonic imaging of the mysterious One from which all existence emanates, the sefirot reflect the probable influence of Gnosticism with its notion of a mythologically rich divine pleroma composed of sundry aeons and personified potencies. The neo-Platonists placed the world of emanation outside the Godhead, but most Kabbalists placed it inside, and so, opened up a fertile realm of theosophical speculation.

Instrumentalist and essentialist understandings of the sefirot. We have been speaking of the distinction between *'Ein Sof* and the sefirot, between the hidden and manifest life of God. But let us refine the picture, noting other ways in which mystics explained this distinction. For some Kabbalists (Ezra of Gerona, TZ/RM, Menaḥem Recanati) the distinction between *'Ein Sof* and the sefirot seems to be ontologically rooted. That is, although the sefirot are part of the divine pleroma and are intimately related to the Godhead, they are not identical with it. Rather, they are *kelim* or vessels, entities which contain the divine essence but do not, strictly speaking, constitute it. They may also serve as *kelim* in a second, related sense; as instruments of *'Ein Sof*. As such, they convey divine energy (*shefa*ᶜ) to the cosmos, helping to create and sustain it.

By way of contrast, such mystics as RaMBaN, Moshe de Leon, the author of *Ma*ᶜ*arekhet ha-'Elohut* and Meir ibn Gabbai, tended towards an 'essentialist' view of the sefirot. They suggested that the distinction between *'Ein Sof* and its rungs is primarily experiential in nature rather than ontological. In essence, *'Ein Sof* and its sefirot are one. As the *Zohar* delights in saying: "It is They and They are It" (3:70a). This unity is generally explained in two ways: (1) It is only the structure of human consciousness that renders them distinct, acting like a prism which refracts and splinters the light of divinity into multiple colors. (2) *'Ein Sof* and the sefirotic rungs must be grasped as inner and outer aspects of a unified Gestalt. To use two favorite similes, the sefirot are bound to *'Ein Sof* like "a flame before a coal" or like "beams of light emanating from the sun."[78] The relation between *'Ein Sof* and the sefirot constituted a supreme mystery for many Kabbalists, even as it led to charges of dualism on the part of some unsympathetic Rationalists.[79]

Sefirotic structure. Outside of a small group of mystically oriented philosophers and the author of *Ma*ᶜ*arekhet ha-'Elohut,* the Kabbalists affirmed the principle of sefirotic change.[80] Prevailing attitudes ranged from the moderate theological dynamism found in Gerona Kabbalah, with its measured choreography of sefirotic movement, to the extreme dynamism—the ever-dancing divine light—celebrated in the writings of Moshe de Leon. On one occasion he likened sefirotic movement to the shifting patterns of light reflected on moving water:

> If you will take a dish with water to the eye of the sun, and shake it, you will see [reflected] on the [adjacent] wall the splendor of the mirrors that are shining [the sefirot]. They "dart to and fro" (Ezek. 1:14), moving with such swiftness that no one is able to fix them.[81]

In short, for most Kabbalists, the ten sefirot are not frozen into a rigid hierarchy in the divine pleroma. In the Zoharic tradition, in particular, they may flow, interact, and recombine in an infinite array of permutations and configurations. The first sefirah may descend unto the last, the last ascend unto the first: for the sefirot represent the dynamic inner life of God, not a static theory.[82] Still, by the early thirteenth century, a hierarchy of sefirot had crystallized, reflecting the order of their emanation from *'Ein Sof*. Using their most common appellations, they may be ordered as follows, moving from first emanation to the last:

(1) *Keter ᶜElyon*: the Supreme Crown or simply *Keter*, the Crown,

(2) *Ḥokhmah*, Wisdom or Sophia,

(3) *Binah*, Intelligence or Understanding,

(4) *Ḥesed*, Love or *Gedullah*, Greatness,

(5) *Gevurah*, Strength or *Din*, Judgement or Rigor,

(6) *Tif'eret*, Beauty or *Raḥamim*, Compassion,

(7) *Neẓaḥ*, Lasting Endurance,

(8) *Hod*, Majesty,

(9) *Yesod ᶜOlam*, the Cosmic Foundation, or *Ẓaddiq*, Righteous One,

(10) *Malkhut*, Kingdom or Royalty, or *Shekhinah*, Immanence.

This terminology was strongly influenced by the verse in I Chronicles 29:11: "Yours, o Lord, are greatness [*gedullah*], strength [*gevurah*], beauty [*tif'eret*], lasting endurance [*neẓaḥ*] and majesty [*hod*], etc." As indicated previously, these terms are rubrics for extensive symbol-clusters, a kind of shorthand employed for the sake of convenience.

Images of the sefirotic totality. Before considering the particulars of emanation, let us consider some of the symbols used to depict the sefirotic Gestalt. One of the earliest and most common images is that of the Cosmic Tree. The roots of this Tree lie in the uppermost reaches of the pleroma, in *Keter*. The Tree grows downward, spreading through those sefirot which constitute its trunk, branches, and crown—its energy ultimately radiating into the lower worlds. *'Ein Sof* is the hidden Root of Roots which sustains the Tree, its power coursing through the Tree like vital sap. The configuration of the sefirot as a Cosmic Tree is commonly rendered in the following—highly stylized—fashion:

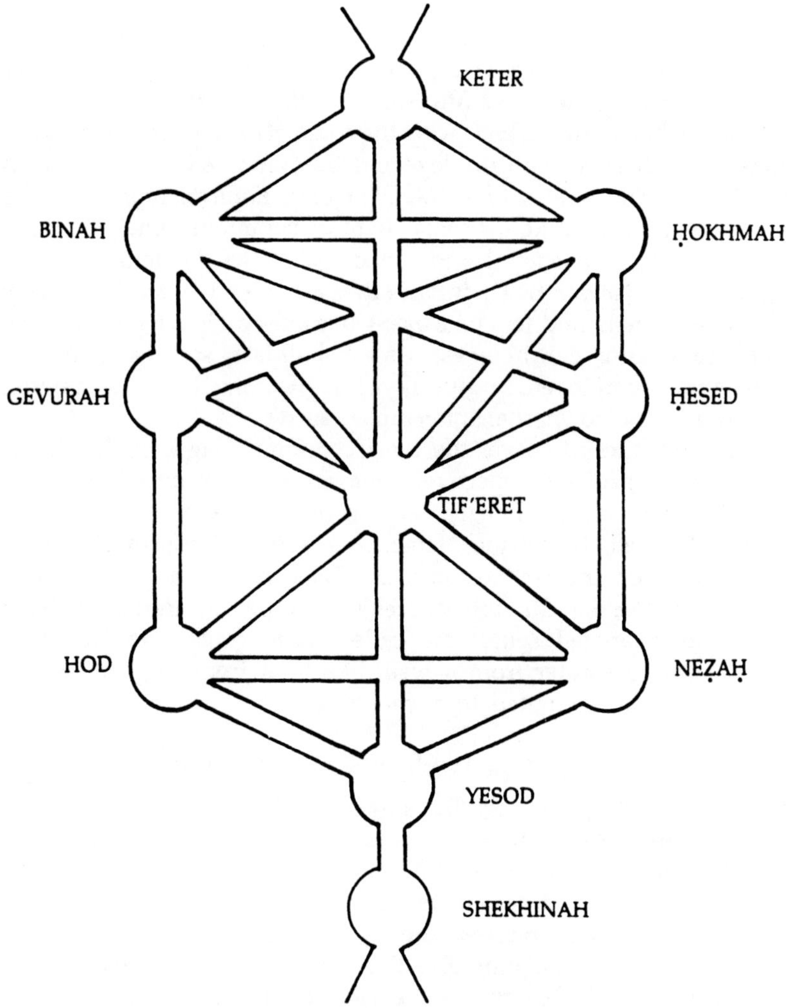

Figure 1: The Sefirotic Tree

Note that the sefirot are not depicted linearly, but in a series of triangles, better suited to depict the complex—indeed, dialectical—interaction between them.

Alongside this picture we find the more common configuration of the sefirot as *'Adam Qadmon*, the Primordial Person, whose symbolic structure serves as the archetype for the human being. The Kabbalists thereby gave precise symbolic expression (and added mythic resonance) to the traditional notion that the human being is created in the divine image. While the Cosmic Tree grows from the top down, this human form has its head on top and is sometimes called the "reversed Tree" (*Kabbalah:* 106). The first three sefirot are generally correlated with the head and in the *Zohar,* with the three cavities of the brain; the fourth and fifth sefirot with the right and left arms, and the sixth sefirah, *Tif'eret,* with the torso. The seventh and eighth rungs are associated with the legs and the ninth sefirah, *Yesod,* with the phallus. The final sefirah, *Malkhut* or *Shekhinah,* represents the totality of the preceding sefirot. It is most commonly imaged as the feminine aspect in general and, on occasion, as the female sexual organ. *'Adam Qadmon* or Divinity is thus portrayed as an androgyne; the union of male and female aspects becomes a cipher for *shelemut,* cosmic completion or wholeness. As we shall later see, this archetype is sometimes employed to give mystical meaning to the institution of marriage and to marital intercourse, as well.

Though these two are the most common images of the divine totality, the sefirot are collectively imaged in many other ways. For example, they are symbolized as a series of sacred letters which collectively spell the Divine Name, as a series of concentric circles emanating from the center-point, as a *menorah,* as a grape-cluster, and as the celestial Chariot of Ezekiel's vision. In another striking image the emanated sefirot are called *hamshakhah* (that which is drawn out), like water from a well, like light from the sun, whose being cannot be separated from its source.[83]

Figure 2: The Sefirot as Divine Name

Y—*Ḥokhmah,* the seed-like letter *Yod* (י) whose tip (connoting *Keter*) points upward to the ultimate Source.

H—*Binah,* the letter *He'* (ה) and Supernal Mother. ה is the womb in which the divine seed י is placed and from whose recesses the lower rungs issue:

> [In the beginning] all the supernal paths and esoteric letters were enclosed within the letter *Samekh* (ס) [*Binah* in Her primal state]. When the Will sought to reveal Itself, the ס opened up, forming the letter ה . . . . Of all the letters none is more perfectly formed to give birth than the ה . (ZḤ Cant. 72b)

W—*Tif'eret*—the so-called Central Column—and the five 'male' sefirot around it, orthographically symbolized as the letter *Waw* (ו). Numerically, the ו is equal to 6; grammatically, it is a copulative, here linking YH with:

H—*Malkhut,* the second ה and Lower Mother from whom all lower existence derives.

The Dynamics of Sefirotic Unfolding: the Sefirot *as Stages of Emanation.*[84]

The process of emanation, the dialectics of God's unfolding, begins with the first *sefirah, Keter,* which is said to be co-eternal with *'Ein Sof. Keter* is the first movement toward self-Revelation, a barely perceptible aura, the first glimmerings of the Divine Will. It is commonly called *'Ayin* (Nothingness) for it is without differentiation and thingness. A late thirteenth century mystic defined *'Ayin* as

> having more being than any other being in the world, but since it is simple, and all other simple things are complex when compared with its simplicity, in comparison it is called nothing.[85]

That is, *'Ayin* is the mystical Nihil that is paradoxically full, the point from which all emanation flows. This may be illustrated by example. The dominant Jewish understanding of Creation in the high Middle Ages was that of *creatio ex nihilo,* God's creation of the World—that which is 'not-God'—out of nothingness. In Hebrew philosophical parlance this process was called *yesh me-'ayin,* literally 'Being out of nothingness.' In a productive 'misreading' so typical of Kabbalistic creativity, *yesh me-'ayin* was interpeted to connote not extra-divine Creation but intradivine Emanation, i.e., Emanation out of divine Nothingness, the unfolding of divine Being from *Keter.*

The first sefirah to emerge from *Keter* is called *Ḥokhmah* (Wisdom): it is but a Point, the tip of the Hebrew letter *Yod* [י], the faintest Thought, the tiniest generative seed. As the first emanation, It is commonly called *Re'shit* (Beginning) in contrast to the eternity of *Keter.* This Point then swells into a Circle, becomes a Palace, or in another image, a womb in which *Ḥokhmah*'s seed is implanted. This womb is the third sefirah, *Binah,* the Divine Mother, from whose recesses the Children—the rest of the sefirotic world—emerge. All active life, all individuation stems from Her. This notion is graphically illustrated in Z 2:42b (RM), where *Binah* is likened to the Great Sea:

> The first rung [*Keter*] is the hidden source of the Sea. A well-spring comes forth from it, making a revolution forming the letter *Yod* [י, sefirotically *Ḥokhmah*]. . . . Then a great vessel is formed, known as the Sea, which is like a canyon dug into the earth, and it is filled by the waters issuing from the springs. . . . This vast basin branches out into seven vessels, seven channels [the seven lower sefirot], and the Sea's waters flow into them. . .

At the end of time, all the lower sefirot, indeed, all of Creation will return to *Binah's* recesses in the drama of *hitballeᶜut*, cosmic re-integration or *apokatastasis*.[86] Thus *Binah* is also called *Teshuvah* (Return), the Cosmic Jubilee, the World-to-Come and the Primordial Sheath.

The upper three sefirot are often grouped together and considered as one unit, in the words of the *Zohar*, *ᶜalma' ᶜila'ah*, the "Supernal World." As the most recondite and mysterious layers of divinity, they are often held to be beyond conscious comprehension, their heights "beyond the ken of even the eagle." (ff. Job 28:7)

Below *Binah* the mysteries of the sefirotic world may more readily be penetrated. Light streams forth from *Binah* and the rungs below Her become accessible through mystical contemplation. These lower seven sefirot are often collectively labelled "the seven days of Creation." They are the more active rungs of divinity, directly involved in the process of Creation and the ongoing functioning of the Cosmos. To return to the organic imagery, *Binah* first gives birth to the fourth and fifth rungs, *Ḥesed* (Love) and *Din* (Stern Judgment). They are imaged as the Right and Left arms of divinity, as two antipodes of the divine personality. *Ḥesed* is free-flowing love and expansive grace, the archetype of Abraham, whereas *Din* is rigor, limitation, and *yir'ah* (awe or fear), the archetype of Isaac. Both aspects are deemed essential to the cosmos' functioning and ideally, a balance is achieved between the two in the sixth sefirah, *Tif'eret*, the archetype of Jacob.[87] When *Din* is not sweetened by Love, however, it may become a punitive force, a valence of evil and destruction that realigns the divine ecosystem and threatens the world below. Out of *Din's* untempered residue, Evil, *Siṭra' 'Aḥra'* (the Other Side), is born.[88]

As the fourth of the seven active or accessible sefirot, *Tif'eret* is at the hub of divine activity. It is the Middle Column, the great synthesizer, modulating the flow of divine energy or *shefaᶜ* as it courses through the sefirotic realm. In the image of the Cosmic Tree *Tif'eret* is the trunk; it is also the torso of *'Adam Qadmon*, the geographical center of the sefirotic universe. It is commonly called Heaven, Sun, the Tree of Life, the Written Torah, King, and the Holy One. It is with this sefirah that the Person-God of Rabbinic Judaism is most closely linked.[89] Along with the ninth sefirah, *Yesod*, it is the quintessentially 'male' sefirah.

The seventh and eighth sefirot are *Neẓaḥ*, and *Hod*, the right and left legs of the body, also identified as the source of prophecy. The ninth sefirah, *Yesod*, is the Foundation of the Cosmos or *Axis*

Mundi and represents the phallus, or procreative force in the world. Through it the blessings of the preceding sefirot—the divine *shefa*ᶜ—are channeled to the final sefirah, *Malkhut,* or *Shekhinah.*

Shekhinah is the divine female, *Binah's* Daughter, the Bride, Spouse, and Lover of the Holy One. She is also the divine limen, alternately attached to and separated from the rest of the sefirotic world. Indeed, Her status becomes a litmus test for the state of divinity and cosmos. Her union with Her Lover *Tif'eret* signals cosmic unity, whereas, Her separation from Him is an index of cosmic brokenness, of "Exile."[90]

While *Binah* represents the active Female, *Shekhinah* is by and large the passive female in Her relations with the rest of the sefirotic world. She is alternately full and empty, rich and poor, depending on Her ties with the sefirot above. She is *ha-kallah ha-kelulah min ha-kol,* the Bride who receives and embodies the divine totality, but also the Moon "with no light of Her own," who can only reflect the luminescence of the Sun. With respect to the worlds below, however, She is an active Presence, the representation of divine immanence and providence. Indeed, She is often depicted as Mother to life below and, more specifically, as the matrix and guardian of Israel's physical and spiritual existence. The souls of Israel are said to issue from Her; they are the fruit of Her holy union with *Tif'eret,* which takes place each Sabbath night.

As may be inferred, the symbol cluster surrounding the tenth sefirah is extraordinarily rich and only a small number of its significations can be touched on here. In addition to the symbols mentioned earlier, She is portrayed as the Rose of Sharon, the terrestrial Garden of Eden, Jerusalem, the Temple, the *Sukkah* (Canopy) of Peace, the Sea into which all rivers flow, the Royal Diadem (*ᶜAṭarah*), the color *tekhelet* (bright blue), the vowel point *ḥiriq* and the Oral Torah. She is occasionally associated with a series of Biblical heroines, with Rachel, Leah, and Ruth, and serves as the paradigm for women, in general: "All women in the world are contained in Her mystery." (Z 1: 228b). *Shekhinah* however, is occasionally imaged as male, too, and is not infrequently associated with King David.[91]

To Israel, below, *Shekhinah* generally represents the loving Mother, though on occasion—when threatened by *Siṭra' 'Aḥra'* and the forces of human sin—She may reflect the terrible side of divinity. Indeed, Gershom Scholem has noted certain parallels between the *Shekhinah* symbolism and the "Great Mother" imagery found in numerous religious cultures.[92]

In one of the most significant of all Her symbolizations, *Shekhinah* is the mystical Community of Israel, the archetype of Israel below. In the Zoharic tradition, in particular, a profound nexus was fashioned between the divine and human Israel: the fate of the one reflecting the fate of the other. The sefirotic symbolism often served to blur the distinctions between the two and, hence, between divinity and devotee. Not infrequently, it is unclear just which 'Israel' is being referred to in a given text, or more precisely, which Israel is the primary referent and which the secondary one, or subtext. This very ambiguity lent *Shekhinah* symbolism extraordinary resonance and power, as shall be seen in subsequent chapters.

In recounting the process of emanation we have necessarily limited ourselves to a few of the central images. As a whole, the process of emanation may be grasped as the genesis of divine articulation; to recall the imagery of Azriel of Gerona, it is the progression of divine life from inarticulate Will—*Keter*—to speech—*Shekhinah*. Or to cite an example from the *Zohar*, emanation may be symbolized as the realization of divine individuation. It is divinity's mysterious progression from *'AYiN* (Nothingness)—*Keter*—to *'ANiY* (Ego)—a cipher for *Shekhinah*—the moment where God as a Person says "I" to Himself and becomes immanent in the devotee's deepest recesses.[93]

The Sefirot *as Stages of Mystical Ascent*

We might gain added appreciation of the sefirot as experiential categories by reversing the process of emanation, by grasping the sefirot as blazes marking the adept's ascent back to the One. It must be reiterated, however, that few Kabbalists used such explicity personal (or self-conscious) language in describing their inner journey. In Medieval Jewish culture, such biographical attestations were considered to be in poor taste, a show of excessive pride.[94]

The primary occasion for such ascent is contemplative prayer. Using the sacred text as a guide the devotee wends his way through the sefirotic world, meditating on the qualities of each sefirah, its evocative cluster of symbols, its myriad inner worlds. *Shekhinah,* the final rung of emanation, is the point of entry. It is the sefirah most frequently experienced by the adept, "the opening to the [divine] Tent," "the gateway to the supernal mysteries." (Z 1:103a) Daniel Matt has written:

> Once inside, the *sefirot* are no longer an abstract theological system; they become a map of consciousness. The mystic climbs and probes, discovering dimensions of being. (D. Matt: 37)

The union of *Malkhut* and *Tif'eret,* the river of divine light or *shefa*ʿ, God's loving and awesome "faces" (*Ḥesed* and *Gevurah*), His innumerable holy names and subtle hues—all these are experienced. Near the top of the sefirotic ladder the adept reaches *Binah: Teshuvah,* Return, the womb beyond which there is no individuation. In the *Zohar, Binah* is called "Who?", the unanswerable question. She is the outermost limit of comprehension, the light which breaks through and glimmers for a split instant. In Moshe de Leon's simile, *Binah* is like "an intuitive flash which illumines the human heart as sunbeams playing on the surface of the water."[95] Beyond lies dark mystery, *Ḥokhmah,* the hidden source of the mystic's nourishment.[96] This rung cannot be known consciously. Indeed, some Kabbalists aver that it cannot be known at all; others maintain that it can only be absorbed, imbibed in some primal fashion. Isaac the Blind, the great mystic of Provençal Kabbalah explained:

> No creature can contemplate [the paths of *Ḥokhmah*] except one who sucks from It. This is meditation through sucking, not through knowing.[97]

Beyond *Ḥokhmah* lies *Keter,* Nothingness, the Annihilation of Thought. As the adept reaches this sefirah, his consciousness expands, the boundaries of ego blur. *'ANiY* has become *'AYiN.*[98]

Further Thoughts on Sefirotic Symbolism

In the course of this brief overview of the sefirot numerous symbol-sets have been alluded to: abstract and pictorial, personal and impersonal. Images have been drawn from mathematics (points, circles); moral imagery and the traditional divine attributes (love, judgment, compassion, righteousness); physiological and sexual imagery; intellectual and linguistic symbolism; cosmology (heaven and earth, sun and moon); botanical imagery (trees, rivers, gardens); and light and color. We have glimpsed symbols drawn from the web of familial relations and from the reservoir of sacred heroes, as well as symbols drawn from Jewish ritual life and theology (Torah, Temple, the Community of Israel, the Holy One, the World-to-Come).

It should be borne in mind that in the Zoharic tradition these symbol-sets rarely exist in self-contained form; many of the most profound mystical texts are dense textures, intricate weavings of different symbolic threads. Contemplation of a specific sefirah or configuration of sefirot may evoke multiple images, drawn from many sources. For as we have noted, a sefirah is really a thick cluster of images and meanings, associatively linked. One image triggers several others; echoes are everywhere heard. Hence, it is not unusual to find mixed metaphors in Kabbalistic texts: lights become rivers; the Temple an Edenic Garden; and Beauty (Heb., *Tif'eret*): the Written Torah, the Groom, the letter *WaW*, the vowel point *shuruq*, myrtle, the color green. In the *Zohar* in particular, there is a remarkable fluidity to the imagery, a looseness of association, even, at times, a kind of synesthesia, all of which attest to (and help create) an altered state of mind, a symbolic consciousness conducive to mystical experience.

Another integral feature of sefirotic symbolism is its considerable affective power. In the more mythically oriented sources especially, the images employed fully involve the adept's senses and emotions: they create a wash of color, evoke a profusion of scents, dramatize and kindle a passionate longing. Such symbols integrate both the affective and ideational poles of meaning. They are truly suggestive, speaking on several levels of signification at once. This phenomenon will be discussed at length in chapters 3 and 4.

Finally, it should be noted that the analysis of the sefirotic symbolism demands the judicious use of multiple interpretive lenses. The reader must adopt the critical posture of historian, philologist, phenomenologist, and psychologist.[99] The last two postures are the most risky from a hermeneutical perspective, yet they offer the possibility of the greatest rewards for the study of religion. One example: until now the sefirot have primarily been surveyed from the adept's perspective, i.e., as stages in the unfolding life of divinity. Yet from a psychological perspective a good deal of sefirotic symbolism may be viewed as the projection of states of soul, stages of consciousness, onto the cosmos. As Arthur Green has noted, inner states are oft described in terms of 'upper' worlds. It is, Green continues, up to the reader to "cautiously turn the mirror around," to hopefully "gain some insight into the mystic's soul."[100] A critical consideration of these inner states remains a *desideratum* for the study of Jewish Mysticism.[101]

SECTION THREE: READING A ZOHARIC TEXT

To give the reader a more visceral sense of sefirotic symbolism, and to specifically illustrate the important role which Torah and homiletics play in so much of the literature, let us consider one *Zohar* text and several possible ways of reading it. The passage chosen is from 3:201b-202a and actually contains a rather consistent set of imagery, botanical in nature.

The selection opens in a pastoral setting. R. Shimon bar Yoḥai, the central figure of the *Zohar,* his father-in-law R. Pinḥas, and the rest of the comrades, have been wandering through the Galilean countryside, speaking words of Torah.[102] Deep in conversation, they come upon a shaded area alongside a gushing spring. This lush setting seems to be "a gift of God" and they decide to tarry awhile; they sit beneath a tree, drink of the spring-water and are delighted. The natural beauty of the spot serves as a springboard to the imagination of R. Pinḥas who recalls a verse from *Song of Songs* and begins to reflect on it:

(1) R. Pinḥas[103] opened and said: "A spring of gardens, a well of living water, rills from Lebanon." (Cant. 4:15) "A spring of gardens": Is this the only kind of spring? There are so many good and precious springs in the world! Ah, but not all pleasures are the same! There is a spring gushing forth in the wilderness, in a parched place. It is a pleasure for one to rest there and drink. But "a spring of gardens," how good and precious! Such a garden nourishes plants and fruit; one who draws near enjoys everything: he enjoys the water, he enjoys the plants, he enjoys the fruit! Such a spring is crowned with everything! So many roses and fragrant herbs all around! How much finer is this spring than all others, "a well of living water!"

(2) We have established that all this refers to the Community of Israel. She is "a spring of gardens." Who are the gardens? The Holy One has five gardens in which He delights and one spring above that waters and drenches them. They are secret and hidden[104] and they all produce abundant fruit and verdure. There is one garden below them; that garden is guarded round on every flank. Beneath this garden are other gardens, bearing fruit of every kind. This garden turns into a spring watering them.

(3) "A well of living water." When the need arises, she becomes a spring; when the need arises, she becomes a well. What is the difference? There is no comparison between water flowing by itself and water drawn for watering.

(4) "Rills from Lebanon." What rills? Five sources issuing from Lebanon above become rills, for when they turn into a spring, water flows, trickles drop by drop. Sweet water, pursued by the soul!

(5) So the Holy One has wrought a miracle for us right here with this spring! For this spring I recite this verse.

The power of this passage lies in its multivocal and sensual symbolism that suggests rather than discursively asserts. It is an interweaving of story and exegesis, of poetry and theosophy, botanical and scriptural imagery. For R. Pinḥas—as for Moshe de Leon—the natural world points beyond itself, the running spring and lush verdure evoking the supernal "gardens," the sefirotic world. Coming upon the spring is a "miracle," a sign of *Shekhinah*—the Cosmic Spring's—blessing and mysterious presence. The significance of the natural setting—that is, its symbolic meaning—is made clear through interpreting the verse from *Canticles*. Read properly, both nature and scripture are able to disclose the mysteries of the cosmos.

The melange of botanical images used here imparts an affective vitality to the passage that a mechanical mapping of sefirotic equivalences could never have. There is a certain indeterminate quality to this imagery, as it moves back and forth between the sefirotic and earthly referents. One generally serves as the primary focus while the other stays below the threshhold of explicit meaning as a kind of subtext.

In the first paragraph R. Pinḥas explicitly marvels at the beauty of the natural setting. The reader familiar with the *Zohar* will be struck by the mention of roses and fragrant herbs. For elsewhere as R. Shimon bar Yoḥai and his circle study, the "fields emit a multi-scented fragrance,"[105] the natural world participating in (and responding to) the sacred activity. The sefirotic meaning of the Scriptural verse remains implicit at this stage of R. Pinḥas' homily; however, it is poised to emerge.

The explicitly mystical exegesis begins in the second paragraph. In successive fashion, the three phrases of the Scriptural verse are 'opened up' to reveal supernal mysteries.[106] As noted in the beginning of the second citation, *Shekhinah*, the mystical Community of Israel, is the prime focus. The first phrase evokes Her twin guises: She is both "garden," the passive vessel that receives the divine energy (or water) from on high, and a "spring," an active force nourishing the worlds (or gardens) below. Consider the former case first. It should be noted that the lower sefirot as a whole are imaged as fertile gardens, drenched by *Binah,* the supernal spring. The irrigation occurs in two stages. First *Binah* nourishes the five rungs (from *Ḥesed* to *Yesod)* that surround *Tif'eret,* "the Holy One"; from there the waters flow unto *Shekhinah,* the garden below. Nourished by the six gardens above Her, *Shekhinah* is fully protected from the demonic forces beyond, truly a well-tended garden.

As an active sefirah conveying blessing to the lower worlds, *Shekhinah* is experienced in two distinct fashions. As is made explicit in other *Zohar* passages (1:60a-b, 235a), when Israel leads a life of holiness, *Shekhinah*'s wellsprings open and blessing streams forth into the world. But when Israel is corrupt, Her blessings remain concealed on high: She becomes a well whose living waters must be drawn out, aroused by the Kabbalist's sacred activity. Thus, the inner life of *Shekhinah* oscillates between moments of revealment and moments of concealment. In times of concealment it is the responsibility of the Kabbalist to draw Her out and make Her present below.

The fourth paragraph is perhaps the most ambiguous. Lebanon here refers to *Ḥokhmah,* the primal point, the source of divine blessing. As the water irrigates the five supernal gardens mentioned earlier, they turn into springs, flowing into *Shekhinah* Herself. All this is clear. But who is the soul here? Is it the adept himself, he who thirstily longs for the sweet waters of divinity which trickle down from *Shekhinah*? Or is it the supernal Soul, as *Shekhinah* is often called?[107] This ambiguity, this blurring of distinction between symbol and archetype, between soul and Soul, invests the text with allusive meaning.

Finally, special attention should be given to the way in which the Scriptural verse was read. The exegetical form—though not content—is firmly within a midrashic framework. That is, each phrase is probed for meaning, no word considered redundant. As in Rabbinic hermeneutics, the parallel structure of the *Canticles* verse—"a spring of gardens, a well of living water"—is ignored, each phrase shown to contain a discrete layer of meaning.[108] Yet unlike the classical midrashist, the Kabbalist directs his exegetical energies not to the world of theology, but to theosophy, the inner life of God.

For example, the Talmudic Rabbis interpreted the *Song of Songs* as a sacred dialogue between the People Israel and God, her lover. Hence, in the Rabbinic exegesis of this verse (Ex. R 20:3), the spring and well are taken as references to Israel. (Note R. Pinḥas' allusion to this in the second citation.) In good Kabbalistic fashion, however, de Leon transforms the People Israel into its sefirotic archetype, *Shekhinah*. The dramatic stage has thereby been shifted from the divine-human border to an intradivine setting. But not all is purely theosophical here; the ties to the earthly, earthy world have in no way been severed. While the midrashist has turned his gaze away from the verse's natural, botanical meaning, the Zoharic author has refocused attention upon it. The flowing spring in the Galilee is perceived as a miraculous emblem of *Shekhinah*'s blessing and bountiful presence, a symbol participating in and pointing to the divine mysteries.

With this we have concluded the introductory chapter. The goal was threefold: to provide an historical overview of the development of classical Kabbalah, to outline the structure and content of sefirotic symbolism, and to introduce the reader to the process of textual interpretation. The aim, in so doing, has been to provide the reader with a conceptual framework for approaching the heart and soul of this book, the Kabbalistic interpretation of the Sabbath.

NOTES TO THE INTRODUCTION

1. English language edition: Philadelphia, 1894. H. Graetz saw Kabbalah as the obscurantist antithesis to those rationalist trends which he felt constituted the essence of Judaism and insured its historical fulfillment.

Interestingly, many of the scholars in the first half of the nineteenth century had a neutral or even positive attitude towards Kabbalah. Key examples include Naḥman Krochmal, Salomon Munk and most strikingly, Adolph Franck who considered Kabbalah "la vie et la coeur" of Judaism. For details see M. Idel's "Remarks on Kabbalah Scholarship" in his forthcoming *Kabbalah: New Perspectives* (New Haven, 1988) and D. Biale, "The Kabbalah in Naḥman Krochmal's Philosophy," *Journal of Jewish Studies* 32 (1981): 85–97.

2. Many of these scholars were also motivated by antipathy to Eastern European Ḥasidism, which retained a Kabbalistic ethos and whose descendants were migrating to Central Europe in increasing numbers.

For discussion of the historiographical approaches of these scholars, proponents of the so-called *Wissenschaft des Judentums,* see B.Z. Dinur in EJ 16: 570–84; G. Scholem, "The Science of Judaism: Then and Now" in *The Messianic Idea in Judaism* (New York, 1971); and the judicious overview in D. Biale, *Gershom Scholem* (Cambridge, MA, 1979): 1–32. For treatment of the larger historical context, see Jacob Katz, *Out of the Ghetto* (New York, 1978); M. A. Meyer, *The Origins of the Modern Jew* (Detroit, 1967); and Jack Wertheimer, *Unwelcome Strangers: East European Jews in Imperial Germany* (New York, 1987).

3. Of course, Scholem's historiography may be placed in historical and biographical relief, as well. See D. Biale's book for the most comprehensive attempt to do so.

4. "Mysticism and Religion: The Case of Judaism" in J. Neusner, *Take Judaism, for Example* (Chicago, 1983): 67.

5. In composing this synthetic overview, I have drawn on numerous secondary sources. Most influential are the writings of A. Altmann, J. Dan, A. Green, E. Gottlieb, M. Idel, Y. Liebes, D. Matt, I. Tishby, and, especially, the work of G. Scholem. Specific references will follow.

6. For more on these two modes of Kabbalah, see M. Idel's succinct "Mysticism" in A. Cohen and P. Mendes-Flohr (eds.), *Contemporary Jewish Religious Thought* (New York, 1987) and the more expansive discussion in *Kabbalah: New Perspectives*, esp. Chapter 9, "Kabbalistic Hermeneutics."

7. Although Scholem's distinction between allegory and mystical symbol is too broadly drawn, it does provide a good preliminary orientation. For discussion, see G. Scholem, *Major Trends in Jewish Mysticism* (3rd ed., N.Y., 1965): 25–28 and idem, *Ha-Qabbalah be-Provans* (Jerusalem, 1970): Lecture 1. On reservations concerning Scholem's depiction of philosophy, see E. Schweid's "Misṭiqah Yehudit le-fi G. Shalom" in *Meḥqerei Yerushalayim be-Maḥshevet Yisra'el*, Suppl. to Vol. 2 (1983) [English: *Judaism and Mysticism* (Atlanta: 1985)]. The most trenchant general critique of G. Scholem's bipolar categorization is M. Idel's "Kabbalistic Hermeneutics" (see n. 6). For reservations from a contemporary literary critical point of view, see Uri Shoham, *Ha-Mashma'ut ha-'Aḥeret* (Tel Aviv, 1982): 61–64. A sophisticated introduction to allegorical and symbolic interpretation in medieval philosophy and Kabbalah may be found in F. Talmadge's "Apples of Gold: The Inner Meaning of Sacred Texts in Medieval Judaism" in A. Green (ed.), *Jewish Spirituality* Vol. 1 (New York, 1986): 313–55.

8. Here I am following the general description put forward by A. Green in "Religion and Mysticism: The Case of Judaism": 70.

9. These assertions will be amply illustrated throughout this study. For a condensed discussion of these points, see G. Scholem, *Major Trends:* 28–34.

10. On the assimilation of A. Bar Ḥiyya's teachings, see G. Scholem, *Ursprung und Anfange der Kabbala* [hereafter, *Ursprung*] (Berlin, 1962): 54–55, 84, 112, and 133. The borrowings from *Ḥasidei 'Ashkenaz* are more extensive. See Ibid.: 85–109, 173–74 and 273–74. (An English translation and revision of *Ursprung* is now available as *Origins of the Kabbalah* [Princeton, 1987].) Also see n. 13 below.

11. To give one pointed example: G. Scholem hypothesizes that an Aramaic work called *Raza' Rabba'* served as a foundational text for the *Bahir.*

This work, whose original form is now lost to us, was frequently referred to in Geonic sources; a Hebrew version of the book (*Sod ha-Gadol*) was evidently preserved in German Ḥasidic literature. Based on extant fragments, *Raza' Rabba'* was part mystical midrash, part magical manual. The imagery employed reveals an affinity to extant *Merkavah* and *Heikhalot* literature from Babylonia (ca. 5th-7th centuries). On its influences on the *Bahir*, see *Ursprung:* 85–109 and index.

12. As I shall later show, the *Bahir*'s sefirotic theory bears a curious resemblance to the Gnostic theory of aeons. It is not altogether clear whether this resemblance is simply a structural parallel or the result of direct historical influence. See G. Scholem's assessment in *Re'shit ha-Qabbalah ve-Sefer ha-Bahir* (Jerusalem, 1962) and the somewhat different view in his later *Kabbalah* (Jerusalem, 1974): 315ff. For detailed discussion of 'gnostic' motifs in the *Bahir*, see *Urpsrung:* 59–85, et al.

13. Evidence suggests that an earlier version of the *Bahir* had circulated in German Ḥasidic circles. These groups were known to have preserved esoteric Jewish traditions from the East. G. Scholem hyphothesizes that some time between 1130 and 1170, leaves from the proto-*Bahir* came from Germany to Provence, where they were recast and combined with other (gnostic?) elements. By the end of the twelfth century, the sources had apparently undergone final redaction, and the book had assumed its present kabbalistic—i.e., sefirotic—form. See *Ursprung:* 85–109, 173–74 and 273–74.

14. Shekhinah's liminality has its roots in several traditions:

(a) The Rabbinic notion of *Shekhinah*, or God's indwelling Presence among the People of Israel. In several accounts *Shekhinah* is portrayed as being in exile with them (see, e.g., TB Meg. 29a). However, the Rabbinic *Shekhinah* is neither distinctively feminine nor, strictly speaking, a hypostasis separable from the Holy One, as in the *Bahir*. (In the *Bahir*, the Holy One is correlated with the masculine aspect of divinity.) Rather, it usually functions as a relational term, a way of connoting divine immanence. For further discussion of the Rabbinic *Shekhinah*, see E. Urbach, *The Sages* (Jerusalem, 1979): Chap. 3 and *Major Trends:* 229.

(b) In all likelihood the Jewish philosophical distinction between *Shekhinah* and the Holy One has influenced the *Bahir* as well. The philosophers preserved the purity of monotheism by correlating the anthropomorphized conception of *Shekhinah* with the "first created essence." It might be said that the *Bahir* maintains the distinction between *Shekhinah* and the Holy One found in philosophy while preserving the divine status accorded *Shekhinah* by the Talmudic Rabbis.

(c) A third possible influence stems from the Gnostic portrayal of the last aeon, the lower Sophia, the "daughter of Light" who falls into the abyss of matter. In several *Bahir* passages, *Shekhinah* is the daughter or princess whose home is in the Realm of Light, but who wanders into far-off lands.

To cite one such example:

> And why is it written "from His Place" (Ezek. 3:12)? Because "there is no one who knows His Place" [ff. TB Ḥag. 13b; here, *Place* is an appellation for *Shekhinah*]. A parable. There was once a princess who came from a distant place. No one knew whence she came, but it was seen that she was a woman of valor, lovely and refined in all her ways. So they said: "Surely, this one is taken from the Realm of Light, for through her deeds she illumines the world." They asked her: "From where do you come?" She replied: "From my place." They said: "If so, the people from her place are great. Blessed is she! And may she be blessed from her place!"
>
> —*Bahir* (Margaliot ed.) sec. 131

For further discussion of this passage, see E. Ginsburg (ed.), *Sod ha-Shabbat* Section 13 (end) and nn. 346-47.

For a comprehensive treatment of *Shekhinah* in the *Bahir*, see G. Scholem's *Ursprung*: 143–59 and the essay "Ha-Shekhinah" in *Pirqei Yesod be-Havanat ha-Qabbalah u-Semaleha* [hereafter, *Pirqei Yesod*] (Jerusalem, 1976), esp. section 4.

15. For more detailed information on the *Bahir*, see G. Scholem's *Ursprung*: Part Two; *On the Kabbalah and its Symbolism* [hereafter, OKS] (New York, 1965): 90–94; and *Kabbalah*: 312–16.

16. In general, such settings are good breeding grounds for mysticism. It should be noted that a parallel spiritual ferment was found in the surrounding Gentile society, as well. It is possible that this group of contemplatives was influenced by the groups of Cathari in the area, though no direct impact has been established to date. For discussion, see *Kabbalah*: 45 and Sh. Shaḥar's articles "Ha-Catarism ve-Re'shit ha-Qabbalah be-Languedoc" in *Tarbiẓ* 40:4 (1971): 483–507 and "The Relationship between Kabbalism and Catharism in the South of France" in M. Yardeni (ed.), *Les Juifs dans l'histoire de France* (Leiden: 1980): 55–62.

The burgeoning of contemplative life in Provence had its parallels elsewhere in the Jewish world in the late twelfth to early thirteenth centuries: among *Ḥasidei 'Ashkenaz* in Germany and Sufi influenced pietists (*Ḥasidim*) in Egypt. Even in the environs of Southern Europe there were other independent forms of mystical experimentation. The most prominent consisted of those anonymous adepts whom G. Scholem has collectively labelled the "Contemplation Circle" (*Ḥug ha-ᶜIyyun*). Both Ḥasidei 'Ashkenaz and the Contemplation Circle developed theosophical symbol systems of considerable potency. The reasons for this sudden efflorescence of mystical-theosophical speculation have not been adequately investigated to date.

On Ḥasidei 'Ashkenaz see *Kabbalah*: 35–42; *Major Trends*: Lecture 3; the many studies of J. Dan, including *Torat ha-Sod shel Ḥasidei 'Ashkenaz* (Jerusalem, 1968); and I. Marcus, *Piety and Society* (Leiden, 1981). On the Egyptian Pietists, see *Kabbalah:* 35–37; S. D. Goitein, "Abraham Maimonides and his Pietist Circle" in A. Altmann (ed.), *Jewish Medieval and Renaissance Studies* (Cambridge, MA, 1967); G. Vajda, "The Mystical Doctrine of R. ᶜObadyah" in JJS 6 (1955): 213–25; and especially P. Fenton's introduction to Obadyah's *The Treatise of the Pool* (London, 1981). On the enigmatic *Ḥug ha-ᶜIyyun,* see *Kabbalah:* 46–48; *Ursprung:* 273–323; J. Dan, *Hugei ha-Mequbbalim ha-Ri'shonim* (Jerusalem, 1980); and the comprehensive study by Mark Verman, "Sifrei ha-ᶜIyyun: The Circle of Contemplation" (Ph.D. thesis, Harvard University, 1984).

17. The conception of *'Ein Sof* is quite similar to the neo-Platonic notion of "the One." Other neo-Platonic elements in Isaac's Kabbalah include the idea (though not the precise details) of divine emanation, and the existence of divine archetypes which are replicated in the lower worlds. The key parallel with the 'Gnostic'-*Bahir* tradition is the notion of infra-divine sefirot which may be 'known' through theosophic contemplation. In Isaac's Kabbalah, however, the sefirot usually lack the personified, mythic qualities found in the *Bahir.*

18. R. Isaac implicitly equated the sefirot with the divine essence itself, going beyond the Bahiric tendency to depict the sefirot as vessels or instruments of divine life. On this distinction, see pp. 26–27 above.

19. For more detailed discussion of Provençal Kabbalah see G. Scholem's *Kabbalah:* 42–48, *Ursprung:* Part Three, and *Ha-Qabbalah be-Provans* (Jerusalem, 1970). On the intellectual backdrop, also see I. Twersky, *Rabad of Posquieres* (Philadelphia, 1980). For an extended example of R. Isaac's contemplative mysticism, see his *Perush le-Sefer Yeẓirah,* published by G. Scholem as an appendix to *Ha-Qabbalah be-Provans.* Also see p. 35 above and the discussion on p. 213 n. 41, below.

20. The role of Judah ben Yaqar has not been adequately assessed in modern Kabbalistic scholarship. The major article remains Soloman Schechter's "Notes on the Hebrew Manuscripts in the University Library at Cambridge," *Jewish Quarterly Review* 4 (1896): 245–55.

M. Idel has suggested that R. Judah, who was known as the teacher of Moses ben Naḥman (Naḥmanides or RaMBaN) in *halakhah,* was also the source for many of the latter's Kabbalistic secrets (see n. 22 below) and the founder of the so-called Naḥmanidean school of Kabbalah. For more on R. Judah, see pp. 108–10 below as well as the germane notes; and p. 175 n. 231.

21. To be sure, many adepts combined several of these elements.

22. RaMBaN, it has been argued, is an excellent example of a conservative Kabbalist. According to M. Idel, RaMBaN held that the Torah contained only a finite corpus of Kabbalistic secrets, some preserved by oral tradition, some now lost. He was therefore cautious in advancing new teachings. Idel has also suggested that RaMBaN used the phrase *ha-mevin yavin* to specifically indicate a possible Kabbalistic explanation for a subject in which no authoritative mystical tradition was known. For further discussion, see Idel's " 'We Have No Kabbalistic Tradition on This' " in I. Twersky (ed.), *Rabbi Moses Naḥmanides* (Cambridge, MA, 1983): 51–74. For another view, one that depicts RaMBaN's Kabbalah in less conservative terms, see E. Wolfson, "By Way of Truth: Aspects of Naḥmanides' Kabbalistic Hermeneutic," to appear in *AJS Review*, vol. 13. Also see G. Scholem, *Ha-Qabbalah be-Gerona* (Jerusalem, 1963/64) and E. Gottlieb, *Meḥqarim be-Sifrut ha-Qabbalah* [hereafter, *Meḥqarim*] (Tel-Aviv, 1976): 88–95.

23. Cited in G. Scholem's *Ha-Qabbalah be-Provans:* 68.

24. For further discussion of the Gerona Kabbalists, see G. Scholem's *Kabbalah:* 48–52; *Ursprung:* Part 4; and his Hebrew University lectures collated in *Ha-Qabbalah be-Gerona* (n. 22).

25. This paradoxical sensation, commonly experienced in moments of mystical ecstasy, is strikingly captured by a latter-day Jewish mystic, the Ḥasidic master, Levi Yiẓḥaq of Berdichev:

> There are those who serve God with their human intellect, and others whose gaze is fixed on Nothing. . . . He who is granted this supreme experience loses the reality of his intellect, but when he returns from such contemplation to the intellect, he finds it full of divine and inflowing splendor.
>
> *Qedushat Levi, "Pequdei":* end, cited in *Major Trends:* 5

26. *Hashva'ah* may here be rendered, "an indistinguishable unity." Azriel characterizes it as *davar ve-hipukho,* "a thing and its opposite," a unity in which all divine opposites are rendered equivalent. *Hashva'ah* is generally said to occur at *'Ein Sof,* though sometimes the first sefirah seems to be connoted as well.

27. Cited in G. Scholem's *Re'shit ha-Qabbalah* (Jerusalem, 1948): 145.

28. Azriel's understanding of the mystical Naught or 'Nothing' seems to have been influenced not only by Isaac the Blind but also the Jewish philosopher Solomon ibn Gabirol and more surprisingly, John Scotus Erigena and Byzantine-Christian neo-Platonism. The contacts between the latter traditions and early Kabbalah deserve further study. For a preliminary treatment see G. Scholem's *Kabbalah:* 391–93 and *Ursprung*: 332 ff., 374, 379, 385 and 388–90.

29. For further discussion of Isaac ibn Latif, see *Kabbalah*: 52–57, passim, and Sarah O. Heller-Wilensky's "Isaac ibn Latif: Philosopher or

Kabbalist?" in A. Altmann (ed.), *Jewish Medieval and Renaissance Studies:* 185–223. On Isaac ibn Latif's understanding of the sefirot, see n. 79 below.

30. Abraham Abulafia was not the only figure who blended several of these disparate traditions. In an oral communication, M. Idel has pointed out the existence of several manuscripts which seem to derive from the circle of Barukh Togarmi, a Kabbalist who served as Abulafia's mentor during the latter's sojourn in Barcelona in the 1270's. One such manuscript, the anonymous *Perush ᶜal ha-Tefillot* (MS Paris 849 fols. 1b-57b) combined the theosophic traditions of *Sefer ha-Bahir* and R. Ezra ben Solomon of Gerona with the mysticism of letter-combination and Names (wherein divinity was symbolized as a texture of letters). It also alluded to a mysticism of colors in which each letter of the Hebrew alphabet was correlated with the visualization of a specific hue and, it appears, with a specific divine rung (see fol. 47a). M. Idel's ongoing research into these traditions should help clarify the intellectual milieu in which Abraham Abulafia functioned.

31. Hebrew, *hu' ve-hu' davar 'eḥad bilti nifrad*. From *Sitrei Torah*, MS Paris BN 774, fol. 140a; English version cited by M. Idel in *Kabbalah: New Perspectives*, Chap. 4 ("Unio Mystica in Jewish Mysticism").

32. See M. Idel's detailed discussion in *Kabbalah: New Perspectives*, Chap. 9 ("Kabbalistic Hermeneutics") and idem, "Infinities of Torah" in G. Hartman and S. Budick (eds.), *Midrash and Literature* (New Haven, 1986). For a psychological analysis that sheds light on this type of mystical consciousness, see Arthur Deikman, "Deautomatization and the Mystic Experience" in R. Woods (ed.), *Understanding Mysticism* (Garden City, 1980): 240–60.

33. Abulafia's influence on Spanish Kabbalah was limited due to the intense attack launched by the esteemed halakhist and Kabbalist RaSHBa. Near Eastern Kabbalists were less affected by these attacks. The anonymous author of *Shaᶜarei Ẓedeq*, Isaac ben Samuel of Acco and R. Shem Ṭov ibn Gaon all seem to have combined elements of Abulafian Kabbalah with the Jewish-Sufi pietism mentioned in n. 16 above. An even greater Abulafian influence may be discerned in Byzantine-Greek Kabbalah, probably due to Abraham Abulafia's extended sojourns there. Ecstatic elements may be discerned in the writings of Isaiah ben Joseph of Greece (1320's), in the *'Even Sappir* of Elnatan ben Moshe Kalkis of Constantinople (1368–70), in the influential *Sefer ha-Peli'ah* (ca. 1410) and, in one intriguing passage, in the *SHOSHaN Sodot* written at the turn of the sixteenth century (see fol. 69 in the printed edition).

Abulafian Kabbalah remained influential in the post-classical period. It enjoyed a renaissance in sixteenth century Jerusalem and Safed, affecting such pivotal mystics as Moses Cordovero and Ḥayyim Viṭal as well as Judah Al-Boṭini. It also exerted an important influence on eighteenth and nineteenth century Ḥasidic piety, e.g., in Beshtian meditation on the divine Name and in the practice of atomizing the letters during contemplative prayer.

For further discussion of Abulafia's life and thought, see G. Scholem's *Major Trends*: Lecture 4; idem, *Ha-Qabbalah shel Sefer ha-Temunah ve-shel 'Avraham 'Abulʿafiah* (Jerusalem, 1968/69); and more recently the groundbreaking studies of M. Idel, including "Unio Mystica in Abraham Abulafia" in I. Twersky (ed.) *Studies in Medieval Jewish History and Literature*, vol. 3 (Cambridge, MA, in press); "Kitvei R. Avraham Abulafia u-Mishnato" (Ph.D. diss., Hebrew Univ., 1976) and the revised English version to appear in several volumes, beginning with *The Mystical Experience in Abraham Abulafia* (Albany, 1988).

34. G. Scholem terms this circle Gnostic for two basic reasons:

a) the Castilians' mythic portrayal of evil as a radical counterforce to divinity; and

b) their depiction of the angelic world as a multiplicity of personified emanations.

35. The *Zohar* assimilated the structure of *Siṭra' 'Aḥra'* but generally employed more impersonal imagery. Two exceptions are the figures of Sammael, the Kabbalistic equivalent of Satan, and his female consort, Lilith. See G. Scholem, *Kabbalah*: 125.

36. For further discussion on the Castilian Gnostics, see G. Scholem's "Qabbalot R. Yaaqov ve-R. Yiẓḥaq ha-Kohen" in *Maddaʿei ha-Yahadut* 2 (1926/27) and "Le-Ḥeqer Qabbalat R. Yiẓḥaq ben Yaaqov ha-Kohen" in *Tarbiẓ* 2–5 (1931–34). A very brief English summary may be found in *Kabbalah*: 55–57. Also see the recent essays by J. Dan: "Samael, Lilith and the Concept of Evil in the Early Kabbalah" in *AJS Review* 5 (1982) and "The Beginning of the Messianic Myth in Thirteenth Century Kabbalah" [Hebrew], Hebrew University Institute of Jewish Studies (Jerusalem, 1981). For an important primary source, see R. Kiener's translation of the "Treatise on the Left Emanation" in J. Dan (ed.), *The Early Kabbalah* (New York, 1986): 165–82.

37. Late thirteenth century Castile was a fertile meeting ground for the full array of Kabbalistic trends.

38. M. Idel has recently called attention to a related aspect of this symbolic creativity. Not only is each sefirah associated with an expanded set of Scriptural referrents, but a given Scriptural term may be associated with an expanded set of divine referrents. That is, in pre-Zoharic Kabbalah the relation between a Scriptural term and its esoteric/sefirotic referrent was relatively stable. However, in the *Zohar* and a few other innovative texts of the period, each Scriptural term is associated with a profusion of sefirotic symbols.

There is a theological underpinning to this symbolic profusion, evincing a more dynamic notion of divine life than held hitherto. It is as though only such polysemy could adequately reflect the vital, ever-changing nature of the Godhead. See p. 27 above and M. Idel, "Kabbalistic Hermeneutics" in *Kabbalah: New Perspectives.*

39. On the *Zohar*'s treatment of *Shekhinah* see *Pirqei Yesod*: Chap. 8 ("Ha-Shekhinah") and I. Tishby, *Mishnat ha-Zohar* (Jerusalem, 1957–61) [hereafter MZ] vol. 1: 219–64. The English reader is advised to consult *Major Trends*: 229–35 and A. Green's "Bride, Spouse, Daughter" in S. Heschel, *On Being a Jewish Feminist* (New York, 1983).

40. Scholem ff. *Zohar* [hereafter, also Z] 3:127b–28a.

41. Ff. *Kabbalah*: 113 ff. Also see *Major Trends*: 160 on the *'Idrot*. In the former source, G. Scholem notes that the *'Idrot* imagery is also an attempt to reconcile the apparently incompatible doctrine of sefirot with the earlier *Shiʿur Qomah* speculation on the mystical *Corpus Dei*. Yehuda Liebes has recently advanced another explanation for the *'Idra'*'s warning against "fashioning a molten image" of the divine. See his important essay, "Ha-Mashiaḥ shel ha-Zohar" in *Ha-Raʿyon ha-Meshiḥi be-Yisra'el* (Jerusalem, 1982): 134–38.

42. G. Scholem notes that this phallic symbolism poses "not a minor psychological problem considering the author's strict devotion to the most pious conceptions of Jewish life and belief." For discussion, see *Major Trends*: 228 and his article "Ha-Ẓaddiq" in *Pirqei Yesod*.

43. G. Scholem (*Major Trends*: 222–23) cautions that this erotic imagery was almost entirely limited to the internal life of God, and was only rarely employed in describing the relation of God and devotee. This view has been challenged by I. Tishby (MZ 2:297–301) who demonstrates that erotic descriptions of divine–human "coupling" (*zivvug*) are by no means uncommon in the *Zohar*. Still, he allows that the most widespread—and basic—sexual imagery is intra-divine. As will be shown later, *hieros gamos* was given archetypal significance in the *Zohar*, serving as the model for the sacred union of husband and wife. On this point see *Major Trends*: 235 and MZ 2: 609ff. For further treatment of sexual symbolism in the *Zohar*, see *Major Trends*: 225–35 and MZ 1:148–49 and 158–61.

44. Here I have been limiting myself to two of the more striking symbol–sets in the *Zohar*. More traditional Kabbalistic images are employed as well: light imagery, linguistic and Torah symbolism, etc. For examples see MZ 1:151–161 and the systematic discussion of sefirotic symbolism later in this chapter.

45. See Y. Liebes, "Ha-Mashiaḥ shel ha-Zohar": 194–98. For G. Scholem's dating of the various strata, see *Kabbalah*: 214–20.

46. Y. Baer has noted certain similarities between this peripatetic form of study—evidently used by contemporary Kabbalists—and the activities of

Franciscan Spirituals in thirteenth century Spain. For further discussion, see Y. Baer, *A History of the Jews in Christian Spain* (Philadelphia, 1961) 1: 266–70.

47. On the narrative aspect of the *Zohar*, in general, see Tishby's comments in MZ 1 (Preface): 25–27. Two recent studies have analyzed the narrative structure of specific sections of the Zohar. On the *'Idrot*, see Y. Liebes, "Ha-Mashiaḥ shel ha-Zohar", esp. pp. 103–04; on the Zoharic treatment of Ex. 1–20, see E. Wolfson, "Left Contained in the Right: A Study in Zoharic Hermeneutics", *AJS Review* 11 (1986): 27–52. The English reader may discover the *Zohar*'s narrative richness in D. Matt's recent translations, *Zohar: The Book of Enlightenment* (New York, 1983) [hereafter cited as D. Matt].

48. The *Zohar* was one of the first Jewish works to interpret Scripture in the four-fold fashion pioneered by Christian exegetes. In the *Zohar* these four levels include the literal-contextual, allegorical-philosophical, Aggadic-homiletical and sefirotic-mystical layers of meaning. See G. Scholem, OKS: 50–65 for further discussion.

49. See D. Matt: 5–6.

50. Ibid: 6–7. See there for a fuller text and translation. On the *'Or Zaruᶜa* and its place in Moshe de Leon's oeuvre, see A. Altmann's introduction to "Sefer 'Or Zaruᶜa le-R. Moshe de Leon" in *Qoveẓ ᶜal Yad* 9 (1980): 219–93, and Asi Farber, "Li-Mqorot Torato ha-Qabbalit ha-Muqdemet shel R. Moshe de Leon," in *Meḥqerei Yerushalayim be-Maḥshevet Yisra'el* 3: 1–2 (1984): 67–96.

51. See *Zohar* 3: 152a:

> R. Shimon said: If a man looks upon Torah as merely a book presenting narratives and everyday matters, alas for him! Such a torah, one treating everyday concerns, and indeed a more excellent one, we too, even we, could compile. . . But the Torah, in all of its worlds, holds supernal truths and sublime secrets. . .
>
> Woe to the sinners who look upon the Torah as simply tales pertaining to things of the world, seeing only the outer garments. But the righteous whose gaze penetrates to the very Torah, happy are they!
>
> Just as wine must be in a jar to keep, so the Torah must be contained in an outer garment. The garment is made up of the tales and stories, but we, we are bound to penetrate beyond!
>
> ff. H. Sperling and M. Simon's translation of *The Zohar* (London, 1933).

52. The bulk of them were written after the *Zohar* and often served as exegesis of doctrine enshrined in it.

53. It should be recalled that pseudepigraphy was a time-honored mode of expression in Castilian Kabbalah. The interesting question is why Moshe de Leon chose to employ it in this particular instance.

54. A financial motive cannot be wholly discounted either (see the evidence in D. Matt: 4 and 28), though this clearly was not a primary consideration as H. Graetz once charged. See his *History of the Jews*, Vol. 4: 1–12 and *Major Trends*: 191–92 for G. Scholem's demurral.

55. Undoubtedly the motives are overdetermined. For further discussion, see D. Matt: 13–14, 25–30; *Major Trends*: 190–204; *Kabbalah*: 233–35; MZ 1: Introductory Section, Chap. 2–3; and Y. Liebes, "Ha-Mashiaḥ shel ha-Zohar": 101ff. Liebes has convincingly shown the special relationship Moshe de Leon felt with the soul of R. Shimon.

56. D. Matt: 27. Also see Y. Liebes, "Peraqim be-Millon Sefer ha-Zohar" (Ph. D. diss., Hebrew University, 1976): 2–3 and idem, "Ha-Mashiaḥ shel ha-Zohar": 141 n. 210.

57. MS Vatican 203 fol. 63b, cited in *Major Trends*: 189.

58. To cite several examples: the TZ/RM tends more towards theism whereas the *Zohar* frequently edges towards pantheism. The former's author engaged in a sharper social critique than did Moshe de Leon and had better knowledge of Talmudic casuistry. The TZ/RM lacks the inspired literary style of the *Zohar* and often employs a different (more dualistic) symbolism.

59. For further discussion on the TZ/RM, see G. Scholem's comments in *Major Trends*: Lecture 5 and *Kabbalah*: 218–19. Books written in imitation of the *Zohar* came to constitute a distinctive literary genre in later Kabbalah. Important examples include Joseph of Hamadan's *Sefer TaSHaQ* and Joseph Angelino's *Livnat ha-Sappir* (both of which imitate the Zohar's language), as well as the aptly named *Zohar Tinyana'* (Second Zohar) of Moshe Ḥayyim Luzzatto.

60. The English reader seeking further discussion on the *Zohar* may consult *Major Trends*: Lectures 5–6; *Kabbalah*: 213–43; D. Matt: Introduction; and A. Green, "The Zohar: Jewish Mysticism in Medieval Spain" in P. Szarmach (ed.), *An Introduction to the Medieval Mystics of Europe* (Albany, 1984). The most comprehensive treatment of the *Zohar* is still I. Tishby's two volume MZ, soon to appear in English translation as *The Wisdom of the Zohar* (in press).

On the study of the *Zohar* in Castile on the eve of the Expulsion, see J. Hacker, "Lamdanutam ha-Ruḥanit shel Yehudei Sefarad be-Sof ha-Me'ah ha-15," *Sefunot* 17 (1983): 52–54. On the popularization of the *Zohar* in this period, see Z. Gries' pioneering article "ʿIẓẓuv Sifrut ha-Hanhagot ha-ʿIvrit be-Mifneh Me'ah ha-16 u-ve-Me'ah ha-17 u-Mashmaʿuto ha-Hisṭorit" in *Tarbiẓ* 56 (1987): 527–81. On the place of the *Zohar* in the present-day Sephardic culture, see A. Bension, *The Zohar in Moslem and Christian Spain*

(London, 1932), passim; S. Deshen and M. Shokeid, *The Predicament of Homecoming* (Ithaca, 1974), passim; and Avraham Shtall's article, "Qeri'ah Pulḥanit shel Sefer ha-Zohar" in *Peʿamim*, Vol. 5 (1980): 77–86.

61. On this Kabbalist, who flourished in the first half of the fourteenth century, see E. Gottlieb in EJ 9:29–30 and A. Goldreich's thesis on *Sefer Me'irat ʿEinayim* (Ph.D. diss., Hebrew University, 1981).

62. For an overview of these philosopher-Kabbalists (who include Moshe Narboni and Joseph ibn Waqar) see G. Scholem, *Kabbalah*: 63–64. For more detailed discussion on Narboni, see A. Altmann, "Moshe Narboni's Epistle on Shiʿur Qomah" in idem, *Jewish Medieval and Renaissance Studies*: 225–88; on Joseph ibn Waqar, see Georges Vajda, *Récherches sur la philosophie et la Kabbale dans la pensée juive du moyen age* (Paris, 1962): 115–97.

63. On the development of this tradition, see G. Scholem, "Me-Ḥoqer li-Mqubbal," *Tarbiẓ* 6 (1939): 334–42.

64. See G. Scholem, *Kabbalah*: 64 for details.

65. Ibid.: 65. The most detailed treatment of the *Peli'ah* and *Qanah* is Michal Oron's Ph.D. thesis, "Ha-Peli'ah ve-ha-Qanah" (1980), recently published by the Hebrew University. An English abstract is appended to her work. Other important studies include I. Ta-Shma, "Heikhan Nitḥabberu Sifrei ha-Qanah ve-ha-Peli'ah" in *Peraqim be-Toledot ha-Ḥevrah ha-Yehudit bi-Ymei ha-Beinayim u-va-ʿEt ha-Ḥadashah* (Jerusalem, 1980): 56–63; Steven Bowman, *The Jews of Byzantium*: 1204–1453 (Tuscaloosa, 1985): 136 and 156–61; and the exchange between M. Oron and S. Bowman in *Tarbiẓ* 54 (1985): 150–52 and 297–98. These works also shed light on broader trends in Byzantine-Greek Kabbalah.

66. Cf., e.g., Shem Ṭov's *Sefer ha-'Emunot*:

> I realized that this doctrine [i.e., philosophy] is a terrible misfortune for the people of Israel and leads to apostasy and atheism. We have seen that when the great catastrophe [the persecutions of 1391] took place and the wrath of persecutions and apostasies was poured out upon us, our learned men and "experts in investigation" at once denied their faith and became converts. There is no doubt that because of their guilt our communities were destroyed. They, the men of knowledge and the philosophizers, were the first breakers of the fence and repudiated the Torah, and many of the common people followed them. And we have remained desolate and forsaken. As soon as they came to the conclusion that "there is no justice and no judge," that neither good nor evil is recompensed, that only philosophical inquiry is important, that it alone brings about the exercise of Providence, they recognized that this can be attained far more easily when one is "liberated" and can lead a free and calm life, not remaining "a slave in Exile."

cited in I. Zinberg, *A History of Jewish Literature,* Vol. 3 (Cleveland, 1973): 199–200.
On the deteriorating situation of Spanish Jewry in the late fourteenth to fifteenth centuries, see Y. Baer, *A History of the Jews in Christian Spain,* Vol. 2. On Shem Ṭov ibn Shem Ṭov, see now David Ariel, "Shem Tob ibn Shem Tob's Kabbalistic Critique of Jewish Philosophy in the Commentary on the Sefirot: Study and Text." (Ph.D. diss., Brandeis Univ., 1981).

67. Perhaps the most outstanding example of this phenomenon is Israel al-Naqawa's *Menorat ha-Ma'or,* which quotes the *Zohar* under the title *Midrash Yehi 'Or* ("Let There Be Light").

68. It might be noted that Italian Kabbalah developed along distinctively intellectualist, contemplative lines, with less stress on those mythic and theurgic elements so common in Spain. For details see M. Idel, "Magical and Neo-Platonic Interpretations of the Kabbalah": 188ff. in B. Cooperman (ed.), *Jewish Thought in the Sixteenth Century* (Cambridge, MA, 1983). For discussion of Spanish Kabbalah prior to the Explusion, see G. Scholem, "Li-Ydiᶜat ha-Qabbalah bi-Sfarad ᶜErev ha-Gerush," *Tarbiẓ* 24 (1954): 174–206 and I. Tishby, *Meshiḥiut be-Dor Gerushei Sefarad u-Porṭugal* (Jerusalem, 1985).
For general discussion of fourteenth and fifteenth century Kabbalah, see *Kabbalah*: 61–67 and Zinberg, Vol. 3 *(The Struggle of Mysticism and Tradition Against Philosophical Rationalism).* On the influence of Kabbalah on the semi-rationalist philosophers of the day, also see Z. Harvey, "Yesodot Qabbaliyim be-Sefer 'Or Ha-Shem le-R. Ḥasdai Crescas" in *Meḥqerei Yerushalayim be-Maḥshevet Yisra'el* 2 (1983) and H. Tirosh-Rothschild, "*Sefirot* as the Essence of God in the Writings of David Messer Leon" in *AJS Review* 7–8 (1982–83).

69. M. Idel has identified some ten works from this school, including the well-known commentary on *Sefer ha-Temunah;* a commentary on the Passover Haggadah, published (with incorrect attribution) in M. Kasher and S. Ashkenazi, *Haggadah Shelemah* (Jerusalem, 1967): 121–32; a commentary on the *Shemaᶜ*; and an explication of the sefirot. All reflect the *Temunah*'s overriding concern with *shemiṭṭah* theory. Until recently, most scholars had accepted G. Scholem's view that *Sefer ha-Temunah* was from thirteenth century Spain. See *Ursprung,* end; and his detailed lectures in *Ha-Qabbalah shel Sefer ha-Temunah ve-shel 'Avraham 'Abulᶜafiah.* Also see E. Gottlieb, *Meḥqarim,* 332–39; and idem, EJ 15:999. More generally on the doctrine of *shemiṭṭot, see Kabbalah*: 118–22 and Sh. Rosenberg, "Ha-Shivah le-Gan ᶜEden" in *Ha-Raᶜyon ha-Meshiḥi be-Yisra'el*": 43–63. Also see pp. 97–100 below and the germane notes.

70. Both G. Scholem and the eminent historian Yitzḥak F. Baer long claimed that the *Qanah* and *Peli'ah* (n. 65) were composed in Spain in the latter half of the fourteenth century. *SHOSHaN Sodot* was written by Moses

ben Jacob of Kiev (1449–1520). Although of Ashkenazic origin, R. Moses studied in Istanbul and later settled in Crimea. As I will later show, *SHOSHaN Sodot* reveals the clear influence of *Sefer ha-Qanah.*

71. On the re-orientation of Kabbalah after the Spanish Explusion see G. Scholem, *Major Trends*: 244–51 and idem, "Le-'Aḥar Gerush Sefarad" in *Devarim be-Go* (Tel Aviv, 1976), Vol. 1: 262–69.

72. For discussion on Safed Kabbalah see *Major Trends:* Lecture 7; R. J. Zwi Werblowsky, *Joseph Karo: Lawyer and Mystic* (Oxford, 1962); L. Fine's anthology, *Safed Spirituality* (New York, 1984) and S. Schechter's classic essay, "Safed in the Sixteenth Century" in his *Studies in Judaism*, second series (Philadelphia, 1908). On other trends in sixteenth century mysticism see B. Cooperman (ed.), *Jewish Thought in the Sixteenth Century.* On the spread of Kabbalah in the sixteenth and seventeenth centuries, see G. Scholem, *Sabbatai Ṣevi* (Princeton, 1973): 66–93 and I. Twersky and B. Septimus (eds.), *Jewish Thought in the Seventeenth Century* (Cambridge, MA, 1987).

73. For further discussion see *Kabbalah*: 67 ff.

74. A more detailed discussion of Meir ibn Gabbai's life and thought may be found in the introduction to my *Sod ha-Shabbat* (Albany, 1989). Also see G. Scholem, EJ 7:233; E. Gottlieb, *Meḥqarim*: index; I. Zinberg, *The History of Jewish Literature,* Vol. 5:39–49; and especially R. Goetschal, *Meir ibn Gabbai: Le Discours de la Kabbale Espagnole* (Leuven, 1981).

75. Some Kabbalists were much occupied with resolving this conceptual conflict, whereas others were not bothered by it in the least, preferring to direct their attention to less theoretical issues.

76. For the sake of completeness it might be noted that some—especially later—Kabbalists did attribute personal qualities to *'Ein Sof,* speaking, e.g., of the "Infinite, Blessed be He"! See also the evidence adduced by M. Idel in "Demut ha-'Adam me-ᶜal ha-Sefirot," *Daᶜat* 4 (1980): 41–55.

77. See, e.g., Azriel's notion of *hashva'ah,* p. 11 and n. 26 above.

78. The most common term for the divine emanation, *'aẓilut,* highlights the organic connection between the sefirot and *'Ein Sof.* Literally, it means that which is near by or with the Source. For further discussion, see *Kabbalah*: 101–03.

It is worth noting that the two modes of explaining the unity of *'Ein Sof* and the sefirot are sometimes conflated. That is, some mystics state that at a lower stage of consciousness, divinity seems complex, variegated but at the highest stage—as the devotee penetrates ever inward—only *'Ein Sof* (or *'Ein Sof* and its outward aspect, *Keter*) remain real. To use a Zoharic simile (3:288a), divinity may be likened to a single spark which radiates multiple beams of light. From a distance one sees these sundry lights but as he draws near the source, "there is nothing but the spark alone."

79. It should be noted that our typology necessarily presents the positions in neater and more discrete fashion than did the classical Kabbalists themselves. Two qualifications to bear in mind: First, the heuristic distinction between essentialists and instrumentalists should not be read too sharply. Although systematic reflection on the nature of the sefirot began in the early thirteenth century, it was only in the late fifteenth to early sixteenth century that the two basic positions were "presented as conflicting stands, and thereby crystallized as independent perceptions." (M. Idel) Not surprisingly, many Kabbalists before (and some after!) unself-consciously alternated between the two basic views.

Secondly, the working typology hardly exhausts Kabbalistic views on the sefirot. For example,

a) Moses Cordovero of sixteenth century Safed attempted to harmonize the two views sketched above, seeing the sefirot both as divine essence and as *kelim*.

b) A few mystically inclined philosophers held an instrumentalist position but saw the sefirot in quasi-philosophical terms: as Separate Intellects (e.g., Abraham Abulafia, Joseph Albo) or as intra-divine Ideas (e.g., Isaac Abravanel, David Messer Leon and other Italian Kabbalists of a Platonic stripe.) They thereby tended to attenuate the sefirotic dynamism found in most other strands of Kabbalah. (See n. 80 below.)

c) A rather different view may be found in ecstatic Kabbalah and in the writings of Isaac ibn Latif, where the sefirot are primarily conceived in immanentist terms: as the structure of divine emanation within created reality. (As shall later be shown, most theosophical Kabbalists saw the sefirot in both transcendent and immanent terms: as the divine Ground *for* reality and the structuring presence *in* that reality. See chapter 2, pp. 190–94.)

For further discussion on the nature of the sefirot, see M. Idel's nuanced typology in *Kabbalah: New Perspectives*, Chap. 6, "Kabbalistic Theosophy."

80. These philosopher-mystics tended to see the sefirot as static, unmoved in their perfection, like Platonic ideas set within the Divine Mind. Accordingly, sefirotic change is only apparent, a function of limited human perception. It might also be noted that some other Kabbalists, e.g., Isaac the Blind and Joseph ben Shalom Ashkenazi (an adept who immigrated to Barcelona in the late thirteenth century) distinguished between the three upper sefirot, which were without activity or change, and the seven lower rungs, which underwent certain changes in time and space. More typical views, however, will be concentrated on here.

81. *Sheqel ha-Qodesh* (London, 1911): 113. Moshe de Leon thus embraces the Heraclitean view that *essentially* "all is flux." To speak of the sefirot, one must arbitrarily freeze and delimit that which can never, properly speaking, be frozen. For other examples of Moshe de Leon's theological

dynamism, see Z 1: 41b, ZḤ 39d and the untitled text published by G. Scholem, "Eine unbekannte mystische Schrift des Mose de Leon," MGWJ 71 (1927): 109–23. For discussion, see M. Idel, *Kabbalah: New Perspectives:* 140–41; and idem, "Le-Gilguleha shel Ṭekhniqah Qedumah shel Ḥazon Nevu'i bi-Ymei ha-Beinayyim," *Sinai* 86 (1980): 5–6.

82. See two sources cited in *Kabbalah: New Perspectives:* 196–97:

> In spite of the fact that it is beneath [the other sefirot], sometimes it [Diadem or *Malkhut,* the "last" rung] ascends to *'Ein Sof* and becomes a diadem on their head; for this reason it is called *ᶜAṭarah* [Diadem].

The second source is from an anonymous commentary on the sefirot from the early fourteenth century. According to it, the enumeration of the sefirot began with:

> *ᶜAṭarah* to let you know that it is also *Keter* [=Crown!—a common name for the highest rung]; and if you reverse the sefirot, then *Malkhut* will be the first sefirah. . . as they have neither beginning nor end.

83. See *Kabbalah*: 102 for general discussion. For detailed treatment of divinity as a series of sacred letters and divine Names, see OKS: Chapter 2 and M. Idel, "Tefisat ha-Torah be-Sifrut ha-Heikhalot ve-Gilguleha ba-Qabbalah", *Meḥqerei Yerushalayim be-Maḥshevet Yisra'el* 1 (1981), esp. 49–84.

84. The synthetic portrait that follows draws primarily on Zoharic, and secondarily on Geronese, traditions.

85. David ben Avraham ha-Lavan in his *Masoret ha-Berit* (ca. 1300), ed. by G. Scholem in *Qoveẓ ᶜal Yad* o.s 1(1936): 31. Translated in *Kabbalah*: 95. M. Idel describes *'Ayin* as the fullness of being which transcends Being itself.

86. *Hitballeᶜut* literally means "swallowing." This cosmic process was discussed first in thirteenth century Spanish sources and at greater length in *Sefer ha-Temunah* (n. 69 above). For explanation of *torat ha-hitballeᶜut,* see *Kabbalah*: 52, 116–22 and G. Scholem's *Ha-Qabbalah shel Sefer ha-Temunah ve-shel 'Avraham 'Abulᶜafiah*. Also see pp. 98–100 and 196 below; as well as E. Ginsburg, *Sod ha-Shabbat,* nn. 335–36.

87. The eight lower sefirot are frequently called by the name of certain Biblical heroes. In this schema, each rung serves as an archetype of its human namesake, often indicating the spiritual rung he or she attained or experienced most intensely. That is, *Binah* is sometimes called "Moses," *Yesod,* "Joseph," and *Malkhut,* "Rachel" or King David. Perhaps the most common hero-symbolism is the one noted in the text, linking the middle triad with the three Patriarchs. For further discussion see *Kabbalah*: 111 and D. Matt: 34 and 38.

For an unusual linking of the seven lower sefirot with the seven prophetesses, see Menaḥem Azariah of Fano's (d. 1620) "Mother of All Life," translated by M. Krassen in *Kabbalah: A Newsletter of Current Research in Jewish Mysticism* 2:2 (1987): 6–7.

88. For further discussion of Evil in classical Kabbalah, see G. Scholem, *Kabbalah*: 122–28 and "Siṭra' 'Aḥra' " in *Pirqei Yesod*.

89. Cf. A. Green in "*Zohar*: Jewish Mysticism in Medieval Spain": 119.

90. According to most Kabbalists *Shekhinah*'s Exile stemmed from the Adamic Sin. G. Scholem explained the Zoharic understanding of this 'Exile' as follows:

> The sefirot were revealed to Adam in the shape of the Tree of Life and the Tree of Knowledge, i.e., *Tif'eret* and *Shekhinah*; instead of presevering their original unity and thereby unifying the spheres of "life" and "knowledge" and bringing salvation to the world, he separated one from the other and set his mind to worship the *Shekhinah* only without recognizing its union with the other sefirot. Thus he interrupted the stream of life which flows from sphere to sphere and brought separation and isolation into the world.
>
> From this time on there has been a mysterious fissure, not indeed in the substance of Divinity but in its life and action. This doctrine has been completely hedged around with reservations, but its basic meaning for all that is clear enough. Its pursuit led to the conception of what the Kabbalists call "the exile of *Shekhinah*." Only after the restoration of the original harmony in the act of Redemption, when everything shall again occupy the place it originally had in the divine scheme of things, will "God be One and His Name, One". . . .
>
> In the present unredeemed and broken state of the world this fissure which prevents the continous union of [*Tif'eret*] and the *Shekhinah* is somehow healed or mended by the religious act of Israel: Torah, *miẓvot* and prayer. Extinction of the stain, restoration of harmony . . . is man's task in this world. In the state of Redemption, however, "there shall be perfection above and below, and all worlds shall be united in one bond." (*Major Trends*: 232–33)

91. To further sample the symbolic richness of this sefirah, see the nearly two hundred *kinnuyyim* (apellations) recorded in *Maᶜarekhet ha-'Elohut*, fol. 67a–74b.

On *Shekhinah* as King David, see, e.g, p. 169 n. 190 below. The Kabbalistic assignment of gender to specific sefirot is often more complicated that appears at first blush. Not only does the gender attributed to *Shekhinah* retain a degree of fluidity—alternating between the dominant female and secondary male referrents—but a certain mutability may be found in the engenderment of other divine rungs. For example, it is not unusual to find the first nine sefirot—including the generally feminine *Binah*—typified as masculine, reserving a specifically feminine identity only for *Shekhinah*. On the other hand, Shem Ṭov ibn Gaon once depicted all ten sefirot as female: "Know that all the sefirot are designated by feminine names for they all *receive* [divine energy] from one another." (*Keter Shem Ṭov*, MS Munich 11 fol. 234a) Quite a different rationale for female engenderment is implicit in the source in n. 87 above, where all seven active rungs were asociated with heroic women.

92. See his essay, "Ha-Shekhinah" in *Pirqei Yesod*, esp. pp. 300 ff. G. Scholem noted, however:

> While *Shekhinah* has certain dark and destructive aspects, they are relatively moderate when compared to [many] other female images found in the history of religion. (Ibid.: 300)

The English reader interested in Shekhinah's "dark" side may consult R. Patai's provocative (though occasionally flawed) analysis in *The Hebrew Goddess* (2nd ed., New York, 1978), chapters 5 and 6.

93. On *'ANiY* as a name for *Shekhinah*, see *Major Trends*: 216. For further discussion on the process of divine individuation see Ibid: 216-217.

94. For other explanations of this reticence, see *Major Trends*: 15–16; and P. Mendes-Flohr's introduction to M. Buber's *Ecstatic Confessions* (San Francisco, 1985): xxiii and xxix n. 58 (citing the views of Prof. Ze'ev Gries).

It may also be noted that certain Kabbalists severely limited the degree of mystical ascent, maintaining that *Shekhinah* was the highest rung open direct experience. Any understanding of the upper sefirot, therefore, was dependent on the mediation of *Shekhinah*. In the Zoharic image, She serves as *'aspaqlariah she-'einenah me'irah*, a darkened mirror or prism through which the more recondite rungs may be glimpsed. For further discussion see D. Matt: 37–38.

95. Quoted in *Major Trends*: 221. See G. Scholem, *Monatsschrift fuer Geschichte und Wissenchaft des Judentums* [MGWJ] (1927): 118–19 for primary sources.

96. Here I am drawing on D. Matt's formulation. See ad loc.: 37.

97. In Hebrew: *derekh hitbonenut—derekh yeniqato, ve-lo' derekh yediᶜato*. From Isaac's Commentary to *Sefer Yeẓirah* (1:1), printed as an appendix to G. Scholem's *Ha-Qabbalah be-Provans*. The English translation is from D. Matt: 37. For discussion of this passage, see G. Scholem, *Ursprung*: 246–47.

98. For further discussion of the sefirot as stages of mystical ascent, see pp. 198–99 and 213 n. 41 below.

99. Here I am building on the remarks of A. Green. See his "Religion and Mysticism": 89–91.

100. Ibid.: 90.

101. For further analysis of sefirotic symbolism, see G. Scholem, *Major Trends*: Lecture 6, and OKS: 100–09; D. Matt: 33–38; I. Tishby's lengthy treatment in MZ 1: 95–282; and now M. Idel, *Kabbalah: New Perspectives*, esp. chaps. 6 and 9.

102. See Z 3:200b–201b for details.

103. This translation is drawn from D. Matt: 180–81. I have departed from his fine rendering in two minor instances only. The paragraph divisions are mine, included for heuristic purposes.

104. I. Tishby (MZ 1:16) reads: "It [the Spring] is secret and hidden."

105. Cited in Y. Baer, *A History of the Jews in Christian Spain*, Vol. 1: 269. Also see Z 3: 144b (IR). The affinity for nature expressed in these sources recalls the writings of the Franciscan Spirituals. See Baer, Ibid.: 268–70 for details.

106. Like a stone dropped into a pond, the verse also "opens out" to its surrounding verses, evoking—in the mind of Moshe de Leon and R. Pinḥas—the paradisical garden of Canticles as a whole. Especially resonant are the surrounding verses, Cant. 4:12–5:1, where the lush, aromatic garden is a metaphor for the beloved bride (kabbalistically, *Shekhinah!*):

A garden is my sister, my bride,
 A fountain locked, a sealed up spring.
Your limbs are an orchard of pomegranates
 and of all luscious fruits,
 of henna and nard—
Nard and saffron,
 fragrant reed and cinnamon
 with all aromatic woods,
 myrrh and aloe—
 all the choice perfumes.
[You are] a spring of gardens,
 A well of fresh water,
 A rill from Lebanon. . . .

107. See D. Matt: 293 and the sources cited therein.

108. As R. Alter has shown (*The Art of Biblical Poetry* [New York, 1985]: 185–203), the semantic parallelism found in the *Song of Songs* is remarkably free and nuanced, employing techniques ranging from verbal repetition to elaboration and intensification. The midrashists and Kabbalists, it could be argued, were preternaturally sensitive to the subtle shifts in meaning created by the latter two verbal forms.

CHAPTER ONE

The Symbolism of the Kabbalistic Sabbath: Motif Studies

Over a period of several centuries, the classical Kabbalists developed a rich body of myth and ritual which articulated a new vision of the Sabbath. Several outstanding examples of this are the re-imaging of the Sabbath as a mystical marriage ceremony, a day on which the divine lovers re-unite; the Sabbath as a cosmic Axis, around which Time is organized and through whose channels the week is ennobled and blessed; and the Sabbath as a festival of spiritual restoration, whereby the Jew is graced with an additional *pneuma,* the Sabbath-soul, enabling him to participate more fully in the mysteries of the divine world. The Sabbath is thus experienced as a multi-leveled process of renewal, whereby Divinity, Time, and Person—indeed the Cosmos as a whole—are transformed and brought near their ideal state.

As we shall see, the mystical Sabbath is a complex melding of tradition and innovation: although the rabbinically ordained praxis was retained, its underlying meaning was significantly altered, recast in line with sefirotic symbolism and distinctively mystical concerns.[1] For example, in the fiery crucible of the Kabbalistic imagination, the traditional blessing over the wine becomes a mythic representation of *Shekhinah* and the Holy One's "coronation," while the three Sacred Meals serve as occasion to partake in the divine Sabbath and to invest the lower worlds with supernal blessing. The Kabbalists transform the Rabbinic Sabbath into a mystery rite; it is a celebration of cosmic renewal, a pilgrimage to the heart of being.

The purpose of this chapter is to classify, describe, and interpret the key mythic motifs of the Kabbalistic Sabbath, paying close attention to the course of their historical development. To provide a broader context for these themes, we will first outline some of the major elements of the pre-Kabbalistic Sabbath and briefly compare *miẓvat Shabbat* among the Rabbinic Sages and their Kabbalistic descendants.

SECTION ONE: AN HISTORICAL OVERVIEW

The Sabbath in Antiquity

Israel's enduring love affair with the Sabbath is first attested in the Biblical corpus. Its authors accorded Shabbat both universal-sacramental[2] and national-social significance, linking the institution with two of the pivotal moments in "Sacred History," Creation and the Exodus from Egypt. In the first instance Shabbat is seen as a day of universal consecration and rest in *imitatio dei* (ff. Gen. 2:1–3 and Ex. 20:11). The Sabbath is both the crown of God's Creation and the climax of each mundane week. By dividing time into a recurring pattern of six ordinary days of labor and a seventh day of heightened sacrality and rest, one lives in accord with the cosmic rhythms established by God "in the beginning."

In the second instance, the Exodus, Sabbath takes on a more distinctly national coloration: it is portrayed as a holiday recalling the liberation of one people, Israel, from Egyptian slavery (Dt. 5:15; cf. Ex. 23:9–12). On the one hand, the Sabbath celebrates freedom from all forms of human servitude; on the other, it is a day necessitating Israel's loyalty before *YHWH*, by virtue of His having redeemed them. The national significance of the day is amplified in several related passages: the Sabbath is seen as a perpetual sign of God's covenant with Israel, ever confirming His special relationship with the community (see Ex. 31:13–17).

In more general terms, the worth of the Sabbath in the Biblical tradition is attested by its place in the Decalogue, the only holy day so honored. The severe punishments Scripture associated with desecration of the Sabbath[3] further indicate the day's singular import.

From an historical perspective, the Sabbath had attained significant institutional status by the period of the Monarchy. It was a popular, joyous festival marked by cessation of agricultural labor and commerce, a day of celebration, both private and public. As many scholars have noted, esteem for Shabbat rose just before, during, and after the Babylonian Exile in the sixth century B.C.E. With the Temple—the sacred center[4]—in ruins and the religious leaders banished, the Sabbath came to serve as a temporary replacement for the defiled Sanctuary. For the Sabbath was an institution that could survive in Exile and one that was peculiarly appropriate to the religious and social needs of a small and scattered people confronted with the growing threat of assimilation. Moshe Greenberg explains that under such circumstances,

> the distinctively Israelite day of rest which allowed of public and private expression and which was not essentially bound up with a sacrificial cult, became the chief vehicle of identification with the Covenant Community. To mark oneself off from the gentile by observing the peculiar, weekly "sign" of God's consecration of Israel was an act of loyalty which might well be counted the equivalent of the rest of the Commandments, while disregard of the Sabbath might well be considered as serious a breach of faith with the God of Israel as the worship of alien gods. (EJ 14:562)

Accordingly, Sabbath observance was seen as the key to national survival, a notion that persisted even after the Temple was rebuilt. Many writers of the Exilic period—Jeremiah, Ezekiel, Exilic Isaiah, and Neḥemiah—singled it out from all the Covenantal obligations and maintained that the fate of the dynasty and Jerusalem, of the individual and the collective, all depended on proper observance.[5] Most of the Pentateuchal references to the Sabbath, including those cited earlier, were products of this turbulent age.[6]

The centrality of the Sabbath as a sacramental and national institution was maintained throughout the Second Temple period, both in the Land of Israel and the Diaspora. The seriousness with which Shabbat was taken is evident in several Apocryphal and Pseudepigraphic passages. According to I Macc. (2:31–38), during the Maccabean revolt the Jews originally allowed themselves to be killed rather than take up arms on the Sabbath, while *The Book of Jubilees* details the severe punishments to be administered for acts of Sabbath-desecration.[7] Sources as diverse as Philo, the *Damascus Covenant* found at Qumran, and Josephus all underscored the sacramental significance of the holy day and evinced marked concern over its proper observance.[8]

This shared concern did not necessarily mean that there was a consensus concerning the *details* of observance, however. Divergent and at times conflicting practices may be noted in the sundry sources.[9] In large part this variety stemmed from the lack of specificity in the Biblical Sabbath-law. Jews had to figure out what it meant to observe the Sabbath—determining exactly which forms of labor were to be prohibited; exactly which activities facilitated 'Sabbath Delight' (ff. Isa. 58:13), and so forth—and, not surprisingly, "different groups of Jews arrived at different answers."[10] As with the details of Sabbath-praxis, there were also significant philosophical differences among the Jewish sects regarding Sabbath's function and spiritual tenor.

Such sources as the *Damascus Covenant* betray a distinct sectarian-legalist orientation, whereas other authors, e.g., Aristobulus and Philo, tended to allegorize and universalize the significance of Shabbat (without detracting from its observance)[11], placing emphasis on its contemplative nature. Philo wrote:

> When He forbids bodily labor on the seventh day, He permits the exercise of the higher activities, namely, those employed in the study of the principles of the virtue's lore. For the law bids us take the time for studying philosophy and thereby improve the soul and the dominant mind.[12]

The Rabbinic Sabbath

Thus far we have established the high importance of Shabbat during the Monarchy and Second Commonwealth period. Still this import falls short of the quintessential status the Sabbath attained soon thereafter, with the rise and spread of Rabbinic Judaism. Rabbinic Judaism emerged out of a series of crises that befell the Jews in Palestine at the turn of the millenium: the sectarian strife of the last centuries B.C.E., the destruction of the Temple in 70 C.E., and the debacle of the Bar Kochba Revolt (ca. 132–35) which effectively dashed any hopes for imminent national restoration. At the heart of this national crisis was a profoundly spiritual one; with the destruction of the Temple the primary means of atonement was lost and the Sacred Center—the axis around which Jewish life was oriented—violated, rendered non-functional. As R. Goldenberg has shown in his article "The Broken Axis," the Rabbis responded to this spiritual crisis in complex, ambiguous fashion. On the one hand they broke with the paradigms of the past, establishing new, enduring modes of sacred living as if in replacement of the Temple; on the other hand they maintained continuity with the past, by maintaining the hope that ultimately, the Temple would be restored. Unable to find any one item that could replace the lost Center, the Rabbis moved on several fronts at once, stating that study, prayer, good deeds, the Day of Atonement, even hospitality, all served in the Temple's stead. As Goldenberg noted, the large number of substitutes reflected the "fear that none of them were really adequate."[13] Yet if no single replacement could be found, A. Green has shown that unofficially, *de facto,*

> the Sabbath gradually supplanted the Temple as the central unifying religious symbol of the Jewish People.[14]

This development may be stated even more pointedly: If the Sabbath became *a* central sacramental and national institution in post-Exilic Judaism (after the Destruction of the First Temple), it became arguably *the* central one in the Rabbinic period, in the wake of the second—more enduring—Destruction. Dispersed, deprived of Sacred Space, primary Jewish allegiance slowly and unconsciously shifted to the Realm of Time, that dimension "left untouched by the conqueror." Indeed, the Sabbath became what A.J. Heschel has called "a Sanctuary in Time," a portable Sacred Center able to withstand the vicissitudes of Exile and wandering.[15] This shift may be explained with reference to Sabbath-law.

With its expansive scope and detailed content, the Rabbinic Sabbath-law ushered in a new stage in Sabbath-celebration. Building on Biblical directives and various oral traditions, observance of the Sabbath was comprehensively defined both *via negationes* (ff. the Biblical prohibition of work) and in positive fashion, often under the rubric of *Menuḥah,* Sabbath-Rest, or *ʿOneg Shabbat,* delighting in the Sabbath (ff. Isa. 58:13). Let us consider the former case first. Going far beyond the sketchy Biblical accounts[16], *Mishnah Shabbat* (ca. 200) lists thirty-nine overarching categories of *mela'khah* or prohibited work. These include:

> sowing, ploughing, reaping, binding sheaves, threshing, winnowing, sorting grain, grinding, sifting, kneading, baking, shearing wool, cleaning it, beating it, dyeing it, spinning, weaving, making two loops, weaving two threads, separating two threads, tying, untying, sewing two stiches, tearing in order to sew two stitches; hunting a deer, slaughtering it, skinning it, salting it, curing its hide, scraping it, cutting it up, writing down two letters, erasing in order to write two letters; building, taking down; extinguishing a fire, kindling a fire, striking with a hammer, carrying out [an object] from one domain to another. (M. Shab. 7:2)

As scholars have noted, this is a highly artificial list which revolves around the basic concerns of human civilization: food and clothing, warmth and shelter, and communication or writing.[17] The rationale that the Rabbis subsequently gave it, however, is of another nature, evincing the aforementioned shift from space-oriented to time-oriented piety.

According to the Talmudic account[18], a Biblical basis for these thirty-nine prohibitions may be found in Exodus 31. Noting the curious juxtaposition of the prohibition of Sabbath-work with the details of constructing the Tabernacle in that chapter, the Rabbis deduced that it was forbidden on the Sabbath to do any work that was required for building this sacred structure. The thirty-nine *mela'khot* detailed above were held to be precisely those needed to construct this portable sanctuary. Arthur Green explained the interpretive process:

> [For the Amoraic Rabbis] the Biblical basis for almost the entirety of the Sabbath prohibitions lies in Ex. 31:13: "Moreover you shall keep My Sabbaths. . . ." This Sabbath command is inserted, seemingly without reason, in the midst of the ongoing discussion of the building of the tabernacle, the Torah's prototype of an ideal Temple. Since the word *'akh* with which this Sabbath verse opens, is a term of exception in the technical vocabulary of rabbinic exegesis (i.e., it comes to teach that what follows is an exception to the previously stated rule), the rabbis conclude that all forms of labor involved in any way in the construction of the tabernacle [i.e., the 39 categories] were meant to be forbidden on the Sabbath.[19]

Green has shed further light on this Rabbinic reading, refuting the notion that it was either obscure or arbitrary. Rather, he argues, the hermeneutical principle is used in a sophisticated manner to reflect (and further effect) the basic change in religious modality:

> By a deft interpretation of an *'akh,* the Rabbis have succeeded in transferring all that Biblical detail from the realm of space, where it had been rendered useless, to that of time. The phenomenon is one of reversal. By *doing* all these labors in the particular prescribed configuration, one creates sacred space. By *refraining* from these same acts, in the context of the Sabbath, one creates sacred time.[20]

This Talmudic definition of *mela'khah* is perhaps the most pointed example of how the Sabbath came to function as the new Sacred Center—quite literally, a Sanctuary in Time—in the centuries following the Temple destruction.[21]

Although Sacred Time may be constructed in this 'negative' fashion, the Rabbis also provided highly detailed guidelines for the 'positive' celebration of Shabbat. They developed an elaborate Sabbath-liturgy with special blessings, refined the lectionary cycle, and implemented ritual acts that emphasized *ᶜOneg Shabbat:* the three festive meals, Torah-study, marital sex, various preparatory rites, and so forth. Like the prohibition of *mela'khah,* these positive Sabbath-miẓvot highlighted the distinction between the holy Sabbath and the profane week; for on Shabbat one's most basic behavior is transformed: one is, e.g., to speak differently, pray differently, walk differently, eat differently, even dress differently and wear special garments.[22]

These behavioral and external changes always point to the underlying sacramental significance of Shabbat, a notion richly developed in the Aggadic literature: The Sabbath is an extraordinary and holy day, the occasion for and sign of God's heightened intimacy with Israel. The Sabbath not only commemorates the Creation and Exodus from Egypt, but recalls that third Sacred Moment: the giving of the Torah (TB Shab. 86b), itself a token of God's special relationship with Israel. Sabbath observance is salvific in nature, serving as "a foretaste of the World-to-Come" and paving the way for Messianic redemption.[23]

The Sabbath itself is given metaphysical status. It is personified as Bride and Queen, portrayed as Israel's spouse. In several *'aggadot* it even reaches a sort of apotheosis:[24] Shabbat is said to originate in the divine world, coming to humankind as "a gift from God's own Treasury"; it is His "Chosen Day," distinguished from the other six. In equally grand fashion, an early midrash equates the Sabbath with the entirety of the work of Creation (*Mekhilta'* "Yitro") while a later midrashic source (PRE 3) goes so far as to identify Shabbat as one of the seven things that existed prior to Creation. The Sabbath is considered inherently meaningful, a sacred entity empowering those who observe it. In the words of *Mekhilta'* ("Ki Tissa' "), whoever keeps this holy day is himself sanctified, "for the Sabbath imparts increased holiness to the People Israel."[25]

The minutiae of the Rabbinic Sabbath were initially observed by the virtuosi alone[26], but over the ensuing centuries their understanding of the day became normative, shaping Sabbath-celebration in almost every Jewish community until the dawn of modernity. Envincing both the centrality of Shabbat and the consolidation of Rabbinic power, Rabbinically-defined observance of Shabbat became an acid test for full membership in the Jewish Community. For example, only Sabbath-observers could serve as legal witnesses in court, while in later centuries the term *shomer shabbat* (one who properly observes the Sabbath) served as the functional equivalent of that distinctively modern designation, "Orthodox Jew."[27]

To sum up, the Rabbinic Sabbath was both an elaborate legal and sacramental institution that defined membership in the community and which effectively served as the central unifying symbol of classical Judaism. As Jewish piety shifted from a spatial to a temporal orientation, the Sabbath came to serve as a Sanctuary in Time: it afforded special access to God and the Sacred, while providing cosmic orientation in a world bereft of a spatial anchor.

From an historical perspective, one of the most striking features of the Rabbinic Sabbath was its structural longevity. Not only did it shape Jewish observance from late antiquity, but it endured for many centuries thereafter, absorbing new movements and modes of interpretation without undergoing a fundamental shift in praxis or behavioral paradigms. Indeed, the most significant of the medieval re-readings of Shabbat, those fashioned by the philosophers and by the Kabbalists, were built on and tended to buttress the Rabbinically ordained halakhah. This is not to say that the inner life of Sabbath-observance remained stable, however; for both the philosophers and the mystics discovered new rationales for *miẓvat Shabbat* and in the process recast its underlying meaning. To these two re-readings we shall now turn.[28]

The Sabbath of the Medieval Philosophers

For the medieval philosophers the Sabbath was a day of heightened joy and intellectual-spiritual renewal, a time to draw near God and to engage in sustained contemplation of Him. Such leading thinkers as Judah ha-Levi and Moses Maimonides (RaMBaM) spoke of the religious significance of Shabbat, regarding it as the "Crown of Israel's faith." Although Judah ha-Levi's great love of the Sabbath is always apparent, it attained an impassioned lyricism in his poetry. In "Shalom lakh yom ha-shevi^ci," e.g., he underscored the Sabbath's sacramental power, its healing light. Combining midrashic simile with imagery drawn from the Song of Songs, ha-Levi personified Shabbat as Israel's "beloved and darling." All week the love-sick poet longs for the "day of my delight." As Sabbath approaches, the spiritual exile and wandering that mark profane time give way to amplitude and rest; isolation, to the reunion of lovers. The poet prepares "apples and raisin-cakes" (ff. Cant. 2:5) and joyously greets the Sabbath, chanting "songs of love unto you, O Shabbat."[29]

In a more prosaic fashion, Abraham ibn Ezra also emphasized the spiritual power of Shabbat, claiming that "on it the [Jew's] soul is renewed" and his rational faculties strengthened.[30] Despite these varied attestations, however, the philosophers tended to treat the Sabbath in a more utilitarian, instrumental vein. This inclination is most apparent when they speak in a discursive mode *qua* philosophers, reflecting, e.g., on the rationales for various *miẓvot Shabbat.*

Specifically as thinkers, they tended to either ignore or rationalize the mythic, apotheosized qualities that the Sabbath attained in the Aggadic literature.[31] Conspicuously absent are those legends that accord the Sabbath metaphysical status within the divine realm. Moreover, most philosophers tended to regard Sabbath observance not so much as an end in itself but as a springboard to some higher purpose. Shabbat, it might be said, was less the goal of the spiritual pilgrimage than a way-station leading to some other destination.

The most complex case is that of the *Kuzari* of Judah ha-Levi. Whereas ha-Levi the liturgical poet celebrated the intrinsic value of Shabbat, ha-Levi the philosopher and defender of the faith moved on two fronts at once. On the one hand, he accorded the Sabbath absolute significance: It is depicted as "the [ripe] fruit of the week," a day of spiritual fullness and communion with the divine (*Kuzari* 3:5). On the other hand, Judah ha-Levi did not shrink from assigning Sabbath-rest utilitarian value: it enables Israel to be exempted from military service and helps them better endure the Exile (3:10). Similarly, it gives Israel respite from the 'slavery' of the week: Rest purifies the body and soul from the dross of the six days past and re-energizes the person for the days lying ahead. (3:5).[32] The instrumental value of Sabbath observance is, not surprisingly, stressed among the more rationally inclined philosophers, as well. According to Saadiah Gaon, Sabbath-observance has a largely social-utilitarian basis. It enables one to:

> obtain relaxation from much exertion. Furthermore it presents the opportunity for the attainment of a little bit of knowledge and a little additional praying. It also affords men leisure to meet each other at gatherings where they can confer about matters of their religion and make public announcements about them, and perform other functions of the same order.[33]

Moses Maimonides found both a utilitarian and a sacramental significance in Sabbath-observance. Sabbath-rest, he claimed, offers respite from weekly toil while it strengthens one's faith in God's creation of the world. But even this second religious rationale has an underlying instrumental-didactic purpose: Shabbat enables the unsophisticated masses to attain a faith that they might not otherwise reach.[34]

Perhaps the most extreme example of the utilitarian Sabbath is that which emerged from the writings of Jacob Anatoli, a Provençal-Italian philosopher of the thirteenth century with a radical Maimonidean orientation. Rather than finding intrinsic value in Sabbath-rest—seeing it, e.g., as the Crown of Creation—Anatoli claimed that it was a means of rendering palatable the workaday week. He de-emphasized key miẓvot (abstinence from *mela'khah;* the festive meals; and so forth) and focused on the Sabbath's intellectual possibilities. As a day uninterrupted by mundane concerns, the Sabbath was an especially efficacious time for Torah-study and intellectual contemplation of God's ways. Indeed, it was such intellection alone that rendered the day meaningful. While the Rabbinic Sages accorded the Sabbath inherent sacral and metaphysical meaning, Jacob Anatoli argued that "time itself lacks significance" and that the Sabbath's holiness derives solely from those intellectual activities pursued on it. The Sabbath, in other words, is a *tabula rasa,* whose character is determined by human activity. In these and other ways, the radical rationalists tended to empty the Sabbath of its mystery and abiding holiness, assigning it a significant but largely functional value.[35]

The Distinctive Features of the Kabbalistic Sabbath

It should be noted that the philosophical interpretations of the Sabbath were far less comprehensive than those fashioned by the classical Kabbalists and exerted far less historical influence. In many ways, the Kabbalistic understanding of the Sabbath was closer to that of the Rabbis than to that of their fellow medieval esotericists. The Kabbalists re-asserted and deepened the sacramental value of Shabbat and its observance and treated the Aggadic legacy with utmost respect, generally adding distinctively sefirotic interpretations to the exoteric meaning. In the ensuing pages of this study, there will be repeated opportunity to assess the Kabbalists' debt to the Rabbinic legal and Aggadic framework; however, to better grasp their unique contribution to Sabbath-celebration, it is useful to outline four points of contrast between theosophical Kabbalists and their Rabbinic predecessors:

(1) For most Kabbalists, Sabbath-observance has theurgic impact, affecting God's inner life and the Cosmos as a whole. By contrast, the Rabbis generally limited the consequences of Sabbath celebration to the human realm. Fulfilling *miẓvat Shabbat* was thought to transform (or purify) the person and to promote Israel's ultimate salvation.

(2) The Kabbalists systematically integrated myth into Rabbinic ritual. While the Rabbis only occasionally correlated mythic paradigms with ritual life, the Kabbalists did so in consistent, comprehensive fashion. For the mystic, each sacred action relates an exemplary story and is part of a larger mythic system.

(3) To the degree that myth is present in Rabbinic ritual it tends to be commemorative in nature, rehearsing events that occured in Sacred History. Kabbalistic ritual, by contrast, tends to dramatize events said to be unfolding in the spiritual realm at this very moment.

These three points will be developed and refined in chapter 2 when Kabbalistic ritual is analyzed.[36] The fourth point of contrast relates more directly to the motif studies presented in this chapter, and hence, merits fuller explication here.

(4) The major conceptual innovation in the Kabbalistic understanding of the Sabbath is the identification of Shabbat with divinity. For the Rabbis, the Sabbath was of heavenly origin, a gift *from* God. For most mystics, the Sabbath was even more sublime; it was an aspect *of* God, a mysterious process within Him. In its Kabbalistic meaning, *Shabbat* refers to that state of intradivine harmony which directs and transforms the cosmos on the seventh day. In a narrower sense, *Shabbat* may also denote a specific sefirah or configuration of sefirot, which reflects this divine harmony most pointedly. This divine or sefirotic Sabbath serves as the archetype and Ground for its earthly manifestation, the traditional Sabbath day.[37]

The Sefirotic Sabbath

Within the Kabbalistic lexicon, *Shabbat* is a dense, multivocal term, able to evoke any number of sefirotic referents and processes within the divine pleroma. In the *Bahir* and other early sources, the primary divine Sabbath was *Yesod*. Two fundamental rationales seem to suggest this association. The first is seventhness, for in the *Bahir*'s accounting, *Yesod* was the seventh rung. The second rationale is more substantive, building on the notion that the Sabbath is the very heart or center of the week, the source of weekly sustenance.

In the Kabbalistic schema, *Yesod* served as the Sabbath of the sefirotic world: standing at the center of the seven 'active' sefirot, *Yesod* nourished the surrounding rungs much like the Sabbath vitalized the six weekdays. Indeed, for the *Bahir*'s author, the seven days of the week are but reflections of the seven lower sefirot or Primordial Days as they are commonly called; just as the weekdays are the temporal symbols of the six sefirot surrounding *Yesod*, the Sabbath-day is the manifestation of the divine Shabbat, the temporal vessel for *Yesod*'s manifold blessings.[38]

When a different sefirotic hierarchy crystallized in Gerona in the early thirteenth century, *Yesod* was reckoned as the ninth rung. This led to certain changes in Shabbat symbolism. Some Kabbalists, e.g., Ṭodros Abulafia, transferred the primary Sabbath to *Tif'eret*, which now stood at the heart of the sefirotic world[39]; other Kabbalists, like RaMBaN and Azriel maintained the link between Shabbat and *Yesod*, whereas still others (like the author of the TZ/RM) moved back and forth between the two rungs as the situation or insight demanded. Those who retained *Yesod* as the primary Sabbath tended to do so on two grounds:

(a) *Yesod* was the seventh sefirah counting from *Binah* or
(b) It was seventh of the so-called active sefirot in the order of emanation, for according to one influential tradition, *Tif'eret* and *Shekhinah* had emerged *du-parẓufin*, as one androgynous entity, and were separated only later.[40]

Although non-Zoharic Kabbalists tended to focus on what might be called the 'male' Sabbath (those quintessentially masculine sefirot, *Tif'eret* and *Yesod*) the notion of a 'female' Sabbath—linked with *Shekhinah*—was present from the earliest days. It is difficult to ascertain the precise motives for this reading: possibly it stems from

Figure 3: Shabbat/*Yesod* amid the Sefirotic "Days of the Week"

Fig. a: ff. *Bahir* 157
see p. 80

Fig. b: ff. *Bahir* 159
see p. 87 for explanation

Fig. 3a and 3b. X = sefirotic "days of the week";
O = *Yesod*, the divine Sabbath.

the fact that *Shekhinah* was also a 'seventh'—of the active rungs—or from the curious fact that *Shabbat* may be either masculine or feminine in Hebrew, or from the presence of certain feminine metaphors (Sabbath as Queen, Bride) in the *'Aggadah*, or more simply, from the *Bahir*'s androgynous image of God.[41] At any event, *Sefer ha-Bahir* (180) interpreted Lev. 19:30, "You shall keep my Sabbaths," as a hidden reference to two divine rungs, *Shekhinah* and *Yesod*. Implicitly, full Shabbat entailed the re-union of these male and female Sabbaths (see *Bahir* 181 for details).

This last notion was given explicit expression in Ṭodros Abulafia's *'Oẓar ha-Kavod* (OK). Abulafia explained that the two divine Sabbaths (here, *Tif'eret* and *Shekhinah*) were originally emanated as one entity—one Shabbat—but were separated thereafter. "Nonetheless," he wrote:

> they are really one. . . the one is included in the other as a flame is bound to the coal.

Each seventh day this essential unity is recovered, primordial androgyny restored:

> On Shabbat the two [sefirotic Sabbaths] unite, for they were originally uttered [emanated] as one. (OK to TB Ber. 20 and to Shab. 33b)[42]

Many Kabbalists depicted this union in rather abstract language while in the Zoharic stream it was given a strongly erotic coloration. For all of these mystics, the union of these two discrete *Shabbatot* symbolized a more comprehensive process: the return of the divine world as a whole to that pristine harmony which may be called "the metaphysical state of Shabbat." We shall return to this important concept, shortly.

As we have noted, most thirteenth century Kabbalists viewed the male Sabbath as primary, commonly referring to it as *Shabbat ha-Gadol* (the Great Sabbath). Moshe de Leon, by contrast, tended to treat *Shekhinah* as the primary Sabbath, the focus of his theosophical and theurgic concerns.[43] This 'feminization'—which undoubtedly had its roots in de Leon's psycho-spiritual make-up[44]—had a profound impact on the later celebration of the day and on the popular imaging of the Sabbath as distinctively feminine: as Bride, Queen, and Lover.

By the late thirteenth century a second feminine sefirah also became associated with Shabbat, namely, *Binah* (the divine "World-to-Come"). (This notion was first found in the writings of Ṭodros Abulafia and in the *Zohar*). As the matrix for the seven lower sefirot and the 'Mother' of the male and female *Shabbatot* below, *Binah* was called "the Sabbath of Sabbaths," "the Jubilee," and soon pre-empted the title, "the Great Sabbath."[45] Whereas the lower Sabbath directed the world on the seventh day, *Binah* remained relatively hidden. She was the divine Sabbath that could only be glimpsed during the present age, vouchsafed at special moments during the Sabbath-day; but in the Messianic Age, She was to hold continuous sway over the entire universe, turning it into a perpetual Sabbath, *ʿolam she-kullo Shabbat* (ff. Mekh. "Beshallaḥ"). The Kabbalists thus gave added resonance to the Rabbinic teaching that the World-to-Come (kabbalistically, *Binah!*) would be "an everlasting Sabbath."[46] In the *'Oẓar ha-Kavod* this future Sabbath assumed yet deeper mystical significance. *Sabbath* was a code-word referring to the post-Messianic apokatastasis,[47] the ultimate re-absorption of all Being into *Binah*. She was to be the point of *teshuvah* (Return), *menuḥah* (final Rest)—the cosmic womb. In cryptic fashion, Ṭodros Abulafia wrote:

> The supernal Sabbath day, the Great Jubilee, alludes to "a cosmos that is entirely Shabbat (Mekh. "Beshallaḥ") wherein "a person shall return to his family [i.e., to *Binah*, the Mother and *Ḥokhmah*, the Father], to the inheritance of his ancestors" (ff. Lev. 25:10) . . . and the upper and lower worlds shall cease from activity (OK to Shab. 33b and RH 31a)

In the end, all will be Shabbat.

Thus far we have concentrated on those individual sefirot which are most commonly called *Shabbat* and on the sefirotic dyad that perhaps best exemplifies the metaphysical state of Shabbat: the union of the divine male and female. However, *Shabbat* may also refer to more comprehensive sefirotic clusters. For example, the Gerona mystic, Asher ben David, was the first author to link all seven of the lower sefirot with Shabbat. Building on Sabbath's etymology, he wrote that on the eve of the primordial seventh day, each of the seven sefirot active in the formation of the world *shabat* (ceased from its labors), thereby ushering in the temporal Sabbath. Every seventh day, this primordial process recurs: the active sefirot once again rest and invest the worlds below with a profound sense of peace.[48] Moshe de Leon took this one step further, explicitly linking Shabbat with all ten sefirot. In his Hebrew tract, *Sefer ha-Mishqal,* he stated that on the Sabbath day "all my crowns are called Shabbat."[49]

In this brief survey, we have seen how the term *Shabbat* may evoke a multiplicity of sefirotic referents, each with its own web of associations and unique shades of meaning. But these discrete *Shabbatot* always direct one's attention beyond the immediate focus to the larger *metaphysical state* of Shabbat, the restored divine Gestalt. One may gaze at a particular sefirah—a particular Shabbat—but he comes to see the All.[50] For the term *Shabbat*—no matter how narrow the explicit meaning—always implies a comprehensive union or wholeness. This inclusive meaning of the divine Sabbath is perhaps best described by the Kabbalists themselves.

In his *Sha^c^arei 'Orah,* Joseph Giqatilia characterized Shabbat as the harmonious union of the eight rungs from *Binah* unto *Malkhut.* As *Binah*'s *shefa^c^*—the "stream of goodness which comes to Israel"—courses downward, all the lower rungs are blessed, suffused with Her celestial music:

> All is Shabbat: the cleaving of the sefirah *Malkhut* unto *Binah.* [This is] "For the leader [*Binah*] whose music comes unto the eighth one [i.e., *Malkhut*]." (Re-reading the obscure verse Ps. 6:1)[51]

In a yet more inclusive image found in the *Zohar* 2:92a (RM?):

> The Sabbath is the mystery of the Whole Faith [the sefirotic totality] which issues from the Supernal Head [*Keter*] and stretches unto the final rung. Shabbat is All.

The inclusive character of the divine Sabbath is stressed yet again in the *Tola^c^at Ya^c^aqov* (TY) of Meir ibn Gabbai. He wrote:

> The entire harmonious configuration is called Shabbat, the mystery of coupling, for [on the Sabbath-day] the lovers [*Tif'eret* and *Shekhinah*] have returned to each other face-to-face. (TY 45a)

Finally, it is conveyed in a striking image fashioned by Moshe de Leon, who suggested that the newly configured divine world literally spells *SHaBbaT*. According to the *Zohar, Shekhinah,* the King's daughter (*BaT*), is in Exile during the week; but each Friday evening She is able to return home, assuming Her rightful place in the divine structure:

> When the supernal Point [*Shekhinah*] ascends and the divine light shines, then She is crowned with the three Patriarchs [*Ḥesed, Gevurah,* and *Tif'eret*].[52] Immediately, She unites with them and becomes one. This totality is called *SHaBbaT:* שׁבת .

Here Moshe de Leon has employed a form of linguistic-orthographic symbolism. The three prongs of the letter *Shin* (ש) correspond to the three Patriarchs while the Hebrew term *BaT* (בת, daughter) connotes *Shekhinah*. As they draw together:

> She is crowned with them and they with the World-to-Come [*Binah*, the "Great Sabbath, and by extension, the Upper Triad]; thus, All is one. (Z 2:204a)[53]

By focusing on sefirotic symbolism, we have been able to glimpse the cosmic dimensions of the Kabbalistic Sabbath. The intra-divine changes alluded to above serve as the Ground for a series of ontological changes that unfold on parallel planes of being: within the lower worlds, within the dimension of Time, and most pointedly, within the Sabbath-observer. These ramifications of the divine Sabbath will be explored in the ensuing pages of this chapter.

With this we have concluded our overview of the pre-Kabbalistic Sabbath and the most salient features of its Kabbalistic re-reading. These preliminary observations will be amplified and refined as the discussion proceeds.

SECTION TWO: MOTIF STUDIES

We are now ready to turn to the major focus of this chapter: the description and interpretation of four key mythic motifs undergirding the Kabbalistic Sabbath. We begin by extending the analysis of the divine Sabbath, concentrating on its role as the Source of Cosmic Blessing. Of special interest here will be the image of the divine Sabbath as 'Sacred Center,' the point of cosmic sustenance and orientation. Thereafter, we shall turn to three motifs which articulate the profound transformations that occur on Shabbat: the Transformation of Time; the Transformation of the Divine World, as dramatized in the Myth of *Hieros Gamos* (Sacred Marriage); and finally, the Transformation of the Sabbath-observer, as portrayed in the Motif of the Sabbath-Soul.

The methodological foci of these studies are primarily historical and descriptive-phenomenological. For example, an attempt is made to trace the development of these motifs in different streams of classical Kabbalah and to assess their relation to various pre-Kabbalistic traditions. We confront the following questions: In what ways are the Kabbalistic interpretations unique? How (and to what extent) have the theosophical Kabbalists developed a new hermeneutic of *miẓvat Shabbat*? Along with these historical concerns, we shall explore various issues in Kabbalistic symbolism, as the symbolic structures underlying these motifs are classified and analyzed. It is asked: what types of imagery are employed in a given motif? What is their specific sefirotic and psychological significance (as understood by the Kabbalists themselves)? And more broadly: what is the larger story these mythic motifs help narrate? Through exploring these issues we can hope to gain a keener sense of the 'deep structure' of the Kabbalistic Sabbath and its place in the Jewish religious imagination.

The historical parameters of this inquiry extend from the late twelfth through the early sixteenth centuries, and hence cover the entire classical period, as it has been defined by the author. The types of literature drawn on include exegesis and pseudepigraphic midrash, disquisitions on sefirotic theory, manuals for contemplative prayer and devotion, and the *ṭaʿamei ha-miẓvot* literature, which provided mystical rationales for the commandments. The following authors and sources have been considered[54]:

(1) *Sefer ha-Bahir* (redacted late twelfth century, Provence?)

(2) Judah ben Yaqar, *Perush ha-Tefillot ve-ha-Berakhot* on the prayers and blessings (ca. 1200, Barcelona)[55]

(3) Azriel of Gerona, *Perush ha-'Aggadot* (early thirteenth century, Gerona)

(4) Idem, *Perush ʿEser Sefirot*[56]

(5) Asher ben David, *Sefer ha-Yiḥud* (early thirteenth century, Provence-Gerona)[57]

(6) R. Moses ben Naḥman (RaMBaN), *Perush ʿal ha-Torah* (mid-thirteenth century, Catalonia and 'Ereẓ Israel)[58]

(7) Jacob ben Jacob ha-Kohen of Soria, *Perush ha-Sefirot* (before 1280, Castile)[59]

(8) Ṭodros ha-Levi Abulafia, *'Oẓar ha-Kavod* (OK) on the Babylonian Talmud (ca. 1280, Castile)

(9) Idem, *Sha^car ha-Razim* on Psalm 19[60]

(10) Moshe ben Shem Ṭov de Leon, *Zohar* (all except the *'Idrot* before 1286; the *'Idrot* after 1291[?], Castile)

(11) Idem, *Sefer ha-Rimmon* (1287) on the rationale for the miẓvot

(12) Idem, *Sefer ha-Mishqal* (1290)

(13) Idem, *Sodot* (ca. 1293)[61]

(14) Joseph Giqatilia, *Sha^carei 'Orah* on the sefirot (before 1293, Castile)

(15) Idem, *Sodot*[62]

(16) Baḥyya ben Asher, *Perush ^cal ha-Torah* (following 1291, Castile)

(17) Idem, *Kad ha-Qemaḥ*

(18) Idem, *Shulḥan shel 'Arba^c* on the miẓvot surrounding the meal[63]

(19) Joseph of Hamadan, *Sefer Ṭa^camei ha-Miẓvot* (late thirteenth to early fourteenth century, Castile?)[64]

(20) Circle of Joseph of Hamadan, *Sefer ha-Yiḥud* (ca. 1295, Castile)[65]

(21) David ben Judah he-Ḥasid, *'Or Zaru^ca* on the liturgy (ca. 1300, Spanish)

(22) Idem, *Sefer Mar'ot ha-Ẓove'ot* on the Torah (early fourteenth century)[66]

(23) Joseph ben Shalom Ashkenazi, *Perush le-Farashat Bere'shit* on *Genesis Rabbah* (German-Spanish-Moroccan? Dating ranges from late thirteenth to mid-fourteenth century)[67]

(24) *Tiqqunei ha-Zohar/Ra^caya' Meheimna'* (TZ/RM) (early fourteenth century, Spanish)

(25) Shem Ṭov ibn Gaon, *Keter Shem Ṭov*, an explication of the Kabbalistic secrets of RaMBaN on the Torah (1298, Castile)[68]

(26) Joshua ibn Shuayb, *Be'ur Sodot ha-RaMBaN,* an explication of Kabbalistic secrets of RaMBaN on the Torah (early fourteenth century, Castile)[69]

(27) Isaac ben Samuel of Acco, *Me'irat ᶜEinayim* (ca. 1305, Palestinian-Spanish)[70]

(28) *Maᶜarekhet ha-'Elohut* on the sefirot (early fourteenth century, Spanish)[71]

(29) Menaḥem Recanati, *Perush ᶜal ha-Torah* (early fourteenth century, Italian)

(30) Idem, *Sefer Ṭaᶜamei ha-Miẓvot*[72]

(31) Joseph ibn Waqar, *Perush le-Shir ha-Yiḥud* (Toledo, mid-fourteenth century)[73]

(32) *Sefer ha-Temunah* (mid-fourteenth century, Byzantium?)[74]; and three works from that circle:

(33) *Perush le-Sefer ha-Temunah,*

(34) *Sod 'Ilan ha-'Aẓilut,* and

(35) *Sod ha-Shem*[75]

(36) Menaḥem Ẓiyyoni, *Sefer Ẓiyyoni* on the Torah ('Ereẓ Israel-Cologne, second half of the fourteenth century)[76]

(37) *Sefer ha-Qanah* on the rationale for the miẓvot (early fifteenth century, Byzantine Greece)

(38) *Sefer ha-Peli'ah* on Genesis (same author, dating and provenance as *Sefer ha-Qanah)*[77]

(39) MS Paris Hebr. 596, untitled commentary on the prayers (fifteenth century, Italy)[78]

(40) Moshe ben Jacob of Kiev, *Shoshan Sodot* (1498, Crimea)[79]

(41) Judah Ḥayyaṭ, *Minḥat Yehudah* to *Maᶜarekhet ha-'Elohut* (before 1510, Spanish-Italian)[80]

(42) Meir ibn Gabbai, *Tolaᶜat Yaᶜaqov* (TY) on the liturgy and assorted rituals (1507, Spanish-Turkish)

Whoever attempts to compass the topic soon discovers that the Kabbalists wrote about Shabbat *ᶜad 'ein sof,* virtually without end! Although it cannot, therefore, be presumed that this study is exhaustive, it is surely extensive, aiming to plumb the most important extant writings. The primary criteria for inclusion are originality, historical influence, and textual focus, i.e., considered reflection on the Sabbath as an institution or mystical symbol. It should be noted that the bulk of the truly innovative interpretations come from the first half of the classical period, from the Provençal-Gerona Kabbalah and, in particular, from the variegated Kabbalah produced in late thirteenth to early fourteenth century Castile. Not surprisingly, the richest reservoir of material can be found in the *Zohar,* the classic work of the Spanish theosophical tradition. A secondary source for fresh material is Byzantine Kabbalah, especially in the mid-fourteenth to early fifteenth centuries.[81] Although a smaller number of vital texts from the final years have come under consideration, the influence of the TY of Meir ibn Gabbai looms large in our discussion.[82]

A final bibliographic note. By the fourteenth century the Kabbalistic understanding of Shabbat had found its way into such exoteric works as David Abudraham's commentary on the prayers (1340) and Israel Al-Naqawah's *Menorat ha-Ma'or* (ca. 1390); its influence was also felt in such philosophically oriented tracts as Joseph Albo's *ᶜIqqarim* (1425) and Isaac Arama's *ᶜAqedat Yiẓḥaq,* a homiletic masterwork of the late fifteenth century.[83] Relevant passages from these sources have been incorporated into the accompanying notes.

motif #1

Shabbat as the Source of Cosmic Blessing

Shabbat, the Kabbalists explained, affords a profound sense of renewal; it is the archetypal source of vitality and blessing. From one perspective, this vision of Shabbat is but an extension of the earlier Rabbinic and philosophical understandings. As we have seen, long before the Kabbalists arrived on the scene, Aggadists, poets, and philosophers had spoken of the Sabbath's edifying, rejuvenating effects on both body and soul. However, the Kabbalistic revision of Sabbath's renewing power may be distinguished from these earlier efforts both in terms of the cosmic scale on which this process occurs and the more sustained, dramatic fashion in which it was articulated. To recall: the medieval philosophers explained Sabbath-renewal in largely social-functional terms, while the Talmudic Rabbis accorded it sacramental significance within the human realm. The theosophical Kabbalists, by contrast, understood Sabbath-renewal in categories that were both sacramental and cosmic. They rooted the Sabbath's life-enhancing powers in the divine Shabbat and extended the province of Sabbath-renewal to the Cosmos as a whole: Shabbat restored and sustained[84] not only the People Israel and each individual Jew, but divinity, Time, and all lower worlds. In conveying this novel vision of the Sabbath's cosmic powers, they developed a rich symbolic language which lent the theme a certain complexity and, as utilized, a systematic coherence heretofore lacking. It is to this deeply mythic vision of the divine Sabbath that we shall now turn.

The primary images articulating the Sabbath's nurturing power are three in number, each with its own web of associations and unique emotional coloration. For example, the divine Sabbath is oft portrayed as a **Cosmic Fountain,** whose holy waters well up and overflow each seventh day. These waters irrigate Being: they suffuse the rest of the sefirotic pleroma and proceed to stream into the lower worlds, enriching and blessing them, as well. In another image, the divine Sabbath is the fecund **Matrix of Souls.** It is the source for both new life—those sacred souls which the devotee and his wife are enjoined to draw into the world through the miẓvah of Sabbath-intercourse[85]—and the source for renewed life, the matrix for the Sabbath-soul which comes to the Jew each Sabbath-day, inspiring him and enhancing his spiritual faculties. The first two images imply the centrality of Shabbat. In the third image, the divine Shabbat is explicitly symbolized as the **Cosmic Axis,** the sustaining Center of the universe: Shabbat is the divine "Jerusalem," the "Eye of the Cosmic Wheel," "the Heart of the World," around which Time and Cosmos are constructed and through which they are blessed.

It is difficult to speak of these three images in isolation, for in the Kabbalistic literature they often run together and interweave[86], forming an extended symbol-cluster, one organic "motif." To better explore this motif, the following organizational strategy has been employed: first a panoramic view of the Sabbath as Source of Cosmic Blessing will be provided by freely drawing on all three controlling images. Thereafter, the analysis will be refined and deepened by concentrating on perhaps the most comprehensive image, that of the divine Shabbat as "Sacred Center."

Thematic Overview

The notion that Shabbat is the Source of Cosmic Blessing is first articulated in *Sefer ha-Bahir.* The *Bahir*'s authors closely correlated the sustaining function of Shabbat with its sefirotic identity as *Yesod,* the seventh of the divine grades. The cluster of symbols accruing to this rung suggests that Shabbat/*Yesod* was seen as the fertile Center—the organizing matrix—of the cosmos: it is called *maʿyan ha-berakhot,* the "well-spring of divine blessing"; the centermost and lushest "royal garden"; "the Foundation of the Cosmos," the "Righteous One upon whom the world rests," i.e., the Axis Mundi. It is also called the "Foundation of Souls"[87] and the source of "creative seed"; finally, it is imaged as the divine "Male," the procreative "phallus." This last image is rarely explicitly employed in the *Bahir*'s discussions of Shabbat, but often serves as a kind of unstated subtext. Let us examine the evidence more closely.

The divine Shabbat is the main reservoir and dispenser of *shefa*ᶜ, the cosmic energy which sustains and sanctifies existence:

> The Holy One gives his abundant Wisdom to the Life of the Cosmos [Shabbat/*Yesod*] which provides [nourishment] for all. (*Bahir* 183)

This notion is amplified in a second passage which weaves together many of the associations cited earlier. The divine Sabbath is both the central axis and the matrix of the cosmos, ordering and sustaining upper and lower worlds:

> The Holy One has a singular *Ẓaddiq* [Righteous One] in the world. This one is beloved for he sustains the entire world and is its Foundation; he sustains it and makes it thrive; he tends it and watches over it. This one is beloved and dear on high, beloved and dear below, awesome and mighty on high, awesome and mighty below. . . . This one is the Foundation of all souls. . . . For is it not written "On the seventh day [here read: through *Yesod*], there was rest and souls"? (Ex. 31:17)

The continuation of this section underscores the integrative powers of Shabbat/*Yesod*, dramatizing its ability to create harmony among the active sefirot:

promotes harmony

> The seventh mediates between them, those six others: the three below and the three above. It modulates between them. (*Bahir* 157)

As it brings peace to the sefirot above and below, so it promotes harmony between Left and Right, "Fire and Water," i.e., the contentious forces of *Din* and *Ḥesed*. Indeed, the *Bahir* asserts, Sabbath "brings joy to them all" (Ibid. 158).

Two Gerona Kabbalists, Azriel and RaMBaN, subscribed to the *Bahir*'s vision of Shabbat/*Yesod* as the central axis and source of cosmic energy.[88] RaMBaN wrote:

> The Sabbath day [*Yesod*] is the well-spring of blessing; it is the Foundation of the Cosmos. "And He sanctified it" [Gen. 2:3], for it [the blessings of the temporal Sabbath] issues from the sacred [the divine Sabbath] . . . .

However, these two mystics added a new wrinkle to Shabbat-symbolism, viewing *Yesod* as the matrix of the special Sabbath-soul, as well. Although Azriel spoke of this soul in allusive fashion alone[89], RaMBaN made crystal-clear that it is not a mere metaphor—as several philosophers had asserted—but rather an "actual [metaphysical] entity," a living symbol of the Sabbath's cosmic blessings.[90] We shall return to this theme later in the chapter, as we analyze the motif of the Sabbath-soul.

The *Zohar* is replete with images of the renewing power of the divine Sabbath. Generally, this restoration is said to spring from the most sublime rungs, the upper Triad, though *Yesod*—the rung of *Musaf*, of divine abundance[91]—and *Shekhinah*—the lower Sabbath—were accorded special status, as well. Throughout, Moshe de Leon was particularly fond of depicting the renewal in images which dramatized the Sabbath's role as active nurturer, as ever-flowing Cosmic Fountain.

For example, on the Sabbath day blessing is said to well up from the supernal Sabbath, *Binah*, "the World that is Coming,"[92] or more generally, from the recesses of the upper Triad. So great is the divine plenitude that it must perforce brim over—like love that cannot be contained—its glory suffusing the grades below. Four related images are commonly employed to dramatize this process:

(1) *Irrigation*: whereby the divine energy or *shefa*ᶜ is likened to a "River going out from Eden [*Binah*]," setting forth "to water the Garden [*Shekhinah* and the lower rungs]." (Gen. 2:10) This image is commonly found in Zoharic interpretations of ᶜ*Oneg Shabbat* and the sacramental meals.[93]

(2) *Illumination*: whereby divine light is said to issue from *Binah*, coursing unto the lower sefirot. For example, as the devotee recites (the prayer), "May the Pleasantness," before Sabbath's end:

> A pleasing radiance issues from the World-that-is-Coming, from which all light streams forth, radiating in every direction. . . . It brings joy and gladness, light and freedom. (1:197b)

(3) *Annointment* is another common image. For example:

> Oil, the liniment of holiness that issues from the Holy Ancient One [*Keter*], gathers in the celestial River [*Binah*] which suckles Her children, [bringing forth] oil to kindle the lamps [the seven lower sefirot]. (3:7b)

and so too,

(4) *Fertilization*: as thrice each Shabbat the supernal dew (i.e., *shefa*ᶜ) emerges from the hidden reaches of *Keter*, coming unto *Tif'eret* and thereafter unto the Cosmic Field, *Shekhinah*. As She receives this vitality, she brings forth fruit, truly becoming the "Field of Holy Apples." (ff. 2:88a)[94]

In the synesthetic imagination of Moshe de Leon these four metaphors often mix, their modalities interweaving and crossing. Consider a passage where the process of divine renewal is simultaneously portrayed in images of light, water, and pearled dew. The light flows, the water flashes, and the dew sparkles and streams forth. De Leon begins:

> "The firmament proclaims [Hebrew: *maggid*] His handiwork." [Ps. 19:2]

His interpretation turns on a word-play, based on *maggid*'s *Aramaic* meaning, viz., "flows" or "streams forth":

> The supernal dew streams forth from all the hidden regions; it is "His handiwork" through which He completes Himself on this day [Shabbat] more than on any other. . . . The "firmament" streams forth [*maggid*] and courses downward from the Head of the King in great abundance. The firmament is that stream issuing from the Cistern, the river going out from Eden [*Binah*] which flows earthward; it is the stream of supernal dew which gleams and sparkles from all sides. This firmament carries all this downward in a stream of love and desire in order to irrigate the field of joy [*Shekhinah*] on Sabbath eve. When this bejewelled dew streams down, the entire [divine world] becomes full and complete. . . . (2:136b)

These mysterious intradivine processes serve as archetype and Ground for the consequent blessing of the lower worlds. In Moshe de Leon's rich mythos, Sabbath-observance in general, and the three sacramental meals in particular, enable the devotee to reflect this supernal drama, to make immanent its spiritual riches:

> Three kinds of blessing well up from the three supernal sources . . . the Holy Ancient One [*Keter*], the Small Face [*Tif'eret*] and the Field of Holy Apples [*Shekhinah*]. . . . Three times these sources well up and flow into each other . . . so that all is blessed as one. . . . The festive table becomes a vessel in which to receive this blessing. . . (2:88a)

According to another *Zohar* passage, weekly time—and its archetype (here: the angelic worlds)[95]—is only sustained by the surfeit of blessing which fills the Sabbath (sefirotically, *Shekhinah*)[96]:

> R. Judah said: Every day the world is blessed through that supernal Day, the seventh. For the six days [Kabbalistically, the six angelic rungs under the aegis of the arch-angel, Meṭaṭron] receive blessing from the seventh, and each gives of its blessing on its appointed day. (2:63b)

Similarly:

> All supernal and earthly blessings depend on the seventh Day. And it is further taught: Why was there no manna on the seventh day? [ff. Ex. 16:26] Because all six supernal days are blessed through it. Each one sustains the world below on its appointed day, imparting that blessing which it received on the seventh. . . . For the weekly blessing is prepared at this time so that all six weekdays may be blessed. . . . The rest of the days are nourished by this overflow of Sabbath-bounty. (2:88a)[97]

In other words, not only does the divine Sabbath renew Time and cosmos on the Sabbath day, but its overflow extends into the week, sustaining mundane existence and according it a degree of sanctity. The point could not be made more forcefully: the Sabbath is the life-blood of the cosmos, upon which all existence depends. Extending the metaphor, it might be said that Sabbath-observance is that which keeps the cosmic channels open, stimulating and maintaining the proper circulation (or flow).[98]

We may round out our thematic overview by considering two texts written at the turn of the fourteenth century. In the *Shaᶜarei 'Orah* of Joseph Giqatilia, the divine Sabbath (here associated with *Yesod*) is imaged as the fount of blessing that vitalizes both *Shekhinah* and the Jew who attunes himself to this process through Sabbath observance:

> The Sabbath [*Yesod*] is the well-spring of Good and the source of all emanation as concerns *'Adni* [*Shekhinah*] and the Jew who cleaves to this rung.[99]

Shabbat/*Yesod* serves as the gateway to the sublime blessings of the ultimate Sabbath (*Binah*) and its temporal correlate, the World-to-Come:

> Through Shabbat a person may enter the World-to-Come, the mystery of the Jubilee. . . . This is the Great Sabbath, the supernal Seventh. . . . The Sabbath [*Yesod*] draws down the emanation and the great Good: Life and Redemption [i.e., the most profound blessings] from the World-to-Come. . . . (1:111–12)

This last text illustrates the multivocal quality of Kabbalistic symbolism. On one level, Joseph Giqatilia is simply restating the Rabbinic notion that the Sabbath is a taste of and portal to the splendors of the World-to-Come, here understood as "the future Age."[100] At the same time, he is disclosing a Kabbalistic *sod:* whoever attains the spiritual rung of Shabbat/*Yesod* on the Sabbath-day receives the holiest blessings of all, those which are drawn down from *Binah,* the cosmic Jubilee, the archetypal "World-to-Come." Here, the World-to-Come is not so much another aeon as it is another already extant dimension of being, open to the devotee each Sabbath-day.[101]

Finally, the motif was given an unusual coloration by Menaḥem Recanati in his *Perush ʿal ha-Torah.* Because he maintained that the sefirot were the instruments rather than the essence of God[102], he more readily attributed definable qualities to *'Ein Sof,* the so-called "Master of the sefirot." On Shabbat, Recanati claimed, the *shefaʿ* of *'Ein Sof* overflows into *Malkhut,* the seventh Day:

> "Therefore, the Lord blessed the seventh day and hallowed it" [Ex. 20:11]: the word *blessing* [*BeRaKHah]* alludes to the overflow of blessing from the Pond [*BeReKHah*: *'Ein Sof*]. . . .

As the divine Sabbath is blessed, She is transformed from passive receptacle into cosmic fountain, conveying Her holy *shefaʿ (qedushah)* to the world below:

The term *blessed* comes before the term *hallowed* [*QDSH*] because the Blessing comes from *'Ein Sof* and Holiness [*QeDuSHah*] from the Holy [*Shekhinah*].[103]

In sum, the divine Sabbath attests to the simultaneous enrichment of the divine pleroma and the person, the angelic and the lower worlds, the Sabbath-day and the mundane week. Everything in this process points to cosmic plenitude, a palpable fullness of Being. In Moshe de Leon's apt expression: "On Shabbat all worlds overflow with blessing" (Z 3:94b).[104]

The Sabbath as Sacred Center

The sustaining function of Shabbat is related in yet more detailed fashion through the controlling image of the Sacred Center. Any critical study of the symbolism of the Sacred Center is indebted to the pioneering work of Mircea Eliade. Several of his insights have been drawn on in this section.[105]

As we have seen, in the Rabbinic period the Sabbath gradually came to serve as "the central unifying religious symbol of the Jewish people."[106] Shabbat became a "Sanctuary in time," a focus of holiness around which cosmos and time were ordered and blessed. Perhaps nowhere is this notion of the sacred center more dramatically symbolized than in the classical Kabbalah.

The Kabbalists expanded and transformed the symbolism of the Sacred Center in two basic ways. First, although retaining the reference to the earthly institution of Shabbat, they transferred the focus to its ultimate source, the divine Shabbat (for them the truly cosmic axis). Hence, Kabbalistic discussion of the Sacred Center takes on a richly ambiguous quality, now referring to the divine Shabbat, now to its temporal reflection, the "Sabbath day," and on still other occasions, to both. Secondly, it was the Kabbalists who were responsible for raising the Sabbath's implicit centrality to the status of an explicit category.

That is, in the pre-Kabbalistic period Shabbat functioned as a Sacred Center but was rarely acknowledged as such in the imaginative literature; with rare exception (e.g., TB Shab. 49b and 96a) its centrality operated on a more implicit—less self-conscious—level.[107] The Kabbalists, by contrast, fashioned a full array of colorful images that deliberately underscored the Sabbath's identity as Sacred Center.

First, they linked Shabbat with those Sacred Spaces which had traditionally served as *axes mundi:* e.g., Eden, Jerusalem, the Temple;

'Even ha-Shetiyyah, the Founding Stone from which the world was fashioned[108] (all sefirotically *Shekhinah*); and even in several accounts, the Holy of Holies (generally, *Binah*). To give another example, the TZ/RM homologized the arrival of the temporal and divine Sabbaths to the salvific return to Zion, the overcoming of homelessness and Exile. Traditional spatial categories of holiness were thereby re-read and relativized, preserved on a new *symbolic* level of meaning.[109]

In addition to these sacred *topoi,* the Kabbalists utilized a series of natural and geometric images which further dramatized the Sabbath's centrality: Shabbat was portrayed as the centermost and lushest royal garden; the central column of the (sefirotic) tree; the heart and soul of the cosmos; its *omphalos;* the pupil of the world's Eye; the center of the circle; the center of the Cosmic Wheel; and the cosmic pillar upon which the world rests. (Interestingly, many of these images had been applied to Jerusalem in Biblical and Aggadic sources, and further evince the symbolic equation of Zion, Temple, and Shabbat in theosophical Kabbalah.)[110] Sacred objects associated with the Tabernacle—that portable Sacred Center—were also homologized to the Sabbath: Shabbat was *ha-bariaḥ ha-tikhon,* the central bar that supported the entire structure[111] and the middle stem of the seven-branched *menorah,* the chief source of illumination.[112]

Just as these images were used to emphasize the sefirotic Sabbath's centrality within the divine and lower worlds, so were they used to portray the centrality of the seventh day in the world of Time. Time was said to revolve around Shabbat: the spiritual week was commonly seen as extending from Wednesday to Tuesday[113], while some adepts taught that even festival time was nurtured by Shabbat, emanating from its holiness like branches from a tree.[114]

Figure 4: The Conventional Structuring of Weekly Time[115] versus the Kabbalistic Model

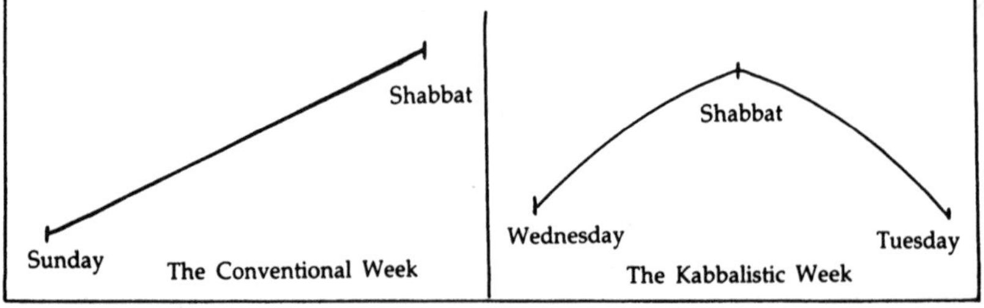

Let us now turn to the more detailed illustrations of this symbolism. Because "Sabbath as Eden" and "Sabbath as Temple" will

be treated elsewhere in this study, other key metaphors will be concentrated on here.

The image of Shabbat as the sustaining Center is first found in *Sefer ha-Bahir.* It has already been alluded to it earlier (*Bahir* 157)[116] but it is more explicitly developed in two other passages, where it is associated with *Yesod,* the fourth of the seven active sefirot and the divine Axis Mundi:

> *Ẓaddiq,* the Foundation of the World is at the Center. . . . It is the Life of the Cosmos. All creation is done through it, as it is written: *Shabat va-yinnafash* [Ex. 31:17] [meaning], there was Sabbath and animation. This is the attribute of the Sabbath day. (*Bahir* 180)

Section 159 employs the typical *Bahir* simile whereby the seven lower sefirot are likened to royal gardens. The Sabbath/*Yesod* is the central one, whose well-spring irrigates the six others:

> [Shabbat] may be compared to a king who had seven gardens, and in the garden in the middle, a flowing spring welling up from a living source [the upper sefirotic world]. Three gardens stand to the right and three to the left. As soon as it accomplishes its work, [the spring] fills up and overflows. Then all [the gardens] rejoice, and say: "For our sake does it overflow!" It waters them and makes them thrive while they wait and rest.

Immediately thereafter the *Bahir* explains that Shabbat/*Yesod* sustains the "heart" of the divine corpus (*Shekhinah,* the feminine Sabbath); as they unite these two Sabbaths nourish and restore the lower sefirotic world:

> Does [the spring] water all seven? Is it not written: "from the East [kabbalistically, *Yesod*][117] I will bring your seed"? [Isa. 43:5]. . . . Say rather [the spring] waters the Heart, and the Heart then waters them all.

In his *'Oẓar ha-Kavod* (OK), Ṭodros Abulafia underscored the centrality of Shabbat by likening the divine Sabbath *(here, Tif'eret)* to the middle stem of a menorah:

> "Knowledge" is the chief source of light for the seven days because it is at the center. . . with three days to its right and three to its left. Because it is the seventh it is called the Sabbath of "Remember." (OK to TB Ber. 33a)[118]

Joseph of Hamadan extends this image, explicity identifying the divine Sabbath (here *Tif'eret/Yesod*) as the living center of the sefirotic and temporal week. His interpretation is a model of Kabbalistic multivocality, as the passage may be read both with reference to the divine Sabbath and its temporal reflection:

> The Sabbath day is a Soul for the other six days; they derive their nourishment, the blessing of *shefaᶜ*, from it. It is at the center, the essence and foundation [*Yesod*] of all. It is the middle stem [*qav ha-ᶜemẓa'i*] of the candelabrum, upon whose [energy] the six candles draw.[119]
>
> So the Sabbath is in the middle: Sunday, Monday and Tuesday are called the "Conclusion of Shabbat" and Wednesday, Thursday and Friday are called "Sabbath eve." The Sabbath is in the middle, imparting *shefaᶜ* to the six days of activity. . . .

In a sense, the entire week is one long Sabbath whose intensity ebbs and flows with rhythmic regularity. The light of Shabbat rises on Wednesday, reaches its peak on Saturday, and gradually grows dimmer, to be relieved in the middle of the week by the rising light of the next Sabbath[120]. Time and cosmos may be said to unfold from Shabbat:

> The Sabbath is the middle point from which the world was fashioned. (*Sefer Ṭaᶜamei ha-Miẓvot* [SṬM]: 296)

Like the Jerusalem of the Aggadists (from whose concentrated essence the world was born), Shabbat is the cosmic center: *Urstoff* and matrix of creation.[121]

This last notion is elaborated by Joseph of Hamadan's older contemporary, Joseph Giqatilia, who likened the Sabbath both to the pupil of the world's Eye[122] and to the center of the cosmic Wheel. Using the second image he wrote that:

> All God's creation and all His Creatures are the mystery of the Wheel [*galgal*]. He created everything from one point which is the mystery of Shabbat, the mystery of the center. . . .

Extending this simile, he likened the six profane days to the spokes of the wheel, while the Sabbath is the hub—the cosmic glue—holding them together. Without Shabbat, time and cosmos are *ḥalulim, meḥullalim ve-ḥalalim,* empty and profane:

Figure 5: The Sabbath as Cosmic Center
(ff. de Vidas' illustration)

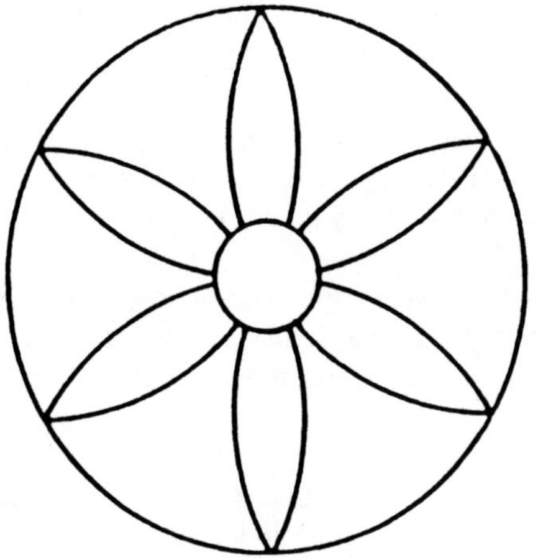

> The six days radiate from the Sabbath [kabbalistically, *Yesod*] and the Sabbath, in its holiness, is in the middle, [alone]: "It has no mate"[123]: It is the source of all *shefa*ᶜ and goodness for the spheres. There is no celestial sphere that does not contain the secret of Shabbat. . . . The six profane days are called the hollow [*ḥalal*] of the wheel. . . . For should the center be removed, all would be hollow, empty and profane [*meḥullalim*], like a body emptied of its soul . . . its very center. . . . This is the mystery of the six profane days and the holy Shabbat. [quoted in Elijah de Vidas, *Re'shit Ḥokhmah:* Gate of Holiness, Chap. 2]

The image of the Sabbath as center of the cosmic circle was particularly well-developed in the writings of Moshe de Leon.[124] Three brief examples will be considered here, beginning with the most tightly circumscribed cosmic circle and ending with the most expansive one. In the *Zohar* (1:5b–6a; cf. 3:296a–b [IZ]), the divine Shabbat, here *Shekhinah,* is the "square inside the [divine] circle" (here limited to *Yesod*); it is also called "the point at the center," "the innermost point," and the "Holy of Holies"—the center (ff. M. Kelim 1:6–9) from which blessing flows. In *Sefer ha-Mishqal,* the entire divine world is envisioned as a circle of holiness, its dimensions defined by the three "sefirotic points called Shabbat": *Binah* (the Great Sabbath) at the acme[125]; *Malkhut* (Sabbath night) at the nadir; and *Tif'eret* (Sabbath day) at the center.[126] *Tif'eret* is the essential Sabbath: the "axis around which the circle revolves," "the middle point and foundation of the Structure" (pp. 110–11):

> So the Lord chose this day from among all others, for through it they [the divine rungs] all unite; by virtue of [Shabbat]. . . the chain rounds into a circle. (p. 115)

In other words, Shabbat is the organizing principle of the sefirotic world, transforming a linear structure into a perfect circle; bringing the discrete aspects into harmonious relation. Order gives birth to blessing:

> There is no proper circle without a center situated in the hollow. From it all is built properly; it is the essence. From it, branches [carrying *shefa*ᶜ] spread out, extending below in all directions.

To profane the Sabbath is to breach the divine circle, threatening the well-being of cosmos and self:

> Concerning [Shabbat], Scripture says: "*Meḥalaleha,* whoever profanes it, shall be put to death." [Ex. 31:14] Whoever enters into the space [*ḥalal*] belonging to the Point of the Structure to uproot any of its *tiqqunim* or aspects [promotes death].[127] (pp. 110–11)

Finally, in *Sefer ha-Rimmon* the cosmic wheel expands to include all worlds: Shabbat (now *Shekhinah!*) becomes the center-point, the linch-pin holding together supernal and lower worlds. It is Shabbat that creates a *uni*verse, a single unified field.

> The mystery of Shabbat is [contained in] the lowest of the three points. . . . She is *'Even ha-Shetiyyah,* the Founding Stone through which the world was established, the center for all seventy nations [of the world]: She dwells in the middle. . . . All Her branches, tendrils and roots describe a circle around Her. . . a wheel. . . a sphere. . . . Without Her, there could be no circle.

Shekhinah/Shabbat is the source from which the lower world emanates:

> Heaven and earth, all the lower entities, derive from and are sustained by the mystery of the Point. She is the mystery of *Bere'shit*. . . the beginning of all things. (MS Brit. Mus. 90b)[128]

On several occasions, there is a darker undertone to the image of Shabbat as Sacred Center. For example, in *Perush ᶜal ha-Torah* (Ex. 20:8), Menaḥem Recanati spoke of the female Sabbath, *Malkhut*, as the surrounded center, beset by the hostile *qelippot*.[129] Her liminal, and hence, precarious status as the meeting place between upper and lower worlds, and between sacred and profane, is underscored. Menaḥem Recanati's interpretation is based on a word-play on the root *ḤLL*, which may mean either "profane" or "the space" within the circle:[130]

> "Those who profane Her [i.e., Shabbat] shall be put to death." [Ex. 31:14] Some explain that it is written *meḤaLaLeha* [with a feminine suffix] to indicate that the Community of Israel [*Malkhut*/Shabbat] is the center of the circle and that the seventy nations [kabbalistically, the profane *qelippot*] surround Her, as it is said: "I set Jerusalem in the midst of the nations, with countries round about her." [Ezek. 5:5] Concerning Her it is said: *Meḥalaleha*: those who profane Her [Shabbat/*Malkhut*], meaning those who encroach upon Her sacred space [*le-ḥalalah*] to uproot that which is ordered and which rightfully belongs to Her. . . .[131]

Finally, let us consider a passage in Baḥyya ben Asher's *Kad ha-Qemaḥ*[132] which conflates many of the images that have been noted:

> Shabbat is both fourth [the midpoint of the week] and seventh like the Great Light, the sun. . . .

Here Baḥyya is referring to the feminine Sabbath, *Shekhinah*, which is the fourth sefirah from *Binah* in the order of Emanation and the seventh of the lower rungs in the order of final placement. He continued:

> Because Shabbat is at the midpoint, it is superior to the other days, for whatever is at the center is holier and more sublime than its neighbors, like the Tree of Life at the center of the Garden, and the middle candle in the menorah which corresponds to the *Shekhinah*. Hence, since the Sabbath is the mid-point it is called *holy*. . . .[133]

Moreover, Sabbath observance enables the devotee to live one day out of seven at the Sacred Center, whereas profaning it—treating the Sabbath like a weekday—entails spiritual Exile, life at the periphery. This notion is intimated in a cautionary tale referring to its historical analogue, the physical Exile of Israel from the Land:

> It is written in the *Sefer Yeẓirah* [4:4]: "The Holy Sanctuary corresponds to the middle." And Israel was not exiled from the Holy Land, the center of the world, till they profaned the Sabbath. They deserved this for the Holy One metes out measure for measure.[134] They profaned the Sabbath for they made the epicenter into one of the radii [*qeẓavot*]; and so they were banished from the Land, the omphalos of the world, unto its extremities.[135]

To conclude: in this section we have seen the orienting, redeeming power which the Sabbath assumed in the mystical imagination. Shabbat (in its full array of meanings) is the cosmic Jerusalem, the Center that holds: it creates life, renews it, re-orders and sustains it, fills the world with blessing.[136]

SABBATH TRANSFORMATIONS

This work has thus far suggested that the Myth of Sabbath-Renewal is not a smooth narrative but an allusive, many-faceted one. Indeed, one might think of it as a kind of cubist portrait or montage filled with splintered sequences and mysterious resonances. For the Kabbalists tell the Story of Shabbat from multiple and constantly shifting angles of vision: different mythic subplots and episodes weave in and out, and attention fluidly shifts from one 'protagonist'—one level of being—to another. In actuality, the Story of Shabbat is a family of stories, a great weave of dramatic symbols, fashioned into a significant whole.

To gain fuller and more adequate understanding of this decidedly complex conception of Shabbat, the initial motif study will be supplemented by focusing on three additional themes or angles of vision: those which most cogently relate the transforming effects of Shabbat in three of their most critical dimensions. We shall first consider the transformations within the realm of Time, a topic that has been broached before but which merits more systematic attention. Thereafter, we shall turn to two other, highly nuanced motifs: the myth of Sacred Marriage—the union of divine Male and Female—which will more precisely mark the progressive changes occuring within the divine Gestalt, and the motif of the Sabbath-soul, which dramatizes the ontological changes undergone by the Sabbath-observer. These initial portraits will be refined in chapters 3 and 4 in our extended discussion of Sabbath-ritual.

By focusing more clearly on the motif of Transformation in these pages, the distinctions between the Sabbath-cosmos and profane existence will necessarily be highlighted. It should be noted, however, that not all Kabbalists were of one mind regarding the degree of transformation. Some Kabbalists, whom we might call the dualists, saw the change as being radical in nature. These mystics—like the Castilian Gnostics discussed in the Introduction—tended to see good and evil as absolutely distinct and opposing forces, and highlighted the ontological gap between the profane week and the holy Shabbat. In this schema, the entrance of Shabbat marks a kind of Changing of the Cosmic Guard, as the harsh Profane realm that holds sway during the week gives way to the blessed rule of divinity. The authors of the TZ/RM and the *Qanah/Peli'ah,* e.g., tended towards such a position.

Other Kabbalists, however, described the changes as being more gradual and continuous in nature. Holding a more harmonistic view of the relations between Sacred and Profane, and between the week-day-world and Shabbat, they saw the Sabbath cosmos as more clearly pervading the week as well. The Sabbath-cosmos increased in intensity as Sabbath neared, and faded only gradually thereafter. Sabbath, in this gradualist schema, is the most fully actuated time, the acme of the unbroken weekly round. David ben Judah he-Ḥasid,[137] Joseph of Hamadan, and the *Me'irat ᶜEinayim* all inclined towards this position.[138]

As shall be seen in subsequent chapters, however, too simple a distinction should not be drawn between the harmonists and the dualists: for at various times any given Kabbalist will feel compelled to stress the radical separation of Shabbat from the week (especially, as he is about to enter Shabbat) whereas at other moments he will highlight the infusion of the Sabbath-cosmos into the week (e.g., as he is about to leave Shabbat on Saturday night). For the experience of Shabbat is complex, and its rhythms multiple.[139]

SABBATH AS PERFECTED TIME

The Sabbath is the dream of perfection. . . the sign of Creation and the first revelation. . . the anticipation of redemption. . . .

> Indeed, on the Sabbath the congregation feels as if it were already redeemed. . .
>
> F. Rosenzweig, *The Star of Redemption*[140]

The Kabbalists conceptualized Time in varying fashions. They employed cyclical models and linear ones, even at times, oscillating ones, to suggest the alternation between sacred and profane time, and between different orders of the sacred.[141] The Sabbath may be said to occupy the center of two basic geometric models. Imaging Time as an endless round of seven-day cycles, the Kabbalists depicted Shabbat as the point around which weekly time revolved, its Sacred Axis. Some adepts widened the circle, seeing the Sabbath as the source for festival time, and the hub of the yearly cycle as well.[142]

But the Kabbalists also imaged Time in more obviously historical fashion, as a system of linear co-ordinates mapping the progression from Creation to Cosmic Redemption (see the figure below). Within this schema—which shall concern us here—each Shabbat is seen as a rupture, a break in the unidirectional procession of history. For on this day Time reverses its course and, as it were, "conflates": the paradigmatic first and last moments erupt into the present; the past, present, and future converge.[143]

To further illustrate this second schema: the Sabbath is said to be a reflection of the primordial seventh day, a day on which the sefirotic totality returns to its pristine harmony, wherein

> the supernal entities are gladdened, and the spirit of Knowledge [*Tif'eret*] and the Fear of the Lord [*Malkhut*] unite, as during the primordial Creation. (Ṭ. Abulafia, OK to TB Shab. 119b)

It is a day on which *Shekhinah*, the diminished Moon, recovers Her Edenic lustre, shining once again with a brilliance that matches that of the Sun *(Tif'eret)*.[144]

Figure 6: Two Geometric Conceptions of Time

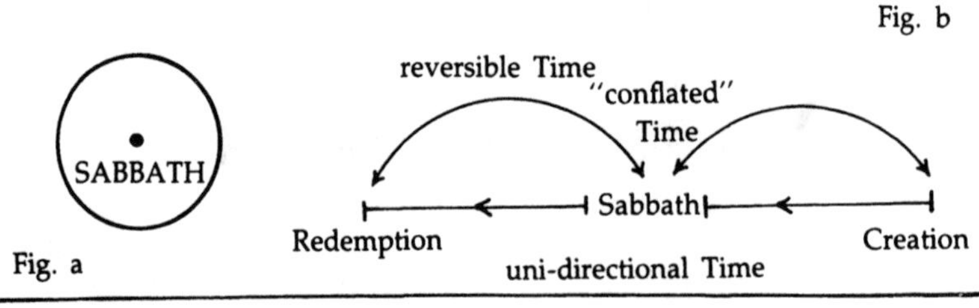

Similarly, Zoharic sources—especially the TZ/RM—liken the Jew's entrance into Shabbat to a return to Eden. Through preparatory acts, the devotee purifies himself of the stain of the week and its spiritual "Fall"; he is wreathed with a Sabbath-soul scented with "the perfume of celestial Garden." According to other sources, he even delights in *'or ha-ganuz,* the lost Edenic light that "enabled Adam to 'see' from one end of the world to the next."[145] For one day the Jew becomes primordial Adam, entering that time beyond "the fiery ever-turning sword."[146]

According to the *Zohar,* each Shabbat partakes of the very first. Moshe de Leon grounded the seemingly non-mythic Rabbinic custom of beginning the Sabbath on Friday afternoon—"while it is still day"[147]—in the primordial event. At the end of Creation, a kind of cosmic battle ensued. A residue of evil (*Siṭra' 'Aḥra'*) from within the Tree of Knowledge (*Malkhut*) rebelled against the Holy One. Left as disembodied spirits, these evil ones sought bodies for themselves, concrete forms in which they could better pursue their aim of controlling the world.

> When the Holy One saw this He raised a wind out of the Tree of Life [*Tif'eret*] which blew and lashed against the other Tree so that the Side of Good was aroused.

To insure that Good prevailed in the world, God ended the work of Creation and began the Sabbath early:

> But had *Siṭra' 'Aḥra'* prevailed over the Side of Good on that night, the world could not have withstood it for even one minute. But the Holy One provided the cure in advance: He caused the holy day [Shabbat] to arrive early, before *Siṭra' 'Aḥra'* could take control, and the world was established.

In commemoration of that event and so as to prevent further encroachments of evil—which threaten the nascent Sabbath-cosmos each week—Israel is bidden to begin Shabbat early. Through this re-enactment of the primordial myth, Evil is driven off, Time purified and renewed, and the Cosmos refounded. Shabbat thus takes on the qualities of Eliadean Sacred Time: it is "primordial mythical time made present," reconstituting the archteypal passage from (threatened) Chaos to harmonious Cosmos.[148]

But if Shabbat is a return to what Eliade calls *illud tempus,* it is also an adumbration of *ᶜolam ha-ba',* the "World-to-Come." This term—now used with willed precision, now with dreamy vagueness—may signify any number of temporal realms in the Kabbalah; five basic ones will be isolated here.

(1) In its most modest associations, the weekly Sabbath is a taste of that already extant "World of Souls," the celestial Eden in which the righteous dwell and to which the adept will ascend upon his death.[149]

But *ᶜolam ha-ba'* also refers to a telescoping series of future worlds, each more fantastic (and expansive) than its predecessor. By probing these visions of the future, a better appreciation of the utopian element in the weekly Sabbath can be attained.

(2) To begin with the most proximate future-age: The Sabbath is a reflection of the Messianic Redemption and "homecoming," when earthly and divine Israel "go forth from the darkness of Exile and the rule of strangers, and behold the light of the Living."[150] This is the age of the People's return to Zion, of national restoration and the rebuilding of the Temple, culminating in the Resurrection. Theosophically, it connotes *Shekhinah*'s release from the clutches of *Siṭra' 'Aḥra'*, and Her return to the divine realm and growing vivification there.

(3) But the weekly Sabbath is also a foreshadowing of that post-Messianic era, the so-called "seventh millenium"[151] or "perpetual Sabbath," wherein divine harmony will become complete and human existence will be reconstituted on a purely spiritual plane. Moshe de Leon explained: If the Messianic era marked the return to physical Zion, this age marks the "true," i.e., spiritual ingathering when the "divine Sabbath. . . the *celestial* Jerusalem" shall gather unto Herself the souls of the righteous and nourish them directly. (*Sefer ha-Mishqal*: 92–94)[152]

The TY proclaims that a comprehensive spiritual healing will occur at this time as the last barriers to intimacy (between divinity and devotee, and between the divine Lovers) melt away:

> "Then your Guide will no longer be kept under wraps, but your eyes shall behold your Guide" [Isa. 30:20]. . . . Then "Death [kabbalistically, *Siṭra' 'Aḥra'*] shall be utterly consumed" [Isa. 25:8]. . . the two lovers shall be united. . . (*Sod ha-Shabbat*: end)

According to *Maᶜarekhet ha-'Elohut* (185a), it is the weekly Sabbath which alludes to the unfolding of this utopian age:

> "when darkness and light [kabbalistically, the divine female and male] shall be the same" [Ps. 139:12] [and] "the Moon's light will

> be equal to that of the Sun. . . as during the seven days of Creation." [Isa. 30:26]

The ritual candlelighting which inaugurates each Sabbath dramatizes *Shekhinah*, the "cosmic candle's," weekly renewal, even as it points to Her millenial radiance.[153]

Sabbath celebration points to the devotee's perfection as well. By actively participating in Shabbat—through Torah study, through prayer—the Jew may fleetingly partake of his ultimate state in the World-to-Come: he becomes "purely spiritual. . . like an angel of the Lord of Hosts"; one "feasting on the splendor of the *Shekhinah*."[154] But this future Sabbath may also be intimated through eloquent non-action: by resting[155] or by observing the halakhic prohibition against cooking on Shabbat. During other festivals one can prepare the food required for the day; not so on Shabbat for:

> the Sabbath [alone] is a foretaste of the World-to-Come. . . the seventh millenium, the Great Sabbath. . . when all [embodied] activity will cease. . . There will be no food or drink, but the righteous will sit with crowns on their heads and feast off the splendor of the *Shekhinah*. . . . They will bask in *'Or ha-Ganuz*, [Her!] primordial light, which was hidden expressly for them. (*Ma-ʿarekhet ha-'Elohut* 185a)

In many ways, the Sabbath intimates both the climax and closure of history. Time, it seems to suggest, will come full circle, spiralling towards pristine beginnings. David ben Judah he-Ḥasid's description of the future Sabbatical age is exemplary:

> Then the righteous will dwell as saplings [nourished by] the "river [that] goes forth from Eden to water the Garden." (Gen. 2:10) They will rejoice and luxuriate in the delights of Eden. All holy souls will dwell there, set in rows around the primordial stream. . . (*Mar'ot ha-Ẓove'ot*: 102)

It is the weekly Sabbath which affords the adept a foretaste of his soul's once and future reward.

(4) The Sabbath of the Cosmic *Shemiṭṭah*. Moshe de Leon held that the delights of the seventh millenium will continue in perpetuity; it is, he said, "a continuous day," "a new world without death" or dissolution.[156] But many adepts disagreed, uncovering yet deeper layers of Shabbat, other Worlds-to-Come. Although the dominant exoteric tradition limited creation to one cycle, these Kabbalists spoke

of seven cosmic cycles or *shemiṭṭot,* each with its distinctive nature and attributes.[157] Drawing on the medieval notion that cosmic ages or aeons were governed by specific planets, some Kabbalists held that the cosmic cycles are governed by the seven active sefirot emanating from *Binah,* the "Mother of the Cosmos."[158]

Starting with *Ḥesed* and concluding with *Malkhut,* each of the lower rungs successively activates a creation-cycle, and by imparting something of its own unique nature to it—"something of its own soul" (*Sefer ha-Temunah* 28b)—each rung sets the tone for the age.[159] Each aeon was said to last for 7000 years, i.e., a cosmic week of God, for whom "one thousand years are like a day." (Ps. 90:4)

According to one line of thought developed in *Sefer ha-Temunah,* on the eve of the seventh millenium (= *ᶜErev Shabbat!*) time progressively slows so that *SHaBbaT* is eventually reached: "The doors of the [cosmic] market close" (Eccles. 12:4), the sefirot cease functioning—*SHoBTim*—and the lower worlds revert to *tohu va-vohu,* primordial chaos.[160] This millenial Shabbat is a timeless time, without external manifestation or dramatic display. All remains fallow, pure potentiality. Subsequently, the world is renewed by the quickened power of the succeeding sefirah.

In other speculations, the seventh millenium proceeds along somewhat different lines.[161] To recall, some adepts saw the onset of the seventh millenium as a time of spiritual fulfillment, for Israel and the divine androgyne alike. Many held, however, that before the millenial Sabbath reaches its end, this fullness will be transcended, mystically "swallowed up" in the higher unity of *hitballeᶜut* or apokatastasis. In one common schema, all Being—from the lower worlds to the seven active sefirot—is reabsorbed in *Binah,* the cosmic Womb and Quarry, the "ancient stream," "supernal Shabbat." At this future time,

> the righteous. . . who have been basking in the splendor of *Shekhinah.* . . will adorn themselves to enter the Great Sabbath, the Mother of the Children. . . . And all worlds, rungs, and chariots will be drawn up into *Binah,* as it is written: "For dust you are and unto dust you shall return." (Gen. 3:19) All the rivers [lower sefirot] shall return to that ancient stream, the stream that flows out of the depth of Thought. (*Mar'ot ha-Ẓove'ot*: 102–04, ff. D. Matt's translation, Ibid.: 32–33)

According to the *Maᶜarekhet ha-'Elohut,* all finally reverts to absolute rest; the individuation that marks existence shall be overcome:

> The divine androgyne [*du-parẓufin*] will return to its primordial [i.e., pre-formed] state in the world of emanation, as when the bond was complete. This is the Great Sabbath, Rest in Eternal Life. All entities will rest therein and cease to exist [*yitbaṭṭelu*]. Because [the weekly] Sabbath alludes to this [cessation], it is said that the Sabbath day is a taste of the World-to-Come. (185a)

Still, this Sabbath is not the ultimate one, as *shemiṭṭah* follows *shemiṭṭah*, aeon following aeon, seven creation cycles in all. In most accounts, full mystical absorption is reserved for the final World-to-Come:

(5) the Great Jubilee of the fiftieth millenium, the so-called "Sabbath of Sabbaths." Most accounts intensify the symbolism for *hitballeᶜut* here, speaking (ff. Lev. 25) of "familial restitution," and of liberation and release:

> The supernal Sabbath day, the Great Jubilee, alludes to "a cosmos that is entirely Shabbat" [Mekh. "Beshallaḥ"] wherein "a person [the human soul] shall return to his Family [*Binah*, the Mother and *Ḥokhmah*, the Father], to the inheritance of his ancestors [ff. Lev. 25:10]. (OK to Shab. 33b and RH 31a)

And:

> All the sefirot ascend unto *Binah* which is the world of Freedom. . . in which all the slaves are set free. . . . They go out to freedom and ascend to their rung, as at first. (*Mar'ot ha-Ẓove'ot*: 104–05)

> This is the Great Liberation. . . . For [all] return from their exile, and rest; they bow down to the Lord in Jerusalem. (*Temunah* 24a)

As emanated life (all souls, worlds and rungs) ascend on high, they behold the "face of the divine"[162] and gain release, or absorption/annihilation in the primal source. Unio mystica indeed!

Other accounts push to the very limit, collapsing all Being into the Nihil, *Keter*, and its "innermost core,"[163] *'Ein Sof*:

> From there all being ascends unto the Sabbath of *Binah* and from *Binah* to *Keter* which is called the Sabbath for all Sabbaths and the Infinite, " 'Ein Sof." (*Temunah* 68b)[164]

Here the ultimate Sabbath is ushered in; Shabbat is all.

The Sabbath of *hitballeᶜut* forms a striking counterpoint to the *Shabbatot* that have been studied until now. In place of the Sabbath of cosmic plenitude and abundant blessing, we witness the Sabbath of radical emptying. All turns inward: the world *shabat*—literally ceases to pulse—and is reabsorbed in the recondite Source. Sefirotic dynamism has given way to utter stillness, fulfillment to transcendence, the "music of Shabbat" to the "world of whispers" and "silence."[165]

As the day of rest and quietude par excellence, the current Shabbat participates in and becomes a symbol of that deepest return, in RaMBaN's telling phrase, "the end of [all] Exile" (to Gen. 2:3). Although this understanding of Shabbat is historically overdetermined, it surely has profound psychological roots, evincing the mystic's longing to overcome the sense of exile or alienation brought about by individuation, revealing his desire to merge back into the All.[166]

Most Kabbalists spoke of the nexus between this ultimate Shabbat and its weekly symbol in allusive fashion only. Although intimated by a few Sabbath prayers and ritual gestures,[167] it is perhaps most powerfully suggested via negationes. By refraining from *mela'khah*—desisting from active labor—the adept may "cleave unto this supernal Sabbath" and attain a small measure of its profound rest.[168]

Let us recapitulate. Each Shabbat partakes of and symbolizes perfected time: both Eden and Redemption, origins and endings, history resolved and, even, history dissolved.[169] It is a temporary glimpse of the ultimate and at its most far-reaching points to the mystery of perpetual Shabbat, *yom she-kullo shabbat*, "the aeon that is entirely Sabbath."[170] In its fluid, multidimensional structure, Sabbath-time allows the adept to live both backwards and forwards, to transcend the bounds of profane (unilinear) experience.[171]

A final observation. The Kabbalists' insistent emphasis on origins and endings is rather striking when we consider that the Rabbinic tradition claims that the Sabbath not only commemorates Creation and foreshadows the World-to-Come, but also recalls the Exodus from Egypt and the Giving of the Torah. These last two historical moments are seldom as crucial in the celebration of the Kabbalistic Sabbath as the first two. The Zoharic tradition does correlate leaving the week to *Shekhinah*'s escape from "the Narrow Straits of the Sea" (*meẓar yam*—or *Siṭra' 'Aḥra'*—a play on *Miẓrayim*, Egypt), but the Exodus is by no means a dominant motif.[172] Similarly, although images of Torah abound in the Kabbalistic literature on Shabbat, there is surprisingly little emphasis on recovering the Sinaitic moments, per se. An exception that proves the rule: In *Zohar* 2:206a–b, each reading of the Torah is likened to *ma^camad har Sinai*. Although the Sabbath is therefore included in what the Kabbalists viewed as the ongoing Sinaitic moment,[173] it is in no way singled out.[174] Hence, from one perspective at least, the Kabbalistic framing of Sacred Time is surprisingly "narrow"!

DIVINE TRANSFORMATIONS: SABBATH AS *HIEROS GAMOS*

> [The Sabbath] is the perfection of Male and Female. . . the Mystery of One. . . . On Shabbat all is one entity.
>
> Moshe de Leon, *Sefer ha-Rimmon*

The transformation of the divine world on Shabbat is perhaps most dramatically articulated by the myth of Sacred Marriage, the holy union of the masculine and feminine aspects of God. The Exile of the week is overcome as *Tif'eret/Yesod* and *Shekhinah* enter into that relationship which the *Zohar* calls *zivvuga' qaddisha'*, and historians of religion, hierogamy or *hieros gamos*.[175] In the rich and fluid Kabbalistic imagery Male and Female become the archetypal Bride and Groom donning evershifting masks and personae: now they are the king and his consort, now the male and female *Shabbatot* returning to primordial androgyny, now the two lovers, Solomon and the unnamed shepherdess of the Song of Songs, or Jacob and Rachel, or the Holy One and the mystical Community of Israel; such are the guises of the protean Groom and Bride.[176]

The re-imaging of Shabbat as a marriage festival is one of the most significant contributions of the classical Kabbalistic tradition to the later Jewish celebration of Shabbat. It laid the groundwork for the ritual innovations of the Safed mystics and has greatly influenced the popular celebration of Shabbat in recent centuries.

In this section we shall trace the historical development of the Marriage Motif and its ancillary themes. We shall, moreover, see some of the ways in which this myth was made real for the Kabbalist by examining its articulation and embodiment in Sabbath ritual.

Historically, three critical stages within the evolution of this motif may be noted:

(1) **Rabbinic pre-cursors.** This oldest stratum consists of a few passages in the Talmud and Midrash which framed the Sabbath in marital terms. These scattered sources had been largely ignored or apologized for by the pre-Kabbalistic rabbis; however, they were brought together and presented in a new light by the Kabbalists.

(2) **The *Bahir*** with its lavish mythic imagery. Here two contributions stand out: its novel understanding of divine androgyny and its use of coupling as a symbol for divine wholeness; and its mystical symbolization of *'Aggadah,* that is, the penchant in the *Bahir* for re-reading Rabbinic legends concerning the relationship of the Holy One and Israel as references to intradivine processes; and

(3) **The contributions of Moshe de Leon** who, in his boundless mythic imagination, developed the Sabbath into a three-fold mystical drama embracing:

(a) *Shekhinah*/Shabbat's liberation from Her entanglement in the demonic forces of *Siṭra' 'Aḥra'* (the Other Side), suggestively symbolized as the six profane days,

(b) Her marriage/reunion with Her lover, the Holy One, and

(c) Their coronation and attirement in garments of divine light.

Let us examine the literary evidence.

Rabbinic Pre-Cursors

Scattered through the Rabbinic literature are several passages that explicitly frame the Sabbath in marital terms and several which could easily be interpreted as such by the Kabbalists.

Passages framing the Sabbath in marital terms.

(1) Sabbath as Bride. Two virtually identical Talmudic passages, TB Shab. 119a and BQ 32a-b, personify the Sabbath as Bride. They explain that on Sabbath eve at sunset various rabbis used to wrap themselves in special garb and go forth to greet "the Sabbath Bride," some proclaiming. "Come, O Bride! Come, O Bride!" A similar personification is found in the Amoraic midrash Genesis R 10:9. Through a clever word-play, the phrase "And God completed (*va-yekhal*) on the seventh day" (Gen. 2:2) is rendered "And God made a bride (*kallah*)[177] of the seventh day":

> This may be compared to a king who made a bridal chamber which he plastered, painted and adorned. What was the chamber lacking? A bride to enter it. Similarly, what was the world lacking [at the end of the six days]? Shabbat![178]

(2) Sabbath and marital imagery. Genesis R 11:8 attests to the love affair between Israel and the Sabbath by likening them to husband and wife. According to this midrash, God paired all the days of the week: Sunday had Monday, Tuesday had Wednesday, Thursday had Friday. Only Shabbat was left alone.

> The Sabbath came before the Holy One and said: "Sovereign of the Universe. All the other days have a mate; am I to be without one?" The Holy One said to it: "The Community of Israel shall be your mate." As it is said, "Remember the Sabbath day *le-qaddesho* [here read]: to betroth it." (Ex. 20:8)[179]

In another source (Lev. R 27:10; alternate version, PRK 78a) it is God who is wed to Shabbat. To use the midrashic simile, Shabbat is God's beloved Queen, the King's *Maṭrona'* or "Lady."

Passages that could easily be re-read by the Kabbalists to allude to sacred marriage. Of the many sources, the two most influential are:

(1) The Talmudic source, TB Shev. 20b. It is explained that the two versions of the Sabbath Command in the Decalog, "Remember" and "Keep" were spoken as one.

(2) TB Ket. 62b. This source says that Torah-scholars used to perform marital intercourse specifically on Friday nights.

Admittedly, these sources are few and their symbolism disparate. It is only after the Kabbalists developed a mystical hermeneutic—new lenses though which to see the ancient sources—that the sources could be brought together and given symbolic coherence.

Heikhalot *Mysticism: The Evidence of* Seder Rabba' di-Vre'shit

Another important layer in the development of the *hieros gamos* motif derives from *Heikhalot* mysticism, specifically from a composition entitled *Seder Rabba' di-Vre'shit.*[180] Though a precise dating of this work has eluded scholars, it was completed no later than the Geonic period and in all likelihood contains material dating from late antiquity.

The *Seder* is a work of cosmogonic speculation, marked by the metrical rhythms and magniloquence typical of the *Heikhalot* genre. After describing the Work of Creation during the first six days,[181] the text states that God, having completed His labors, ascended to the heaven called *ma^con shel simḥah* (the Habitation of Joy) to sit on His celestial Throne. As He arrived, all the angelic princes (*sarim*) who were appointed over the cosmos came before Him in great joy,

> revelling and rejoicing, dancing and singing and praising Him in all manner of praise and song. All the levels of the firmament were filled with joy, chanting before Him as *shabat va-yinnafash* [Ex.

> 31:17], "He ceased working and was refreshed." (Schaeffer ed., sec. 849–52)

At that very moment,

> The Holy One ushered in the princess of the Sabbath [*sarat ha-Shabbat,* in the feminine!] and sat her on His Throne of Glory [i.e., alongside Him]. He brought before her each and every prince of each and every firmament and lower expanse. They danced [*me-raqqedin*] and exulted before [the Sabbath] and said: *Shabbat hi' la-YHWH:* "The Sabbath, she is the Lord's" [Lev. 23:3]. . . . The Holy One even lifted up Adam to the heights of the highest heavens *la-sos u-le-sammeaḥ be-simḥatah shel Shabbat,* to regale her and rejoice in the Sabbath's joy. (sec. 852)

By implication, the Sabbath is God's Queen and Bride. Her ascent to the Throne clearly marks her coronation alongside Him, while key phrases subtly evoke a wedding: Shabbat is called "the Lord's," surely a cipher for marriage. Moreover, the angelic dancing (*me-raqqedin*) brings to mind the Talmudic phrase *keiẓad meraqqedin lifnei ha-kallah*—"how does one dance before the bride"—(TB Ket. 16a), even as the terms *la-sos u-le-sammeaḥ* and *maᶜon shel simḥah*—site of the supernal rejoicing—echo the pharaseology of the traditional nuptial benedictions (TB Ket. 8a).[182]

The continuation of the *Seder* (sec. 853) serves to qualify Sabbath's apotheosis, making clear that, despite her exalted status, YHWH is still *'Elohei ha-Shabbat,* the God of the Sabbath. The Sabbath Bride, in other words, remains quasi-divine here; only in theosophic Kabbalah does her divinization become complete. Although this myth of the celestial Sabbath wedding was not commonly cited in the Kabbalistic literature, it did exert a strong influence on such pivotal mystics as R. Judah ben Yaqar, the teacher of the RaMBaN, and in all likelihood, R. Moshe de Leon.[183]

Medieval Understandings of the Marital Imagery Prior to the Kabbalah

Two distinct attitudes towards the personification of the Sabbath as Bride existed in the rabbinic literature of the High Middle Ages. On the one hand, most authorities ignored, de-emphasized or apologized for this motif. Many of them preferred to speak of the Sabbath as King, rather than Bride, or even the more stately, Queen (cf., e.g.,

RaMBaM in *Mishneh Torah* "Shabbat" 30:2 and *Sefer RaVYaH* 1:392). Perhaps the classic example of such a rereading is that of RaSHI in his commentary to the Talmud. Of it A.J. Heschel wrote:

> Rashi, the classical commentator, afraid lest the feminine metaphor lead to misunderstandings, tried to rob it of any literal meaning by changing either the gender or the object of the metaphor. Rabbi Ḥanina, he said, behaved "like one who goes out to meet a King." [to BQ 32a] Or: "Out of affection he calls the celebration of the Sabbath 'Queen' "! [to Shab. 119a] Similarly, Rashi states that R. Naḥman bar Isaac welcomed the Sabbath "like one who welcomes his teacher."[184]

On the other hand, a different attitude may be discerned in a few late midrashim and a handful of Ashkenazic commentaries on the *siddur* (prayerbook). Two tenth-eleventh century midrashic fragments using marital imagery have been preserved in Israel Al-Naqawa's *Menorat ha-Ma'or* (ca. 1391). To cite the more striking example:

> We read in the midrash: The Sabbath may be compared to a bride. Just as a bride appears before her groom lovely, adorned and perfumed, so Shabbat comes before Israel lovely and adorned, as it is said: "The seventh day, it rested and was refreshed." [re-reading Ex. 31:17] Scripture juxtaposed [to this verse]: "And He gave unto Moses *ke-khalloto le-dabber 'itto*" [Ibid: 18] [conventionally, when He had finished speaking to him]. It is written *ke-KhaLloTO,* [which may also be rendered] *ke-KhaLlaTO,* "as his bride". . . .

The responsibilities of Israel, the groom, are then enumerated:

> Just as a groom wears beautiful garments, so too, a person wears beautiful garments on Shabbat. Just as a groom rejoices all [seven] days of his wedding, so too, a person rejoices on Shabbat. Just as a groom is at leisure and does not engage in labor, so too a person is at leisure on Shabbat.[185]

Despite their literary value, these midrashic fragments seemed to have exerted minimal historical influence. Of greater historical import is the renewed interest in marital imagery evinced in several Ashkenazic *siddurim* and halakhic anthologies, beginning in the late eleventh century. These works were apparently the first to correlate the marital terminology found in the Rabbinic literature with specific Sabbath prayers. For example, the concluding prayers on Saturday night were occasionally likened to a ritual escorting of the Bride or Queen.[186] Similarly, the prayer *'Attah 'Eḥad* (You are One) was sometimes read in marital terms. An early example of unitive imagery is contained in the so-called *Sefer Pardes le-RaSHI*: 229–30, where *'Attah 'Eḥad* was said to intimate the union of the singular God, the singular people, Israel, and the singular day, the Sabbath. More specific nuptial imagery is found in the work published as *Siddur Rabbenu Shelomoh ben Shimshon mi-Germaiza'*.[187] This text, which dates from twelfth century Mainz,[188] stated that "the basis for this prayer [*'Attah 'Eḥad*] is found in Genesis Rabbah [11:8]." According to the *siddur's* version of the midrash, Sabbath, the bride, was given to Israel, her groom.[189]

These sources suggest that the early Kabbalistic interest in marital imagery was part of a more widespread phenomenon. Still, the distinctions between the Ashkenazic literature and the early Kabbalah must not be blurred. First and foremost, only in Kabbalah is the theosophic significance of the Sabbath-Bride developed. More subtly, only in Kabbalah does bridal imagery become a controlling—rather than intermittent—motif, coloring virtually every Sabbath ritual. Finally, even Ashkenazic sources tended to give significant weight to the simile of Sabbath as king. Although this trope was never eliminated in the Kabbalah,[190] a marked shift of emphasis can be detected. The Kabbalists reveled in the imagery of the feminine Sabbath, discovering in it a great mystery. To understand the origins of these transformations, it is necessary to turn to *Sefer ha-Bahir* and thereafter, to the school of RaMBaN.

The Impact of Sefer ha-Bahir

The 'feminization' of divinity and the myth of divine androgyny. As noted, one of the basic features of the *Bahir* is its consistent use of masculine and feminine imagery in speaking of divinity. The sefirot are often arranged in what Gershom Scholem has termed "binomial fashion." In what is surely one of the most audacious contributions of the *Bahir* to Jewish theology, divine unity is expressed through sexual *coincidentia oppositorum*: in the coupling of masculine and feminine sefirot and in images of divine androgyny.

The tenth sefirah in particular is depicted in distinctively female terms: as Daughter, Sister, Mother, and Princess; in gender-linked symbols such as Moon and Field; and, most significantly for the purposes of this study, as Bride. More traditional Jewish theological symbolism is also employed but is subtly, even strikingly, transformed. The tenth rung is identified with *Shekhinah*, the traditional term for divine immanence, but here for the first time given specifically feminine characteristics. Moreover, She is also called the mystical "Community of Israel," traditionally a feminine but non-divine category. In the *Bahir, Shekhinah* becomes the hypostasis of and archetype for the actual People.[191]

Coupling as an image for divine wholeness. As the final sefirah, the divine Feminine has a paradoxical relationship to the rest of the Godhead. She is truly liminal, in the *Bahir*'s words, "cleaving and not cleaving." The Daughter is alternately bound to and separate from the King: She is the Sister/Bride of the Song of Songs "gazing through the window" (Cant. 2:9) at her lover. Giving a kind of Gnostic twist to the Rabbinic notion of *Galut* (Exile) *ha-Shekhinah,*[192] the tenth sefirah is depicted in a state of Exile which is periodically overcome. The goal of intradivine life is union, the end of fragmentation and separation. Redemption signifies a return to the world of Creation, the continual coupling of the masculine and feminine potencies.[193]

The androgyny of divine Shabbat. As we have seen, the *Bahir* located the archetypal Sabbath within divinity. If the primary Sabbath was the seventh sefirah, *Yesod,* the quintessential male rung, *Shekhinah,* the seventh of the active sefirot, was portrayed as the feminine Sabbath. It will probably never be known precisely what complex mix of forces motivated such a re-reading.[194] It is known, however, that the *Bahir* explicitly associated the androgyny of the divine Shabbat with three Scriptural verses.[195] The first is Lev. 19:30, where the enjoinder to "Keep my Sabbaths" is held to refer to the two divine Sabbaths. The other two come from Ex. 20:8 and Dt. 5:12. A mystical rationale is given for the differing versions of the Sabbath command, which, according to Rabbinic tradition, "were uttered as one" (TB Shev. 20b and RH 27a):

> Why is it said: *Remember* [the Sabbath] [Ex. 20:8] and *Keep* [it] [Dt. 5:12]? *Remember* [*Zakhor*] refers to the Male [*Zakhar*] and *Keep* refers to the Female. (*Bahir* 182)[196]

The *Bahir* explicitly states that these two aspects reunite on the Sabbath:

> A parable. . . . A king had a beautiful bride, and every week she would set aside one day to be with him. . . . The king also had lovely sons [other sefirot]. . . . He said to them. . .: "You, too, should rejoice on the day of my joy." (181)[197]

In terse, allusive fashion, the *Bahir* has created the basis for imaging the Sabbath as the time of *hieros gamos*, the union of the divine king and bride.

But the *Bahir* has done even more than this. Its authors have created a symbolic vocabulary and a set of hermeneutical lenses that other Kabbalists can use. Through its complex symbolization of the tenth sefirah throughout the book (and not just in passages pertaining to Shabbat), the *Bahir* created a symbolic nexus between *Shekhinah*, Shabbat, Bride, and the mystical Community of Israel. It was upon this symbol-cluster that later Kabbalists were to build.

Marital Imagery in the Naḥmanidean Tradition

Another important stratum in the evolution of the marital motif is found in the veiled writings of Judah ben Yaqar, his student RaMBaN and in the so-called Naḥmanidean school. Scattered throughout R. Judah ben Yaqar's *Perush ha-Tefillot ve-ha-Berakhot* (Barcelona, ca. 1200) are some seven or eight half-hints and allusions that intimate the presence of a developed myth of *hieros gamos* on Shabbat, one that is intimately linked with the liturgy and other Sabbath rituals.[198]

To provide a striking example here: R. Judah interpeted the Sabbath morning hymn *La-'el 'asher shabat ba-yom ha-shevi^ci* as an allusion to the union of the Bride Shabbat and Her Groom, the Holy One. In terse, encoded fashion, Judah wrote:

> *La-'el 'asher shabat*, etc.: "To God who rested on the seventh day and ascended to sit upon His Throne of Glory". . . In the *Heikhalot* [*Seder Rabba' di-Vre'shit*] it is written, "He ascended and sat on his Throne of Glory"[199] for He had completed His work. . . . [The prayer continues] *Tif'eret ᶜaṭah le-yom ha-menuḥah*: "He cloaked the Sabbath day with beauty". . . . This intimates [*ramaz*] that He was "like a groom serving in a garment of glory" [(and She, the divine Sabbath) "a bride bedecked in her finery"] (Isa. 61:10) on the Sabbath, for the Sabbath [here *Shekhinah*] was given as a mate to *Ẓaddiq Yesod ᶜOlam*.

Here R. Judah has drawn on the imagery pioneered in *Seder Rabba' di-Vre'shit* and given it a more clearly theosophic coloration. As the larger context makes clear,[200] the royal Bride Sabbath is now part of the divine pleroma, Her apotheosis complete.

In the continuation of this passage the Rabbinic dictum to change one's garments on the Sabbath (TB Shab. 113a) is accorded symbolic significance: it is a means of reflecting the supernal regarbing, an intimation of the divine nuptials. In all likelihood, a theurgic valence is present as well, suggesting the adept's power to adorn Bride and Groom:

> This [garbing of divinity] intimates that one's garments on Shabbat should not be like those of the week. As it is written concerning the garments of priestly service,[201] "they are *le-Khavod u-le-Tif'aret* [Ex. 28:2], conventionally, for glory and beauty,

but kabbalistically, for the sake of *Shekhinah*, the divine Glory, and *Tif'eret/Yesod*, the divine Groom. (*Perush ha-Tefillot ve-ha-Berakhot* 1:103.)

R. Judah's writings also contain the earliest literary evidence for a theosophic reading of Genesis R 11:8 (cited on pp. 102–03 above). In the following example—as distinct from the source just analyzed—it is the divine Male who is designated as *Shabbat*:[202]

> Our miẓvah of marital coupling is [symbolically] derived from that which the Holy One said to the Sabbath: "The Community of Israel [sefirotically, *Shekhinah*] will be your mate." And [the Sabbath] is *Ẓaddiq Yesod ʿOlam*.[203]

The marital motif is also intimated in the laconic writings of R. Judah's student, RaMBaN. Drawing on the *Bahir*, he further refined the images of the androgynous Sabbath and the feminine Sabbath as Bride. He also made explicit use of the famous Talmudic sources cited earlier, finding authority for the new Kabbalistic vision in them. RaMBaN wrote:

> In the Midrash of R. Neḥunia ben ha-Qanah [the *Bahir*] a great mystery is mentioned concerning "Remember" and "Keep". . . . "Remember" refers to the Sabbath day [*Yesod*] and "Keep" to the Sabbath Night [*Malkhut*]. *So say the Sages* [emph. mine]. For it is said of Sabbath eve [now, *Malkhut!*]: "Come O Bride!". . . and "Let us go forth to greet the Sabbath Bride, the Queen!" (to Ex. 20:8)

The influence of R. Judah ben Yaqar was more subtly registered, appearing in RaMBaN's writings without attribution. In three discretely worded passages,[204] however, RaMBaN—like his mentor—

interpreted Genesis R 11:8 as an allusion to the divine wedding. One such text reads:

> According to the path of Truth: "For God made the six days [the six sefirot counting from *Binah*], the heaven and the earth" [ff. Ex. 20:11]. The seventh day was Shabbat [*Yesod*] and it was without a mate [ff. Gen. R 11:8]; but the Community of Israel [*Malkhut*] became its mate, as it is written: "the heaven [*Yesod*] *ve-'et*—together with[205]— the earth [*Malkhut*]." (RaMBaN to Lev. 23:36)

The central themes developed by the *Bahir*, by R. Judah and RaMBaN, namely, the divine Sabbath as androgyne and the Sabbath day as marriage festival, are marvelously captured by R. Baḥyya ben Asher, heir to the Naḥmanidean tradition. Commenting on Ex. 20:8 he wrote:

> According to the path of the Kabbalah, "Remember the Sabbath day": Know that the Sabbath is the final sefirah [*Malkhut*], for the Sabbath day is the ultimate perfection of the Work of Creation. It is called the Community of Israel. In this vein our Rabbis of blessed memory said: "The Community of Israel is the Sabbath's [*Yesod*] mate: [Gen. R 11:8] . . . For the Sabbath is also called "Covenant". . . . When Scripture speaks of *Zakhor,* "Remember," the reference is to the great Sabbath, the rung of *Yesod.* . . When Scripture speaks of *Shamor,* "Keep," the reference is to the Sabbath called the Sanctuary/Temple. This is the meaning of "You shall keep my Sabbaths." [Lev. 19:30]

The androgyny of the divine Shabbat, developed in the *Bahir* and refined by RaMBaN, is now given added legitimation, based on the Masoretic hermeneutical principle, *qere' ve-la' ketiv*[206]:

> Consider the verse in Jeremiah [17:24]: "and do no work *bah* [i.e., on Sabbath]": it is written *bah,* on her, but read *bo,* on him.

Each Shabbat the two divine Sabbaths become one:

> Hence, it is also said; "The seventh day [*Yesod*] is a Sabbath unto the Lord your God." [Jer. 17:10] The seventh day is the Foundation of the World which is the seventh sefirah, and the Sabbath [*Malkhut*] is in it, for all [*kol: Malkhut*] is in the all [*ba-kol: Yesod*].

Finally, another fascinating Naḥmanidean interpretation of Sabbath-marriage is found in *Be'ur Sodot ha-RaMBaN* to Gen. 2:3. Attention is drawn to the grammatical irregularities found in Gen. R 11:8, where Shabbat is referred to first in the feminine and thereafter in the masculine:[207]

> The Sabbath came before the Holy One and *'amrah—she* said: . . . "All the other [days] have a mate; am I to be without one?" The Holy One said *lo*—to *him*: "The Community of Israel will be your mate!"

This grammatical androgyny becomes the springboard for speculation on the gender and nature of Shabbat. Underlying this speculation is the culturally embedded identification of activity with the distinctively masculine and passivity and receptivity with the feminine. The *Be'ur* reads:

> "Through the seventh day" [Gen. 2:2]. . . the Structure was completed. [*Yesod*] served as a reservoir [*miqveh*] for divine blessing, the gathering place enjoined by *YHWH* [*Tif'eret*]. This was alluded to in the verse "Let the waters under heaven be gathered unto one place" [Gen. 1:9]. For [*Yesod*] received all the *shefa^c*. But [*Yesod*] lacked a partner and so She [!]. . . .

That is, as the recipient or reservoir of divine blessing, *Yesod*/Shabbat is functionally 'feminine.' At present She lacks an outlet for her overflow, a partner, one to whom She could transmit Her *shefa^c*.

> For this reason, the Aggadah [Gen. R 11:8] referred [to the Sabbath in the feminine]: "The Sabbath *'amrah, She* said [before the Holy One: All the others have a mate.]" For [*Yesod*] received but did not bring down *shefa^c* at that time.

In the continuation of the midrash, however, Shabbat is referred to in the masculine: "The Holy One said *lo—to him*—the Community of Israel will be your mate." Kabbalistically, this shift implies the subsequent transformation of *Yesod*: upon gaining a mate, it becomes an active rung (he!) bringing *shefa^c* to *Shekhinah* below. *Hieros gamos*, quite specifically then, was the means whereby the sefirotic realm was first completed and blessing—Sabbath-blessing—brought to the world.[208]

Hieros Gamos *in the* Zohar

The motif of *hieros gamos* received its fullest expression in the *Zohar*, the next major source. In its mythic richness, dramatic range, and scope the *Zohar* represents a quantum leap beyond the earlier material. (These new ideas were further mined in Moshe de Leon's Hebrew works, especially the *Rimmon* and *Mishqal;* occasional reference will be made to these works, as well, primarily in the accompanying notes.) The major contributions of de Leon may be summarized as follows:

(1) Discussion of the marital motif is greatly expanded; (2) the motif becomes a dynamic drama with a kind of plot rather than a static image or tableau[209]; (3) the drama of hierogamy is comprehensively correlated with Sabbath ritual; (4) it is portrayed in pictorial and sometimes erotic imagery; (5) the marriage motif is closely correlated with two other salient themes: the liberation of *Shekhinah* from Exile and the coronation of *Tif'eret* and *Shekhinah*; and (6) for the first time the feminine Shabbat, rather than the masculine one, becomes the primary sefirotic focus. Although there has been previous occasion to examine points four and six, points one through three and five may be briefly illustrated here.

(1) There is a tremendous expansion in the sheer quantity of material dealing with this theme. Or to put it in another way: Prior to the *Zohar* the wedding motif consisted of a few circumspect allusions. Now it has become a major theme with scores of references that articulate and deeply color Sabbath celebration.

(2) The *Zohar* transforms a rather static nuptial image into a nuanced drama with a kind of mythic plot, a sense of development: e.g., there is a moment when the Bride is prepared for the wedding, there are specific moments when the two lovers unite, and so forth. Virtually all previous sources, e.g., the *Bahir,* RaMBaN, and, even, the OK (one of the few pre-Zoharic sources to associate the Bridal Motif with actual ritual), treat divine union as a state rather than a dynamic process.[210] Examples of this dynamic are provided below.

(3) These supernal events are comprehensively absorbed into and correlated with the stream of Sabbath ritual: e.g., into Sabbath preparation, prayers, the sacramental meals, and marital intercourse. This greatly aided the integration of the Bridal and Marital imagery into Sabbath celebration. Moreover, on a phenomenological level, these rituals afford the devotee living contact with the unfolding supernal drama. This process may be briefly illustrated:

As the devotee prepares his home for Shabbat, his abode, like the celestial world it reflects, becomes a Marriage Canopy ready to receive the Bride who is at once Shabbat and *Shekhinah:*

> "Observe the Sabbath throughout the generations [*DoRoTaM*]." [Ex. 31:16]. . . . The word *DoRoTaM* hints at the notion of dwelling [*DiRoTaM*]: When the Sabbath enters, the dwelling place must be prepared like the chamber of the bridegroom set to receive his bride. . . .

In so doing the Bride is welcomed into the devotee's hearth and home, and Her numinous presence felt:

> The Holy Bride is ushered into Israel's abode, to be in their midst, as the Sabbath begins. (3:300b–301a)

The opening Friday night prayer, the *Barekhu,* marks the completion of the Bride/Queen's nuptial preparations and Her incipient union with Her mate. As the Sabbath begins, *Shekhinah* enters the divine Palace. She is escorted both by Her angels on high—

> those supernal maidens who . . . decorate *Maṭronita'* and escort Her in the presence of the King (2:131b)—

and by Israel below. As the people break forth into prayer, they crown Her and so, adorn Her for the royal wedding:

> She is crowned from below by the holy people. . . . They bless Her with joy and beaming faces, reciting the prayer: "*Barekhu 'eT YHWH ha-mevorakh,* Bless *'eT* [*Shekhinah*] *YHWH* [*Tif'eret*], the blessed One,". . . blessing Her first. (2:135a–b)

According to the *Zohar,* the mystical meaning of this prayer is that Israel must attend to the *Shekhinah* first and to *YHWH* thereafter. The appellation את/*'eT,* indicating the fullness of divine speech (from א/*'alef* to ת/*Tav*) symbolizes *Shekhinah's* renewed perfection on Shabbat. By reciting this prayer Israel attests to this perfection and initiates Her union with the King.[211]

The *Qiddush* and Friday night meal are seen as sacramental acts, enabling the devotee to partake in the coronation of *Shekhinah* and the Holy One and in the mystery of their union. Implicitly the *Qiddush* serves as the marriage ceremony, the moment "when the Bride enters the Canopy."[212] In another *Zohar* account (3:95a) the

Qiddush wine symbolizes the *shefa*ᶜ which now issues forth from the *Binah* and comes unto *Tif'eret*. The proof-text for this supernal mystery is Cant. 3:11:

> Go forth, daughters of Zion, and gaze upon King Solomon, [adorning] him with the crown that His Mother gave him on his wedding day.

The repast itself, the Meal of the Perfect Bride, highlights the mystery of *hieros gamos* as "the supernal dew descends from the Ancient Holy One" unto *Tif'eret* and thereafter unto *Shekhinah*, the fertile "Orchard of Holy Apples."[213]

An interesting variant to the Zoharic vision is found in Moshe de Leon's later *Sefer ha-Rimmon* (MS Brit. Mus. 759 fol. 29b). There the *Qiddush* over wine more clearly dramatizes *Shekhinah*'s betrothal as well as Her royal adornment and annointment. The melodious recitation of the prayer serves to arouse divine love as She prepares to unite with the King. The wine of *Qiddush* now represents the blessing of *Gevurah*, its vitalizing qualities:

> We betroth Her with the *Qiddush*[214] over wine which is the rousing of [supernal] Love. . . . Such arousal can only come from the Left Side [*Gevurah*].[215] Surely this is the hour of the mystery of Love, "when the Ark came to rest" [Gen. 8:4] from all Her labors [of directing the lower worlds] as is proper for all who are annointed as royalty.[216] We must arouse Her holy [powers], "Her perfumes and Her rations. . . given to Her from the King's palace" [Esth. 2:9][217] and enter the "bond of holiness" [the now harmonious sefirotic realm]. . . .

Annointed by the forces of *Gevurah* on high and by Israel below, supernal love kindled, *Shekhinah* is ready to unite with Her Beloved.[218]

The deepest union of Bride and Groom is attained at midnight as the Talmudic miẓvah to engage in marital sex on Friday night (TB Ket. 62b and BQ 82a) is linked with hierogamy. The devotee and his wife symbolically become *Tif'eret* and *Shekhinah* and mirror this divine mystery. This motif will be discussed at greater length in Appendix II of this of this study (pp. 289–93) and in *Sod ha-Shabbat*, Section 12.

Although the primary emphasis on divine Marriage is on Friday night, the "Night of the Bride," the image carries over into Saturday as well. The *Zohar* occasionally associates it with prayers such as "And Moses rejoiced" and "You are One"; with the two Sacramental

Meals; and with Torah Study. But it exists as a *subtext* throughout the day. Indeed, de Leon likened the entirety of Shabbat to "wedding feast."[219]

Athough the discussion has been restricted to these examples, the contribution of the *Zohar* to both Sabbath ritual and to the wedding motif is clear. Newly re-read in line with Kabbalistic concerns, ritual evokes the celestial drama of *hieros gamos* and grants the devotee living contact with it.

(4) The motif of Sacred Marriage is amplified by the inclusion of two related themes, the coronation of the royal pair and even more significantly, the motif of Liberation. While the former is a supplementary image to that of coupling, the latter serves as prelude to it. Before the wedding can take place, *Shekhinah* must be liberated from Her Exile amidst the profane weekly forces, most radically symbolized as *Siṭra' 'Aḥra'*. Influenced by the Castilian 'Gnostics,'[220] Moshe de Leon introduces a kind of dualist tension into the Sabbath-drama not found in earlier thirteenth century writings.

In this view, sefirotic union is the culmination of *Shekhinah*'s transformation or restoration. By focusing on the twin myths of Liberation and Union, de Leon has shifted the theological focus to the limen, to *Shekhinah*. Poised between worlds, Her status serves as an index for the state of the Cosmos and, by implication, for the state of the Jew.

Because the resolution of *Malkhut*'s status depends on the identity of Her contiguous partner, the state of the Cosmos may be formulated in binary fashion: *Shekhinah/Siṭra' 'Aḥra'* versus *Shekhinah*/ Sefirot. Her exile and entrapment among the demonic forces represents the broken state of the Cosmos; Her reunion with Her lover, *Tif'eret*, is a measure of cosmic harmony (and spiritual renewal for the Jew who participates in this drama through the Sabbath-miẓvot). In other words, Her restoration depends on two processes: first, the separation of holy and demonic potencies and the setting of clear boundaries between them—i.e., *Shekhinah*'s liberation—and second, the re-aggregation and fusion of all holy aspects, i.e., *hieros gamos*.

The *Zohar*—and the TZ/RM in its wake—portrays this transformation in highly pictorial language: during the week, when She is among profane or demonic forces, *Shekhinah* is said to be like a closed rose, but on Shabbat, She "opens to receive spices and fragrances"—a reference to Her union with *Tif'eret*—"and to give souls and joy to Her children." During the week, *Malkhut* is called "the closed womb," and in allusion to the Bride in Song of Songs (4:12), "the locked garden, the sealed spring"; on Shabbat She opens to meet Her lover. During the week, She is called "Fear"; on Shabbat "Love." During the week she is in *niddah* (the time of menstrual 'impurity') and hence, "off-limits to Her Husband"; but on Shabbat, separation is overcome and the two lovers reunite.[221] The following passage from *Zohar* 1:175a–b is exemplary:

> R. Shimon opened the verse: "The gate of the inner (Temple) court [*Shekhinah*] that faces east shall be closed on the six working days; but on the Sabbath day. . . . and on the day of the New Moon it shall be opened." [Ezek. 46:1]. This verse. . . .contains a great mystery. Why is She "closed on the six working days"? Because She is then among the Profane Days [the demonic forces or *qelippot*]; She remains closed lest the profane take hold of the holy. "But on the Sabbath day. . . and in the day of the New Moon it shall be opened": for [on Shabbat] the holy takes hold of the holy. At this time the Moon [*Shekhinah*] is illumined and unites with the Sun [*Tif'eret*].[222]

Through the drama of Shabbat the Bride is re-integrated in the divine world and the cosmos placed under a sacred Canopy. In a striking image, fashioned by Moses Cordovero from Zoharic sources, the newly configured divine world is seen as if within a *ḥuppah:*

> The entire divine emanation is likened to a Wedding Canopy. . . . *Keter* is the awning. . . . And *Ḥokhmah,* its walls; *Binah* is the entry and *Ḥesed, Gevurah, Neẓaḥ and Hod* are like the poles that support it; *Tif'eret* and *Malkhut* are the Groom and Bride underneath the canopy, ushered in by *Yesod,* the attendant. (*Pardes Rimmonim:* Gate 23)[223]

The Marital Motif after the Zohar

Friday night remained the focus of the Marital motif in most of the later Kabbalistic sources under consideration here.[224] Bridal imagery tended to coalesce around several events: preparing for and ushering in the Sabbath, the Friday night meal—especially the recitation of the *Qiddush*—and marital intercourse. To these themes we shall now turn.

Sabbath Preparation and Ushering in the Bride. Much like the *Zohar,* the RM likens the newly ordered house to a bridal chamber:

> One must prepare a comfortable seat with several cushions and embroidered covers from all that is found in the house, like one

> who prepares for a bride. For the Sabbath is a Queen and a Bride. (RM 3: 272b)[225]

Consider also *Sefer ha-Qanah* where each of the major furnishings mentioned in the Talmudic paradigm alludes to the divine coupling:

> "Your table should be set, your bed made-up, and the candles burning" [TB Shab. 119b]: The table alludes to the Community of Israel which is set in the sphere of Compassion [*Tif'eret*]; the bed alludes to the Community of Israel who is made-up, adorned for the Groom[226]. . . . The burning candles are the Eastern Candle, an allusion to *Tif'eret* which burns with (i.e., unites with) the Western Candle, the Community of Israel.[227]

As Sabbath is about to begin, the *Qanah* suggests actually going forth to greet the Sabbath Bride and Queen, in consonance with the Talmudic ritual. In a rather unusual statement, the wife and household are specifically included in this sacred act[228]:

> Next he wraps himself in his *ṭallit* and calls together his friends, his wife, and household, saying: "Let us go forth *li-qra't* [conventionally, to greet] the Bride, the Sabbath Queen!" They all join together and say: "Come, O Bride! Come, O Bride!"

This act has theurgic import, for the greeting below causes a welcoming from on high. As they recite "Come O Bride!", She is lifted up into the World of Compassion. The stage is thereby set for the ultimate union (also *qeri'ah!*) of Bride and Groom. The author wrote:

> We wish to lift up the Queen unto the King, though this *qeri'ah* is not yet that *qeri'ah* meaning union. . . . Rather, our *qeri'ah* is one of [supernal] rousing, that She be summoned [*li-qra'tah*] from on high.[229]

Many Kabbalists located the mystery of sacred marriage in the evening prayers that followed. The author of the *Qanah/Peli'ah* called the whole service *qiddushei 'ishah, Shekhinah*'s betrothal and consecration (*Peli'ah* 36b). Other adepts focused on specific sections of the prayers. The "Standing Prayer" or *ᶜAmidah* was said to constitute a mystical wedding ceremony, its seven benedictions paralleling the seven traditional nuptial blessings.[230] Most commonly the Kabbalists would focus on the *ᶜAmidah*'s middle benediction *'Attah Qiddashta*, inserted expressly for Shabbat. Their interpretations are based on the double meaning of the root *QDSH,* indicating both sanctification and betrothal. Israel betroths Bride to Groom through reciting the prayer and more generally, through sanctifying the Sabbath. The following passage from the *'Or Zaruᶜa* of David ben Judah he-Ḥasid [OZ] illustrates this well:

> *'Attah Qiddashta:* "You sanctified [the seventh day]." We now betroth the Sabbath day, the Diadem [*Malkhut*]. She is the exalted and lovely Bride, resplendent in Her beauty. She is the Bride of the King, the Lord of Hosts who approaches Her to enter into the supernal union each Shabbat. So we must betroth Her and bring Her to the supernal *qiddushin* [here, both wedding and sanctification], [showering] Her with light, hues and the luminosity of the supernal world.[231]

The Friday Night Meal and *Qiddush*. In the post-Zohar literature, the Friday Night meal was almost universally accepted as the Meal of the Bride,[232] a time to rejoice with Her. The full array of food indicates Her full joy on this day,[233] while the traditional *zemirot* (or table hymns) become a kind of mystical epithalamium: "While at the festive table one must sing to [the Bride] and regale Her." (Z 3:272b [RM])[234]

But it is the *Qiddush* that inaugurates the meal that attracts the most attention, as it is now explicitly likened to the wedding ceremony itself. One of the first sources to do so was the TZ:

> "And God blessed the seventh day and sanctified it" [Gen. 2:3]. In honor of this blessing and betrothal we are bidden to go forth to greet the Bride. . . . For at this time there is "the voice of the Groom and the voice of the Bride" [Jer. 7:34]. . . . We must bless Them and betroth Them through the Sanctification over the Wine. . . . We must add the greeting *le-ḥayyim,* "Unto life", so that She may be bound unto the Tree of Life [*Tiferet*]. (TZ 24 [69a])

According to OZ (MS JTSA 2203 fol. 40a/55a), the seventy words of the *Qiddush* comprise a supernal Seven Nuptial Blessings for *Shekhinah* and *Tiferet,* each word drawing down a different aspect of celestial blessing. The OZ resolves the halakhic debate as to whether one should recite the *Qiddush* while standing[235] by recourse to this marital motif:

> The Friday night Sanctification is "the *Qiddush* of the Bride"[236]. . . . One should recite it standing in honor of Her and in honor of

Him. . . . For this is like the Seven Nuptial Blessings which are always recited standing.

The TZ, as well, likens the *Qiddush* to the Seven Blessings. All the sefirotic blessings are gathered by *Yesod,* the seventh day and divine "phallus," who brings together Bride and Groom in holy union:

Blessing is the entirety of the seven sefirot. These are the 'Seven blessings' of the. . . Seventh Day, *Ẓaddiq,* of whom it is said: "Blessings upon the head of the *Ẓaddiq*" [Prv. 10:6]. He inherits them from the supernal Mother. . . . The seven blessings received by Groom and Bride are included in *Ẓaddiq,* the seventh day, through whom Bride and Groom are united. (TZ 47 [84a])[237]

One of the most interesting sources, SṬM: 296–97, depicts the *Qiddush* as the moment of betrothal, and a kind of prelude to the moment of sefirotic coupling:

Through the miẓvah [of sanctifying Shabbat] Israel arranges for the betrothal of the. . . Groom, who is the Lord, the King of Hosts, to the Bride, the Community of Israel, the most perfect one, arrayed in beauty. This is the hidden meaning of the *Qiddush* that we recite on Friday nights as it is said: " 'Remember the Sabbath day *le-qaddesho,* to sanctify/betroth it' " [Ex. 20:8]: "Remember it over wine." [TB Pes. 106a]

The wine that is drunk at *Qiddush* both indicates the consummation of the betrothal[238] and alludes to the divine *shefa*ᶜ that will later annoint the Bride at the moment of sacred union:

Likewise, our Rabbis of blessed memory state that the prescribed time for marital intercourse for Torah-scholars is on Friday nights [TB Ket. 62b]. Because the Groom pours the fine oil [*shefa*ᶜ] over the Bride, and divine blessing and well-being thereby come into the world, our Sages say: " 'Sanctify and commemorate the Sabbath over wine': upon its inception." [TB Pes. Ibid.] For it is the way of the world to arrange the betrothal [*qiddushin*] first, after which time He pours the precious oil onto the Bride, the Community of Israel. . .[239]

The Special Case of the *'Or Zaru*ᶜ*a.* Perhaps the most consistent treatment of the marital motif is found in the OZ of R. David ben Judah he-Ḥasid, which was briefly cited above. This text is noteworthy for at least two reasons: for its use of well-developed bridal imagery in the weekday setting and for its systematic use of wedding imagery throughout Shabbat.

Like certain Castilian adepts,[240] R. David ben Judah carried bridal imagery into the week. The weekday morning prayers comprising the *Yoẓer* serve as a mystical bedecking of the Bride, a means of arraying Her in angelic garments. The primary setting for this bedecking is the *'El Barukh*, an acrostic whose first twenty-two words follow the alphabetical order. "Each word," R. David wrote, "forms a garment for the Bride." However, this weekday ceremony lacks the sublime quality of the Sabbath nuptials, something intimated by the liturgy itself. On Shabbat *'El Barukh* is replaced with the much longer acrostic hymn, *'El 'Adon*, in which each succeeding phrase begins with the appropriate letter. This expanded format esoterically indicates that She is now bedecked in multi-layered holy raiment drawn from the supernal (rather than angelic) world, on high:

> During the week She wears special garments, but on Shabbat She wears layered and thoroughly lovely garments, with many folds, raiment of the supernal Kingdom. For on Shabbat, the mystery of the Upper World, the mystical alphabet is manifold and complete. . . . The expanded acrostic of *'El Adon* intimates this fullness.[241]

Most mystical sources use wedding imagery systematically on Friday night only, preferring to merely allude to it afterwards. By contrast the Wedding Ceremony serves as the leitmotif for the entire Shabbat in the OZ. Because of the richness of this source I have decided to translate it in full. Note that the focal point of the interpretation is the special Sabbath blessing found in each of the five *ᶜAmidot* or "Standing Prayers":

> The [special] prayers that we recite each Shabbat parallel that which a groom does in concert with his bride. What does the groom do? When they are first engaged, he sanctifies her through the *qiddushin*, saying: "Behold, you are betrothed [*mequddeshet*] unto me." Parallel to this we recite in the [evening] Prayers "You Sanctified" [*'Attah qiddashta*] through which we bring the beloved Bride [*Malkhut*] into the supernal *qiddushin*.
>
> What does a groom do next? He sends his betrothed nuptial presents. Correspondingly, we recite [at *Shaḥarit*] "And Moses rejoiced in the gift," for the King, the Lord of hosts, who is Moses [*Tif'eret*] sends Her supernal lights from "the joyous Mother of the

> Children." [Ps. 113:9] As it is written, "A River goes out of Eden [*Binah*] to water the Garden [*Malkhut*]." (Gen. 2:10)
>
> What does the groom do after this? He makes preparations for the wedding feast. So we pray [at *Musaf*], "You commanded Moses" concerning the sacrificial offerings. Why? Because the King, the Lord of hosts, sends Her a meal of the celestial bread [i.e., *shefa*ᶜ] as it is written: "Its bread shall be rich" [Gen. 49:20]. For this reason, it is said of sacrificial offerings: "Bread unto a woman" [Lev. 3:11 and 16; Heb., *leḥem 'isheh*—an offering by fire—but here read "*leḥem 'ishah*"!]
>
> What does the groom do next? He offers the Seven Nuptial Blessings and unites with his bride. Correspondingly, we pray [at *Minḥah*] "You are one and Your Name one" for [at this hour] the King joins with the Queen [*Maṭronit*] in perfect union. Then He and She are one, as it is written, "And the Lord [*Tif'eret*] shall be king over all the Land [*Malkhut*]." [Zech. 14:9]
>
> Thereafter what does he do? He comes into her in the miẓvah of coupling and then separates from her.[242] Correspondingly, we pray [at Sabbath's close] "You favored us with knowledge," the essence of the *Havdalah*, the ritual of Separation. For as Sabbath departs, the supernal King withdraws from the Queen.[243]

R. David now homologizes the departing Sabbath-soul to the King and the terrestrial soul to the Queen:

> For this reason, the soul remaining below is bereft, for she remains alone, without her mate [the Sabbath-soul]. So we strengthen her with fragrant scents at Havdalah.
>
> So you see that we recite our prayers on Shabbat in the manner that a groom acts with his bride, thereby alluding to the renowned Groom and Bride. [MS JTSA fol. 39b/54b][244]

TRANSFORMATION OF THE PERSON: THE SABBATH-SOUL

> "You have blessed this day above all others"[245]: This refers to the additional soul which a person receives on Shabbat. For it brims over with blessing, with song and jubilation [*rinnun*] drawn from on high. (MS Paris Hebr. 596, fol. 35a [fifteenth century, Italy])

As the realms of time and divinity are transformed on Shabbat, so is the Sabbath-observer. The most graphic and certainly the best-known marker of this ontological transformation is the assimilation of the *neshamah yeterah*, the 'additional' or Sabbath-soul. This motif, which was to play such a central role in the later understanding of Shabbat, owes a great deal of its richness—and not a small part of its influence—to its Kabbalistic interpretation.[246]

Pre-Zoharic Developments

The Sabbath-soul is mentioned but once in the Rabbinic literature, in TB Beiẓah 16a (and in Taᶜan. 27b where it is repeated verbatim). Because it is such a spare source it is difficult to know precisely what this Sabbath-soul is or what it does:

> On Sabbath eve the Holy One gives the human being an additional soul and on Saturday night He takes it away. Thus, R. Shimon ben Laqish said: "Why is it written: 'He ceased from work and rested, *shabat va-yinnafash*' [Ex. 31:17]? This may be read: Once the rest has ceased, *vay-nefesh:* woe! that soul is gone."

The *neshamah yeterah* remained a minor motif through much of the medieval period. A few references to a Sabbath-soul are found in the Ashkenazic literature that preceded the rise of Kabbalah[247]; these sources, however, are highly laconic and add little to our understanding of this motif. Most leading authorities—especially those from Spain and Provence—tended either to ignore this motif or to rationalize it, purging it of any mythic qualities.[248] A good example of the former response may be found in RaMBaM's *Mishneh Torah* ("Hilkhot Shabbat" 29:29):

> Why is a blessing recited over fragrant spices at the conclusion of the Sabbath? It is to cheer the soul which is saddened at the departure of the *day.* [emph. added]

Mention of the Sabbath-soul is nowhere to be found.

A few sources read the admittedly ambiguous term, *neshamah yeterah,* as "an *enlarged* soul." This, in turn, was taken as a metaphor for some temporarily increased capability. For example, RaSHI (to Beiẓ. 16a) described the *neshamah yeterah* as an increased capacity for *ᶜOneg Shabbat:* "an expanded heart for repose and joy, . . . for eating and drinking."[249] Abraham ibn Ezra, the sole philosopher to make use of the term, essentially rationalized it. In his commentary to Gen. 2:3, he explained that the Jew is granted an extra measure of wisdom and intellectual power on Shabbat, "an increase in one's rational faculties (*yitron ha-sekhel*)."[250]

For most Kabbalists, by contrast, the Sabbath-soul is no mere figure of speech, but a metaphysical entity issuing from the heart of the sefirotic world.[251] In the Zoharic tradition, where it received its fullest elaboration, the *neshamah yeterah* is both emblem and cause of an inner change; it represents the internalization of the Sabbath-cosmos and indicates that the human microcosm now fully mirrors the divine archetype. Having received this soul, the devotee can participate in the proper way in the supernal mysteries that are unfolding; with this soul, the devotee attains his full spiritual stature.

Because of ambiguous wording in several early sources, it is difficult to ascertain which Kabbalistic text first referred to the Sabbath-soul as an emanated entity.[252] Not surprisingly, the earliest candidate is the *Bahir*. I. Tishby (MZ 2:487–88) avers that sections 157 and 158 might possibly be allusions to the Sabbath-soul.[253] The latter passage is especially suggestive. Referring to *Yesod*, the "Source of all souls," the *Bahir* states:

> "On the seventh day, *shabat*" [Ex. 31:17]: Each day has a Logos that is its master. The seventh day *[Yesod]* comes and does its task, making all [the sefirot] rejoice. Not only that but it causes souls to grow, as it is said: "On the seventh day He rested *va-yinnafash*: and there were souls."

It is difficult to identify the "souls" referred to here. Although they may connote the *neshamot yeterot*, they may plausibly refer to those offspring produced during Sabbath marital intercourse. Given the explicit discussion of the latter elsewhere in the *Bahir*, this second reading seems more likely. Perhaps a more ambiguous case is that of Azriel of Gerona, who seems to occupy a middle ground between the metaphorical interpretation of Abraham ibn Ezra and that of RaMBaN, the first Kabbalist to unequivocally speak of the *neshamah yeterah* as an actual emanated soul. More precisely, Azriel seems to waver between viewing the *neshamah yesterah* as a distinct metaphysical entity—a soul—emanating from *Yesod* (*à la* RaMBaN) and as an added measure of spirituality, a position closer to that of ibn Ezra. In his *Perush ha-'Aggadot* (to TB Taʿan. 27b: pp. 34–35), Azriel wrote:

> On Shabbat the soul is more deserving of being visited with this spirit than during the week. . . . By the *neshamah yeterah* is meant an additional holy spirit *[ruaḥ ha-qodesh ha-yeterah]*, more sublime than any other, as it is written: "[Daniel surpassed the others] by

> virtue of his *ruaḥ yeterah.*" [Dan. 6:4] For when this spirit is present in the soul, [the soul] is given power to understand and grasp. . . . And on Shabbat, the holy spirit is over all and the soul reaches its full potential *[koḥah]*. . . for the soul's power is enlarged in consonance with the seventh day [*Yesod,* its source].[254]

From this it is clear that the *neshamah yeterah* strengthens and supplements the ordinary soul. On this point, Azriel and ibn Ezra are in agreement; however, as I. Tishby pointed out, for Azriel this means having added spiritual-mystical powers, rather than heightened rationality. (This is underscored by Azriel's usage of the term *ruaḥ ha-qodesh.*)[255] Another difference is that Azriel of Gerona accorded this Sabbath-spirit ontic reality: it is an emanation from *Yesod.* The real question is whether this spirit constitutes a soul or not. Tishby maintains that the answer is "no": that, like ibn Ezra, Azriel referred only to an increase in one's contemplative capacity and not to the assimilation of "an ontic reality *qua soul.*" (emph. mine; cf. MZ 2:488)

Tishby's argument is not completely convincing. He stakes his claim on Azriel's use of the term *ruaḥ,* which he interprets as "spiritual power" and which he implicitly contrasts with "soul" (*nefesh* or *neshamah*). Azriel, however, does not make a clear distinction between *ruaḥ, nefesh,* and *neshamah* in this passage.[256] On the other hand, Azriel did speak of receiving this Sabbath-soul in proper measure (*ʿal matkuntah*), a phrase more apt for describing the influx of spirituality than that of a distinct soul. The ambiguity in Azriel's position is captured in his closing words to this discussion:

> But on Saturday night the holy spirit [*ruaḥ*] that visits the person returns to its place *[Yesod]*. . . Hence, the *Gemara'* says: "When the rest ended, a soul was lost." That soul [*nefesh*] that was received in [proper] measure on Shabbat withdraws and returns to its place. . . . returning to God who imparted this holy spirit.

As noted, the first Kabbalist to unambiguously speak of the Sabbath-soul was RaMBaN. In his commentary to Gen. 2:3 he refuted the position of ibn Ezra, maintaining that each Shabbat a real Sabbath-soul issues from *Yesod* and is assimilated by the devotee. He concluded:

> Understand that on Shabbat one [receives] *nefesh yeterah be-'emet:* an actual Sabbath-soul.

Elsewhere he wrote:

> This is the meaning of *shabat va-yinnafash* [Ex. 31:17], referring to the additional soul *[neshamah yeterah]* that comes from the Foundation of the Cosmos "in whose care is the Soul of all Life". [Job 12:10][257]

Still, the *neshamah yeterah* was not a major Kabbalistic motif until the *Zohar* became widely disseminated. If Moshe de Leon and the TZ/RM are excluded from consideration, a surprising fact emerges: in the literature following the RaMBaN until ca. 1400, there are only a handful of references to the Sabbath-soul. Among the sources consulted in this study there is one allusion in OK (12a), one in Joseph Giqatilia's *Sodot,*[258] two passing references in OZ (MS JTSA fol. 39a/54a and 39b/54b),[259] a paragraph in the *Me'irat ᶜEinayim,*[260] and a brief allusion in Menaḥem Recanati's *Perush* (5b). More strikingly, Baḥyya ben Asher, heir to the Naḥmanidean tradition, spoke not of an extra Sabbath-soul,[261] but of the ordinary soul's reception of added divine blessing, or *shefaᶜ*, on Shabbat. As *Yesod,* the divine Shabbat, pours blessing into the soul, the soul ceases being a stranger, a wanderer on earth. Infused with Shabbat, it (and by extension, the Jew) comes home; the weekly Exile is overcome:

> According to the path of the Kabbalah, the seventh day is the seventh sefirah [counting from *Binah*] called "the world of souls," for there lies the origin and power-source [*koaḥ*] for the soul; it is the well-spring of blessing. During the week the soul may be likened to a wanderer without a home; but on Shabbat it is like a wanderer who has found one. Hence, it is written: "And He blessed" [Gen. 2:3], for He emanated [*shefaᶜ*] unto it from the source of blessing, and so "sanctified it" [Ibid.], for the soul draws [this influx] from the Sacred. (Baḥyya to Gen. 2:3)

From this source, two things are learned: (1) that the *neshamah yeterah* was not necessarily a commonplace in the early stages of the Kabbalistic Sabbath, and (2) that there were other ways of speaking of the soul's (and the person's) transformation during Shabbat.[262]

The Sabbath-Soul in the Writings of Moshe de Leon and in the Tiqqunei ha-Zohar/Raᶜaya' Meheimna'

The development of the motif of the *neshamah yeterah* is primarily due to the mythic imagination of Moshe de Leon, and secondarily, to that of the author of the TZ/RM. Their views differ in several significant ways and it is worthwhile to sketch out the major points of divergence before proceeding:

Frequency of reception. According to the *Zohar*, the additional soul is received on Shabbat only; on several occasions, the TZ/RM includes other holidays, as well.[263]

Ontological structure of the additional soul. With one exception,[264] the *Zohar* does not distinguish between the terms *nefesh, ruaḥ,* and *neshamah*—the traditional terms for the tripartite division of the soul[265]—when speaking of the Sabbath-soul; because the Sabbath-soul was considered simple in structure, Moshe de Leon used the terms interchangeably. The TZ/RM, on the other hand, generally maintains the tripartite schema for the additional-soul.[266]

Point of origin. The *Zohar* never fixes a single point of sefirotic origin for the Sabbath-souls. In various passages, they are said to issue from:

(a) *Shekhinah*: "This spirit is the expansion of this Point, issuing from Her and setting forth into the world." (2:204b)

(b) *Yesod:* "The Sabbath-soul flies forth from Cosmic Life" (2:138a); and

(c) *Tif'eret,* the "Tree of Life from which souls blossom." (2:98a and 3:173a)

But as I. Tishby points out, in most cases these choices merely denote the launching point, the rung from which the souls are sent forth into the lower world following their progressive descent through the divine realm. Ultimately they are said to stem from either *Binah* (1:48a–b) or *Keter* (2:205a).

The TZ/RM, true to its more hierarchical view and systematic treatment of the extra-soul, usually identifies *nefesh yeterah* with *Malkhut, ruaḥ yeterah* with *Tif'eret,* and *neshamah yeterah* with *Binah.*[267]

The degree of transformation: the additional soul as supplement to versus supplanter of the ordinary soul. According to the *Zohar,* the *neshamah yeterah* descends to strengthen and augment the permanent soul. As the Sabbath-spirit resides within the soul the latter is "enlarged, with greater power than before." (cf. 2:204b) The ordinary soul is no way displaced:

> As the Holy One provides a person with a soul at birth, so also does He provide him with this other soul [for Shabbat]: [He does

so] without diminishing the food and raiment for his original [i.e., weekday] soul. (2:98a)

In the TZ, however, the Sabbath-soul—with its complete threefold structure—actually replaces the weekday one.[268] The more gradualist transformation spoken of in the *Zohar* gives way to a more radical change. It might be said that the difference is between receiving a spiritual "pacemaker" and undergoing a pneumatic "transplant." In the TZ, entering Shabbat takes on the structure of a full *rite de passage:* one's old pneumatic self must die so that one may enter the higher order of Shabbat, newly reborn. In a remarkable passage (TZ Add. 5 [141b]), the ordinary soul is likened to a corpse which must be buried on Shabbat:

"You must not let his corpse remain on the Tree[269] overnight." [Dt. 21:23] This refers to the Sabbath when a person is bequeathed an additional soul; the soul that holds sway during the week should not be seen on it, doing that labor [*mela'khah*] which is prohibited on Shabbat. Rather, "bury it on that day," [Ibid.] for it should not be seen before the "Remember" and "Keep" of Shabbat.

Entering the Sabbath is like coming before the burning Bush. To stand on the holy ground of Shabbat, one must put off the habitual, the *na^cal:* conventionally, "shoe," but here also meant hyperliterally as that which constrains and confines one. This *na^cal* is none other than the ordinary soul:

Thus, it is said: "Remove your shoes [*ne^calekha*]—that [soul] which confines you—from your feet, for the place on which you stand is holy ground." [Ex. 3:5][270] Indeed, "you shall not defile your land": for the Sabbath-soul is the celestial Land of Israel [i.e., from the divine realm], the "holy ground," of which it is said: "Israel was holy to the Lord." [Jer. 2:3]

It is important to note that this passage is intentionally ambivalent, alluding to two parallel transformations. Sefirotically, it refers to the changes taking place within *Shekhinah,* the sefirotic Soul, the Tree alluded to in Dt. 21:23. At the same time it underscores the changes taking place within Her symbol, the human pneuma. As *Shekhinah* divests Herself of the harsh aspects of *Din* that surround Her during the week,[271] so the devotee removes or 'buries' his lesser soul.[272]

The degree of differentiation among Sabbath-souls: egalitarian versus hierarchical conceptions. The *Zohar* does not distinguish between the *neshamot yeterot* received by different Jews: all contain the same ontological structure. In contrast, the TZ/RM claims that "one receives a *neshamah yeterah* according to one's deeds" and spiritual rung.[273] For example, the highest Sabbath-souls are distributed by the Supernal *Shekhinah (Binah)* and are symbolized as fledglings (*'efroḥim*), whereas the less developed souls—received by ordinary Jews—derive from the lower *Shekhinah* and are called eggs (*beiẓim*).[274] According to one TZ passage (21 [46a]), the surplus of souls available on Shabbat are given to Torah-scholars—i.e., Kabbalists—who occupy the highest spiritual rung:

> Additional entities, called "extra souls," descend with Her; She gives them to the students of Torah. . . .

This enables them to maintain some degree of what may be called Sabbath-consciousness during the week:

> The surplus of souls afforded the Holy People on Sabbath eve are received by the students of Torah during the week; with these [souls] the profane is made holy.[275]

Imagery Used

One of the best ways to appreciate the transforming effect of the Sabbath-soul in the Zoharic tradition is to note the images that are used to describe the presence of this *neshamah,* and to convey their 'feeling-tone' or emotional significance. All the ensuing images are elaborated below.

Images of envelopment. The additional soul is symbolized as an enveloping, maternal presence: one enters into it as one enters a shelter (Z 2:204a–b). Its reception is time and again correlated with the numinous presence of *Shekhinah* overhead, She who "spreads her wings and shelters Israel as a mother [bird] does her fledglings." (Ibid.; cf. *Rimmon,* MS Brit. Mus. fol. 29b)

Images of Edenic garbing. The TZ likens the additional soul to an Edenic garment of light for the ordinary soul. This returns the primordial lustre lost after the Adamic sin (TZ Intro. [11a]).[276] It is through the *neshamah yeterah,* in other words, that the devotee regains access to Eden. (This notion is found in the *Zohar,* as well, albeit in less explicit fashion.)

Images of coronation. In the *Zohar,* the Sabbath-soul is said to form a crown of kingship for the devotee and for his ordinary soul. (Z 2:135b, 204b and 3:173a; cf. *Rimmon:* Ibid. and *Mishqal:* 114) For example:

> What is this *neshamah yeterah?* A holy spirit that hovers over a person and adorns him with a holy crown, the crown of angels. (ZḤ 29a [MN])

Images of internalization: the *neshamah yeterah* as honored guest. According to the TZ (6 [22b]), the Sabbath-soul is to be housed within the abode *(dirah)* of one's heart. According to the *Zohar,* it is to be welcomed into one's soul (2:204b). Like a beloved and honored guest, the Sabbath-soul is to be cared for and regaled.

Light imagery. The *Zohar* likens the Sabbath-soul to the flickering Sabbath candles and to those supernal sparkling flames called the *ẓaḥẓaḥot,* which confer enlightenment upon the righteous. (1:48b and 2:209a)

The Sabbath-souls as fledglings. The Sabbath-souls are imaged as tiny birds, the tender offspring of *Shekhinah,* who closely guards and nourishes them. As noted, the TZ uses the image of bird-eggs as well. Both underscore the familial bond between the Mother and one's soul. Consider, e.g., TZ 6 (22b):

> Many additional souls descend with Her to dwell with Israel. . . . The souls that are from the supernal *Shekhinah* are called fledglings [*'efroḥim*]. . . . She is the supernal Mother, forming a Canopy of Peace as She watches over them.

The Sabbath-souls as celestial blossoms. The *Zohar* describes the souls as blooming forth from the Tree of Life (*Tif'eret*). (3:173a)

Images of expansion. The *neshamot* are imaged as expansions of the supernal Point *(Malkhut),* swellings of light. When assimilated by the devotee, they enlarge his spiritual being, expand his consciousness.

The final example. The last association to bear in mind is not so much a pictorial image as it is a kind of aroma, an instance of olfactory symbolism. Moshe de Leon repeatedly spoke of the Edenic scent that the *neshamot yeterot* take on, as they stop to bathe in the perfumes and spices in the celestial Garden en route to the Sabbath-observers. For example:

> As this spirit descends, it bathes in the spices and perfumes in the Garden of Eden and then proceeds unto the Holy People. . . . (2:204a)

Although the nexus between aroma and soul is clearly articulated in connection with the Havdalah ceremony,[277] the *Zohar* seems to use this association in a subliminal fashion here.

We are now ready to see how these images are employed in their ritual setting. In so doing, we shall see how the motif of the *neshamah yeterah* is dramatized and made real for the devotee. First to be analyzed are the Zoharic descriptions of the moment of transformation (when the *neshamah yeterah* is actually received). Thereafter, we will examine the transforming effects of the Sabbath-soul during the subsequent hours of its sojourn.

Reception of Neshamah Yeterah *as the Existential Beginning of Shabbat*

It has previously been argued that the Sabbath-cosmos emerges in increments. To return to the earlier simile, it is like a light that begins to grow in anticipation of the day and reaches its climax on the Sabbath itself. Still, the Kabbalists ritually noted certain benchmarks: privileged moments that demarcate between the Sabbath and the profane, or between the almost-Shabbat and the fully Shabbat. So it must be asked: When does the Sabbath-cosmos fully arrive into the Sabbath-observer's life? Although ritual candlelighting unequivocally marks the beginning of Shabbat from a halakhic standpoint,[278] the existential beginning of full-Shabbat may be correlated with the reception of the Sabbath-soul. As perhaps befits an existential marker, the Zoharic tradition refrains from rigidly fixing this moment and records a number of alternatives.[279] Moshe de Leon himself linked the reception of the extra soul with several critical moments: most clearly, with the inception of the Friday night prayers (Z 2:135a–b and *Mishqal:* 114)[280] and the recitation of the prayer *Hashkivenu* (Z 1:48a). He also correlated the descent of the souls with the recitation of the *Qiddush ha-Yom* (Sanctification of the Day) in the ᶜ*Amidah,* a traditional halakhic marker for those males not present at candlelighting (cf., e.g., 3:173a). On still other occasions, he associated the reception of the Sabbath-soul with the emergence from the Friday afternoon bath (2:204a; 136a); and by implication, with candlelighting (1:48a).

In this section, several Zoharic accounts of the reception of the Sabbath-soul will be analyzed. This should provide us with significant clues towards a phenomenology of de Leon's Shabbat experience.

Drawing on the imagery found in the *Hashkivenu*, the *Zohar* portrays the assimilation of the Sabbath souls in warm, enveloping, maternal imagery.[281] As this prayer is recited the numinous presence of *Shekhinah* is felt overhead. As She draws ever nearer, She spreads Her wings and graces Her children Israel with new souls:

> The [*Hashkivenu*] is then recited. . . . Come and see: As Israel blesses and welcomes this "Canopy of Peace," the Holy Guest. . . . the supernal Holy One [*Shekhinah*] descends and spreads Her wings over Israel, sheltering them as a mother [bird] does her fledglings. . . . As [*Shekhinah*] hovers over them, wings outstretched over Her children, She brings forth new souls for each and every person. (1:48a)

Similar imagery is found in another source, Z 2:204a:

> On this [Sabbath] night, this supernal Point [*Shekhinah*] spreads forth light, spreading Her wings over the world. All other dominions pass away. The world grows secure.[282]

Sheltered in the divine Sabbath, the devotee receives his Sabbath-soul and is emotionally renewed:

> At this moment, an extra-soul is imparted to each member in Israel. With this Sabbath-soul all sadness and anger are forgotten. Joy reigns on high and below.

According to several other passages, the moment of transformation occurs shortly after one's emergence from the Friday afternoon bath.[283] The purpose of this bath is spiritual purification: through it the stain of the week (and its cosmic correlate, *Siṭra' 'Aḥra'*) is removed. This is a necessary prelude to being crowned with the Sabbath-soul:

> As the Sabbath approaches the holy People must wash their bodies of the mark of the profane week. For what reason? Because during the week Another Spirit [*Siṭra' 'Aḥra'*] goes forth and rests upon the People. [On Shabbat] one needs to get out from under that Spirit and enter into the other, holy spirit; so, one must bathe, that the supernal holy spirit may rest on him. (2:204a)

Typifying the *Zohar's* multivocality, this enveloping spirit seems at once to connote the realm of holiness, *Shekhinah,* and the additional soul.

The devotee's purification seems to parallel that of his Sabbath-soul, which is now bathing in the Garden of Eden. As the Sabbath-souls arrive in the Garden, they rouse the souls which dwell there, and the spiritual world as a whole awakens:

> When this spirit that burgeons within a person descends, it bathes in the spices of the Garden of Eden [in the angelic world] whence it wends its way down to rest on the holy People. As this spirit descends, sixty chariots [ten for each of the six sefirot from *Ḥesed* to *Yesod*] descend with it into Eden, [each one] crowned on six sides. When it arrives in the Garden, all the Edenic spirits and souls stir, roused by that spirit. (Ibid.)

Sometime after the devotee emerges from the water, he is wreathed with the fragrant soul: Sabbath has begun.

One of the most striking accounts of the reception of the Sabbath-soul may be found in *Zohar* 2:136a–b. Just before Sabbath's inception, the entire heavenly world is caught up in a whirl of incessant activity and spiritual commotion "with souls coming and souls going; souls ascending and souls descending."

The drama is two-fold. The *Zohar* explains that on Shabbat the righteous souls in lower Eden are also transformed. As the *neshamot yeterot* descend to earth, the souls of the righteous ascend, lifted up by winged angels and escorted by fiery Chariots bearing aloft the divine Throne. They mount up until they reach the celestial Garden of Eden. As they arrive, "other holy souls—the *neshamot yeterot*—crown the Holy People" below.[284]

The mention of the Chariots and the incessant rushing back and forth seems to echo Ezekiel's vision (Ezek. 1). The whirl of ecstatic supernal activity and rapt anticipation parallels—and for a historian of religion is a projection onto the cosmos of—the devotee's joyous anticipation as he is about to enter the holy day. The ensuing passages convey the internal rhythms of Sabbath eve in exemplary fashion:

> Souls come and souls go. Souls ascend and souls descend. . . .wreathing the holy People. On the very eve of Shabbat, there is a great procession [*gilgul*] of souls, some coming, some going, some in ascent and some in descent. And who can behold

the innumerable holy chariots perpetually speeding to and fro, all delighted, all filled with desire?. . . . (2:136a)

This vision of spiritual agitation and ecstasy[285] is restated in a neighboring passage:

When R. Hamnuna Sava used to come out from the river on Friday afternoon he would rest a little on the bank, and raising his eyes in gladness, he would say that he sat there in order to behold the joyous sight of the heavenly angels ascending and descending.[286] At each arrival of the Sabbath, he said, man is caught up into the world of souls [a cipher for ecstasy]. Happy is he who experiences the mysteries of his Lord! (2:136b)[287]

Then, of a sudden, the incessant activity ceases, the souls enter their new homes and the world knows a deep and joyous rest:

So it proceeds until that moment when the voice proclaims: "Sanctified! Sanctified!" Then rest and tranquility fill the cosmos. Even the wicked in Gehinnom enjoy this repose. And all the souls crown themselves, those above and those below. Happy is the People who may partake of this! (2:136a)

Our final passage correlates the reception of the Sabbath-soul with the Sanctification of the Day found in the *ᶜAmidah.* It combines many of the symbols which have been alluded to before: Edenic imagery and scents, coronation and botanical imagery, metaphors of spiritual awakening. The overall picture is one of sensual joy:

As Israel below is sanctifying the day, the Tree of Life [*Tiferet*] rouses. Its leaves rustle as a breeze comes forth from the World-to-Come [sefirotically, *Binah*]. The branches of the Tree sway and waft forth the scent of the World-to-Come. The Tree of Life is further aroused and at this moment, brings forth holy souls which it gives to the world. Souls exit and they enter, each rousing the other. They exit and they enter, and the Tree of Life is filled with joy. All Israel is wreathed with crowns, which are these holy souls. Now the cosmos is joyous, and at rest. (3:173a)

The Impact of the Sabbath-Soul During Shabbat

Through the presence of the *neshamah yeterah* the devotee is able to align himself with the transformations that have occurred in the divine world and within the realm of time; human microcosm comes to mirror the divine archetype. For example, the Sabbath-soul is said to be a "crown of kingship" reflecting the coronation on high. It is the symbol of sefirotic harmony, or in the words of Moshe de Leon, "the embodiment of the divine totality" (Z 2:88a). The Sabbath-soul enables the devotee to exemplify the Sabbath-cosmos, the so-called "World of Souls." For

> the *neshamah yeterah* is the soul containing the totality of perfection. . . . Indeed, this soul is called *Shabbat.* (2:88b)

Through the presence of the *neshamah yeterah* the devotee reaches his full spiritual stature. It is a "symbol of the World-to-Come" (Ibid.) enabling the devotee to become his ideal (i.e., ultimate) self:

> The supernal spirit joyously descends onto a person on Shabbat and fills his soul with joy. *His soul is lifted onto the same rung it will be on in the World-to-Come.* (emph. mine). . . . This spirit will give him delight in the future world. As it is written: "Then shall you delight yourself in the Lord" [Isa. 58:14] and "He will satisfy your soul with sparkling flashes [ẓaḥẓaḥot]" [Ibid.:11] (2:208b–209a),

the light of enlightenment.

Not only may one speak of the Sabbath-soul in terms of the World-to-Come, but one may speak of the World-to-Come in terms of the Sabbath-soul:

> During the Messianic era . . . an expanded spirit will be roused and added to Israel. . . . They will enjoy freedom from the [oppression] of the Nations . . . like on the Sabbath [*ke-dugmat Shabbat*], when one is given an extra-soul. (2:88b)

The Sabbath-soul spiritually empowers the devotee, expands his insights:

> Each person has a soul which takes in a spirit on the Sabbath eve. This spirit resides within one's soul all Sabbath long and the soul is enlarged, with greater power than before. (2:204b–05a)

It transforms his emotional bearing, uprooting sorrow and pain, as it brings joy.[288] According to the TZ (21 [57a]) this soul endows husbands and wives with harmonious relations. It is for this reason, the author claims, that Friday night is the ideal time for marital intercourse.[289]

Moreover, according to the *Zohar*, the presence of the Sabbath-soul increases fertility and ensures holy offspring:

> When Torah-scholars dwell within this holy and supernal spirit, they must engage in marital intercourse, for as this spirit descends it draws down all the holy souls [produced by the supernal coupling of the Groom and Bride]. Through the [Sabbath-spirit] the holy supernal entities impart sacred souls to Their children below. (2:204b–205a)

A symbiotic relationship is said to exist between the Sabbath-soul and his host. Each gladdens and takes care of the other. Through Torah-study (3:173a and 173b–74a) and through partaking in the earthly delights of the Sabbath repast (2:204b), one regales his Sabbath-soul and comes to experience increased joy:

> Happy is the one who regales his spirit on Shabbat! During the six days of the week this soul delights in the supernal spirit [the *shefa*ᶜ] of the Ancient of Ancients. On the Sabbath, after [the soul] descends and bathes in the Garden of Eden at dusk, it takes delight in the bodily enjoyments afforded by the Meals of Faith. This spirit is then crowned from on high and from below, from all sides. . . .

The devotee is bidden to take care of his honored guest:

> Since it dwells with the person, he must take care of it, as it is said: "The Children of Israel should keep the Sabbath ['*et ha-Shabbat*]." [Ex. 31:17] "Sabbath" refers to the Lower Point [*Malkhut*]; '*et ha-Shabbat,* [where the particle '*et* is understood to *include*[290] the *neshamah yeterah*] refers to the expansion of this Point.

According to another *Zohar* teaching, the *neshamah yeterah* divides in two as the Sabbath arrives: one part remaining in the celestial world, while the other descends to crown Israel below:

> As it is written, "It is between Me and Israel" [Ex. 31:17], meaning: It is a portion and a heritage to be shared by us jointly.
>
> On this day the supernal portion is crowned with a holy sublime Delight, resplendent in the Glory of the Ancient of Ancients. The lower portion is crowned with earthly delights, derived from the festive meals. So one must regale it with sumptuous food and drink, fine raiment and with the joy felt by all [participants].

When this portion is crowned below . . . . it ascends on high and unites with its [supernal] portion. Thereupon, the Point gathers all the divine light from above and below, and the soul is perfected on all sides. (2:204b)

So it is that a symbiotic relationship is nurtured. Through delighting in the Sabbath, the devotee helps crown the *neshamah yeterah* and renders it whole. And the Sabbath-soul, in turn, lifts up the devotee, enabling him to enter the pneumatic world and to share in its secrets.[291] Indeed, Moshe de Leon elsewhere avers that the Sabbath-soul enables the adept to make the deepest penetration of all, to become one with the sefirotic Gestalt:

to become bound up in the "bonds of holiness," *le-hitqasher be-qishrei ha-qodesh*, in the mystery of the People "glorious in holiness." [Ex. 15:11] (*Rimmon* 29b)[292]

Another dramatic example of this spiritual ascent may be found in a neighboring *Zohar* text. Through the aid of the Sabbath-soul, the ordinary soul embarks on a nighttime voyage:

After midnight, when the Torah-scholars have consummated their marital intercourse, and sleep overcomes them, their ordinary souls wish to ascend on high to behold the King's glory. So the supernal spirits that entered them at the arrival of Shabbat take those souls and bear them aloft. These souls bathe in the perfume of the Garden of Eden, and see what they see. (2:204b)

The *neshamah yeterah* then ushers the ordinary soul back in time for the waking hours.

Thus we have seen that the Zoharic tradition ascribes transformative powers to the Sabbath-soul: changing the person spiritually, psychologically, emotionally, even physically (so that he feels safe, protected). But as Sabbath leaves, so does the Sabbath-soul. The ordinary soul that was enlarged and exhilarated throughout the day now is left weakened and bereft. According to one account, it is but two-thirds of a "soul": "When the Sabbath departs, the bond [uniting the three aspects of soul] is severed; the *neshamah* ascends and the *nefesh* and *ruaḥ* [the two lower parts] are left estranged and saddened." (Z 3:35b)

The Kabbalists devised a series of strategems to attenuate this loss, but that is another story, one which we shall treat in chapter 4.

A COSMOS THAT IS ENTIRELY SHABBAT: SOME CONCLUDING THOUGHTS

"Call the Sabbath a delight" (Isa. 58:13): a delight unto both the body and the soul, a delight unto the celestial and lower realms. (*Zohar* 2:47a)

The multiple changes which have been discussed throughout this chapter point to a transformation of the entire Cosmos. According to the Zoharic tradition, not only are Time, Divinity, and Person renewed, but the angelic worlds and even Gehinnom. As the Sabbath enters, all the demonic forces that pervade the weekday universe shut down and hide, confined to "the Cavern of the Great Abyss":

All evil spirits and demons, indeed, the entire Realm of Defilement [*Siṭra' 'Aḥra'*], hide within the eye of the millstone of the Cavern of the Great Abyss. For when the spirit of holiness spreads over the world, the spirit of defilement cannot remain. . . . The entire world is under the [shelter] of the supernal Peace. (Z 1:48a)[293]

Even the sinners in Gehinnom are protected. The fires of Hell are extinguished[294] and the travails of the week cease. According to one source (ZḤ Ber. 29b [MN]), even these unfortunates are wreathed with a Sabbath-soul.[295] The angelic worlds are transformed, as well: in one striking passage (Z 2:208a) they are re-integrated into divinity itself and lose all individuation. "Absorbed into the supernal Flame [*Malkhut*]," they must be *re-created* at Sabbath's end.[296]

"Indeed," Moshe de Leon wrote, "the upper and lower worlds are in union" (as in Time primordial) and Complete Compassion (*raḥamim gemurim*) everywhere holds sway. (Z 2:205a) This Sabbath-cosmos—this newly redeemed world—is marvelously evoked in that well-known *Zohar* passage, *Raza' de-Shabbat* (2:135a–b); it is a fitting finale to this chapter:

The Secret of Shabbat. She [*Shekhinah*] is Shabbat! United in the secret of One to draw down upon Her the Secret of One. . . .[297]

When the Sabbath arrives, She is placed by Herself, separated from the Other Side. All judgments are removed from Her. Basking in the oneness of holy light, She is crowned over and over in the presence of the King. All wanton tyrannies and lords of affliction flee from Her and vanish. There is no power in all the cosmos aside from Her. Her face shines with a light from beyond.

> On earth She is crowned by the holy people, and all of them are crowned with new souls. They bless Her with joy and beaming faces. . . .

NOTES TO CHAPTER ONE

1. Although the great bulk of their creative energy was devoted to the re-reading of extant rituals, the classical Kabbalists also developed a number of novel rites and gestures to further dramatize their mystical understanding of Shabbat. Several of these will be treated in chapters 3 and 4.

2. Following M. Greenberg (EJ 14:558 ff.) and I. Tishby (MZ 2:481 ff.), I am for the moment using *sacramental* in its most general sense, to signify the Sabbath's peculiarly sacred, numinous power. Both M. Greenberg and I. Tishby use the term to distinguish the Sabbath's holiness from its social or utilitarian import.

3. Cf. Ex. 31:15, 35:2; Num. 15:32–36; Jer. 17:27; and Ezek. 20:10–13.

4. I am using the term in its Eliadean sense, to denote a locus which affords uniquely powerful access to the divine and which serves as the cosmic axis around which life is organized. Sacred Centers, it might be said, provide cosmic orientation. For details see M. Eliade's *The Sacred and the Profane* (New York: 1959) Chap. 1. On the Temple as Sacred Center, see Ibid.: 40–44, 58–61, and 75; M. Fishbane, "The Sacred Center" in idem and P. Flohr, *Texts and Responses* (Leiden, 1975): 21 and 24–25; R. Goldenberg, "The Broken Axis: Rabbinic Judaism and the Fall of Jerusalem" in *JAAR* XLV/3, Supplement (Sept. 1977): 870 ff.; and J. D. Levenson's recent *Sinai and Zion* (Minneapolis, 1985): 111–84, passim.

5. See Jer. 17:27 where it is warned that profanation of Shabbat *will* cause the destruction of Jerusalem and Neh. 13:15–18 which states that failure to observe the Sabbath *had* caused the Destruction and Exile. Also see Isa. 56:2,4,6; 58:13–14; Ezek. 20 and 22:26; Jer. 17:19–27; and Neh. 13:14–22.

6. For an overview of the Biblical Sabbath, see M. Greenberg's article in EJ 14: 558–62 and J. Tigay, *'Enẓiqloppediah Miqra'it*, Vol. 7: 504–21. For fuller treatment see N. A. Andreassen, *The Old Testament Sabbath* (Missoula, 1972) and the comprehensive bibliography therein. Also see R. de Vaux, *Ancient Israel* (New York, 1961): 475–83; and M. Tsevat, "The Basic Meaning of the Biblical Sabbath" in *Zeitschrift Altestatmentliche Wissenschaft*, Vol. 84:4 (1972): 447–59. M. Fishbane's *Biblical Interpretation in Ancient Israel* (Oxford, 1985): 98–100, 130–34 and 478–79 affords insight into the exegetical elaboration of Sabbath law in the Exilic and post-Exilic periods.

7. See *Jubilees* 2:25–33 and Chap. 50.

8. See, e.g., Philo's *De Abrahamo* 5; *De Cherubim* 85–87; *De Migratione Abrahami* 89–90; *De Opificio Mundi* 30; *Quod Omnis Probus Liber Sit* 72–91; *De Fuga et Inventione* 173–74; and *De Specialibus Legibus* 2.65–69. Also see *Damascus Covenant* 10:14–11:18; and Josephus' *Antiquities* 14.10.12, 20, 21, 23 and 25, 16.2.3, and 16.6.2–4; *Wars* 1.7.3 and 7.5.1; and *Against Apion* 2.22 and 2.40.

The sacramental power of the Sabbath is a recurring theme expressed in extant sources from the late second Temple period. In addition to the well-known sources cited above, see Aristobulus' teaching preserved in Eusebius's *Praeperatio Evangelica* 13.12, translated in J. Charlesworth (ed.), *Old Testament Pseudepigrapha* Vol. 2 (Garden City, NY, 1985): 841–42. There the Sabbath is equated with the Logos; it is the first created entity, "the genesis of light in which all things are created." The cosmic Sabbath is said to give true rest to those that observe it; through Shabbat one attains knowledge of divine things.

The sacramental quality of Sabbath observance is also highlighted in two Essene sources, fragments of which were found at Qumran:

In the aforementioned *Jubilees* (Chap. 2) Shabbat is depicted as God's "chosen day," the sign binding Israel unto God and unto the angelic realm. This text relates that the Sabbath was originally given unto the angels, allowing them to rest in imitatio dei. Later God granted the gift of this day to one earthly community—"to Israel alone, that they might eat and drink" and "bless the Creator" thereon. According to the angelic pronouncement, Israel was chosen "from among the nations that they might keep the Sabbath together with us." In other words, Sabbath observance brings together God's chosen day with His chosen people; it also brings Israel into alignment with higher orders of being: enabling the Jew to attune himself to the divine rhythms and to participate in the angelic order.

The transformative powers of Sabbath observance are implied in a second Qumran text, 4Q *Shirot ᶜOlat ha-Shabbat* (the angelic hymns for the Sabbath). In all likelihood these songs served as a liturgical vehicle enabling the devotee to attain communion with the angels and to partake in their Sabbath celebration in the celestial Temple. For discussion, see C. Newsom, *Songs of the Sabbath Sacrifice: A Critical Edition* (Atlanta, 1985) and L. Schiffman, "Merkavah Speculation at Qumran: The 4Q Serekh Shirot ᶜOlat ha-Shabbat" in J. Reinharz and D. Swetchinski (eds.), *Mystics, Philosophers, and Politicians* (Durham, 1982): 15–47.

9. One striking example is the divergent attitudes towards eating on the Sabbath. Whereas *Jubilees* (2:21 and 50:12) notes the importance of festive meals and forbids fasting, Josephus (*Against Apion* 2:40) and various Roman sources report that Sabbath-fasting was widespread. On this question, see R. Goldenberg, "The Jewish Sabbath in the Roman World" in W. Haase and H. Temporini (eds.), *Aufstieg und Niedergang der Romanischen Welt* (Berlin, 1979), Vol. 2: 439–41; and Y. Gilat, "Taᶜanit Shabbat", *Tarbiẓ* 52:1 (1983): 1–15.

10. This was noted by R. Goldenberg, Ibid.: 415. As previously noted, early attempts to specify the exact nature of Sabbath-law may be found in the inner Biblical exegeses of the Exilic and post-Exilic periods. See M. Fishbane in n. 6 above.

11. Aristobulus maintained that the Sabbath expresses aspects of cosmic reality which have universal significance; Sabbath is meaningful for all people. By way of example, he averred that both Homer and Hesiod viewed the seventh day as holy. Philo also underscored the universal significance of Sabbath-celebration, noting that it is "a day of festival for all people, the birthday of the world." (*De Opificio Mundi 30)*

12. *De Specialibus Legibus* 2.61. The contemplative nature of Philo's Sabbath is also apparent in *De Decalogo* 20; *De Vita Mosis* 2.215–216; and *De Vita Contemplativa* 3–4.

For fuller discussion of the Sabbath in the late Second Commonwealth period, see R. Goldenberg, "The Jewish Sabbath in the Roman World": 414–47 and the sources cited therein. R. Goldenberg's study extends through the early fourth century and also treats early Christian attitudes. For other treatments of Sabbath in Judeo-Hellenistic sources, see the references cited under "Sabbath" in the index to J. Charlesworth (ed.) *The Old Testament Pseudepigrapha* (2 vols., Garden City, NY, 1983–85). On the Sabbath in Essene-pietist circles, also see L. Schiffman, *The Halakhah at Qumran* (Leiden, 1975), esp. chap. 3–4; B. Sharvit, "The Sabbath of the Judean Desert Sect" [Hebrew], *Beit Miqra'* 21 (1976): 507–16; and the sources cited in n. 8 above.

13. For details see "The Broken Axis" (cited in n. 4): 875–77.

14. See his "Sabbath as Temple": 293, in S. Z. Fishman and R. Jospe (eds.), *Go and Study: Essays and Studies in Honor of A. Jospe* (New York, 1982).

15. Ff. A. Green, Ibid.: 292–93. For A. J. Heschel's classic evocation of Shabbat, see *The Sabbath* (New York, 1951). The image of the Sabbath as a sanctuary or cathedral in Time was previously employed by H. N. Bialik in his famous essay, "Halakhah ve-'Aggadah" (1917). See his *Divrei Sifrut* (Tel Aviv, 1954): 84ff. [abridged English version in N. N. Glatzer (ed.), *Modern Jewish Thought* (New York, 1977): 58ff.].

16. In a famous Tannaitic dictum (M. Ḥag. 1:8), the Rabbis likened their expansive Sabbath-law to "mountains hanging from a hair", *ke-hararim ha-teluyin be-saᶜarah.*

17. See R. Goldenberg, "The Jewish Sabbath": 423–24 and Y. Gilat, "ᶜAl 39 'Avot Mela'khot Shabbat", *Tarbiẓ* 29 (1960): 222–28.

18. See TB Shab. 49b. Also cf. Ibid. 97b and Mekh. de-R. Shimon bar Yoḥai to Ex. 35:1.

19. See A. Green, "Sabbath as Temple": 294.

20. Ibid. See the discussion therein.

21. Although it was the Rabbis who explicated and systematically developed the symbolic link between Sabbath and Temple, it seems clear that they were building on earlier precedents and allusions. The Biblical roots of the Temple-Sabbath nexus is discussed by J. D. Levenson in his *Sinai and Temple,* esp. pp. 142–45 and 178–84. Building on M. Cassuto and J. Blenkinsopp, Levenson argues that a series of linguistic parallels and symbolic correspondences were artfully employed by the redactor to link Tabernacle and Temple—perfected space—with Creation and its fulfillment, Shabbat—perfected time. Moreover, Levinson suggests, the resultant experience of entering the Tabernacle/Temple is deemed parallel to that of entering Shabbat. Each affords God and person, *menuḥah:* profound rest and inner harmony.

Another possible cross-indexing of Temple and Sabbath may be found in the writings of the Dead Sea Sect, who in many ways anticipated the later Rabbinic transfer of Temple symbolism to the temporal realm. Barukh Bokser has recently suggested that the Sabbath was symbolized as a temporal Temple at Qumran, as various proscriptions traditionally applied to entering the Temple were transposed into the setting of Shabbat. See B. Bokser's "Approaching Sacred Space," *Harvard Theological Review* 78:3–4 (1985): 284–85.

Although the Rabbis explicated the link between Sabbath-law and the Temple/Tabernacle only in sources edited in the Amoraic period, implicit connections may be found in the Mishnah. J. Neusner has recently argued that the operating principle for much of Mishnaic Sabbath-law is the simile of the Temple for the village, as the norms of restricted movement and behavior applicable in the Temple setting become transposed into the village during the context of sacred time. He maintains that the detailed Sabbath-laws of carrying and the rigid definition of social space are "not a return to a perfect time" so much as "a recovery of perfect being," recalling the sanctity attained at the Temple. For further discussion, see J. Neusner, "Innovation Through Repetition: The Role of Scripture in the Mishnah's Division of Appointed Times" in *History of Religions* 21:1 (1981): 48–76. The historical evolution of Sabbath as "symbolic Temple" requires further investigation.

22. See TB Shab. 113a–19b, passim.

23. See TB Ber. 57b and Shab. 118b.

24. The phrase is I. Tishby's; see MZ 2: 484–85.

25. See I. Tishby, MZ 2: 481–83 for more sources. For a larger sampling of Rabbinic *'aggadot,* see Y. L. Barukh, *Sefer ha-Shabbat* (Tel-Aviv: 1980): 27–46 and *'Oẓar ha-'Aggadah* (Jerusalem, 1982): 918–26.

26. See, e.g., J. Neusner, *A History of the Jews in Babylonia* Vol. 4 (Leiden, 1969): 178. In those areas of Babylonia under Rabbinic supervision, public celebration of Shabbat (refraining from work, observing the Sabbath limit, and such like) was nearly universal. It cannot be assumed, however, that the masses observed (or were even familiar with) all the details of Rabbinic Sabbath-observance that pertained to the private domain.

27. I am basing these remarks on A. Green's formulation in "Sabbath as Temple": 293.

28. For further treatment of the Rabbinic Sabbath, see G. F. Moore, *Judaism* (New York, 1971), 2: 21–40; E. Urbach, *Ḥ̣aZaL* (Jerusalem, 1971) [English version: *The Sages*]: index; I. Tishby, MZ 2:481–83; and J. Neusner's more historically self-conscious account in *A History of the Jews in Babylonia* (Leiden, 1966–70), 1:24–25 and 155, 3:243–52, and 4:171–82.

On the spirituality undergirding Sabbath halakhah, see R. Goldenberg, "Law and Spirit in Talmudic Religion" in A. Green (ed.), *Jewish Spirituality* 1:232–52. On differing Rabbinic conceptions of *ᶜOneg Shabbat,* see Y. Gilat, "Taᶜanit Shabbat" [On Fasting on the Sabbath], *Tarbiẓ* 52:1 (1983): 1–15. A comprehensive analysis of the historical development of the Rabbinic Sabbath remains a desideratum.

29. The text of this poem may be found in *Sefer ha-Shabbat:* 304–05. See there also ha-Levi's poems "Yom shabbaton" and "Yeqar yom ha-shabbat tagdil", pp. 305ff. For a complete collection of ha-Levi's Sabbath hymns, see now D. Yarden, ed., *Shirei ha-Qodesh le-R. Yehudah ha-Levi,* Vol. 3 (1986): 441–49.

30. See Abraham ibn Ezra's commentary to Gen. 2:3 and Ex. 20:8. Also see " 'Iggeret ha-Shabbat," an epistle written to the Sabbath, wherein ibn Ezra proclaims his great love of the day.

31. The philosophers' rationalizing of Shabbat is stressed in I. Tishby, MZ 2:483–87. I have drawn on his insights throughout this section. Nonetheless, I. Tishby oversimplifies matters by failing to take into account the sacramental emphasis found in the poetry of Judah ha-Levi and Abraham ibn Ezra, e.g. In the case of these two authors, at least, it is necessary to distinguish between their liturgical voice and their philosophical stance; literary genre (and performance context) seems to have influenced their attitudes and formulations. I. Tishby's comments retain greater validity when restricted to the more overtly discursive literature.

32. A more spiritual (though still instrumental) significance is accorded Sabbath observance in *Kuzari* 2:50. There it is suggested that Sabbath observance is a means of exhibiting and strengthening one's faith "in God's omnipotence and. . . . His creation of the world through the Word." See *Kuzari* 2:50 for details.

A fuller analysis of the *Kuzari* necessitates discussion of the rhetorical strategies employed by Judah ha-Levi in this apologetic classic. A close reading must also distinguish between the two major personae found in this work (a rabbinic sage and the Kuzari king in search of a new faith) and attempt to relate their statements to the author's own hierarchy of values and attitudes, insofar as they can be inferred. Clearly, such an interpretive endeavor is beyond the scope of the present discussion. It may simply be noted that the rabbi oscillates between intrinsic and instrumental rationales for Sabbath-observance (cf. 2:50 and 3:5) whereas the Kuzari king advances largely instrumental rationales (3:10).

33. *Beliefs and Opinions*, Book 3:2. Here I am using the S. Rosenblatt translation (Yale Judaica Series, Vol. 1 [New Haven, 1948]). It is interesting to note that Saadiah ascribes these functions not only to Shabbat but to the festivals in general.

34. See his *Guide of the Perplexed* 2:31 and 3:43. The former reads:

> Therefore we have been commanded inactivity and rest so that we should conjoin two things: the belief in a true opinion—namely the creation of the world in time, which at the first go and with the slightest of speculations, shows that the deity exists—and the memory of the benefit God bestowed upon us by giving us rest "from under the burdens of the Egyptians" (Ex. 6:7). Accordingly the Sabbath is, as it were, of universal benefit, both with reference to a true speculative opinion and to the well-being of the state of the body. (Sh. Pines transl.)

35. J. Anatoli's views on Shabbat are found in his *Malmad ha-Talmidim* (Lyck, 1886). For sources and further discussion, see I. Tishby, MZ 2:486–87.

The survey of philosophical approaches to the Sabbath has necessarily been brief, limited to *ra'shei peraqim*. A more detailed study remains a desideratum.

36. See pp. 187–90 below.

37. By *Ground* I mean that the divine Sabbath makes the earthly Sabbath ontologically possible: the changes within the divine Source effect changes in the human realm. By *archetype* I mean that the primal structure of the divine Sabbath serves as the model for the structure of the earthly Sabbath. These two features of Kabbalistic theory will be treated more systematically in chapters 2 through 4.

38. For further discussion of the sefirotic Days, see p. 32 above. See also *Sod ha-Shabbat:* Prologue and Section 14, and the accompanying notes, esp. n. 6 and nn. 358–64. For early Kabbalistic views, see *Bahir* 57, 82 and 158, and I. Tishby's analysis, MZ 1:144. A summary of thirteenth and fourteenth century Kabbalistic views is found in Joseph ibn Waqar's *Perush le-Shir ha-Yiḥud*, in A. Habermann, ed., *Shirei ha-Yiḥud ve-ha-Kavod* (Jeru-

salem, 1948): 116–17. A sophisticated discussion is also found in the late fifteenth century Spanish adept Joseph Alcastiel's "Teshuvot le-She'elot ᶜal Derekh ha-Qabbalah she-sha'al R. Yehuda he-Ḥayyaṭ" in G. Scholem, "Li-Ydiᶜat ha-Qabbalah bi-Sfarad ᶜErev ha-Gerush," *Tarbiẓ* 24 (1954): 191–93.

39. See page 32 and the chart on page 29 above.

40. For discussion see MZ 2:493–94 and the sources cited therein. For other links between *Yesod* and "seven," see J. Giqatilia, *Shaᶜarei 'Orah* (Ben Shlomo ed.) 1:107–08; Joseph of Hamadan, *Sefer Ṭaᶜamei ha-Miẓvot* (MS JTSA Mic. 1722) fol. 117b; and the Joseph ibn Waqar source cited in n. 38 above. J. Giqatilia also provided more substantive rationales for *Yesod*'s identity as Shabbat. He stressed *Yesod*'s functional centrality and its ability to hold together the sefirotic world. For examples, see n. 53 below and the striking teaching on pp. 88–89 above.

I have found two other (more unusual) numerological explanations for *Yesod*'s "seventhness":

(1) In his *Perush ha-Sefirot,* R. Jacob b. Jacob ha-Kohen of Soria, suggested that the upper triad properly constitutes a single pneumatic entity, the tripartite divine soul. (In medieval thought, the soul was generally divided into three aspects.) Thus, although *Yesod* is the ninth sefirah in ordinary perception, it is, ontologically speaking, the seventh rung:

> [*Yesod*] is called "the seventh day." How so? *Ḥesed* makes one; *Din* two; *Raḥamim* three; *Neẓaḥ* four; *Hod* five; *Maḥshavah [Keter]*, *Ḥokhmah* and *Binah* form [the tri-partite divine] soul; they are considered as one, making six. *Yesod* is the seventh . . . the one that binds.

(Brit. Museum MS Version B, cited in G. Scholem, "Qabbalat he-Ḥakham R. Yaaqov he-Ḥasid b. Yaaqov ha-Kohen," *Maddaᶜei ha-Yahadut* 2 [1927]: 227 and 230.)

(2) Two closely related sources associated with the *Sefer ha-Temunah* Circle, *Sefer Sod ha-Shem* (Constantinople *Zohar Ḥadash,* 1740: fol. 171c) and *Sefer Sod 'Ilan ha-'Aẓilut* (G. Scholem, ed.; *Qoveẓ ᶜal Yad* n.s. 5:85), suggest that in terms of historical manifestation *Yesod* is the seventh rung, the last of the seven sefirot which generate and govern the cosmic cycles or *shemiṭṭot.* According to this esoteric teaching, each of the six sefirot from *Ḥesed* to *Malkhut* successively hold sway over a 6,000 year cycle, determining its fundamental tenor. These six *shemiṭṭot* of activity culminate in the cosmic Shabbat. As *Yesod*'s rule approaches, time progressively slows and—in some accounts—reverses its course. When *Yesod* finally holds full sway, time and matter, even the six active sefirot, cease to exist; all are absorbed into the primal ground of *Yesod.* This is "Cosmic Rest," the "Sabbath of Sabbaths."

The foregoing precis should alert us to the idiosyncratic Shabbat-symbolism of the *Temunah* circle. *Yesod* is typically the ninth of the ten sefirot and the active rung par excellence; *Binah* is generally the point of return during apokatastasis. In the *Temunah* circle, *Yesod* is marked by tenthness and radical passivity; in the texts cited it serves as the Ground for apokatastasis. I plan to systematically analyze the *Temunah* Circle's understanding of Shabbat in a separate article.

41. In all likelihood, the motives are overdetermined. For yet another possibility see p. 107 above and n. 196 below.

42. Cf. the parallel in Ṭodros Abulafia's *Shaʿar ha-Razim* MS Munich 209 fol. 48a–49a (ad Ps. 19:3). Also see the *Keter Shem Ṭov* of Shem Ṭov ibn Gaon which states that initially the seventh rung was bi-sexual, "*sheviʿi u-sheviʿit*—the male-and-female seventh." (Coriat ed., fol. 38a) The androgyny of the divine Sabbath is neatly captured in Moshe de Leon's image of the Sabbath as a date-palm (*tamar*), a tree distinguished by its bi-sexual nature. See *Sefer ha-Rimmon,* MS Cambridge Add. 1516 fol. 41b.

43. This is especially true in the *Zohar.* In *Sefer ha-Mishqal,* however, Moshe de Leon maintained *Tif'eret* as the central Sabbath. For an example see J. Wijnhoven's critical edition, *Sefer ha-Mishqal: Text and Edition* (Ph.D. diss., Brandeis, 1964): 110.

44. On Moshe de Leon's attraction to feminine symbolism, see A. Green, "Bride, Spouse, Daughter": 257; and pp. 16–17 above.

45. The major exception to this trend is the Naḥmanidean School. See, e.g., *Maʿarekhet ha-'Elohut* (Mantua, 1558) fol. 183b: "The seventh day corresponds to *Yesod,* the Great Sabbath which is the World-to-Come, cosmic life. . . ."

46. It might be noted that in Rabbinic theology the term *ʿolam ha-ba',* World-to-Come, had an ambiguous meaning. Sometimes it was construed as the Messianic eschaton, an interpretation frequently followed by the Kabbalists and relevant for our purposes here. For Rabbinic examples of this usage, cf. TB Zev. 118b, Tos. Ar. 2:7, TB Ar. 13b, et al. More frequently the Rabbis used *ʿolam ha-ba'* with reference to the hereafter: the "World of Souls" which the individual enters upon the termination of his earthly life. In this sense, the World-to-Come is a spiritual state which already exists, another dimension of present-day reality. Cf. e.g. Tanḥ. "Va-Yiqra'" sec. 8 (cited in D. Matt: 267):

> The wise call it *ʿolam ha-ba'* not because it is not now in existence, but because for those who are today in this world it is still "to come." So it is the "world that comes" after a person leaves the world. But one who says that this world is destroyed and afterwards *ʿolam ha-ba'* will come—it is not so.

For further discussion on the ambiguity surrounding *ʿolam ha-ba'* in Rabbinic thought, see EJ 12:1355–57. The dual meaning of the term is perhaps most strikingly underscored in the Kabbalist Meir ibn Gabbai's *ʿAvodat ha-Qodesh* (AQ) 2: 41–43, where he self-consciously distinguishes between that *ʿolam ha-ba'* connoting the extant World of Souls and the one connoting the aeon following the Resurrection.

Finally, it should be noted that the Kabbalists reflected the ambiguity surrounding the World-to-Come in their sefirotic usage of the term as well. At times it refers to the spiritual state currently flourishing within *Binah;* at other times to the future Jubilee, the ultimate cosmic aeon under *Binah*'s aegis. For a germane example see J. Giqatilia's usage on p. 84 above. For further layers of temporal signification, see the discussion on the Sabbath as *ᶜolam ha-ba'*, pp. 95–100.

47. According to a notion originating in Gerona Kabbalah, the process of Redemption will consist of several distinct stages. First, Messianic redemption (including the ingathering of the exiles) will occur; sometime thereafter, the resurrection of the righteous; and finally, at the very end of the cosmic aeon, *hitballeᶜut:* the reabsorption of all Being into the divine Source.

48. For Asher ben David's interpretation, see his *Sefer ha-Yiḥud* (I am relying on the version printed in *Ha-Segullah* [1937], p. 4, lines 29–33). Also see Baḥyya ben Asher's recasting of this source, *Perush ᶜal ha-Torah* ad Num. 15:32. An interesting variation on this theme may be found in OK to Shab. 69b and in *Shaᶜar ha-Razim* fol. 48a-b where Ṭodros Abulafia found a geometric rationale for calling all lower seven *Shabbat*. The OK passage reads:

> "Said R. Huna: If one is travelling in the wilderness and does not know when it is the Sabbath, he must count seven days and observe that one as Shabbat." This discloses a great mystery concerning the ten logoi with which the world was created. Six of them correspond to the six days of Creation and "the seventh is a Sabbath unto the Lord." The three above cannot be perceived; for they are entirely bright and pure light, sparkling unto infinity [*'Ein Sof*]. . . . But the seven remaining [logoi] may be envisioned as a circle drawn from seven points, without beginning or end. Each one is the seventh depending on where one begins. . . . Hence, one counts seven and observes that one, for it too is a Sabbath. . . . This is a great secret pertaining to the six days of Creation and their hidden fountain. . . . Surely, this is the mystery of "You shall keep my Sabbaths." (Lev. 19:30)

The explanations of R. Asher and the OK are combined in Menaḥem Recanati to Ex. 16:26; *Peli'ah* 85c–d; and in the TY. See *Sod ha-Shabbat:* Prologue and nn. 9–11 for further discussion. For an interesting variation, see *Shoshan Sodot:* 80b–81a (item 28).

49. Originally printed under the title *Ha-Nefesh ha-Ḥakhamah* (Basle, 1608), fol. 8a.

50. For theoretical discussion of how certain discrete symbols may come to evoke the Totality, see V. Turner, *The Forest of Symbols* (Ithaca,

1967): chap. 1–2 (passim) and J. Fernandez' article "The Performance of Ritual Metaphors" in J. David Sapir (ed.), *The Social Uses of Metaphor* (Philadelpha, 1977), esp. p. 126. For an illustration, see my article "The Sabbath in the Kabbalah," *Judaism* 31:1 (1982): 34–35.

51. *Shaʿarei 'Orah*, edited by J. Ben-Shlomo (Jerusalem, 1970) 2:50. Although only eight sefirot are mentioned here, elsewhere Joseph Giqatilia extends the Sabbath-unity to all ten rungs. See n. 53 below.

52. In this instance *Tif'eret* includes *Neẓaḥ*, *Hod*, and *Yesod*.

53. This notion of Shabbat as a *multi-tiered* sefirotic union is also found in Joseph Giqatilia, *Shaʿarei 'Orah* 1:108. There it is the two discrete sefirotic "Sabbaths," *Binah* and *Yesod*, which bind the divine world into one. He begins:

> Shabbat is the essence of the Tree moving from below to on high. . . . It is the mystery of the unification of all the sefirot . . . for the Sabbath [here *Yesod*] binds the final sefirah, *'Adni*, with all the rungs on high.

In the continuation of the passage, he clarifies that this sefirotic union is actually a joint effort of the two discrete "Sabbaths": As *Yesod* (the lower Sabbath) integrates *Malkhut* into the divine Gestalt, "*Binah* [the supernal Sabbath] binds the two sefirot above Her with the six below."

Finally, on the correlation of Shabbat with the divine totality, see the Spanish-Italian adept Joseph ibn Shraga's *Sod Qiddush le-Maʿalei Shabbeta'* (ca. 1500). Combining sefirotic and letter mysticism (see p. 30 above), ibn Shraga wrote:

> Shabbat . . . is composed of the ten sefirot which are the ten letters [in the divine Name written *plene*]:
>
> יוד הא ואו הא
>
> (printed in Abraham Elmalik, *Liqquṭei Shikheḥah u-Fe'ah* [Ferrara, 1556] fol. 39a.)

54. For full documentation of the editions used see the Bibliography.

55. On this Kabbalist, see p. 9 and p. 44 n. 20 above. Also see the sketch in EJ 10:354 and the bibliography there; the EJ's claim that R. Judah ben Yaqar studied under Isaac the Blind is, however, most unlikely.

56. On Azriel, see p. 11 above. For additional information, see G. Scholem, *Ursprung:* 324 ff. and *Ha-Qabbalah be-Gerona;* and I. Tishby, *Ḥiqrei ha-Qabbalah u-Sheluḥoteha* (Jerusalem, 1982): 3–35.

57. On R. Asher ben David, one of the critical links between Provençal and Catalonian Kabbalah in the early thirteenth century, see EJ 3:706 and *Ursprung:* index. For collected sources, see J. Dan (ed.), *Ha-Qabbalah shel R. 'Asher ben David* (Jerusalem, 1979).

58. This work was begun in Catalonia in the 1250's but completed in Acco, following Naḥmanides' escape from Spain in 1267.

59. G. Scholem attributes authorship to "the circle of R. Jacob." On this mystic and his circle, see pp. 13–15 above.

60. On Ṭodros Abulafia see p. 15 and G. Scholem, *Kabbalah:* 53ff.

61. I have used 3 MS sources for the *Rimmon:* Brit. Mus. 759; Moscow 219; and Cambridge Add. 1516. Unless specifically indicated, my citations will follow the Brit. Mus. MS. Happily for the reader, two critical editions of the *Rimmon* have become available recently. See now Elliot Wolfson's complete edition of the work, (Ph.D. diss., Brandeis Univ., 1986) and Dorit Cohen-Aloro's edition, *Sefer ha-Rimmon: Miẓvot lo' taᶜaseh* (Jerusalem, 1987).

On *Sefer ha-Mishqal* (also called *Ha-Nefesh ha-Ḥakhamah*) see the doctoral dissertation of J. Wijnhoven (Brandeis Univ., 1964). The *Sodot,* mystical varia on the Sabbath and holidays, has been preserved in two MSS, Schocken 14 fol. 78–99 and Vatican 428 fol. 19a–48b. Citations will generally follow the Schocken edition.

62. A version of Joseph Giqatilia's *Sodot* is printed at the back of the 1817 Lemberg (Lwow) edition of the *Noᶜam 'Elimelekh.* I have also consulted JTSA Mic. 1609 fol. 117a-20a; MS Vatican 214 (fol. 64a); and the version in *Sefer Heikhal ha-Shem* of R. Yeḥiel Ashkenazi (Venice, 1601): 40a–b.

In his early years Joseph Giqatilia (1248–ca. 1325) was a leading student of Abraham Abulafia; he later became a theosophic Kabbalist, a close associate of Moshe de Leon. On Giqatilia, see p. 15 above; G. Scholem, *Kabbalah:* 409–11; E. Gottlieb, *Meḥqarim:* 96–131 and 257–343; J. Ben-Shlomo's introduction to *Shaᶜarei 'Orah;* and A. Farber, "Qetaᶜ Ḥadash me-Haqdamat R. Yosef Giqaṭilia le-Sefer Ginnat 'Egoz," *Meḥqerei Yerushalayim be-Maḥshevet Yisra'el* 1 (1981): 158–76.

63. I have used the Cheval edition of Baḥyya ben Asher's writings throughout. On R. Baḥyya ben Asher as a Kabbalist, see E. Gottlieb in *Tarbiẓ* 33 (1963/64): 287–313 and idem, *Ha-Qabbalah be-Khitvei R. Baḥyya ben 'Asher* (Jerusalem, 1970).

64. This work is divided into two sections, only the first of which has been edited. For the miẓvot of commission, I have relied on the Menaḥem Meier critical edition (cited below); for the miẓvot of omission, I have used MS JTSA Mic. 1722, esp. fol. 114a–17b.

Little is known regarding the life of R. Joseph of Hamadan. This innovative Kabbalist was most likely Castilian, despite his Persian appellation (Hebrew: *R. Yosef ha-ba' mi-Shushan ha-birah*). On his thought see E. Gottlieb, *Meḥqarim:* 248–56; Menaḥem Meier's dissertation on *Sefer Ṭaᶜamei ha-Miẓvot*/Section 1 (Ph.D., Brandeis Univ., 1974); J. Zwelling's introduction to "Sefer Tashak: Critical Text with Introduction" (Ph.D. thesis, Brandeis Univ.,

1975) and M. Idel, "Perush ᶜEser Sefirot u-Seridim mi-Ketavim shel R. Yosef ha-ba' mi-Shushan ha-Birah," *ᶜAlei Sefer* 6–7 (1979): 74–84.

65. On this work, see M. Idel, Ibid: 82–84.

66. On R. David ben Judah see G. Scholem, "Peraqim le-Toledot Sifrut ha-Qabbalah," KS 4 (1926): 286–327; D. Matt (ed.), *The Book of Mirrors: Sefer Mar'ot ha-Ẓove'ot* (Chico, 1982) and idem in HUCA (1980): 129–72. On the *'Or Zaruᶜa* see A. Marmorstein, "David ben Jehuda Hasid" in MGWJ 71 (1927): 39ff. On R. David's circle, see M. Idel, "Ḥomer Qabbali mi-Beit Midrasho shel R. David ben Yehuda he-Ḥasid," *Meḥqerei Yerushalayim be-Maḥshevet Yisra'el* 2 (1983): 169–207 and idem, "La prière kabbalistique et les couleurs" in R. Goetschal (ed.), *Prière, Mystique et Judaisme* (Paris, 1987): 107–19.

67. M. Idel has suggested that R. Joseph ben Shalom was active in the last two decades of the thirteenth century, probably in conjunction with R. David ben Judah he-Ḥasid (oral communication). M. Ḥalamish has argued for a mid-fourteenth century dating (before 1358). On R. Joseph ben Shalom Ashkenazi, see M. Ḥallamish's introduction to the critical edition of the *Perush* (Jerusalem, 1985) and idem, EJ 10:236–37.

R. Joseph ben Shalom's writings on Shabbat appear to have had a certain influence on the *Temunah* circle.

68. In his youth Shem Ṭov ibn Gaon of Soria was a student of RaSHBa and Isaac ben Ṭodros. He later immigrated to Safed and wrote a work of ecstatic Kabbalah, *Baddei ha-'Aron.* For details see EJ 8:1174–75.

The *Keter Shem Ṭov* was a prime example of the so-called Naḥmanidean supercommentaries (explications of the RaMBaN's *sodot* on the Torah) which constituted an important Kabbalistic literary genre between 1290–1330. Other examples included in the present study are the *Be'ur Sodot ha-RaMBaN* of Joshua ibn Shuayb and the *Maᶜarekhet ha-'Elohut* (both written by students of RaSHBa and Isaac ben Ṭodros); and the *Me'irat ᶜEinayim* of Isaac ben Samuel of Acco. The earlier *Perush ᶜal ha-Torah* of R. Baḥyya ben Asher contained explications of the RaMBaN's *sodot* but was not limited to this endeavor. For further discussion of these supercommentaries, see G. Scholem, *Ursprung:* Chap. 3; E. Gottlieb, *Ha-Qabbalah be-Khitvei R. Baḥyya ben 'Asher;* and M. Idel, "Perush Lo' Yaduᶜa le-Sodot ha-RaMBaN," *Daᶜat* 2–3 (1978–79): 120–26.

69. Attributed to his disciple, Meir ben Solomon ibn Sahula. See G. Scholem, *Kabbalah:* 61; E. Gottlieb, *Meḥqarim:* index; and Z. Galili's article in *Meḥqerei Yerushalayim be-Maḥshevet Yisra'el* 4 (1985): 83–96.

70. On R. Isaac ben Samuel, see p. 21 and p. 51 (n. 61) above.

71. On this work, see E. Gottlieb, EJ 11: 637–39 and *Meḥqarim:* 289–343.

72. On Menaḥem Recanati, see E. Gottlieb, *Meḥqarim:* 573–75 and the sources therein.

73. On Joseph ibn Waqar see p. 20 above; *Kabbalah:* 63–64; and A. Habermann (ed.), *Shirei ha-Yiḥud ve-ha-Kavod:* 99–123.

74. On the *Temunah,* see p. 23 and p. 52 (n. 69) above.

75. The *Perush* is generally held to be written shortly after the *Temunah.* On the two other titles, variant recensions of the same text, see the sources cited in n. 74. Also see n. 40 above. As noted, the Sabbath-symbolism of this Circle is complex and idiosyncratic. Although I will refer to these works in the motif studies, a more sustained analysis will be undertaken elsewhere.

76. Menaḥem Ẓiyyoni, a Palestinian-born adept who flourished in the late fourteenth to early fifteenth century, combined theosophic Kabbalah with the esoteric theology of Ḥasidei 'Ashkenaz. For details see J. Dan, EJ: 1313–14 and idem, *Torat ha-Sod shel Ḥasidei 'Ashkenaz:* 259f.

77. The dating and location follow the conclusions drawn by Michal Oron in her recent study "Ha-Peli'ah ve-ha-Qanah" and are supported by the findings of I. Ta-Shma and S. Bowman. See p. 51 n. 65 above.

78. On this manuscript, see G. Sed-Rajna, "De quelques commentaires kabbalistique sur le rituel dans les manuscrits de la Bibliothèque Nationale de Paris," *Revue des Etudes Juives* 124 (1965): 307–51.

79. This work incorporates material from various mystical streams, including Ḥasidei 'Ashkenaz, the *Bahir,* Gerona Kabbalah, Abraham Abulafia, and Byzantine Kabbalah (e.g., the *Qanah*). Citations follow the (partial) edition printed in Koretz in 1784. Comparison with the complete MS (Oxf. Bodl. 1565) revealed only the most minor differences in matters concerning *sod ha-Shabbat.*

On R. Moshe ben Jacob and his writings, see p. 23 and p. 52 (n. 70) above. Also see EJ 12:420–21. On *Shoshan Sodot,* also see Ḥayyim Lieberman, *'Ohel RaḤeL* (Brooklyn, 1980) 1:93ff.

80. On Judah Ḥayyaṭ, a leading Kabbalist of the Spanish Exilic period, see G. Scholem, "Li-Ydiʿat ha-Qabbalah bi-Sefarad ʿErev ha-Gerush," *Tarbiẓ* 24 (1954): 167ff. and E. Gottlieb, *Meḥqarim:* 439–75 and 493–505.

81. This conclusion is based, in part, on my provisional assignment of the *Temunah* circle to the Byzantine setting. See p. 23 above.

82. The relative dearth of fresh Spanish sources from the mid-fourteenth to late fifteenth centuries raises a series of questions. Is this paucity the function of a diminished literary interest in Sabbath ritual (as opposed to sefirotic theory, e.g.) or of diminished bibliographic evidence (the loss of manuscripts in the strife-torn decades preceding and following the Expulsion)? To what extent may the dearth be correlated with the general dissipation

of creative energy in the Spanish Kabbalah of this period? Finally, how is the paucity of Spanish sources explained in light of the rising influence of earlier Kabbalistic interpretations of the Sabbath, including those of the *Zohar*, TZ/RM, and Baḥyya ben Asher? (As noted, some of these ideas had penetrated into more exoteric Spanish works.)

83. A few passages may be noted here: See *Menorat ha-Ma'or* (Enelow ed.) 2:182 on divine union during *Mova'ei Shabbat* and on a mystical reading of Ps. 96:10 (ff. views held by Jacob bar Sheshet in *Sefer ha-'Emunah ve-ha-Biṭṭaḥon* [*Kitvei RaMBaN* 2:363] and David ben Judah he-Ḥasid in OZ, MS JTSA fol. 39a); 2:197 on the mystical meaning of *Havdalah* (ff. Baḥyya); 3:570 on "keeping Shabbat" (ff. *Bahir* and the *Zohar*); and 3:602–03 (ff. TZ on the Sabbath). Also see Joseph Albo's *ʿIqqarim* (Husik ed.) 2:11 and 3:64–65 for a philosophical recasting of the sefirotic Shabbat; and *ʿAqedat Yiẓḥaq* "Va-Yaqhel" for a Zoharic view of the divine Sabbath (ff. Z 3:94a–b).

84. To clarify the terminology: *Restore*, like its near synonym *renew*, refers to the intensive vivification experienced during the Sabbath day. Through Renewal/Restoration, Being is transformed and brought back to its ideal. *Sustain* is a broader term, referring not only to the Sabbath-renewal but to its longer-range effects which endure, albeit in diminished fashion, into the week.

85. On this miẓvah, see Appendix II below; Z 1:112a (MN); and *Sod ha-Shabbat:* Section 12.

86. This is especially true in the *Bahir* and *Zohar*.

87. See *Bahir* 57, 58, and 158.

88. The concept of the divine Sabbath as axis mundi was probably alluded to by RaMBaN's teacher, R. Judah ben Yaqar, although the extreme brevity of the text precludes certainty. Consider the following discourse on the prayer *Tikkanta Shabbat* (the middle of the seven *Musaf* benedictions for Shabbat). A theosophic reading of the passage yields:

> In Spain it is written *Tikkanta Shabbat,* [conventionally,] "You have established the Sabbath" for it is written: "[Wisdom] has hewn out her seven pillars" [upon which the world stands] [Prv. 9:1; cf. TB Sanh. 38a and Ḥag. 12b]. Hence Shabbat [sefirotically, *Yesod*] is called a pillar and pillars are said to establish [the world] [ff. Ps. 75:4]. . . . And so, *Tiqqanta*—"You have established"—is said with respect to Shabbat for the pillar of Shabbat is more perfect than the six pillars of the week [sefirotically, the other lower rungs or 'days'].
>
> (*Perush ha-Tefillot ve-ha-Berakhot* 1:110–11)

The theosophic reading suggested here coheres with the view expressed elsewhere in *Perush ha-Tefillot ve-ha-Berakhot* (2:42) that *Yesod* (the male Sabbath) is *Ẓaddiq Yesod ʿOlam,* the Foundation of the Cosmos. It also coheres with the view developed in the *Bahir* (ff. TB Ḥag. 12b) that Shabbat/*Yesod* is the most perfect of the seven sefirotic pillars (or 'Days') on which the world stands. (See G. Scholem, *Origins of the Kabbalah:* 152–53; and cf. Z 1:82a and 186a.) However, a purely midrashic explanation of R. Judah ben Yaqar's words is also possible, extrapolating from the view advanced in TB Sanh. 38a and Lev. R 11:1 that "the seven pillars were the seven days of Creation" and from the dictum that the Sabbath was *ḥemdat yamim,* "the most desired of days" (from the Sabbath liturgy and an old tradition ascribed to *Targum Yerushalmi* to Gen. 2:2).

89. See the discussion on pp. 123–24 above.

90. See RaMBaN to Gen. 2:3. It may be noted that TZḤ 99c also links the Sabbath-soul with *Yesod:*

> From [*Yesod*] comes the abundance of extra-souls that accrues to people on Shabbat.

91. See Z 1: 259b and 3:302b where the *Zohar* correlates the welling up of abundance within *Yesod* most closely with *Musaf,* i.e., the *Additional,* Sabbath service. This conception is, in part, based on the much older association of *Yesod* with "Joseph," Heb. *YoSeF,* which literally connotes, abundance or increase.

Also see the recasting of the *Zohar*'s interpretation in TZḤ 99c:

> An additional portion [*musaf*] issues forth from the aspect of *Ẓaddiq* who is the crown of all *musafin* [abundance]. . . . In it is the surfeit of *Ḥokhmah, Binah, Daᶜat* and all the aspects of the Holy One. . . .

For a different symbolism, see the *Rimmon* text in n. 98 below.

92. "World-that-is-Coming": Heb., *ᶜolam ha-ba'.* I have generally rendered this phrase in the more traditional fashion, World-to-Come. However, it often has a more dynamic connotation in the *Zohar* which I wish to capture here. Cf., e.g., 3:290b (IZ) where *Binah* is described as "the world that is coming, constantly coming and never stopping." For further discussion see D. Matt: 267 ff.

93. See, e.g., 2:63b. Also see Z 3:273a (RM). This image is found in many other Kabbalistic sources of the late thirteenth century. To name but a few: Joseph Giqatilia, *Shaᶜarei 'Orah* 1:113 and *Sodot* section 4; Baḥyya ben Asher to Ex. 20:8; and *Sefer ha-Yiḥud* from the circle of R. Joseph of Hamadan (on "Shalosh Seᶜudot").

94. For further discussion see p. 114 above; and *Sod ha-Shabbat:* Section 15 on *ᶜOneg Shabbat.* On the image of fertilization, also see G. Scholem, OKS: 140 and I. Tishby's explanation in MZ 2:540. On *Shekhinah* as the "Field of Apples," see Y. Liebes, "Ha-Mashiaḥ shel ha-Zohar": 146–47, n. 224.

95. As has been previously noted, the *Zohar* sometimes places the temporal week under the aegis of lower seven sefirot; however, in other

instances, the six weekdays are thought to be under the sway of the angelic worlds below. In this schema, only Shabbat is under the direct influence of the divine realm. On these two interpretations, see MZ 2:498.

96. In typical Kabbalistic fashion, *Sabbath* has double meaning in this passage. On one level it refers to the sefirotic Sabbath (*Shekhinah*) while in a more general sense, it connotes the Sabbath-day.

97. Also see Z 3:144b. According to another passage, 2:61b, this flow of blessing occurs on a reduced scale during the week. There are many parallels in post-Zoharic literature. Cf., e.g., the slightly later *Meᶜirat ᶜEinayim:* 174. One interesting difference is that *Shekhinah goes up* to receive Sabbath-blessing:

> Each Sabbath day the Diadem ascends with the sefirotic Sabbath day unto the supernal King which is *Binah* to receive bounty for the ensuing six weekdays—that [She] may direct the world with this bounty.

98. Moshe de Leon carried the motif of Cosmic Blessing into his Hebrew writings as well, most notably *Sefer ha-Rimmon,* where Sabbath-renewal was linked with certain moments in the liturgy. To cite two examples:

(1) The morning benediction *Yoẓer 'Or* (He who forms light) dramatizes the spiritual abundance enjoyed on this day, when blessing descends like a river of light:

> On Shabbat, [*Yoẓer 'Or*] refers to the surfeit of spirit coming from the "river that goes out from Eden" [the supernal Sabbath], the source whence the souls blossom. All worlds rejoice in this [abundance]; there is plenty of nourishment for all. . . . "For on the seventh day [sic!] He gives you *leḥem yomayim* (Ex. 16:29),"

a double portion of food, spiritual nourishment. Kabbalistically, *leḥem yomayim* refers to the nourishment of the two lower Sabbaths, *Tif'eret* and *Shekhinah,* who are now as one. (MS Brit. Mus., fol. 30b)

(2) During the *Musaf* service cosmic blessing abounds; the devotee's soul is bathed in light as *Shekhinah* recovers Her primordial splendor:

> *Musaf* is the abundance of light in the soul [sefirotically, *Shekhinah*] . . . for the Moon unites with the light of the sun [*Tif'eret,* the masculine Sabbath] as during the seven primordial days. All is set aright, in perfect balance. This service is called the *Musaf* of Shabbat because of the Moon's [i.e., the feminine Sabbath's] abundance, Her perfect fullness. . . . Surfeit, expansion and divine plenitude are found on Shabbat more than on other days. . . . The branches and boughs [of the sefirotic tree] are united. . . . The Totality is uniquely restored. . . . (Ibid. 32a)

99. Also see *Shaᶜarei 'Orah* 1:106:

> Shabbat corresponds to the sefirah *Yesod,* the rung *'El Ḥai* (the living God). Hence, the Sabbath day is called the fount of all blessings

and holiness, as it is said: " '*Elohim* blessed the seventh day and made it holy, for [the divine] Shabbat is in it [re-reading Gen. 2:3]." The [supernal] Sabbath is the source for all blessings and for the efflux of holiness which streams below.

100. Cf. TB Ber. 57b, AZ 3a, and many others. The presence of the appositive term, *Jubilee*, in Giqatilia's interpretation suggests that he is reading World-to-Come as the future Age rather than "the hereafter."

101. There may be elements of this understanding—minus the specific theosophical meaning—in the Rabbinic teaching itself. Much depends on how the term World-to-Come is construed. See the discussion in n. 46 above and J. Guttmann's comments on the World-to-Come in *Philosophies of Judaism* (New York: 1964): 37. Guttmann, however, overlooks the ambiguity of the term.

102. See pp. 26–27 above.

103. From Menaḥem Recanati's *Perush:* ad Ex. 20:8. Also see ad Gen. 2:3. On the divine Sabbath as source of cosmic blessing in R. Baḥyya ben Asher, see his comments to Gen. 2:3. This source is cited in another context in this chapter. See p. 125 above. For other germane sources, see R. Joseph ben Shalom Ashkenazi, *Perush le-Farashat Bere'shit:* 191; and *Sod ha-Shabbat,* Section 20. R. Joseph ben Shalom maintained that on Shabbat, *Binah* and the upper sefirot hold sway. Indeed, "all the springs [lower sefirot] cease [their activities] and derive enjoyment from the World-to-Come"—*Binah*— "the supernal Sabbath, Sabbath-delight." For "[Sabbath-Delight] is like a Pond which is filled with water from the Spring [*Ḥokhmah*]. From the Pond all the fields are watered. This is true blessing."

104. The notion that divine *shefaᶜ* suffuses the world on Shabbat is also found in at least one work of ecstatic Kabbalah, Abraham Abulafia's *Sitrei Torah,* MS Paris 774 fol. 154a–b, section "Sod ha-Moᶜed ve-Shabbat ve-Khippur." Abulafia correlated the Sabbath day with the increased flow of supernal energy from the Active Intellect and hence, with heightened mystical understanding for the person whose intellect cleaves to its Source. See there for details.

105. See Eliade's *The Sacred and the Profane:* Chap. 1 and *Patterns in Comparative Religion* (New York, 1958): Chap. 10 for general discussion.

106. A. Green, "Sabbath as Temple": 293.

107. This is seemingly true of pre-Kabbalistic medieval writers as well. A rare exception is Abraham ha-Kohen, an early eleventh century liturgical poet from Palestine, who wrote about a narcissus "encircled by six petals like the Sabbath is by the weekdays." See T. Carmi, ed. *The Penguin Book of Hebrew Verse* (New York, 1981): 304.

108. According to Aggadic tradition the world was created out of this point, spreading forth in all directions. In one account, the Stone was likened to the navel of an embryo around which the fetus grows. Tradition identified the Founding Stone with the ground on which the Holy of Holies was erected. For sources see Tanḥ. B. "Qedoshim" 10 and Mid. Ps. 50:2. Cf. TB Sanh. 37a, Cant. R 7:5, Eccles. R 1:1, et al.

109. Arthur Green has noted this mystical relativization of Space in his "Sabbath as Temple": 302.

110. Images traditionally associated with Jerusalem include the lush garden at the center (Zion as Eden), the world-*omphalos,* the pupil of the world's eye, the cosmic pillar, etc. It is my contention that Shabbat became a kind of "cosmic Jerusalem" in the Kabbalistic tradition. This thesis will be supported throughout this section.

111. Cf. the *Me'irat ᶜEinayim:* 22. Drawing on the vocabulary of sacred architecture, R. Isaac of Acco likened the sefirotic world to the *mishkan.* Its various sections are held together by the divine Sabbath (here *Yesod*), which gives the shrine structural integrity:

> The seventh day, Shabbat, corresponds to *Yesod,* through which the realm is perfected. It completes, binds and unifies all; it is "the central bar between the planks running from one end to the other" (Ex. 26:28) . . . it brings together "heaven and earth" [the upper and lower rungs]. . . . By means of [Shabbat] all ten [aspects] become one.

112. *Menorot,* of course, were present in the two Temples, as well.

113. Perhaps there is a halakhic basis for this Kabbalistic view, stemming from the notion that preparing for Shabbat should not start later than Wednesday. Cf. TB Shab. 19a. For another possible legal impetus, see the definition of the week found in TB Giṭ. 77a; Pes. 106a and RaSHI ad loc.

114. See *Me'irat ᶜEinayim:* 175 where Shabbat (associated with *Tif'eret/ Yesod*) is called the "essence of the matter" and the Central Column or main artery of the cosmic Tree. The festivals (identified with *Ḥesed, Gevurah, Neẓah* and *Hod*) are Sabbath's branches, "drawing from [its] holiness . . . its unbounded heritage." In a startling simile, R. Isaac of Acco likens Shabbat to divinity (*YHWH*) and the festivals to "*'eilim,*" angelic beings in need of divine sustenance:

> Hence, Scripture states: "Who is like You, *YHWH* among the *'eilim;* who is like You, majestic in holiness." [Ex. 15:11] "You, *YHWH*" alludes to the inner essence, the Central Column, the "majestic holiness." None among the *'eilim* are as exalted as You. For they draw from Your holiness. . . .

Also see the earlier source, Z 3:94a–b, wherein the three pilgrimage festivals (sefirotically, the peripheral rungs) are nourished by the holiness of Shabbat, here *Tif'eret*, the hub of the sefirotic world. The *Zohar* explains that Shabbat is always called *qodesh* in the Torah; for it is, by nature sacred, in perpetual contact with the source of holiness, *Ḥokhmah*. The festivals, by contrast, are termed *miqra'ei qodesh*, conventionally, "holy convocations," but here: days that must be called unto holiness, periodically invited to partake of it. Their sacrality is attained by cleaving unto Shabbat: "All the [other] sefirot ["festivals"] are invited unto Holiness; they link themselves unto Shabbat and are crowned with it."

For more on the ontological distinction between Sabbath and the Festivals, see p. 280 n. 24 below.

115. The conventional model derives, of course, from Gen. 1–2:3. Also see Mekh. "Ba-Ḥodesh" 7 (to Ex. 20:8):

> R. Isaac [alt. version, R. Judah ben Beteira] says: . . . Count the days towards the Sabbath . . . saying, the first day of Shabbat [= Sunday], the second day of Shabbat [= Monday], and so forth, as it is said: "Remember [i.e., daily] the Sabbath day" [Ex. 20:8].

Also see RaMBaN to Ex. 12:2 and to 20:8. Many Kabbalists drew upon both models, viewing the Sabbath as now the endpoint and now the center of the week. For example, Baḥyya ben Asher (ad Ex. 12:2) upheld the conventional model of the week as the *peshaṭ* of Ex. 20:8, but spoke of the "Sabbath at the center" in his more esoteric interpretations. For illustrations see pp. 91–92 above and nn. 120 and 135 below.

116. See p. 80 above.

117. See *Bahir* 155.

118. That is, the seventh sefirah is called the Sabbath of "Remember" (*Shabbat shel Zakhor* ff. Ex. 20:8) because it is the quintessentially male rung (Heb., *zakhar*). This mystical word-play may be traced to the *Bahir*'s rendering of Ex. 20:8, *Zakhor 'et yom ha-Shabbat:* "Correlate the Sabbath day with the male rung." (sec. 180 and 182).

119. The use of the menorah as a symbol for the seven lower sefirot goes back at least as far as *Perush Shem ha-Meforash* of R. David ben Asher, printed in *Ha-Segullah* (1932). For discussion, see E. Gottlieb, *Meḥqarim:* 564f.

120. On this image cf. G. Scholem, OKS: 137 and the *Shenei Luḥot ha-Berit* (SHeLaH) of Isaiah Horowitz, "Massekhet Shabbat." The centrality of Shabbat in the spiritual week is also expressed by R. Baḥyya ben Asher in his commentary to Ex. 1:2–3:

> The Sabbath is the middle day of the week . . . three come before and three after. . . . It is known that Sabbath eve begins on Wednesday [ff. TB Shab. 19a?]. . . . Thus, the seventh day is also the midpoint, the fourth.

That is, it is like *Malkhut,* which is both fourth (in emanation) and seventh (in the final ordering of the active sefirot). Cf. also *Sod* 13, appended to the printed edition of Moshe de Leon's *Ha-Nefesh ha-Ḥakhamah.*

The notion that each day partakes of Shabbat is given a specific moralistic coloration in the *Re'shit Ḥokhmah* of the sixteenth century Kabbalist, Elijah de Vidas. In "Shaᶜar ha-Qedushah," Chapter 2, he wrote:

> Because the holiness of Shabbat is present each day one must think of it and reflect on its holiness daily. . . . One must act each day in accord with the holiness of Shabbat . . . for it is the centerpoint around which the six days revolve.

This notion is further extended in later Kabbalistic and Ḥasidic sources. See Judah Aryeh Leib Alter, *Sefat 'Emet,* "Ki Tissa'" for a striking example.

121. Joseph of Hamadan's terminology clearly evokes the legend of the Founding Stone (n. 108 above). His earlier comment that the week is nourished by Shabbat may also be influenced—at least in part—by *'aggadot* of the sacred center. According to Rabbinic sources, the Founding Stone is also the omphalos which nourishes the surrounding world. Cf. Tos. Suk. 3:15; TJ Suk. 54d; TB Suk. 49a; Eccles. R 1:1; and "Midrash be-Ḥokhmah Yasad 'Areẓ" in A. Jellinek, *Beit ha-Midrash* 5:63. It is also possible that R. Joseph, like other thirteenth century Kabbalists surveyed here, was influenced by the remark in *Sefer Yeẓirah* 4:4: There "are seven dimensions: the six *qeẓavot* [directions], up, down, east, west, north and south, with the Holy Sanctuary [the seventh dimension!] in the center, supporting them all." On this passage, see also p. 92 above.

122. Once again, this image was previously used with respect to Jerusalem. Cf. *Massekhet 'Ereẓ Zuṭa'* 9 and *Maḥzor Viṭri* (Ish-Hurwitz ed.) p. 723 where the world is likened to the human eye: the white is the ocean which encompasses the earth; the iris is the earth upon which humans dwell; and the pupil is Jerusalem.

123. The reference here, of course, is to the midrash in Gen. R 11:8; it is quoted on pp. 102–03 above.

124. My surmise is that Moshe de Leon was, in fact, the prime innovator of this imagery. Given the dating of the germane literature, it is probable that his thinking exerted an influence on Joseph Giqatilia. It is virtually certain that de Leon influenced Menaḥem Recanati's circle imagery (discussed on p. 91) as well. Compare!

125. The two upper rungs are secreted within.

126. In addition to the geometric significance highlighted here, the term *points* (Heb., *nequddot*) has a linguistic meaning, denoting the Hebrew vowel-points. (Like the Hebrew alphabet, vowels were given mystical weight in Kabbalah.) In both the *Mishqal* and *Rimmon,* Moshe de Leon correlated the three divine Sabbaths with specific *nequddot. Ḥokhmah/Binah* (the Great

Sabbath) was symbolized as the *ḥolam,* a point or tiny circle written above the consonant. *Tif'eret/Yesod,* the so-called Sabbath day, was correlated with the *shuruq,* a point written alongside the consonant at mid-staff. The third Sabbath, *Malkhut* (Sabbath night), was denoted by the *ḥiriq,* a vowel-point written beneath the consonant. The following illustration is based on the description in *Rimmon,* MS Cambridge Add. 1516 fol. 30a-b:

Figure 7: The Divine Shabbat as a Configuration of Vowel-Points (illustrated with the letter *WaW*)

The symbolism of the "Sabbath at the center" was extended in the ensuing *Rimmon* passage (fol. 32a). Each vowel-point was said to nestle within a larger point or circle:

> The first Sabbath is the lowest vowel-point, the Sabbath-Night. The Sabbath that stands with Her and in which She is encompassed is the Sabbath Day [*Tif'eret*]. And if you say that the [Sabbath] Day is the Life-of-the-Worlds [*Yesod*], in any event, [*Yesod* too] is contained in the middle vowel-point [*Tif'eret*]. And this is the [mystery of the *consonantal* symbol of the divine Male, the letter] *WaW* [written *plene* as וו], i.e., two sefirot that are one. . . .
>
> The Great Sabbath is the highest vowel-point for in that point [here *Ḥokhmah*] is contained the supernal one [*Binah*]. In actuality, however, the three vowel-points are one . . .

suggesting the possibility that the entire sefirotic pleroma was envisioned as a series of concentric circles with *Malkhut* at its innermost core. For a likely parallel, see *Me'irat ʿEinayim* (Goldreich ed.): 118.

127. *Ḥalal* may also be rendered 'womb,' thereby introducing a sexual dimension into the discussion.

Also see *Sefer ha-Rimmon* (MS Brit. Mus. fol. 90b) where the danger of encroaching on the Center is clearly both personal and cosmic. To enter the Point (here *Shekhinah*), that Sanctuary which is Shabbat, one must first love Her:

> Whoever seeks to disrupt the empty space which is the Center Point called Shabbat, that person's punishment is death [ff. Ex. 31:14]. . . . Scripture says "*Meḥalaleha,*" those who profane Her, i.e., enter Her chamber [*beit ḥalalah:* again suggesting a sexual organ or womb] without guarding Her. . . . One must not enter into the hollow of the Circle, without keeping and revering it [Shabbat]. . . . For She is the Hub of the [cosmic] circle, holding all entities together.

The consequences of profaning Shabbat (and the sacred Center) are also discussed in Z 1:5b–6a. See there for details. On the sexual overtones attached to Sabbath profanation, see also n. 131 and Appendix I, below.

128. For a variant of this *Rimmon* passage, see Ibid. MS Cambridge Add. 1516 fol. 31b–32a. For Zoharic parallels, see Z 1:71b, 72a, 231a and 2:222a.

129. For a fascinating variant, see Joseph Giqatilia, *Shaᶜarei 'Orah* 2:46–48 where it is the male Sabbath, *Yesod,* that is threatened!

On the *qelippot,* the "husks" or "shells" that surround divinity, see I. Tishby, MZ 1:298–301; and *Sod ha-Shabbat,* n. 591. Also see A. Altmann, "The Motif of Shells in Azriel of Gerona" in idem, *Studies in Religious Philosophy and Mysticism* (Ithaca, 1969): 172–79.

130. Cf. its usage in Moshe de Leon's *Mishqal* and *Rimmon,* cited above.

131. As in the *Rimmon* passage quoted in n. 127 above, there may be sexual overtones to this notion of profanation, suggesting improper union or rape. On the sexual connotations of entering the cosmic center/*Shekhinah*—variously imaged as the supernal Jerusalem, Temple, sacred chamber, and Holy of Holies—see Y. Liebes, "Ha-Mashiaḥ shel ha-Zohar": 194.

132. *Kitvei R. Baḥyya ben 'Asher* (Jerusalem, 1970): 392.

133. Kabbalistically, *Holy (QaDoSH)* is a common appellation for *Malkhut.* See p. 85 above.

134. Cf. TB Soṭah 8b and the Scriptural passages noted in n. 5 above.

135. On the *qeẓavot* cf. n. 121 (end) above. For another example of Baḥyya ben Asher's symbolic equation of Holy Land/Jerusalem/Temple and Shabbat, see his *Perush* ad Ex. 1:2–3:

> The earth is divided into seven climactic zones; the seventh is the Land of Israel, which is at the center of the inhabited world. It has the most perfect balance between cold and hot of all regions for it is equidistant from the extremes. . . . The Temple is in the seventh climactic zone. . . . Now some scientists have written that the Land of Israel is actually the fourth zone. All arrive at the same conclusion, however; for the Land is at the center, with three zones flanking it on this side and three on that. It is thus the fourth from either end, the middle zone, and the seventh. This is similar to the Sabbath which is the middle of the week and the seventh day.

136. Throughout this chapter, we have seen how the symbol of the Sacred Center may be transferred from the realm of space to the realm of Time and even—in the Kabbalah—to the "realm" of the Divine. It is interesting to note a related development, the Zoharic use of that simulta-

neously "temporal" and "divine" trope—Shabbat—to indicate human centrality, to mark a person as an axis mundi or salvific figure. In the *'Idra' Rabba'* (Z 3:144b–45b), the six comrades are likened to the six sefirot stretching from *Ḥesed* to *Yesod,* while R. Shimon is their Shabbat: the instantiation of *Binah,* the mystical Matrix who sustains the lower rungs. Cf., e.g., 3:144b (IR):

> R. Abba said: We are the six shining lights illumined by the seventh. You [R. Shimon] are the seventh unto [us] all, for the six exist only by virtue of the seventh. All depend on the seventh.
>
> R. Judah called [R. Shimon] "Shabbat," for all six were blessed through him [cf. 2:63b], as it is written: "A Sabbath unto *YHWH*" [Ex. 16:23]. Just as the Sabbath is holy unto *YHWH,* so is R. Shimon Shabbat, holy unto *YHWH* [sefirotically, the six *qeẓavot* from *Ḥesed* to *Yesod*].

As the temporal Shabbat blesses and sustains the world, and paves the way for redemption, so does its human symbol. According to Z 3:145b (IR):

> You, R. Shimon, the seventh unto the six [comrades], will be crowned and blessed more than all others. . . . Through you these righteous comrades will experience delight in the World-to-Come [sefirotically, *Binah*]. For it is written: "If you call the Sabbath 'delight', the Lord's holy ["day"] 'honored' ". Who is the Lord's holy ["day"]? R. Shimon bar Yoḥai, who is called honored in this world and in the World-to-Come.

This Shabbat symbolism is used more broadly—generically—in the RM. In 2:142b, e.g., sage-mystics as a group are designated as "Shabbat" whereas the common folk are "the weekdays." According to 3:29a, "the sage is like the Sabbath day." He maintains the quality of Shabbat throughout the week, for "his *nefesh* [soul] is called the Sabbath-Queen, the additional Sabbath-soul."

This motif of the righteous person as Shabbat had a certain impact on later Jewish thought, e.g., in Ḥasidic *Torat ha-Ẓaddiq.* For a succinct example, see *'Or Yiẓḥaq* of R. Yiẓḥaq of Radwil (Jerusalem, 1961), "Parashat Noaḥ": 24a.

137. In his OZ. In *Sefer Mar'ot ha-Ẓove'ot,* R. David tended towards a more dualistic view. See D. Matt, *Book of Mirrors:* 29–31 for details.

138. See e.g., *Me'irat ʿEinayim* (Goldreich ed.): 21, 165 and 366. Although the 'dualists' held that the union of *Tif'eret/Yesod* and *Malkhut* is rent asunder during the week, here it is stated that "*Ẓaddiq* is always with the Diadem without pause. [Hence, Evil has no operative role here.] Were there to be even a second's pause [in their union] the world would be reduced to emptiness." The distinction between the union of the week and that of Shabbat is only a matter of degree: "On Shabbat the Diadem and all the Structure ascends unto *Binah,*" becoming part of a higher, more inclusive unity.

For discussion of the theoretical differences between the harmonists and dualists, see I. Tishby, MZ 1:289–301 and 321–26 and *Sod ha-Shabbat,* nn. 591–92 and n. 605.

139. For example, the relatively harmonistic OZ stresses the separation of Shabbat from the week in its interpretation of the special version of *Hashkivenu* recited on Friday nights:

> During the week we must recite "He who guards His people Israel forever" because the world is under the control of the Princes [the harsher angelic realm] and so we must plead for Compassion upon the world. But when the Sabbath arrives, the world gets out from under that rule and all become subjects of the Holy One. (fol. 39a/54a)

On the other hand, the TZ/RM, which often stresses the radical separation of Shabbat from the week (cf. MZ 2:494–95), softens the distinction in TZ 21 (46a) by allowing that, on Shabbat, Torah-scholars receive a plurality of Sabbath-souls which last into the week. See p. 128 and n. 136 above for details.

Moshe de Leon is even harder to categorize. He regularly alternated between a harmonistic and dualistic view of the Cosmos. That is, in some *Zohar* passages (e.g., 2:204a on bathing) he emphasized the fact that the Counter-World of *Siṭra' 'Aḥra'* holds sway during the week; in other passages, this weekday rule is assigned to Meṭaṭron or the angelic worlds, which are continuous with, if inferior to, the divine realm. (See 1:20b–21a; 2:207b–208b.) In some sections, the *Zohar* underscores the radical separation of the divine lovers, *Tif'eret* and *Shekhinah,* during the week. *Shekhinah* suffers in Exile during this time and can return to Her lover only on Shabbat. (Cf. 1:75a–b, 257a, 2:63b, etc.). Elsewhere, however (2:204b–05a), de Leon claimed that these two enter into sacred union daily, at the propitious hour of midnight. Here, the difference between Shabbat and the week is relative and not absolute. As in the *Me'irat ʿEinayim* (n. 138), the divine couple (merely) reaches a higher rung of union on Shabbat.

140. *Star of Redemption,* transl. by William Hallo (Boston, 1972): 313–15. Holding a decidedly anti-historical view of "Jewish" Time, this great theologian independently developed an understanding of Shabbat that is at times astonishingly close to views developed in classical Kabbalah.

141. For a theoretical perspective on the symbolic representation of Time, see Mircea Eliade, *Sacred and Profane:* Chap. 2; E. Leach, "The Symbolic Representation of Time" in W. Lessa and E. Vogt (eds.), *A Reader in Comparative Religion* (3rd ed.: New York, 1972); and E. Zerubavel's *Hidden Rhythms* (Chicago, 1981), which reflects specifically on the case of Shabbat.

142. See n. 114 above.

143. One of the most succinct examples of this notion is found in a later Kabbalistic work, the *Shenei Luḥot ha-Berit* of Isaiah Horowitz (Tractate Shabbat: "Torah 'Or"). He wrote:

> It is written: "It is a Sabbath unto the Lord [*YHWH*]." As God's Name indicates Past, Present and Future [*HaYaH, HoWeH, YeHeH;* cf. Ex. R 3:6], so does Shabbat. For it refers to the three Sabbaths: The Sabbath of Creation, the Sabbath of the giving of the Torah, and the Sabbath of the future time, a day that is entirely Shabbat.

Following the lead of Ṭur OḤ 292 and other works, he associated the three intermediate blessings of the Sabbath ʿ*Amidah* with these three Sabbaths. "You sanctified" refers to the Sabbath of Creation, "Moses rejoiced" to the Sabbath of the giving of the Torah, and "You are One" to the Future Sabbath. Horowitz continued:

> The Sabbath of Creation attests to the aspect of *HaYaH* . . . the Sabbath of the Giving of the Torah to the aspect of *HoWeH* [our current aeon]: for our ancestors, ourselves and for our children. And the future Sabbath refers to [*YeHeH*], "the day on which the Lord will be one and His Name one." [Zech. 14:9] These three principles of Shabbat contain all the principles within the essence of the divine Name.

144. See *Rimmon* (MS Brit. Mus.) fol. 32a, partially translated in n. 98 above. According to Rabbinic tradition, the moon's light was originally equal to that of the sun. On the legend of the moon's diminution, see TB Ḥul. 60b, Pes. 68a, Shev. 9a; and Gen. R 6:3. For more on its Kabbalistic reinterpretation, see *Sod ha-Shabbat:* Prologue and Section 22 (end), as well as the germane notes.

145. On *'or ha-ganuz,* see TB Ḥag. 12a. On its Kabbalistic usage with reference to Shabbat, see *Perush le-Sefer Temunah* 68b and esp. *Peli'ah* 36b. In mystical sources, beholding this hidden light often signifies enlightenment, experiential knowledge of the divine mysteries.

146. For more detailed discussion of Edenic/Adamic imagery, see e.g., pp. 96, 128, 129–30, 132 and 135 above; and pp. 264–67, 271–72, 281 (n. 29), 282 (n. 33) and 289–92 below. On the cross-indexing of Shabbat and Eden in pre-Kabbalistic sources, see, e.g., Gen. R 16:5.

147. Ff. TB Ber. 52a, Shab. 118b and Mekh. "Yitro" to Ex. 20:8. The Zohar's re-interpretation is a good example of the Kabbalistic mythicization of Rabbinic ritual.

148. The quotation is from *The Sacred and the Profane:* 68. For further discussion see Ibid. chap. 2, and idem, *The Myth of the Eternal Return* (rev. ed., Princeton, 1971).

149. See the discussion in n. 46 above and cf. p. 136 above and Appendix II, pp. 294–96 below.

150. From *Sod ha-Shabbat:* Section 13, pp. 39–40. Meir ibn Gabbai is commenting on the significance of reciting Ps. 124 during the Sabbath morning service. See there for details.

Also cf. Z 2:88b, translated on p. 134 above.

151. Following the formulation in TB Sanh. 97a: "Six thousand years shall the world exist and for one [thousand] it shall lay desolate." Speculation on the nature of this seventh millenium was widespread in medieval thought. Some Kabbalists interpreted the seventh millenium not as "non-existence" but rather as an era of pure spirituality. It was clearly distinguished from the era of Messianic Redemption and Resurrection which was said to occur at the end of the sixth millenium. See, e.g., Moshe de Leon's *Sefer ha-Mishqal:* 92–95.

152. Here, the "divine Sabbath" and "celestial Jerusalem" signify *Binah*. This is a bold claim as most other Kabbalists located the immediate source of the soul's nourishment in *Shekhinah.* See the examples in the ensuing discussion.

153. Citing the Talmudic dictum (TB Shab. 23b) that one should light candles each Sabbath eve because of *shelom bayit,* domestic tranquility, the *Maʿarekhet ha-'Elohut* goes on to disclose its *sod:*

> It is a miẓvah to light candles for it is truly *shelom bayit:* the union of *Shalom* [*Tif'eret/ Yesod*] with *Bayit* [*Malkhut*], the divine "Home." (Ibid.)

Judah Ḥayyaṭ in his *Minḥat Yehudah* (ad loc.) adds:

> It is a miẓvah to light candles [on Sabbath eve] for the Sabbath alludes to the seventh millenium when the Moon's light will be equal to that of the Sun.

154. See OK to TB Ber. 11b; *Sefer Mar'ot ha-Ẓove'ot:* 102; and cf. *Sod ha-Shabbat:* Section 18.

155. *Sod ha-Shabbat:* Section 14.

156. *Mishqal:* 92. Moshe de Leon pointedly rejected the doctrine of periodic creation cycles (or *shemiṭṭot*). For details, see there, pp. 92–95.

157. This doctrine is a curious amalgam of ideas and influences: a mystical re-reading of the Sabbatical [Heb., *shemiṭṭah*!] and Jubilee cycles discussed in Lev. 25, Dt. 15, etc.; combined with Aggadic motifs and speculations on the existence of earlier worlds; and certain Greco-Arabic astrological ideas concerning planetary influence over given cosmic ages.

For Aggadic sources, see TB Sanh. 97b; Gen. R 9; and PRE 51 which speaks metaphorically of cyclical creation—of the continuous rolling and unrolling of the "cosmic scroll."

On astrological (and related philosophical) influences, see G. Scholem, *Ha-Qabbalah shel Sefer ha-Temunah* and idem., *Ursprung:* 408 ff. [*Origins of the Kabbalah:* 462ff.].

158. The three upper rungs remain concealed, without generating aeons that are apparent.

159. That is, the first *shemiṭṭah* was governed by the attribute of grace, *Ḥesed,* and so nourished by the stream of divine love; the second *shemiṭṭah* (according to the *Temunah,* the aeon in which we live) is governed by *Gevurah/Din,* with its harsher admixture of good and evil, etc.

160. That is, the seven lower sefirot remain intact, though their active powers are annulled. For an interesting parallel, see Jacob bar Sheshet, *Meshiv Devarim Nekhoḥim* (Vajda ed.): 94–95 and E. Gottlieb, *Meḥqarim:* 106ff.

161. The variety, complexity, and occasional opacity of these esoteric speculations on the cosmic Sabbath is remarkable. I intend to call attention to only a few salient examples here.

162. See *Mar'ot ha-Ẓove'ot:* 107: "When the Jubilee arrives all souls will ascend to behold the Face of God; [then] they will return unto their [ancestral] holding and to their family (ff. Lev. 25:13)."

163. Hebrew, *tokh tokho.* See *Temunah* 38b.

164. Also see *Perush* ad loc.; and Baḥyya ben Asher ad Num. 10:35: "When the Great Jubilee arrives all ten [rungs] will return to their Source, *'Ein Sof.*"

165. On the "music of Shabbat," see *Shaʿarei 'Orah* 2:50 (cited on p. 73 above); Z 2:88b (cited in the Epilogue, p. 277 below); *Rimmon* 30a; and MS Paris Hebr. 596 fol. 35a (cited on p. 121 above.) On the "world of whispers" and "silence," see *Mar'ot ha-Ẓove'ot:* 224.

166. It is tempting to read this longing for apokatastasis in a Freudian vein, as part of the purported conflict between "Eros" and "Thanatos." In his late work, *Beyond the Pleasure Principle,* Freud posited a lifelong conflict between the human instinct for life/individuation and the yearning to return to the quiescence which preceded existence. Richard Rubenstein has commented on the affinity between this Freudian conception and the attestations of various Kabbalists:

> The mystics tended to see the very same conflict in terms of the polarities of the maintenance of the self and the return to the Source. (*After Auschwitz* [Indianapolis, 1966]: 220)

For RaMBaN and other Kabbalists, life—separation from divinity—implies a kind of "Exile," a cosmic alienation that is only fully overcome by the ultimate reabsorption of Being in its primal Ground. From a psychological perspective, it might be said that the Kabbalists have mythicized the conflict between individuation and the longing to return by projecting it onto the cosmos. For further discussion, see *After Auschwitz:* 218ff. and 231ff., where Rubenstein provides a similar reading for the Lurianic mythos.

167. See, e.g., *Mar'ot ha-Ẓove'ot:* 102 and *Sod ha-Shabbat:* Section 13, pp. 42 and 49–50 (ad Ps. 136; and Ps. 29 and 24:7). This last passage will be analyzed in chap. 2, pp. 196–97 below.

168. Ff. *Temunah* 89b and *Perush* ad loc. (This is one of the few instances in which the *Temunah* circle explicitly connected the concept of Shabbat with *mizvot Shabbat.*) Also see *Sod ha-Shabbat:* Section 14; and the *Ma'arekhet ha-'Elohut* passage cited on pp. 98–99 above.

It is possible that the *Peli'ah*'s emphasis on contemplative silence during Shabbat (fol. 36b) is related to this quietistic aspect of the supernal "seventh day."

169. For most Kabbalists the weekly Sabbath is associated with a cluster of temporal values, ranging from the fullness of time to its transcendence or cessation. In the words of the *Bahir* (159) " '*Shabat va-yinnafash*' [Ex. 31:17]—it is both cessation and animation." Some adepts, however, strongly inclined to one side or the other. Moshe de Leon consistently portrayed Shabbat as "fullfilled time": rich dynamic, "extroverted"—filling the world and the week with blessing. Joseph ben Shalom Ashkenazi and the *Temunah* circle, by contrast, tended to associate Shabbat with Time that is "emptied out" or purely "inward." For them Shabbat points to a metaphysical "time beyond time" without external manifestation—it is a time of lying fallow, of "complete rest, without change." Here we discover two distinct models for Sabbath-sanctification, for personal and temporal renewal.

170. This Rabbinic phrase (M. Tamid, end) is widely employed by the Kabbalists, as is its variant, *'olam she-kullo Shabbat* (ff. Mekh. "Beshallah").

171. This ability to mythically enter into different "time zones" is the temporal correlative to G. Santayana's notion that Religion provides us with another—indeed, several other!—worlds to live in. By participating in the mythic re-enactment or anticipation of sacred moments, and by identifying with the various sefirotic heroes and mythic protagonists of these events, the Kabbalist is able to discover and express his "many selves," to use the Freudian term. Freud noted that there is a deep-seated human need to live out or "body forth" one's many selves; for, he argues, the Self is not a simple entity but a composite community of selves—some acknowledged, others generally repressed—which ideally exist in some integrated fashion. Herbert Fingarette, in his *Self in Transformation* (New York, 1963), builds on Freud, stating:

> There can be no development into a *human* being without the incorporation into the Total Self of a variety of lives and part–lives. The more these are fully lived, the more rich and deep a Self. (190)

One might argue that Kabbalistic myth and ritual (like dreams, play, fiction and various art-forms) enable the participant to evoke and weave together this "plurality of lives" and part-lives. Moreover, he is able to do so in a manner that is both disciplined (in accord with a "sacred structure") and, generally speaking, below the threshold of conscious intention. The Kabbalist can therefore enact or "play at" that which he could never assert in ordinary experience. For example, as the adept mythically represents and comes to identify with the plight of *Shekhinah,* say, or glimpses his post-Messianic self, he surpasses his ordinary self and unself-consciously partakes of other—heretofore submerged—aspects of his identity. The more intense the emotional identification, the more fully he 'becomes' those other selves.

For further discussion, see S. Freud, "Thoughts for Times of War and Death," *Complete Works* (New York, 1953–74) Vol. 18: 291 and H. Fingarette's suggestive analysis in *The Self in Transformation:* 184–198.

172. Interestingly, a similar de-emphasis is found in the exoteric interpretation of Judah ben Yaqar (*Perush ha-Tefillot ve-ha-Berakhot:* 1:115), replicated verbatim in *Sefer 'Abudraham:* 148. R. Judah noted that although Shabbat is both *zekher le-maʿaseh bere'shit* and *zekher li-yẓi'at miẓrayim,* the Friday night *ʿAmidah* mentions only the Sabbath of Creation. This is because "the essence of *miẓvat Shabbat* is [the Sabbath of Creation] when He rested, for Shabbat occurred *before* the Exodus from Egypt."

173. On the Kabbalistic doctrine of perpetual Revelation, see G. Scholem, "Revelation and Tradition as Religious Categories" in *The Messianic Idea in Judaism* (New York, 1971), esp. pp. 298–303.

174. The major exception I have found is the TY, written at the end of the classical period (1507). Meir ibn Gabbai specifically correlated Sinaitic time with Shabbat, treating it as a major motif. See, e.g., *Sod ha-Shabbat:* Section 13 (pp. 46–47) where the Sabbath morning Torah service is portrayed as a symbolic re-enactment of Revelation:

(1) The paragraph that is chanted as the Torah is removed from the Ark contains eight verses. Ibn Gabbai explained its symbolic import:

> The first seven correspond to the seven *qolot* [revelatory Voices] with which the Torah was given (Ex. R 28:6 et al.) . . . while the eighth verse corresponds to the concluding portion or *Mafṭir,*

kabbalistically, a reference to *Shekhinah* and Her symbol, the Oral Torah also revealed at Sinai.

(2) The opening verse of this paragraph, Dt. 4:35, contains ten words, "corresponding to the Decalogue." He added: "This verse refers to the receiving of the Torah and the Torah was given on the Sabbath."

(3) Seven basic lectionary portions are read, again "paralleling the seven *qolot* with which the Torah was given."

(4) The Torah is to be read in rapt silence, to signify the awesome silence during Revelation. Symbolically, the reader on the raised *bimah* evokes God above, while the congregation gathered below becomes Israel "standing at the foot of the mountain" (ff. Ex. 19:17).

A much briefer correlation of Sabbath ritual with Sinaitic Revelation is found in M. Recanati's *Perush* to Ex. 20:8.

175. On Sacred Marriage in the Kabbalah see G. Scholem, OKS: 104, 131, 138ff., 153, 163ff. For general discussion see Mircea Eliade, *Myths, Dreams and Mysteries* (New York, 1967): 158 and 171–83, and *The Myth of the Eternal Return:* 23–27 and 57–58. Also see the extensive treatment in W.

D. O'Flaherty, *Women, Androgynes, and Other Mythical Beasts* (Chicago, 1980): index, s.v. "hierogamy."

176. Ff. n. 171, it might be said that these mythic guises represent assorted personae which the Kabbalist may play at and in varying degrees, "become."

A programmatic note. The fluidity of the *Zohar*'s imagery—and its use of symbol clusters—poses organizational problems for any motif study. In a given passage *Shekhinah* may be imaged as the Bride, the Moon, the Throne, etc. Images of marriage may give way to images of illumination and coronation. Sometimes the metaphors mix, as in the famous passage *Raza' de-Shabbat* (2:135a–b) where the sacred union of Male and Female is imaged as the seating of the Holy One upon the Throne!

These shifting and mixed images all dramatize sacred union, however; they are identical from a cognitive point of view, even though they differ aesthetically and in emotional impact. As I discuss the Zoharic evidence in this section, I concentrate on, but do not limit myself to, those passages which 'foreground' nuptial, marital, and sexual imagery.

177. Both *va-yekhal* and *kallah* share the same root, *KLH.*

178. For Kabbalistic interpretations of Gen. R 10:9, see Ṭ. Abulafia's *Shaʿar ha-Razim* to Ps. 19:6 and Menaḥem Recanati's *Perush* ad Gen. 2:2. It may be noted that there is at least one other midrashic source likening Sabbath to a Bride, viz., Ex. R 41:6. It was not, however, frequently cited by the Kabbalists and did not seem to exert a major influence.

179. The midrash turns on the double-meaning of *le-qaddesho,* meaning both "to sanctify it" and "to betroth it." Gen. R 11:8 is preserved in many versions. (For a partial listing, see the Theodor-Albeck edition of *Bere'shit Rabbah* [Jerusalem, 1965] Vol. 1: 95–96.) In some MSS Sabbath is the bride and the Community of Israel, the groom; in others, it is just the opposite. For more on the linguistic features of this midrash, see p. 111 above. For a later version of this midrash cf. *Pesiqta' Rabbati* 23:7.

For another possible instance of marital symbolism, cf. TB Shabbat 33b which relates that one Friday evening R. Shimon bar Yoḥai and his son saw a man carrying two myrtle sprigs in honor of Shabbat. Since myrtle was sometimes used in wedding ceremonies this passage may have had overtones of marriage symbolism, as suggested by J. Lauterbach. ("The Origin and Development of Two Sabbath Ceremonies," HUCA: 15 [1940]: 367–424). Surely, it did for the Safed Kabbalists. It was not, however, a crucial source for the classical Kabbalistic discussion of Sabbath as marriage festival.

180. This work has been preserved in several versions. The most complete is MS Oxf. Bodl. 1531 which has been published in P. Schaeffer's *Synopse zur Hekhalot Literatur* (Tübingen, 1981). All citations will follow the section number in Schaeffer's book.

For a brief summary of *Heikhalot* mysticism and its influence, see *Kabbalah:* 14–22 and 30–35.

181. See sections 842–48.

182. *La-sos u-le-sammeaḥ* recalls the fifth and sixth nuptial benedictions, which begin *sos tasis* and *sammeaḥ tesammaḥ*. Also see the seventh blessing: ". . . 'asher bara' sason ve-simḥah ḥatan ve-khallah" (Who created gladness and joy, groom and bride). The phrase *maᶜon shel simḥah* recalls the festive *zimmun* for the Grace after the wedding meal: "Blessed be our God, in whose *maᶜon* is joy", *she-ha-simḥah bi-mᶜono.*

183. Interestingly, these two Southern European Kabbalists were unusually well acquainted with the traditions of Ashkenaz, where the *Seder Rabba' di-Vre'shit* was transmitted and preserved. The influence on R. Judah ben Yaqar will be discussed shortly; also cf. n. 189 below. The matter of its influence on Moshe de Leon is more complicated. It is clear that he knew some version of the *Seder,* as evinced by an extended reference to the simultaneous coronation of the Holy One and Shabbat in ZḤ "Bere'shit" 17b (MN): "The Holy One did not sit on his Throne of Glory until the Sabbath came and sat on His Throne of Glory, etc." I suspect that the *Seder* also had a subtle influence on the famous passage *Raza' de-Shabbat* (Z 2: 135a-b), wherein marital and coronation imagery are fused: "The Holy One does not sit on His Throne of Glory [now *Shekhinah*!] until She enters the mystery of One. . . ."

184. *The Sabbath:* 111.

185. Cited in H. Enelow, "Midrash Hashkem Quotations in Alnaqua's Menorat ha-Maor," HUCA 4 (1927): 327. The midrash cited here (XIa) is actually an anonymous text. See also midrash XI, probably from *Midrash Hashkem.*

186. See, e.g., *Siddur RaSHI:* 267 (sec. 534) which likens Shabbat to a queen; and the S. Ish-Horowitz ed. of *Maḥzor Viṭri* [MV]: 116 which likens it to a queen and bride. Though MV often contains later materials (see n. 189 below), this interpretation appears to be pre-Kabbalistic.

187. Ed. M. Hershler (Jerusalem, 1971): 182.

188. See A. Grossman, *Ḥakhmei 'Ashkenaz ha-Qadmonim* (Jerusalem, 1981): 82.

189. The marital motif was further developed in thirteenth century Ashkenazic sources, concurrent with its development in Kabbalah. See, e.g., the interpretations of *'Attah 'Eḥad* found in MV: 109–10 (which may contain Kabbalistically influenced material); the teaching ascribed to R. Tam in Isaac ben Moshe of Vienna's *'Or Zaruᶜa* ("Hilkhot Moẓa'ei Shabbat"); and the tradition attributed to Eleazar of Worms, quoted in n. 231 below.

The relationship between Ashkenazic and Kabbalistic views of *hieros gamos* has not been adequately investigated to date. It is clear that some of the Ashkenazic traditions (including esoteric views not committed to writing) were known to Judah ben Yaqar who, in the third quarter of the twelfth century, studied with R. Isaac ben Abraham of Dampierre, heir to the Tosafist and German Ḥasidic traditions. It also is likely that that Ashkenazic traditions were known by the likes of Moshe de Leon and David ben Judah he-Ḥasid. See n. 183 above and n. 244 below.

190. A good example may be found in the *Rimmon* (29b) of Moshe de Leon. This mystic, who was so strongly drawn to the feminine Sabbath in the *Zohar*, here freely mixed masculine-kingly imagery with feminine-bridal symbolism. Concerning Sabbath's arrival, he wrote:

> The supernal holy Ḥasidim . . . would long to glean their [Sabbath-] soul and to enter into the mystery of the Canopy of Peace [i.e., *Shekhinah*] and dwell in Her Shelter. They would beckon their Lord, King David [another symbol for *Shekhinah/Malkhut*] as He approached. They would cry out, "Come, O bride! Come, O bride!"

Of the Sabbath-night meal, the meal of *Shekhinah*, Moshe de Leon wrote:

> The treasured people . . . insure Her joy with a great feast. . . . They rejoice in the happiness of the King who comes to their home, dwelling in their very midst.

191. For further discussion, see G. Scholem's *Ursprung/Origins of Kabbalah*, Section Two; and *Re'shit ha-Qabbalah ve-Sefer ha-Bahir:* Lectures 12 and 13.

192. See the discussion on pp. 42–43 (n. 14) above.

193. See, e.g., *Bahir* 86. There the verse "as long as the sun shines, YiNnoN (ינון) is his [the Messiah's] name" (Ps. 72:17) is reinterpreted through mystical letter symbolism. Redemption will come only when the male aspect of divinity, graphically symbolized by the elongated final *NuN* (ן), will unite with its feminine counterpart, symbolized by the curved *NuN* (נ).

It should be noted, however, that the *Bahir* frequently tries to lessen the sexual overtones in its more anthropomorphic imagery, by referring, e.g., to the cleaving of the King and Daughter. A more unbridled sexual imagery is first found in the *Zohar*.

194. See, e.g., the grammatical considerations and Aggadic associations listed on pp. 70–71. Also see n. 196 below for another possibility.

195. Cf. *Bahir* 181–83.

196. In addition to the word-play between *zakhor* and *zakhar*, there may be a halakhic rationale for these associations. In the medieval Rabbinic tradition, all the miẓvot are fancifully subsumed under *miẓvat Shabbat:* "Remember" refers to the positive commandments and "Keep" to the negative

commandments. Although women are exempted from most time-bound positive commandments, they are expected to keep the negative commandments. The author of the *Bahir* may be drawing upon this conceptual link between "Keep" and females in this passage. For further discussion, see *Sod ha-Shabbat:* 86–87 n. 4.

197. It is conceivable that the *Bahir* has here been influenced by the description of the nuptial rejoicing in *Seder Rabba' di-Vre'shit* (p. 104 above). This requires further investigation.

198. I am preparing for publication a full-length article on *hieros gamos* in R. Judah's writings. The recondite nature of his *sodot* requires careful and extensive analysis, a task better undertaken in a separate paper. The present discussion will be limited to a few striking examples of his Kabbalah. All citations follow the second edition of R. Judah's *Perush ha-Tefillot ve-ha-Berakhot,* published in two sections and edited by S. Yerushalmi (Jerusalem, 1979).

199. Cf. the MS Oxford version of *Seder Rabba' di-Vre'shit* published in P. Schaeffer, *Synopse zur Hekhalot Literatur,* sections 837 and esp. 849. Judah ben Yaqar's writings are replete with references to the *Heikhalot* literature.

200. This will be demonstrated in detail in my article on R. Judah.

201. Worn when entering the Tabernacle, a fit metaphor for entering Shabbat. Cf. pp. 62–64 and 85–92 above.

202. Apparently, R. Judah—like the *Bahir*—conceived of the divine Sabbath in bi-sexual terms.

203. From *Perush ha-Tefillot ve-ha-Berakhot* 2:42. For other Kabbalistic readings of this midrash, see ibid. 1:11–12 and 1:124–25.

204. RaMBaN to Gen. 2:3; Lev. 23:36; and Dt. 5:15.

205. The grammatical function of the Hebrew copulative *ve-* is given mystical significance here.

206. That is, "read though not written." Such glosses indicate that a Biblical phrase should be read in a different manner from its written form. For further discussion, see EJ 16: 1419–20 and 1571.

207. This grammatical irregularity appeared in many medieval MSS of Gen. R; it has been "corrected" in most printed editions.

208. This reading is also found in Shem Ṭov ibn Gaon's *Keter Shem Ṭov,* fol. 25a-b (ad Gen. 2:3). For other parallels, see *Peli'ah* 85c–d; Joseph Albo, *ᶜIqqarim* 2:11; and *Sod ha-Shabbat:* Prologue. For discussion, see *Sod ha-Shabbat* nn. 14–24.

For other examples of the marital motif in the Naḥmanidean tradition, see *Keter Shem Ṭov* ad Ex. 20:8 (fol. 37b–38a in the printed ed. or fol. 256a-b in the superior MS Munich 11 version.) Also see the *Derashot* of Joshua ibn Shuayb (Krakow, 1596) fol. 27c and 60a.

209. This dramatic dynamism may be directly related to Moshe de Leon's theological dynamism, discussed on pp. 27 and 54 (n. 81) above.

210. The major exception is noted in n. 223 below.

OK's interpretations are significant in that they represent one of the earlier attempts to correlate the marital motif with Sabbath ritual: specifically, with candlelighting and the blessing over the two *ḥallot* (cf. ad Shab. 25b and Ber. 39b). Of the former Ṭodros Abulafia wrote:

> "R. Abbahu said: [*Shelom bayit,* domestic peace] refers to the candles to be lit on Shabbat [ff. TB Shab. 23b]": R. Abbahu calls the Sabbath candles "Shalom" because [on Shabbat] the supernal Sabbath unites with the Community of Israel, His mate, and consequently, all is peace. This is "Righteousness [*Malkhut*] and Peace [*Tif'eret/Yesod*] kissed." [Ps. 85:11]

Nevertheless, these rituals are taken as an allusion to the state of divine union. They do not describe a dynamic event with ebbs and flows, or something unfolding at the moment of ritual performance. The symbolic and theurgic significance of Sabbath-ritual remains general here. Indeed, it is Sabbath observance in general that promotes and partakes of divine union. To cite one example:

> Through the merit of Israel, when they keep the Sabbath and scrupulously keep its miẓvot . . . the supernal entities are gladdened, and the spirit of Knowledge [*Tif'eret*] and the Fear of the Lord [*Malkhut*] unite, as during the primordial Creation. [ad Shab. 119b]

211. Ff. the insightful commentary of D. Matt: 258. According to I. Tishby, MZ 2:535, the moment of union corresponds to the recitation of the *Shemaᶜ*.

Interestingly, *Sefer ha-Rimmon* (MS Brit. Mus. fol. 29b) correlates this incipient union with two other rituals of Friday evening, one domestic (here the province of women) and the second, synagogal (the province of the men). The domestic ritual is, of course, the candlelighting which ushers in Shabbat; regarding it, the *Rimmon* laconically notes:

> The candle which is the symbol of the Soul [sefirotically, *Shekhinah*] is lit in the home. According to the [Sages], candles are lit because of *shelom bayit,* domestic tranquility [but kabbalistically, the union of divine Male and Female] concerning which the woman is commanded. The matter of candlelighting is well-known, insuring that joy be given unto the Canopy of Peace [the divine "Woman"] [through *hieros gamos*]. This is sufficient for the enlightened.

In the synagogal setting the focal point is the special benediction recited during the Sabbath evening *ᶜAmidah, 'Attah qiddashta 'et yom ha-sheviᶜi* ("You sanctified the seventh day"). Moshe de Leon's interpretation turns on the double meaning of *qiddashta*, which can also signify betrothal:

> And so when the Chosen People are sanctifying Her, they recite *'Attah Qiddashta* . . . that She be betrothed and joined [*nizmedet*] in the mystery of supernal holiness,

sefirotically, the union of *Tif'eret* and *Malkhut*. As in the *Zohar* passage, Israel serves as Her bridal attendants, partaking of and adding to Her joy. This motif is given added nuance in the later *Qiddush* over the wine. See *Rimmon* Ibid. and the ensuing discussion for details.

212. Cf. *Sod ha-Shabbat*, Section 10 (s.v. "According to the path of truth.") ff. Z 3:272b.

213. See 2:88a-b and 234b, et al.

214. Hebrew, *meqaddeshin 'otah ba-qiddush*. The multivalent term *meqaddeshin*, conventionally 'consecrate,' here seems to connote Her 'separation' from the profane realm and more pointedly, Her formal 'betrothal' or *qiddushin* (a ceremony which must be performed over wine).

215. See *Rimmon* 30a, et al.

216. A *maqama*-like rhyme: *va-tanaḥ ha-tevah mi-kol ha-mela'khah, kedat kol nesukhah. Nesukhah* here has the connotations of both 'annointed' and 'of the status of royalty' (i.e., a Queen). On *Shekhinah* as *nesukhah*/ royalty, also see *Rimmon* on *Barukh she-'amar: "Va-yehi ro'sh nesikhot 'ha-yoshevet ri'shonah be-malkhut'* (Esth. 1:14)": "She was the Queen [holding sway over the world], and 'occupied the first place in the Kingdom.' "

I would like to thank my colleague Elliot Wolfson for calling this latter source to my attention and for generously sharing with me his deep knowledge of the *Rimmon*.

217. The Biblical verse refers to Esther as she prepared to come before the king for the first time. Kabbalistically, of course, the reference is to *Shekhinah*'s supernal adornment.

218. I shall return to the *Rimmon*'s reading of the *Qiddush* shortly, in my analysis of the Sabbath-soul, p. 136 above and n. 292 below.

219. See Z 3:105a–b and 2:207a–b as well as *Mishqal*: 115 and *Rimmon* 30a. In the *Mishqal* source especially, *hieros gamos* imagery is extended throughout the day:

(1) *Shekhinah*, the Bride, is escorted at Sabbath eve: "Our sages would say 'Come O bride', waiting for the bride in order to escort her to the marriage canopy."

(2) The wedding and union takes place on Sabbath night: "The night [sefirotically, *Shekhinah*] is like a bride who enters the wedding canopy with her mate. When they [*Shekhinah* and *Tif'eret*] are together all is one mystery, one entity."

(3) During Sabbath day, their union persists, "Nighttime and Daytime [sefirotically, *Tif'eret*] forming one day." Moshe de Leon portrayed them as royal lovers, "a film of dew encircling their heads, which were wreathed 'with a diadem of beauty, a crown of glory.' [Isa. 28:5]."

I have recently come across a more fully realized treatment of the *hieros gamos* motif. In his *Sodot* (MS Schocken 14 fol. 88a-b and MS Vatican 428 fol. 40a-b), Moshe de Leon systematically correlated specific moments in Sabbath worship with stages in the divine marriage. For example, the Sabbath evening prayer *'Attah Qiddashta* dramatizes the betrothal and adornment of the Bride, while the subsequent prayers represent Her entry into the marital canopy (the sefirotic realm). The prescribed marital intercourse of Sabbath night promotes *Shekhinah*'s union with Her lover, *Tif'eret/Yesod,* and enables Her to "bring forth fruit in season"—to give birth to "holy souls" drawn down by the couples below. The morning prayer "And Moses rejoiced" dramatizes the Groom's rejoicing of the Bride who becomes, in the words of the prayer, "a corona of beauty" resting on His head. This coronation/union is completed during the *Qedushat Keter* (Crown Sanctus) of *Musaf.* In the late afternoon, as the prayer "You are One and Your Name One" is recited, the deepest union of Bride and Groom is achieved, one now embracing all seven active rungs.

220. See, e.g., Moshe of Burgos' teaching summarized in n. 223 below.

221. Most of these allusions, and their sources, may be found in MZ 2:494–95. See there for further interpretation.

222. The theme of Liberation and Sacred Union is highly elaborated in the TZ. A succinct example:

> When *Shekhinah* is in Exile, it is said of Her: "The dove did not find a resting place." [Gen. 8:9] But on Shabbat and holy days, She couples with Her husband. . . . (TZ 6 [22b])

Also see TZ 48 (85a–b) and p. 217 below. One motif which plays a far greater role in the TZ/RM than in the *Zohar* proper is that of re-garbing *Shekhinah.* As Sabbath enters *Shekhinah* is divested of Her constraining garb of *Siṭra' 'Aḥra'* and cloaked in garments of majesty and holiness. For further discussion see MZ 2:495 and esp. chapter 3, below.

223. Cf. the similar formulation in M. Cordovero's *'Or Yaqar,* "Terumah" sec. 5.

It is important to recall that the marital motif was not necessarily restricted to the Sabbath setting in Zoharic Kabbalah; for, as noted in n. 139 above, Moshe de Leon alternated between a dualistic and a harmonistic view of sefirotic relations (see there and p. 93 above for definitions). According to the harmonistic schema, divine marriage is possible throughout the week; indeed, the ultimate function of all prayer and Torah-study is to promote the union of feminine and masculine aspects of the Godhead (ff. I. Tishby,

MZ 2:262). Only thus can the world be sustained, for "blessings reside only when Male and Female are found in the mystery of union." (Z 1:165a)

A dynamic marital motif was already associated with the weekday liturgy in *Sod Semikhut Ge'ulah li-Tfillah,* written by Moshe of Burgos, one of the Castilian "Gnostics" who influenced de Leon. See Scholem's edition of this text in "Le-Ḥeqer Qabbalat R. Yiẓḥaq ben Yaaqov ha-Kohen" in *Tarbiẓ* 5 (1934): 322–23. There the entire morning service marks different symbolic stages in the divine union and coupling. Through the prayers, the adept progressively redeems *Shekhinah* the Bride from the impure cosmic forces; adorns Her in pure garments (the angelic worlds); lifts Her up to the sefirotic realm to meet Her Groom; and brings about their joyous union. At the peak of the prayers, the adept causes Her to ascend through the pleroma unto "the Supernal Heights" (*Keter*), so that "all is in perfect union."

This *hieros gamos* motif was greatly elaborated in the *Zohar* and the ancillary Hebrew writings of de Leon. It was associated, by turns, with the briefest of rituals and with extended periods of sacred time. For example, Z 2:133b–34b (on *Qeri'at Shemaᶜ*); *Rimmon,* MS Oxf. Bodl. 1607 fol. 16a; and *Maskiot Kesef* (ed. J. Wijnhoven): 23–25, all associated *hieros gamos* with spiritually intense sections of the daily prayers. A more leisurely or temporally extended nuptial myth was developed in conjunction with certain holiday periods. According to Z 3:100b, the ten Days of Awe are symbolized as stages in the divine wedding, consummated on *Yom Kippur.* Z 3:214b extends the nuptial period an additional twelve days, through "*Shemini ᶜAẓeret* which is the rejoicing of the Torah . . . the union of the [divine] Boḍy . . . and the perfection of All." Finally, the most extended nuptial myth is associated with the seven week period from Passover to Shavuᶜot. The Zohar source, 3:97a–98b, infuses the Biblical narrative with powerful physiological-sexual imagery. The Exodus at Passover marks the redemption of *Shekhinah* (the divine Community of Israel) from the impurity of *Siṭra' 'Aḥra'*/Egypt; or, to use the physiological trope, the cessation of Her period of menstrual bleeding. The ensuing seven weeks of "wandering," in which the ᶜOmer is counted (ff. Lev. 23:15), is associated with the seven "clean days" of waiting following the end of the menstrual flow (ff. Lev. 15:28). During this period of spiritual purification, *Shekhinah*/Community of Israel moves from the forty-nine Gates of Impurity to the forty-nine Gates of *Binah,* ascending through the sefirotic realm. Finally, on Shavuᶜot, the day of divine Revelation, the union of the perfected Bride and Groom is consummated.

Comparatively speaking, then, the *hieros gamos* of Shabbat is of intermediate length; it is more extended and all-encompassing than the episodic *hieros gamos* associated with the profane week, but less extended (although perhaps more intensely felt) than the nuptial dramas associated with the New Year and the Seven Weeks. A final point: only on Shabbat is there direct symbolic representation of the myth of *hieros gamos,* through the sexual union of the adept and his wife.

224. Because I referred to Moshe de Leon's Hebrew writings in the preceding section, I shall exclude them from the present analysis.

225. See TZ 24 (70a) for a parallel. On several occasions the TZ builds on this symbolization of the home, specifically correlating the festive table, menorah, and couch with the sefirotic world and with different aspects of the upcoming *hieros gamos*. Cf. I. Tishby, MZ 2:502 for some examples.

226. Cf. Menaḥem Recanati ("Va-Yeḥi") who claims: " 'The spread couch' "—this is the bed of King Solomon [in the Song of Songs]", i.e., the bed of *Tif'eret*.

227. Medieval authorities associated the two candles with "Remember" and "Keep" (kabbalistically, *Tif'eret* and *Shekhinah*) which, according to Rabbinic tradition, were "spoken as one." (Shev. 20b) On its Kabbalistic implications, see also *Peli'ah* 36a and *Sod ha-Shabbat:* Section 8, end.

228. On the *Qanah*'s attitude towards women and the miẓvot, see Talya Fishman, "Women and Torah Study" in *Kabbalah: A Newsletter of Current Research in Jewish Mysticism* 2:2 (1987): 4–6.

229. It is likely that the unusual usage of *QR'* in this passage is based on its use in Esther 4:11. See there.

The act of ritual welcoming described in the *Qanah* may be compared with the one found in *Zohar* 2:135a–b where the *Barekhu* is thought to set the stage for the divine union. See p. 113 above.

230. See David ben Judah he-Ḥasid, *'Or Zaruᶜa*, MS JTSA Mic. 2203 fol. 40a. Also cf. *Shoshan Sodot* (79a) which makes a similar point with the *meᶜein shevaᶜ*, the public summation of the seven benedictions, recited at the end of the *ᶜAmidah:*

> The esoteric meaning [of this prayer] is to unite *Shekhinah* with [*be-*] the seven blessings.

Although on one level this implies that *Shekhinah* is consecrated *through* our recitation of the seven blessings, sefirotically it intimates Her union *with* the seven divine rungs above!

> Thus [we understand] the traditional rationale [for reciting this prayer], namely, *mi-sakkanot ha-mazziqin* [RaSHI to Shab. 24b; conventionally, due to "danger of demons" but here: "danger *to* the demons"] for as She unites with the supernal rungs, all the opposing forces *safu tammu*—are snuffed out and gone.

231. Many were the Kabbalists who interpreted *'Attah Qiddashta* as an intra-divine wedding. A cryptic allusion to this motif is probably ensconced in Judah ben Yaqar's early work, *Perush ha-Tefillot* 1:89. A clearer example, perhaps, is the *Rimmon* extract cited in n. 211 above. Subsequent examples include SṬM: 297, *Maᶜarekhet ha-'Elohut* 184b–85b, Menaḥem Ẓiyyoni's *Sefer Ẓiyyoni* 36c, and the anonymous fifteenth century Italian text, MS Paris Hebr. 596 (34b and 35a) which provides two distinct interpretations

of the sacred union. The marital interpretation of *'Attah Qiddashta* entered more exoteric works as well, e.g., David Abudraham's commentary on the prayers, *Sefer 'Abudraham:* 147. It is unclear, however, whether Abudraham understood the prayer sefirotically. For further discussion, see *Sod ha-Shabbat* n. 122.

The tradition of reading this prayer in marital terms may well have originated in German Ḥasidic circles, thereby possibly predating its appearance in Spanish Kabbalah. The early sixteenth century work *Shoshan Sodot* (79a) reports the following:

> Each of the [middle blessings of the] Sabbath Prayer is different from the other. During *ᶜArvit* one recites "You sanctified"; during *Shaḥarit,* "Moses rejoiced" and during *Minḥah,* "You are one." The sage R. Eliezer (!) ha-Roqeaḥ explained that one who marries, first betroths her; then rejoices with her; and finally unites with her. So too, the Holy One on the Sabbath day.

This source raises many pertinent questions: is it an authentic source of the Roqeaḥ (d. 1230), an old Ḥasidic tradition? If so, who is the bride here? Shabbat, in all likelihood, but how are the wedding and union of Shabbat and the Holy One to be understood? Does this union have any theosophic connotations? Alternatively stated, how does the Roqeaḥ's interpretation compare with the Kabbalistic readings? Did it have any influence on them? Should the antiquity of the Roqeaḥ tradition be borne out, it would again point to the crucial links between early Kabbalah and Ashkenazic Ḥasidism.

232. For a succinct example, see *Shulḥan shel 'Arbaᶜ, Kitvei R. Baḥyya:* 482. The only exceptions I have come across are a) *Sefer ha-Yiḥud* (from the circle of Joseph of Hamadan), wherein the Friday night meal is associated with *Ḥokhmah;* and b) the dissenting view expressed by R. Hamnuna Sava [alt. version: R. Abba] in Z 2:88a–b, where the meal is associated with *Keter.* For discussion, see *Sod ha-Shabbat* n. 514.

233. See, e.g., *Sod ha-Shabbat,* Section 11:

> Therefore one must grace [the table] with plenty and show great joy at the festive meal on Sabbath night, so as to point to the Bride, the Glory of the Night who is filled with all good and who is encompassed by supernal Eden. To [partake of] this mystery, one should sample all the foods prepared for Shabbat [ff. Z 1:48b], [further] alluding to the Bride who is encompassed by All.

234. In accord with the miẓvah of gladdening the bride (cf. Ket. 16b–17a, e.g.)! On the mystical re-reading of this tradition, see also *Sod ha-Shabbat,* Section 10, where *Shekhinah* is regaled through the *Qiddush* over wine, too:

> According to the path of Truth, we are obligated to sanctify [the Sabbath] over wine because when the Bride enters the bridal canopy [simultaneously, the devotee's home and the sefirotic world on high!], She must be gladdened . . . for therein lies the mystery of "the wine that brings joy to *'Elohim* and humankind." [Judges 9:13]

Sefirotically, the red *Qiddush* wine symbolizes *Gevurah* whose *shefa*ᶜ flows into *Shekhinah/'Elohim* at this hour, strengthening Her and giving Her cheer.

235. On this debate, see *Sod ha-Shabbat:* Section 9 (s.v. *Va-Yekhullu*) and n. 124.

236. On this theme, also see Menaḥem Recanati to Gen. 2:3:

> "And heaven and earth were completed [*YeKhuLlu*]": . . . According to the path of Truth, *YeKhuLlu* is written without a *WaW* in allusion to the Bride [*KaLlaH*] who is perfected [*KeLuLaH*] on all sides.

237. On *Ẓaddiq* as the link between Groom and Bride also see OK to Ber. 6; TZ 6 (21b) and 21 (45b); MS Paris Hebr. 596, fol. 34b; et al.

238. Also cf. *Peli'ah* (36b) where the wine completes the nuptial ceremony:

> One should take care with the wine that is used in the *Qiddush* of the day, for a Bride without *qiddushin*—what is her virtue? With the wine, matters are completed.

239. On *Qiddush* anticipating the ultimate union of Bride and Groom, also see *Yalquṭ he-Ḥakham ha-Maskil* (late thirteenth century, Gerona), MS Moscow 131 fol. 14a, cited in A. Goldreich (ed.), *Me*ᶜ*irat* ᶜ*Einayim:* 364.

240. For example, Moshe of Burgos and Moshe de Leon. See n. 223 above.

241. On the notion that each word of Sabbath prayer bedecks and adorns the Bride, see pp. 200–01 and esp. 236 below. Also cf. OZ, MS British Museum 771 fol. 51b, s.v. *Tikkanta Shabbat.*

The OZ elsewhere suggests a causal connection between the adornment of *Shekhinah* in refined, layered garments and the cosmos' spiritual enrichment (or vestment) on Shabbat:

> On Shabbat She wears two layers of lovely garments, raiment of the supernal kingdom. . . . [Accordingly, as Israel chants *'El 'Adon*] the divine energy descends from the supernal world in two-fold measure, twice that which is received during the week . . . [during recitation of] *'El Barukh.*" (OZ, MS Brit. Mus. 771 fol. 47a and 22b)

242. According to Jewish law, the groom is to separate from his virginal bride following sexual consummation. (Because of the discharge of blood, she becomes taboo, "unclean"). For details, see TB Nid. 65b; and Ṭur YD 193 and EH 63.

By implication, *Shekhinah* is perpetually a "virgin," entering Marriage for the first time each Shabbat.

243. Compare with OZ (MS Brit. Mus. 771) fol. 51b. There R. David interpreted the first six words of the *Musaf* prayer *Tikkanta Shabbat* as a prècis of the entire wedding celebration:

Tikkanta Shabbat, "You established the Sabbath." That is, You [*Tiferet*] adorned the Bride who is the Sabbath in all sorts of jewelry (*tiqqunim*), as befits Her. *Raẓita Qorbanoteha,* "You desired her *qorbanot* [conventionally, "her sacrifices" but here read etymologically, as "her acts of drawing near"]. That is, You wanted Her to be *with* the King, the Lord of Hosts [a cipher for sexual union]. *Ẓivvita Perusheha,* "You enjoined her distinct duties," referring to when She separates (*poreshet*) from the King. This is the mystical meaning of "A man who engages in the miẓvah of sexual intercourse must then separate from her [ff. TB Nid. 65b]."

244. Apparently, this imaging of Shabbat as Wedding Ceremony was assimilated in the *Menorat ha-Ma'or* of Israel Al-Naqawa (d. 1391), who dropped the more obvious sefirotic associations but retained the basic framework. (Cf. the Enelow ed. of this work, 2:191.) Al-Naqawa's text is partially translated in A. J. Heschel's *The Sabbath:* 112.

On a different note: I suspect that R. David's portrait of Shabbat as a multi-tiered wedding ceremony derived inspiration from Moshe de Leon's *Sodot* (cited in n. 219 above); indeed, the OZ is replete with uncited borrowings from this work. It is also likely that both adepts were influenced by Ashkenazic-Ḥasidic sources. An intriguing piece of evidence is the teaching attributed to R. Eleazar ha-Roqeaḥ of Worms, cited in n. 231 above. This merits further investigation.

245. From *'Attah Qiddashta,* the middle benediction of the Sabbath evening Prayer.

246. Other motifs used in dramatizing the person's transformation are discussed in Appendix I below. See there for details.

247. The notion that the *neshamah yeterah* constituted an additional soul was present in *Siddur RaSHI:* 524; *Pardes le-RaSHI:* 26; and MV sec. 151 (p. 117), as well as in the halakhic sources listed in n. 263 below. Similar views were also present in later, i.e., thirteenth century, Ashkenazic (or Ashkenazi influenced) works, including *Shibbolei ha-Leqeṭ* sec. 130 and the *'Or Zaruʿa* of Isaac ben Moses of Vienna, "Hilkhot Shabbat" sec. 92. It must be noted, however, that these sources did not develop the Rabbinic image to any appreciable extent.

248. The widespread neglect of or apology for the Sabbath-soul has been demonstrated by I. Tishby in MZ 2:488ff. Tishby, however, did not distinguish between these tendencies and the more positive view evident in the Ashkenazic sources cited above.

249. It seems highly probable that Tos. to Beiẓ. 33b (which refers to the loss of the *neshamah yeterah* on Saturday night) follows RaSHI's interpretation of the term.

250. Some thinkers spoke of an internal reconfiguration of the tripartite soul on Sabbath. See the view of Asher ben Saul of Lunel (brother of the early Kabbalist Jacob Nazir) recorded in S. Assaf, ed., *Sifran shel Ri'shonim* (Jerusalem, 1935): 176–77 and discussed by G. Scholem in *Origins of the Kabbalah:* 232.

The understanding of *neshamah yeterah* that is perhaps closest to Kabbalistic models is that of the Ashkenazic pietist-mystic Eleazar ha-Roqeaḥ of Worms (see nn. 231 above and 282 below). Although he did not speak of an extra Sabbath-soul, he used the term *nefesh yeterah* to indicate the expansion of the ordinary soul, which enables the Jew to attain a higher spiritual rung. In his *Sodot ha-Tefillah* (MS Oxf. Bodl. 1595/96, fol. 42b), R. Eleazar wrote:

> All the days of the week the soul is on the lower rungs, but on the Sabbath it ascends to the top, becoming expansive and happy. This is *nefesh yeterah.* But when Sabbath departs, the soul descends. This is *shabat va-yinnafash:* When the Sabbath ceases, woe to the soul that has lost [so much]." [TB Beiẓ. 16a] So the person is sad, but when it is Shabbat the person's heart rejoices.

I will return to the motif of the soul's ascent on Shabbat in the discussion of Zoharic sources.

251. This understanding exhibits both the Kabbalists' affinity with popular religion and some of the critical distance from it. From the meagre evidence available, it seems likely that the folk-understanding allowed that each Sabbath a Jew actually received another soul. Most Kabbalists adapted this understanding but gave it a sophisticated (indeed, esoteric) coloration. The Sabbath-soul is part and parcel of the sefirotic system, an emanation deriving from the divine Ground.

252. It should be noted that some early Kabbalists like Jacob Nazir did speak of the *neshamah yeterah* as a real entity, but treated it in non-Kabbalistic (i.e., non-sefirotic) fashion. Jacob Nazir saw it as a "second soul" whose function is to increase one's desire to fulfill *ᶜOneg Shabbat.* See I. Tishby, MZ 2:488–89 for further discussion.

253. Later Kabbalists, to be sure, generally read the *Bahir* passages in this fashion. Cf., e.g., Menaḥem Recanati to Gen. 2:3.

254. Elsewhere in this passage Azriel claimed that "on Shabbat one is filled with the spirit according to its rung," a clear reference to *Yesod.*

255. Cf. MZ 2:488 n. 67. On this term in early Kabbalah cf. A. J. Heschel, "ᶜAl Ruaḥ ha-Qodesh bi-Ymei ha-Beinayim" in *Sefer ha-Yovel li-Khvod Alexander Marx* [Hebrew Volume] (New York, 1950): 190–93.

256. Several Kabbalists who clearly believed that the Sabbath-soul was an ontic entity did not distinguish between these terms either. Moshe de

Leon, e.g., used *nefesh, ruaḥ* and *neshamah yeterah* interchangeably. See p. 126 above.

257. RaMBaN to Ex. 31:13, ff. *Bahir* 180. Also see ad Ex. 20:11.

258. Cf. Section 5 which reads:

> Intercourse, the mystery of "Remember and Keep [were uttered as one]" [Shev. 20b] and *Shabbat Shabbaton* [Ex. 31:15, et al.; kabbalistically, the union of *Tif'eret* with *Malkhut*]. The holiness of the union is due to the presence of the *neshamah yeterah* in the person.

259. The second OZ source is cited on p. 121 above; the first, in n. 282 below.

260. See n. 272 below.

261. The term *nefesh-* or *neshamah-yeterah* is nowhere used.

262. On the reception of added *shefa*ᶜ on Shabbat as a cipher of personal transformation, see the motif study in Appendix I below. See also Baḥyya to Ex. 20:8, beginning with his interpretation of Isa. 58:13.

On another Naḥmanidean understanding of *nefesh yeterah,* cf. *Be'ur Sodot ha-RaMBaN* to Gen. 2:3. Unlike Baḥyya, the *Be'ur* does make use of the term *nefesh yeterah* (ff. RaMBaN). However, it is not at all clear that this term denotes a separate "soul":

> "On the Sabbath there is a *nefesh yeterah*" [RaMBaN ad loc.]: The Rabbi was referring to that which sustains souls [*nefashot*] by bringing *its* blessing [emph. mine] into them on Shabbat. Hence, at Sabbath's departure the soul says: "Woe, a soul is [has?] lost." [ff. TB Beiẓah 16a]

263. For sources pertaining to these other holidays, see TZ Intro (11a); 21 (45b), etc.; but cf. TZ 6 (22b) for another view. The earlier commentators were similarly divided on the frequency of reception. Cf., e.g., Tos. and RaSHBaM to TB Pes. 102b.

264. See Z 3:35b, quoted on p. 136 above.

265. On the three aspects of soul in Medieval Jewish Philosophy see EJ 15: 172–73; in the *Zohar,* see MZ 2:11–19.

266. For further discussion, see MZ 2:499.

267. See, e.g., TZ 6 (22b); 18 (34a); and 24 (69a). For the exceptions see I. Tishby, MZ 2:500. This hierarchical view of the soul is maintained during the week; according to TZ 6 (23b) the ordinary tripartite soul is said to come from the three lower worlds: *Beri'ah, Yeẓirah* and *ᶜAsiyyah.*

268. According to one account the *neshamah yeterah* supports not the ordinary soul, but *Shekhinah* in Her earthly "Exile":

> On Friday nights, the *neshamah yeterah* descends to support the Lower *Shekhinah* in *Galut* . . . and when the Sabbath departs, the *neshamah yeterah* within Her leaves: *"Va-yinnafash"* [Ex. 31:17]: . . . Woe to the Soul [*Malkhut*], for there is none to support Her. (TZ Add. 6 [143b])

269. Usually rendered "stake"; the TZ translates the Hebrew *ʿeẓ* hyperliterally for mystical reasons that will become clear.

270. This usage of *naʿal* as a confining, even defiling presence, recurs several times in the *Tiqqunim.* Cf., e.g., TZ 48 (85a–b), translated on p. 240 below.

271. On the regarbing of *Shekhinah* each Shabbat see MZ 2:495; and chap. 3, below.

272. The notion that the Sabbath-soul supplants the ordinary pneuma is also intimated in the *Me'irat ʿEinayim:* 106. R. Isaac of Acco suggests that the plenitude of Sabbath-blessing is so great that it—qua Sabbath-soul—completely fills the devotee's body and utterly transforms him:

> Through his inwardness the devotee [*ḥasid*] draws forth an additional soul from the influx of holy spirit; it courses from the Well-springs of Holiness [sefirotically, *Ḥokhmah*], the foundation of *Binah,* through the paths of Truth and Faith [*Tif'eret* and *Malkhut*] into the devotee's body [I would contend: completely filling him]. [In the process] the created world and all its space [*ḥalal*] is blessed, suffused with divine energy.

Accordingly, the stakes for profaning Shabbat are raised to the limit: to do so is to empty one's very self and by theurgic extension, to empty *Shekhinah,* the divine Sabbath. R. Isaac's interpretation turns on the now-familiar wordplay between *meḥallel*—one who profanes—and *ḥalul*—to be emptied out, made hollow:

> When a wicked person profanes the Sabbath, he profanes/empties himself, *for his inner space was previously filled with the Sabbath-soul* [emph. mine]. Now it is emptied and he becomes *ḥalul,* a spiritual void. [Moreover] he makes all the entities that were full, empty, and empties Shabbat. [Before] the Diadem was full, blessed with Compassion. . . . But this person creates emptiness; he "severs the shoots" and creates separation [between the Lovers] on high.

273. Of course, it could be argued that the *Zohar* need not do this because it regards the *neshamah yeterah* as a supplement to the already differentiated souls that Jews normally possess. In other words, a kind of hierarchy of souls and of spiritual levels may be maintained by dint of the permanent soul. Still, it might be said that the TZ/RM foregrounds the differing spiritual levels of people by consciously maintaining a hierarchy of Sabbath-souls, whereas the *Zohar* de-emphasizes it by implying the equality of Sabbath-souls.

274. Cf. TZ 6 (22b).

275. Cf. Z 3:29a–b (RM) for a parallel teaching. Also see my comments on the RM in n. 136 above.

276. See I. Tishby's remarks, MZ 2:499.

277. See chap. 4, pp. 262–67 below.

278. Cf. Ṭur OḤ 263 and the sources therein.

279. It sometimes seems as though the *Zohar* were saying: the moment that Shabbat enters the devotee's life varies from week to week, from person to person. I must caution, however, that this last reading is probably too modern for the *Zohar*. In part, the variety of accounts may be attributed to the Aggadic status of the Sabbath-soul, which precludes the need for precisely fixing the moment of its arrival. The non-systematic, dynamic nature of Moshe de Leon's thinking also plays a role.

280. The *Zohar* passage holds that this crowning occurs just prior to the *Barekhu:*

> She [*Shekhinah*] is crowned below by the holy people, and all of them are crowned with new souls. Then the beginning of the prayer to bless Her with joy and beaming faces: *Barekhu 'et YHWH ha-mevorakh.* (transl. D. Matt, *Zohar:* 132)

The *Mishqal* implies that the reception occurs *during* the *Barekhu.*

281. Some of the liturgical phrases that are suggestive to a Kabbalist are: "Spread over us Your Sukkah of Peace; "Shelter us in the shadow of Your wings," etc.

282. Also cf. *Mishqal:* 112–13. The safety that the Sabbath affords is also articulated by David ben Judah he-Ḥasid in OZ 39a/54a (to *Hashkivenu*). Explaining why this prayer is altered on Shabbat, R. David wrote:

> During the week we must recite "He who guards His people Israel forever" because then the world is under the control of the Princes [the angelic world] and so we must plead for compassion upon the world, to guard against the ruling Princes. But when the Sabbath arrives, the world gets out from under their rule and [all] become subjects of the Holy One. For this reason we recite "He who spreads a *Sukkah* of Peace," referring to *Binah,* the "rejoicing Mother of the children" [Ps. 113:9] who spreads forth Her wings over Her children. At this point She "shelters them under the shadow of [Her] wings [*Malkhut*]," for they have already gone under the supernal *Shekhinah.*
>
> A parable. To what may this be compared? To a shepherd who daily leads his flock through wilderness and forest where beasts of prey lurk. For this reason, the shepherd takes along [sheep]dogs [the "Princes," or angelic emissaries of *Din*] to protect the flock from the wolves and lions and other wild beasts [radical *Din, Siṭra'*

> 'Aḥra']. But when he brings the sheep beyond the wall to a safe abode, there is no need for further protection.
>
> So it is during the week. The world is given unto the Princes for safekeeping. For this reason Israel must recite the prayer "He who guards His people Israel" each evening. But on Shabbat the world does not need protection for the Canopy of Peace . . . protects us; the Holy One Himself watches over the world, over events large and small. He sends forth His supernal light to the world through an abundance of divine energy and the additional Sabbath-soul. For this reason we say *"Shabat va-yinnafash"* [Ex. 31:17]: He ceased from labor and imparted souls.

Incidentally, R. David ben Judah's interpretation again seems to build on earlier Ashkenazic sources. See the parallels in MV, *Siddur RaSHI,* and esp. Eleazar of Worms' *Perush ha-Tefillot* (MS Oxf. Bodl. 124, fol. 133a) which contains a lovely version of the parable of the Shepherd and the Sheep.

283. In the TY, where the traditional Friday afternoon bath has become an act of ritual immersion (*ṭevilah*), the Sabbath-soul is actually received as one is emerging from the water. For further discussion, see pp. 229–30 below; and *Sod ha-Shabbat:* Section 5.

On the custom of bathing before Shabbat, cf. TB Shab. 25b (s.v., "Judah bar Ilai") and 113b; RaMBaM, MT "Shabbat" 30:2; etc.

284. Also see the parallel (and equally rhapsodic) description in Z 2:89a.

285. One is tempted to call it a "rush."

286. As above, the paradigm for this experience seems to be Ezekiel's vision of the Chariot. The "joyous sight of the heavenly angels ascending and descending" recalls the *raẓo' va-shov* of Ezek. 1:14. (The image also brings to mind Jacob's ladder, esp. Gen. 28:12.)

287. "Caught up in the world of souls [a cipher for ecstasy]": On the origins of this imagery, see G. Scholem's discussion "Four Who Entered Paradise and Paul's Ascension" in his *Jewish Gnosticism, Merkabah Mysticism, and Talmudic Tradition* (New York, 1965). Also see I. Gruenwald, *Apocalyptic and Merkavah Mysticism* (Leiden, 1980).

In the *Zohar* passage, entering Shabbat is depicted as a moment of ecstatic spiritual ascent. Both the setting and the imagery used—the river bank, the procession of angels—suggest the possible influence of a contemporary meditative technique. As M. Idel has recently shown, the *Merkavah* tradition of gazing on a pool (or bowl) of moving water [see *Re'uyyot Yeḥezqe'l* in I. Gruenwald: Ibid.] was still used by mystical visionaries in thirteenth century Spain. This practice was consciously linked with the paradigm of Ezekiel's vision at the river Kevar. The presence of moving water—its surface shimmering with dancing light—was used to evoke the *raẓo' va-shov* of the angels or even the dynamic movement within the

Godhead. Moshe de Leon refers to such practices in his *Sheqel ha-Qodesh* (Greenup ed.: 113). For a partial translation of this source, see p. 27 above. For further details on these meditative techniques, see M. Idel, "Le-Gilguleha shel Ṭekhniqah Qedumah shel Ḥazon Nevu'i bi-Ymei ha-Beinayyim" in *Sinai,* Vol. 86 (1980): 1–7 (esp. pp. 6–7).

288. E.g., see Z 3:95a:

> On Shabbat, all sorrow and anger depart from the world; for it is the day of the King's wedding; a day on which [Israel receives] additional souls.

And 2:204b:

> With the *neshamah yeterah* one forgets all pain and the heat of anger; instead, joy is found on high and below.

And finally, 2:89a. On Sabbath eve,

> a breath/breeze/soul [*ruaḥ*] from the delectation of the Holy Ancient One [*Keter*] courses through all the worlds, ascending and descending, spreading forth unto all the holy children, unto those who observe Torah. Then they attain complete rest; trouble, travail, the weekly struggle to make ends meet—all these are forgotten. Thus, Scripture says: "On this day YHWH has given you rest from sorrow and trouble and from the harsh labor that you endured." (Isa. 14:3)

289. Also see *Rimmon* 29b on *ᶜonat talmidei ḥakhamim.* On Sabbath as the time for marital intercourse for scholars, see TB Ket. 62b and BQ 82a.

290. On the inclusive properties of *'et* in Rabbinic hermeneutics, see EJ 8:371.

291. The *Zohar*'s conception of the reunification of the bifurcated soul bears an affinity to an idea developed in ecstatic Kabbalah. According to the anonymous author of the *Shaᶜarei Ẓedeq,* during *devequt*—mystical communion—the human soul regains its primordial wholeness, uniting with its other half, God, the supernal Soul. See M. Idel, *Kabbalah: New Perspectives:* 63–64. This notion was widespread in contemplative Ḥasidism, too. Cf. the Maggid of Mezritch's famous teaching in *Maggid Devarav le-Yaᶜaqov,* section 24, summarized in G. Scholem, *The Messianic Idea in Judaism:* 226–27.

292. *Qishrei ha-qodesh* is a Hebraicized version of the Zoharic *qishrin ᶜila'in qaddishin* (2: 244a–b), an epithet for the unified sefirotic world. See Y. Liebes, "Peraqim be-Millon Sefer ha-Zohar": 398.

The fuller *Rimmon* text makes clear that the Sabbath-soul imbues the adept with added theurgic responsibility, even as it enables him to become part of the supernal Gestalt. It is as though there were a double coronation and double wedding ceremony each Shabbat: both adept and *Shekhinah* are coronated, while the ensuing intra-divine union is paralleled by the union/communion of the devotee with the sefirotic realm. Here are some excerpts from this remarkable source, beginning with the moment of earthly "crowning":

> Each person in Israel is imbued with an additional soul on Sabbath eve; "with crowns on their heads" [ff. TB Ber. 17a!] they enter the Canopy of Peace [*Shekhinah*/Shabbat] that arches overhead.

The crowned devotee serves as an attendant unto *Shekhinah*, preparing Her for the royal wedding unto the King. As he recites the *Qiddush* over wine the adept brings down *shefa*ᶜ from *Gevurah*, annointing Her and kindling divine love (see my comments on p. 114 above):

> The [people] consecrate [or: betroth] Her in the *Qiddush* over the wine which is the rousing of Love. . . . Surely this is the hour of the mystery of Love, when the "Ark rested" [Gen. 8:4] from all Her labors, as is proper for all who are annointed as Queen. We must arouse Her holy [powers], "Her perfumes and Her allotted portions . . . that come from the King's palace." [Esth. 2:9]

Through participating in the supernal mystery, the adept is borne aloft, to

> become bound up in the "bonds of holiness," in the mystery of the People "glorious in Holiness." [Ex. 15:11]

Here the erstwhile "participation mystique" intensifies, edges towards unio mystica.

293. Also see 2:135b; and 2:203a–b, where the demonic fires must be hurled down to the Cavern of the Great Abyss.

294. Ff. TB Sanh. 65b. In an interesting parallel, Z 2:252b holds that even the *nehar di-nur*, the "river of Fire" (Dan. 7:10) that flows through supernal Eden abates on Shabbat! During the week, souls are ritually immersed in this stream and cleansed; all impurities are burned up and consumed, while all that is pure passes through unscathed. But on Shabbat, this river—like a celestial Sambatyon—rests:

> Every day of the week the River of Fire flows, singeing some seraphim and [angelic] overseers. When Sabbath arrives, a tribunal goes forth and the River of Fire quiets, its storms and sparks cease.

295. The passage reads:

> Even the wicked in Hell are crowned [with a *neshamah yeterah*] on Shabbat. They enjoy quiet and rest; for there is no one so wicked as to be without some good deeds which might aid him in the World-to-Come. When is he aided? On the Sabbath, so that all may be adorned with the Crown of Shabbat.

296. Hence the *Havdalah* blessing "*bore'* me'orei ha-'esh," "*Creator* of the flames of fire." See pp. 272–73 below for further discussion.

297. A reference to the sacred union of the Bride/Queen with the King. The phrase "United in the secret of One" indicates Her newly perfected state.

CHAPTER TWO

Aspects of Meaning in Kabbalistic Ritual: With Special Reference to the Case of Shabbat

A PROGRAMMATIC INTRODUCTION TO CHAPTERS 2 THROUGH 4

In recent years anthropologists and historians of religion alike have devoted much energy to the study of ritual: its symbolic structure, societal function, and the reasons for its powerful ability to mobilize desire and create belief. For it is through such concrete acts that religious conviction generally emerges. As anthropologist Clifford Geertz has noted, "[people] attain their faith as they portray it."[1] Within the study of Judaism, new attention has been drawn to the activity of the theosophical Kabbalists, who have been well-known for their creativity in symbol-making and exegesis, and increasingly, for the extraordinary richness of their ritual life. In the ensuing three chapters we shall discuss some of the theoretical issues informing Kabbalistic ritual in general, and Sabbath ritual in particular. We shall focus on two broad hermeneutical questions throughout: what do these rituals mean, and how do they work? To wit: how does a given ritual create a certain sacred order and project it onto the cosmos and into the life of the devotee? What sorts of meanings, explicit and implicit, are stored in the myths that underlie the ritual?[2] What sacred stories are told about society and cosmos, about the nature of being Jewish? What performance factors influence the ritual's meaning and efficacy, its transformative power? In fine, how does ritual construct a world[3] that seems uniquely real to the devotee and legitimate his role in it?

Viewed as a whole, chapters 2 through 4 constitute a kind of triptych, an extended meditation on the nature of Sabbath ritual and the problematics of its interpretation. The chapters assume the following structure. In chapter 2, to orient the reader, a kind of typology of Kabbalistic ritual is provided, placing special emphasis on the Sabbath-setting. Kabbalistic ritual is distinguished, briefly, from its Rabbinic precursors, as innovations and subtle shifts in emphasis are noted[4]; then, the ontology underlying the life of miẓvot is elucidated and the consequences of ritual activity, charted, all as seen by the Kabbalists themselves.

The next two chapters are more concentrated and form the heart of our inquiry. The focus is on those rituals located at Sabbath's margins: the rites of Preparation (chap. 3) and Separation (chap. 4), of entry and closure. As rituals of considerable complexity and dramatic urgency, they contain a wealth of interesting material from a theoretical point of view. All rituals are transformative agents to one degree or another, and these rituals—by dint of their liminal setting—are ontological transformers par excellence, dramatizing and modulating the shift from one modality—one cosmic order—to another. The analyses of these radical transformations will be informed both by the typology presented in chapter 2 and by some of the methodological approaches pioneered in the History of Religions and symbolic anthropology.

A TYPOLOGY OF KABBALISTIC RITUAL

Rabbinic and Kabbalistic Ritual: Some Contrasts

Until recently, ritual studies have tended to be focused on nonliterate cultures. To this day, Kabbalistic ritual has received relatively little scholarly attention from historians of religion[5]; yet Kabbalistic ritual is a significant area of study not only because of its symbolic richness and the insight it affords into varying types of mystical experience, but also because it is largely a mythic re-reading of the rituals of a highly sophisticated and literate (i.e., Rabbinic) culture. Unlike the Lurianic mystics, the classical Kabbalists developed only a small number of new rites to expressly dramatize the mythic elements in their thought. Their creativity is primarily one of revision and re-casting, of "uncovering" new meanings in the old praxis. As Gershom Scholem has noted: "The existing ritual was not changed. It was taken over more or less intact,"[6] enabling the Kabbalists to remain within the traditional nomos even as they transformed it. To express this in other words: outer praxis remained relatively constant while the inner landscape and underlying "story" was significantly altered. In this way, the Kabbalists' re-reading of Tradition was both conservative and boldly innovative, a classic case of "new wine in old skins," i.e., of religious revitalization. For this reason, Kabbalistic ritual is an excellent point of departure for studying the tension between continuity and change that necessarily suffuses a religious Tradition.[7]

The scope of the Kabbalists' "mythopaeic revision" of Sabbath ritual cannot yet be fully gauged, for we still lack a comprehensive phenomenology of the Rabbinic Sabbath in its various expressions. We can no longer unqualifiedly accept Scholem's conclusion that the "strangely dry and sober" Rabbinic ritual is devoid of a mythic substrate.[8] Recent scholarship—e.g., the work of Jacob Neusner and, in a different vein, that of Moshe Idel—has done much to revise this view: disclosing the mythic matrix underlying such activities as Torah-study, the Rabbinic meal, etc.[9] Nor is the Rabbinic observance of Shabbat wholly lacking in mythic models as Scholem suggests. To cite three examples: By resting from labor, the Jew is—very broadly, to be sure—emulating God's behavior at the primordial Shabbat. More narrowly, recitation of certain prayers has mythopaeic resonance: e.g., he who recites the *Va-Yekhullu* on Friday night is considered "as though he had become a partner with the Holy One in the Work of Creation" (TB Shab. 119),[10] while several midrashim suggest that the *Havdalah* is modelled on Adam's actions as the first Sabbath came to a close.[11] These examples, however, serve more to qualify than to fully undermine Scholem's assessment of Rabbinic Sabbath ritual, for no consciously articulated mythology undergirds such rites as candlelighting, the use of wine at *Qiddush,* marital intercourse, and the like. Such meanings—if they do exist—remain buried.[12] Myth, in short, seems to be the occasional (rather than permanent) concomitant of Rabbinic ritual life. Another feature worth noting is the apparently fragmentary nature of these Rabbinic Sabbath myths. Each *'aggadah* constitutes a separate explanation unto itself, an isolated story. Only in Kabbalah is there an integrated mythic system (perhaps because only in Medieval times has Rabbinic Judaism itself become a system.)

Realizing the tentative (and generalized) nature of these conclusions, let us draw several more refined distinctions between Rabbinic and Kabbalistic Sabbath ritual. (The reader is encouraged to review the preliminary assessments made on pp. 68–69 above.)

(1) The first distinction is a matter of degree. The mythic aspect of Rabbinic ritual tends to be commemorative in nature, rehearsing (and in some cases, even recovering) events that occurred in sacred history. On occasion, it may also be anticipatory, pointing towards the eschaton. Kabbalistic ritual does not eschew these dimensions; indeed it frequently intensifies them, as has been seen. Kabbalistic ritual, however, tends to a much greater extent to dramatize sacred

events that are said to be unfolding in the spiritual realm at this very moment or hour. The present qua present is invested with mythic potency,[13] affording the miẓvot great immediacy and—as shall be seen—"metaphysical" urgency. *Miẓvat Shabbat* enables the devotee to fully participate in the *ongoing* mysteries suffusing heaven and earth.

(2) Most Kabbalists integrated myth into ritual in a manner both systematic and comprehensive. As was noted in chapter 1, the Rabbis developed a rich body of lore evincing the Sabbath's status as a sacramental institution. One need only recall the apotheosis of Shabbat as Bride, Queen, King, and divine Treasure; its status as one-sixtieth of the World-to-Come; the notion of the Sabbath-soul, etc. Still, these remained minor motifs in the literature, without elaboration. Moreover, they were never systematically correlated with, or integrated into, the stream of Sabbath ritual. The Kabbalists, by contrast, did so in comprehensive and sustained fashion. Each ritual act dramatized an exemplary story and was part of a larger mythic Gestalt. A brief review of the motif of the Sabbath-soul may highlight some of the critical differences.

The sole Rabbinic discussion of *neshamah yeterah* lacks a story line: we only know when the spirit leaves the devotee but not when it arrives, whence it derives, what it does during the week or during its earthly sojourn; nor do we know how it transforms the devotee and shapes his experience of Shabbat. Zoharic Kabbalah, to give one pointed contrast, tells of this and much more. It transforms the spare Rabbinic allusion—a static image without a plot—into a complex mythic drama and brings the events to life via the mime of ritual.

(3) For most Kabbalists, proper observance of Shabbat has theurgic impact, affecting the Cosmos and God's inner life. For this very reason, the devotee is accorded cosmic responsibility.[14] The following excerpt from the *'Oẓar ha-Kavod* is a good example of how Rabbinic ritual may be re-read towards this end. Commenting on the dictum (TB Shab. 118b) that "If Israel were to properly keep two Sabbaths, they would immediately be redeemed," Ṭodros Abulafia wrote:

> This passage refers to the two supernal Sabbaths, Remember [*Tif'eret*] and Keep [*Malkhut*], for on [Shabbat] they unite and receive divine blessing, the emanation of Compassion which comes from the Master of Compassion [*Keter*]. Indeed, all comes from Him. Redemption depends on this.

Through deft use of sefirotic symbolism, the Aggadic focus is shifted from the human realm to the intradivine. Hence, redemption—now understood as divine renewal—is something that may take place each Shabbat, so long as Israel observes it properly. This new symbolic interpretation does not undermine the original Rabbinic notion, however: it is preserved as another, more exoteric layer of meaning.[15]

(4) Two other basic differences have just been alluded to: the relocation of the Aggadic world in the divine realm, and the resultant multivocality of Kabbalistic symbolism. While for the Rabbis, most *'aggadot* dramatized events transpiring at the juncture of the human and divine realms, the mystics saw the intradivine world as the primary Aggadic stage. For example, the metaphorical marriage of Shabbat and the Community of Israel related in *Genesis Rabbah* is now understood to symbolize the supernal marriage of *Tif'eret* and *Shekhinah.* The Rabbinic image is retained, however, as the marriage of earthly Israel to the Sabbath day is seen as the outward manifestation of the divine process.[16] In dialectical fashion, the earlier Tradition is both re-read and (paradoxically) preserved. This twofold consequence helps explain the multivocal power of Kabbalistic symbolism. One term evokes two referents: at certain times the human referent (or symbol) will be in the foreground; at other moments, the divine one (or archetype) will be highlighted. The other referent always remains in the background, poised to re-emerge. As conceptual and emotional links are formed between the two, the distinct boundaries between symbol and archetype—e.g., between the two Communities of Israel—may blur.[17] The divine and human identities may begin to conflate. For ritual has the ability to make assertions that are unacceptable in other contexts, to subliminally suggest that which cannot be said.

Through even these brief points, the simultaneously radical and conservative valences of Kabbalistic ritual may be inferred. Rabbinic praxis, newly symbolized, is reinforced—indeed, revealed to be cosmically necessary; but as this is done, the old rationale or mythos is transformed and a new inner landscape fashioned for the devotee.

Symbolism and Magic: The Ontological Structure of Kabbalistic Ritual

It is through ritual that the central myths of the Kabbalistic Sabbath are given dramatic voice and made viscerally real, and so incorporated into the life of the devotee. But how does this complex process work? Before analyzing those rituals that specifically chart the entry into Shabbat and the separation from it, it is useful to make some general comments about the structure undergirding Kabbalistic ritual: to see how the Kabbalists themselves viewed the inner workings of ritual and its consequences. This account will necessarily be idealized and rather sharply drawn: it will be fleshed out and refined as the discussion unfolds. For vital ritual life is seldom a tidy affair.

As Gershom Scholem has noted, the ontology underlying ritual life in theosophical Kabbalah is at once symbolic and magical, based on the belief that "everything is *in* everything else" and that "everything *acts on* everything else."[18] All worlds and levels of being are interrelated. The cosmos may be conceived of as an infinitely complex organism linked both via contiguity (in a great Chain of Being)[19] and via symbolic structure. That is, the template of divinity (and in some accounts, *Siṭra' 'Aḥra'*, too) is felt to permeate all levels of existence: "What is above is below and what is inside is outside," heaven and earth reflecting each other.[20] In the opinion of Menaḥem Recanati:

> All created being, the human being and all other creatures in the world, exist according to the archetype [*dugma'*] of the ten *sefirot*. (*Sefer Ṭaʿamei ha-Miẓvot* 3a, cited in G. Scholem, OKS: 124)

Yet, despite this profoundly inter-linked cosmology, the human being is accorded a singular role and essence, which elevates him above other created beings. Only he is truly *Ẓelem 'Elohim* (Gen. 1:27), the specially empowered and obligated image of God. This may be illustrated by reference to both the contiguous and symbolic schemas.

Standing at the end of the Chain of Being, the human being (and more specifically, the Jew) serves as an ontological transformer. Through meditation and proper performance of the miẓvot he is able to draw down the divine energy (*shefaʿ*) into the world, investing it with sacrality; so too, he is able to reverse this divine flow—to return it to its sefirotic source—thereby adorning and completing divinity. If God is the Creator and initiator of the ongoing process, humanity (i.e., Israel) serves as its perfecting agent.

Moreover, the person is uniquely able to reflect and act upon the world of divinity by virtue of three symbolically-charged properties:

(1) The status of the human soul, said to actually derive from the divine matrix;

(2) The person's status as divine microcosm—in the *Zohar*'s words, "the perfection of all, the [only] one containing all" (3:48a); and

(3) His ability to establish a special link with divinity by virtue of ritual life: via Torah and the miẓvot.

The soul as divine. It is the soul which renders the person *'adam,* the perfectable image of God. Whereas the Talmudic Rabbis viewed the soul as a created (non-divine) entity, Kabbalists tended to see it as consubstantial with divinity[21]: in Moshe de Leon's words, "a cosmic spark," "a blossom from the [sefirotic] Tree," "the holy offspring born of the union of the Holy One and *Shekhinah,*" indeed, "part of God above" (re-reading Job 31:2)[22] Nurtured in the sefirotic realm, the soul is sent forth to animate and perfect the body. But this movement is two-directional. As in Neo-Platonism, the soul (by its very nature) is able to ascend on high, to return to its supernal root.[23] We have already seen a specialized instance of this *reversio* in the analysis of the Sabbath-soul (pp. 135–36 above). As the pneuma returns home, borne on the wings of Sabbath-delight, the adept is transported into the divine mysteries.[24]

Person as microcosm. Closely related to the notion of the divine soul is the concept of Person as Microcosm, reflecting the sefirotic archetype. If, as some Kabbalists suggested, all beings symbolize an aspect of the supernal structure, only the person embodies its totality:

> The human being is the symbol of the divine paradigm. *All* worlds, on high and below, are included within him: He is the mystery of the Image of God [*Ẓelem 'Elohim,* ff. Gen. 1:26–27] (*Tolaᶜat Yaᶜaqov* 89b)

Or again: "Only the human being is the perfection of all, the one containing all." (Z 3:48a) Not surprisingly, the soul is frequently portrayed as the microcosm par excellence. This mirrored relation allows the devotee's quest for self-knowledge to simultaneously serve as a means for attaining knowledge of God:

> Whoever wishes to further enter into the King's Palace must first know his own soul . . . which is in the image of its Creator. . . . *When a person knows the measure of his soul and its inner aspects, from thence will he understand and expand his insights into the mysteries of Kingship.* (*Sefer ha-Mishqal:* 35; emph. mine)

Here is a striking example of theological interiority, whereby the encounter with absolute Being unfolds in the depths of one's soul.

It should be recalled that some Kabbalists restricted this microcosmic relationship to the soul. Many, however, periodically asserted that the entire human being, even the body itself, is an image of the divine. Menaḥem Recanati, inspired by the *Zohar,* wrote:

> For this reason the human being is called a microcosm, for he is composed of the divine totality. For all his limbs are the likeness and the emblem of the upper world. As it is said: "*From my flesh* shall I behold God." [Job 19:26][25]

Here it is the human body, properly tuned (via the miẓvot) and properly decoded (via Kabbalistic gnosis), which discloses the mysteries of the divine Corpus.[26]

The central role of ritual life: Torah and the miẓvot. The divinity of the soul and the microcosmic structure of the person provide the ontological foundation for the divine-human nexus; yet they do not explain it entirely. The link to divinity is most clearly actualized through ritual life in the broadest sense: the holy path of Torah and the miẓvot. This process—at the very heart of the Kabbalistic enterprise—may be briefly sketched here. Re-reading the Rabbinic dictum (Gen. R 44:1) that "the miẓvot were given to humankind to purify [*le-ẒaReF*] them," the Kabbalists claimed that they were given to bind (also, *le-ẒaReF!*) persons to God and to bind together worlds.[27] It is important to recall that in the Kabbalistic ontology, the miẓvot are accorded cosmic status. Each miẓvah is seen as originating in the so-called "supernal Torah" or divine essence itself. The miẓvot are not only uttered by God but, in their archetypal form, are part of the divine corpus.[28] The proper performance of a given miẓvah is held to both represent and magically call forth the supernal life contained in its archetype. By contrast, a profaning act is said to weaken divinity, and strengthen its archetype, the antipodal forces of *Siṭra' 'Aḥra'.* In the *Zohar*'s sonorous refrain, *be-'itᶜaruta' di-le-tatta' 'ishkaḥ 'itᶜaruta' le-ᶜeila'*: "a rousing below produces a similar rousing on high."[29] Thus the person is accorded nothing less than cosmic power, cosmic responsibility.

The balance between the symbolic and magical aspects of ritual life constantly shifts. We may better grasp the dynamic between representation and theurgy by considering two interpretations of the life of miẓvot, the first highlighting its symbolic aspect, the second stressing the magical valence, as well. Through proper performance of the miẓvot the devotee aligns himself with divinity and truly becomes the microcosm or symbol of God. Meir ibn Gabbai powerfully illustrated this notion with a musical metaphor. In his ᶜ*Avodat ha-Qodesh* (2:16), he likened devotee and God to two musical strings. He noted that when the strings are perfectly attuned to one another, should one begin to vibrate, the other necessarily follows, resonating at precisely the same pitch. Ritual life, ibn Gabbai suggested, serves as a spiritual 'tuning fork' enabling the devotee to attune himself to the celestial music and so, add to its chorus. In this sense, ritual life is a powerful tool for integrating the devotee into the cosmos, enabling him to participate in the supernal mysteries in the proper way.[30]

The magical aspects of ritual life (and the cosmic responsibility this entails) are neatly underscored by R. Joseph of Hamadan in his *Sefer Taᶜamei ha-Miẓvot*. Combining the traditional notion that the 613 miẓvot correspond to the number of sinews and limbs in the human body with speculations on the mystical *corpus dei*,[31] the Kabbalist audaciously claimed that each miẓvah simultaneously affects a specific limb in both devotee and divinity: in his words, '*ever maḥaziq 'ever*.[32] For example, the miẓvah of keeping the Sabbath

> corresponds to the third joint of the third finger of the right hand of the Holy One, for the 248 miẓvot [of commission] correspond to the 248 [supernal] limbs which correspond to the 248 angelic limbs . . . in which *Shekhinah* is garbed. When one upholds the miẓvot he sustains the holy and pure Chain. This is the mystery of '*ever maḥaziq 'ever*, "one limb strengthens another." (STM: 294)

The Jew and the angelic realm, the Jew and God, person and Person, the one and the All, are thus linked in an intricate web of symbolic and magical action.

Built on the divine archetype, the person has the potential for becoming an exalted image of the divine. Standing at the end of the chain of emanation, he has the unique task and power to actualize a miẓvah, to return the divine flow back to its source, and thus serve as God's partner in the work of cosmic Restoration.

The Multiple Consequences of Kabbalistic Ritual

Until now we have been sketching the broadest contours of Kabbalistic ritual. This portrait may be refined by detailing the multiple consequences of ritual activity as understood by the mystics themselves. Because the list of consequences is long—reaching some ten in number—it is useful to initially group them into three overarching categories, which will then serve as a framework for discussing the more refined distinctions (or sub-categories). Bearing this in mind, Kabbalistic ritual might be characterized as symbolically significant activity which is understood to accomplish one or more of the following:

(1) to dramatize an event in the sacred realm, especially one pertaining to the supernal world;

(2) to theurgically affect the supernal world (most prominently, by helping to restore and augment the divine Gestalt); and

(3) to transform the life of the devotee, by bringing him in alignment with the divine paradigm and by ushering him into a higher state of being.

The first category underscores the symbolic valence of ritual life, whereas the other two evince its magical import. The second category focuses on ritual's cosmic efficaciousness while the third suggests its reflexive power, its "inward magic." To give these three basic categories added texture and nuance, let us now proceed to unpack them, exploring their inner dimensions or sub-categories.

Ritual as Sacred Drama

As a highly-charged symbolic drama, Kabbalistic ritual may dramatize or reflect some event (or myth) currently unfolding in the supernal realm. A distinction may be made between those rituals which articulate myths occurring at this very instant and those rites which allude to an event happening only roughly at this time, in the present in its more extended sense.[33] Several preparatory rituals, e.g., fall into this latter category, anticipating events about to unfold. Other rites are primarily confirmatory, allowing the adept to express, savor and maintain transformations that have been occurring.[34]

Kabbalistic ritual may also rehearse some paradigmatic event that either happened in Sacred Time (be it Edenic, Sinaitic, etc.) or which will happen in eschatological time. In both of these cases, ritual may be seen as a reflecting surface enabling the devotee to re-view the sacred history of the People or to anticipate their ultimate fate. These events may be understood as occurring in some undefined fashion "right now," though in the case of eschatological time, in partial fashion only.

That a given ritual may simultaneously reflect several mythic paradigms may be readily illustrated. Consider, e.g., the *Tolaʿat Yaʿaqov*'s (TY's) analysis of Returning the Torah to the Ark on Sabbath morning (a rite accompanied by the recitation of Psalm 24:7). Meir ibn Gabbai related that, on one level, the participants are re-enacting the symbolic gesture of King Solomon who

> recited this when he brought the Ark into the Holy of Holies, thereby symbolizing the supernal process,

the integration of *Shekhinah* into *Binah*. This ritual is not only a reflection of an earlier event, however, but intimates that which occurs each Shabbat and is taking place in the sefirotic world at this very instant:

> For the Sabbath is the time of returning the supernal Torah [*Tif'eret/ Shekhinah*] into the mystery of the Ark [here, *Binah*], into the Treasury of the Holy One.

As the devotees chant the prayer they intimate (and imitate) the angelic chorus:

> Then the celestial living Creatures [i.e., the angels closest to divinity] who are called by the name of YHWH exclaim, "Lift up your heads, O Gates, [Heb., *sheʿarim*, connoting the seven lower sefirot] so that "the King of Glory [*Tif'eret*] may come in" [Ps. Ibid.] to His Palace.

Thus, the words of prayer and the return of the Torah esoterically indicate that Shabbat is a time for profound sefirotic union, the integration of the divine Torah into the cosmic Ark.

But that is not all. This act is also an allusion to *hitballeʿut*, the perduring cosmic re-integration or "mystical swallowing" which will occur on the ultimate Shabbat. Speaking in circumspect fashion (as befits this esoteric teaching) ibn Gabbai concluded:

> Thus we recite this psalm as we place the Torah in its Palace. This teaches us further of the reabsorption of the Holy [into its primal source] and the ascension of the Glory [*Shekhinah*, but more generally, the seven active sefirot] as it rises from height to height unto the place from which it unfolded,

the cosmic womb, *Binah:*

> the world that is entirely Shabbat.

To summarize: by observing the current Shabbat the Kabbalist attunes himself to a moment in sacred history; to the current divine union; and catches a glimmer of the ultimate oneness of the Sabbath aeon. We have thereby seen how one ritual may evoke multiple myths and conflate several key moments of sacred time. This example also provides us with a glimpse of how a discrete, delimited, well-known ritual symbol may evoke the experience of the unlimited, the mysterious, the All: the physical Torah evokes the sefirotic Torah, and this Shabbat, the ultimate one. In these ways the text richly attests to that central feature of Kabbalistic ritual: its multivocality. A single note may be played, but chords are heard.

This feature will be analyzed in greater detail below; but first, let us turn to the next overarching category.

Ritual as Agent of Human Transformation

Another point, alluded to before, merits articulation. Ritual symbols afford the devotee living contact with the pneumatic world and enable him to participate in its mysteries in the right way. As we noted, ritual life attunes the devotee to the celestial music in dual fashion: it enables him not only to properly hear it but to be filled with it and play it, as well. Ritual, therefore, transforms the devotee and helps him reach his "ideal" self. As he enters the symbolically charged world of ritual, he becomes a kind of symbol, a mirror able—with only rare exception—to reflect the sacred realm.[35] At one moment he may be the embodiment of Edenic Adam; at another, the symbol of divinity in one of its myriad configurations. Indeed, the Kabbalist seems to be the person who, by dint of his ritual life, best reflects the supernal order.[36] Through ritual, he leaves behind profane existence and enters the "zone of paramount reality,"[37] a higher order of being.

The transformations wrought by Sabbath celebration are uniquely powerful. Although all rituals afford temporary contact with the Sacred, the entire Sabbath day is considered one uninterrupted period of holiness, affording ongoing contact with the Sacred. The order of transformation is seen as so significant and enduring that sacred time becomes not a break in the quotidian, profane order, but the new modality, the new "normalcy." One enters into the Sabbath as into a perduring atmosphere; it is a Temple in which one dwells. Hence, the transformed Sabbath-cosmos—and its emblem, the Sabbath-soul—are thought to be present even when one is not engaged in a specific, well-defined ritual, when one, e.g., is merely desisting from labor. For it is Sabbath-observance, in general, that transforms.

Drawing on the Kabbalists' own attestations, it is useful to distinguish between formalized rituals that are felt to radically transform one and those thought to create more subtle changes. For example, the preparatory rituals just before Shabbat are felt to bring about radical changes in the adept's identity, as he shifts from one modality (the Profane) into another (the Sacred). By contrast, the rituals of Shabbat proper create more subtle changes in one's ontological status: for having entered the Sacred, changes are now a matter of degree. Specific rituals, in this sense, maintain and refine the Sabbath-order, whereas radical transformation is only effected by ritual's opposite, the deliberate act of profanation. This counter-transformation is dramatized in several word-plays found in the TZ/RM. Profane activity threatens to turn *ᶜoNeG* (Sabbath-delight) into *NeGaᶜ* (cosmic harm), and to usher the person out of the realm of *SHaBBaT* into that of its antipode, *SHaBBeTa'i* (i.e., *Siṭra' 'Aḥra'*) whose very name spells *'i SHaBBaT:* no Sabbath, at all.[38]

Finally, the life of the miẓvot may also be seen as a spiritual ladder, linking heaven and earth; the commandments are both a means to (and road map for) the devotee's mystical ascent and an instrument for magical descent, for drawing down divine energy from on high.[39]

The mysticism of ascent—the transport of the adept's soul, will or thought—is perhaps most powerfully realized in contemplative prayer, that most inward aspect of devotional life.[40] Although the more practical commandments demand a certain well-defined and outwardly focused action, the realm of prayer leaves room for extended meditation and mystical immersion. It is through such prayer that the devotee most commonly prepares for and moves towards mystical communion or *devequt* with his Source. For one who knows the mystical *kavvanot* (intentions), the words of prayer serve as twofold symbols; not only reflecting life within the upper worlds (as in other rituals), but also providing markers or blazes for the devotee on his otherwise uncharted ascent to the divine. Gershom Scholem explains this more fully:

> The individual in prayer pauses over each word and fully gauges the *kavvanah* that belongs to it. The actual text of the prayer therefore

> serves as a kind of bannister onto which the Kabbalist holds as he makes his not unhazardous ascent, groping his way by the words. The *kavvanot,* in other words, transform the words of the prayer [into angelic rungs and sefirotic grades,] into holy names that serve as landmarks on the upward climb. (*Kabbalah:* 177)[41]

In some instances, the contemplative ascent eventuates in the magic of descent. "The ascent is for the sake of the descent"—to recast the famous phrase—as the devotee's soul (or more simply, his soaring words) calls forth *shefa*ᶜ from on high. A good example of this spiritual enrichment is found in R. Isaac of Acco's account of ushering in the Sabbath:

> For the *shefa*ᶜ comes from *Ẓaddiq* [*Yesod*] by means of the devotee [*ḥasid*] who knows how to bring down the proper flow by saying: "Come, O Bride; come, O Bride!" Through his mystical concentration he [also] draws forth a Sabbath-soul from the influx of holy spirit. It courses [through the supernal rungs and the lower worlds] . . . coming into the devotee's body. [In the process] the created world and all its expanse is blessed and filled. (*Me'irat* ᶜ*Einayim:* 106)[42]

In sum, ritual transforms the devotee by affording him rare intimacy with the supernal realm. Via mystical symbolization—of language, realia, gestures, and the person—a web of semblances is generated, uniting earthly with supernal, ephemeral with eternal, devotee with divinity—microcosm with macrocosm. The controlling images of mystical ascent and magical descent suggest a new proximity between the person and the pneumatic world, as the one moves towards (or even into) the other's realm. The adept may penetrate into the transcendent mysteries or make them wholly immanent so that they "fill his body . . . and bless the created world." (*Me'irat* ᶜ*Einayim:* Ibid.)

Thus far, we have been focusing on the mythico-symbolic aspects of ritual life and their transforming effects on the devotee. Although some Kabbalistic ritual is focused almost exclusively on these matters, most have a theurgic valence, as well. Let us now turn to the final overarching category.

Ritual as Theurgic Act

Mention may be made of four major theurgic consequences which may happen singly or in various combinations. Kabbalistic ritual "magically" acts upon and transforms the supernal realm by setting proper boundaries between the Sacred and the Profane, and between Divinity and *Siṭra' 'Aḥra'*. This act of Separation is essential for the maintenance of Order, or to use Mircea Eliade's term, Cosmos.[43] Most commonly, this theurgic goal takes on two forms, (1) the liberation of *Shekhinah* from Her entanglement in *Siṭra' 'Aḥra'* and (2) the defense of divinity (and by extension the Jew) against the forces of evil by warding evil off and gaining mastery over it. Such rituals function either to appease (and hence neutralize) evil, or else to subjugate it or temporarily blot it out.

It might be said that the first strategy *creates* proper Order, whereas the second serves primarily to *maintain* it.

More frequently, ritual activity is directed to the divine world per se. This may take on the form of returning (or redirecting) the divine energy to its supernal source and so investing the Godhead with added holiness (sub-category 3). The most frequent images used to dramatize this activity are those of adornment and coronation, whereby *Shekhinah* and the Holy One are garbed (or renewed) with the divine light released by holy action. Mystical prayer, in particular, serves this purpose: through meditation the adept returns the sacred letters—and the crowns of light each contains—to their supernal Root.

The theurgic action *par excellence*, however, is that which promotes intradivine union, investing the sefirotic world with an influx of supernal energy so that its polar aspects are integrated and divinity, restored (sub-category 4). Through ritual life harsh *Din* and flowing *Ḥesed* may be harmonized; Male and Female brought into sacred union; or the seven lower and three upper sefirot re-integrated.[44] This may be affected either by descent, i.e., through the downward flow of *shefa*ᶜ from on high, or by ascent, the absorption of the active sefirot—singly or in aggregate—into the uppermost reaches of the Godhead.

This supernal harmony is generally accompanied by a parallel revitalization below, as the *shefa*ᶜ born of the sacred union brims over and streams into the lower worlds. That is, as an epiphenomenon of this union, heaven is brought down to earth, its energy erupting into the profane sphere. If adornment returns the divine flow to its Source, *yiḥud* (sacred union) helps bring it down. Ritual life thus helps maintain the ecology of the cosmos.

All of these theurgic strategies are found in the rituals surrounding Shabbat. It is interesting to note that particular strategies tend to be employed at specific stages during the day; indeed, they help define the rhythm of Shabbat, telegraphing its underlying mythos and conveying its emotional tenor. In the Zoharic tradition, e.g., *hieros gamos* is dramatized throughout the day, yet is the primary motif for Friday night.[45] Images of coronation and adornment are less time-specific, but are mostly confined to the *Qiddush* and prayer services for Friday night and Saturday morning.[46] The downward flow of *shefa*ᶜ from *Keter* to *Shekhinah* is the dominant image used to convey the surfeit of blessing felt to infuse the Cosmos during the three Sacramental Meals.[47] Less common are those ritual strategies highlighting the harmonization of Right and Left, and those effecting the ascent of the lower sefirot unto their matrix on high. Yet both are employed in the Zoharic *Minḥah* ritual and help articulate the conflicting emotions—the polyrhythms—that characterize the waning hours of Shabbat. This notion may be illustrated briefly.

During Shabbat there is little need for the ritual harmonization of Left and Right, for a natural Sabbath-harmony between the two is generally presumed. *Ḥesed* is seen as the dominant modality whereas *Din* operates in a "sweetened" state, nourished by unbounded Love. Nonetheless, as Sabbath draws to a close the harsher aspect of *Din* begins to stir, and there is a need to re-assert Sabbath harmony. According to the TY, the Torah reading at *Minḥah*, accomplishes just that. Meir ibn Gabbai explained:

> On Shabbat we read the Torah twice: In the morning we read the Portion in its entirety, for "[God's] love [*Ḥesed*] persists the entire day" [Ps. 52:3] and [daytime] signifies wholeness. But at dusk we read ten verses or [perhaps a few] more, but not the entire portion; for the complete portion is of the Right, and [the Right] prevails only till the hour of *Minḥah*. Thereafter, the aspect of Judgment [*Din*] normally prevails. We read from the Torah at *Minḥah in order to subsume the Left in the Right*. Indeed, the Torah proceeded from the fusion of these two, as it says: "From His Right [and from] the Fire [i.e., the Left], the Teaching came unto them." [Dt. 33:2][48]

We have already seen how the other strategy, the integration of the lower sefirot in the upper rungs, indicates the deepest sort of divine union, that which will prevail during the "aeon that is entirely Shabbat." This ultimate state is fleetingly attained during the current Sabbath at several moments of overwhelming power: during the Musaf *Qedushah*, and, according to the TY, at the "hour of Supreme Grace," during the late afternoon prayers. It is as if there were a continual spiritual ascent throughout the Sabbath, each of the four prayer services disclosing a new (and ever-deepening) sefirotic drama.

Finally, at *Minḥah* the drama reaches its climax. Meir ibn Gabbai wrote:

> The evening prayer ["You sanctified"] corresponds to the Perfect Bride who is betrothed to the Groom. The morning prayer, "And Moses rejoiced" esoterically refers to the Groom who rejoices "when he is given his Portion [kabbalistically, *Malkhut*], which ascends to unite with him. In this prayer ["Groom"] implicitly includes the supernal Arms [*Ḥesed* and *Gevurah*], as well. The *Musaf* prayer mystically denotes the *Ẓaddiq* of the World, including the two pillars, Yakhin and Boaz [*Neẓaḥ* and *Hod*], upon which the House is firmly established. Hence, [at *Musaf*], all seven [lower] rungs band together in intimate union. But now [as we recite "You are One"], He [the seven lower sefirot] and His Name [*Keter*] "are One."

And so, in the waning hours of Shabbat, full integration is achieved.

While the rituals of Sabbath proper are focused on the intra-divine world, the rituals at Sabbath's boundaries are focused on the sefirotic limen. As the mythic stage shifts, the two anti-demonic strategies are the primary ones employed. The rituals of preparing for the Sabbath tend to concentrate on the liberation and purification of *Shekhinah,* and conversely, on the suppression of *Siṭra' 'Aḥra'.* This tendency is most pronounced in the Zoharic tradition (especially in the TZ/RM and the TY) and in the *Qanah-Peli'ah,* as well. In the rituals marking Sabbath's end, apotropaics[49] play a major role, too: not so much to suppress *Siṭra' 'Aḥra'* as to ward it off, to keep the devotee from harm and divinity's borders from Evil's polluting influence. It should be noted that these ritual strategies are restricted to Sabbath's limens and to *ḥol* (the profane week). During Shabbat itself they are seen as highly inappropriate, "out of sync" with the sacred mythos, constituting acts of profanation.

There will be ample opportunity to illustrate these points in chapters 3 and 4.

A final observation. In constructing this typology we have focused on distinctively *Kabbalistic* interpretations of ritual. It should be noted, however, that virtually all adepts accorded a limited place for ordinary, i.e., non-mythic, non-symbolic ritual. Even so theurgically oriented a Kabbalist as the young ibn Gabbai left room for *ʿavodah le-ẓorekh hedyoṭ,* worship to satisfy specific human needs.[50] Such straightforward rituals sound like single notes amidst the thick chords of mystical ritual.

A CONCLUDING EXAMPLE

Finally, the characterization of Kabbalistic ritual can be sharpened by distinguishing ritual life from both ordinary and profaning activity, and by drawing a distinction between two sorts of sacred acts, which may be termed *strong* and *weak* ritual, or alternatively, *formal ritual* and *ritual-like* activity. These distinctions emerged from study of numerous sources, but may be illustrated in condensed fashion by considering a *Zohar* text (3:105a) on Sabbath-speech and the TY passage (55a) that builds upon it. These two sources provide a distinctively Kabbalistic rationale for the enjoinder to transform one's speech on the Sabbath (TB Shabbat 113a–b). This Rabbinic teaching—like the *Zohar* after it—distinguishes between three categories: Sabbath-speech, weekday (or mundane) speech, and that which stops before the threshhold of speech: unstated thoughts in general. The *Gemara'* reads:

> "And you shall honor it . . . not finding your own affairs, nor speaking your own words" [Isa. 58:13], meaning that your speech on the Sabbath should not be like your speech on weekdays [*ḥol*]. "Nor speaking": [Mundane] speech is forbidden but thought [about profane matters] is permitted.

In the *Zohar*'s re-reading, these three categories take on mythic proportions. Consider the case of mundane thought first. This is an example of what may be called ordinary behavior: activity that is neutral, without representational value or cosmic valence. Unlike the two other behavior types, it is symbolically and magically silent. The *Zohar* explains:

> While all speech has a supernal archetype or Voice that it arouses, mere thinking does not produce any effect or Voice. (3:105a)[51]

By contrast, profane speech is an example, albeit a mild one, of an anti-nomian or profaning act. During the week, this would constitute a neutral activity. But in the holy context of Shabbat it becomes a symbolic and magical act, like ritual but with a critical difference: its impact is de-cosmosizing. The *Zohar* explains:

> There is no uttered word that does not have a Voice that ascends on high and rouses its other [i.e., its celestial counterpart], that which is called *ḥol*, Profane, belonging to the Profane Days [below the sefirotic world]. When the Profane is aroused on a holy day, surely, there is a diminution in the world above.

Meir ibn Gabbai maintained that such an act defiles the Temple that is Shabbat and sullies its archetype, *Shekhinah*, by mixing sacred and profane:

> As the profane entity is aroused on high, "It defiles the sanctuary of the Lord." [Num. 19:20]

Sacred speech, however, has a symbolic and magical valence that is restorative, enhancing divinity. The *Zohar* reads:

> But if one utters a holy word, a word of Torah, it becomes a Voice which ascends and arouses the holy beings of the supernal King. They place a crown upon His head and there is rejoicing above and below.

This Zohar interpretation was elaborated by Meir ibn Gabbai. Rereading Cant. 3:11, he imaged the holy words uttered by Israel as "the daughters of Zion" which "go forth" to adorn King Solomon [*Tif'eret*] from below. As they do so, "His Mother [*Binah*] adorns Him," bestowing on Him blessing from above "on this His wedding day."

From this example we may learn not only of the three-fold division between ritual, ordinary and profane activity, but of two distinct morphological types of ritual. Sabbath-speech may be considered a low-grade, weak ritual, or perhaps more precisely, a *ritual-like* activity. Formally, it has only some of the traits generally associated with well-defined or strong ritual. Compared to the latter, sacred speech is relatively fluid: both in terms of its temporal setting (it may occur throughout Shabbat, rather than at a precisely fixed hour) and in terms of its content: there is much greater latitude for spontaneity and variation (i.e., individuality) in expression. Precisely coded language is not essential: there is no text to be rehearsed or precisely repeated. Yet, both the *Zohar* and the TY are at pains to stress the impersonal or formal quality of Sabbath-speech. Meir ibn Gabbai called it "words of *Torah*" while the *Zohar* suggests that holy-speech is somehow not one's own. It cites Isa. 58:13, generally understood as the classic source proscribing profane speech on Shabbat:

> "You shall call the Sabbath a delight . . . and you shall honor it . . . not finding your own affairs, nor speaking *your own words.*"

In its ontological structure, as well, Sabbath-speech is both similar to and different from more strictly formal ritual: similar, in that it is given precise symbolic and magical significance; different in the degree of its efficaciousness. That is, its impact is considered less significant than formal ritual and the impact of its antipode, less deleterious. For example, Meir ibn Gabbai wrote that although "an insignificant [profane] word" threatens divine unity "a more serious act . . . threatens the upper and lower worlds."[52]

Psychologically, it is not surprising that Sabbath-speech serves as a *low-grade* ritual. Insofar as it takes on many of the qualities of more formal ritual, it exemplifies the Kabbalistic tendency to transform human activity (and especially, Sabbath-activity) into a sacred modality. Yet, to place too great a formal emphasis on something as ubiquitous as speech would threaten other aspects of Sabbath observance. Neither Moshe de Leon nor Meir ibn Gabbai ever stressed its import to the degree that interpersonal communication would be rendered impracticable. One may assume that this teaching on Sabbath-speech was only intermittently focused on, remaining in the background the rest of the time, sounding like a drone beneath the melodic line of the more formal Sabbath-ritual.[53]

Having concluded the typology, let us turn to the rituals of Preparation, performed on Friday afternoon.

NOTES TO CHAPTER TWO

1. See C. Geertz's *The Interpretation of Cultures* (New York, 1973): 114.

2. As was noted on p. 69 above, many Kabbalists associated each Sabbath ritual with a mythic substrate. More will be said on this matter later in this chapter.

3. I am using this term in its phenomenological sense, ff. M. Scheler, A. Schutz, P. Berger, et al. For explication see P. Berger's *A Sacred Canopy* (Garden City, NY, 1967), Chap. 1: "Religion and World Construction."

4. I hope to note, for heuristic purposes, distinctive tendencies and emphases found in each of these variegated traditions. Sometimes it is possible to sharply distinguish between trends in Rabbinic sources and theosophical Kabbalah; frequently, however, the distinctions are a matter of degree, as certain ideas, motifs and categories appear in both but in different "frequency distributions."

5. Although few trained in History of Religions methodology have any expertise in Kabbalah, those trained in the history of Kabbalah have remained relatively untouched by the recent ferment in the study of religious symbolism, ritual, and myth. Still, several pioneering studies in Kabbalistic ritual are currently available, largely the work of an earlier generation of scholars. Of special note are several essays by I. Tishby and G. Scholem.

See the former's MZ and esp. the latter's two German volumes, *Zur Kabbala und ihrer Symbolik* and *Von der Mystischen Gestalt der Gottheit,* subsequently translated into one Hebrew volume as *Pirqei Yesod be-Havanat ha-Qabbalah u-Semaleha.* (The first of the two German volumes is available to the English reader under the title, *On the Kabbalah and its Symbolism*). I have drawn upon G. Scholem's numerous insights and theoretical formulations in developing my typology.

Special mention should also be made of Moshe Idel's forthcoming *Kabbalah: New Perspectives,* which should prove to be a landmark study in the field. M. Idel's work has also exerted an influence on my thinking here.

6. OKS, "Tradition and New Creation in the Ritual of the Kabbalists" [hereafter, "Tradition and New Creation"]: 126.

7. These questions are succinctly broached in G. Scholem's essay, "Revelation and Tradition as Religious Categories" in *The Messianic Idea in Judaism.*

8. "Tradition and New Creation," OKS: 121. On the distinction between mythically inflected ritual and ritual devoid of any mythic content ("pure ritual"), see now J. Z. Smith, *To Take Place* (Chicago, 1987) Chap. 5.

9. For discussion of the mythic paradigms underlying the early Rabbinic meal see J. Neusner's, *From Politics to Piety* (New York, 1979): 73–74 and 78–90. For more wide-ranging discussion of the myths underlying Amoraic piety see his *A History of the Jews of Babylonia* (Leiden, 1966–70), Vol. 3: Chap. 3, Vol. 4: Chap. 5, and Vol. 5: Chap. 5–7; also see "The Study of Religion as the Study of Tradition: Judaism" in *History of Religions* 14 (1974): 191–206. Many of these insights are treated in more popular fashion (and with greater emphasis on the category of "Myth") in the author's *There We Sat Down* (rev. ed., New York, 1978): Chap. 2–5 and *The Way of Torah* (3rd ed., Belmont, CA, 1979): Part Two.

M. Idel has located remnants of theosophy and mythical thought in Amoraic and post-Amoraic sources, and has speculated on the correlations between these traces and the Rabbinic conception of the miẓvot. See *Kabbalah: New Perspectives,* esp. Chaps. 6 and 7: "Kabbalistic Theosophy" and "Ancient Jewish Theurgy"; see also his various studies in *Meḥqerei Yerushalayim be-Maḥshevet Yisra'el.* Although Scholem tended to stress the distinctions between Kabbalah and Rabbinic Judaism, Idel—in good dialectical fashion—has sought to uncover points of continuity. Hence, two separate hermeneutical "wagers" can be witnessed, each with fateful consequences for constructing the history of early Kabbalah and analyzing its relation to prior Tradition.

10. It is difficult to know exactly what the Talmudic author meant by this phrase. Perhaps one difference between him and a Kabbalist is that the latter would remove the caveat "as though," asserting boldly where the Rabbis must hedge. As has been shown, the mystics claimed that the pristine time of *Maᶜaseh Bere'shit* actually re-enters the world each Sabbath eve.

11. Cf., e.g., PRE 20. For other suggestive sources see p. 65 above.

12. That is, some myth probably underlies the use of myrtle in welcoming the Sabbath (TB Shab. 33b), but its meaning is currently lost to us.

13. James Kugel has argued that the central miẓvah of Torah-study, of doing midrash, enabled the Rabbinic Jew to bask in the sacral time of the past, to enter into the world of Scripture. In so doing, the quotidian present is overwhelmed by the Bible's (mythically potent) time. "The Bible's time is important, while the present is not." He cites E. E. Urbach's view that, for the Rabbis, "God acted (in the past), will act (in the eschatological future), but is not acting in between." Although Urbach's view is too sweeping—exceptions may readily be marshalled—it does point to an interesting difference in stress. For the Zoharic Kabbalist, e.g., Torah-study/midrash always enables one to uncover currently unfolding mysteries. The goal is not to obliterate the present but to "tap into" it in the proper (theosophically sophisticated) way. For the details of J. Kugel's argument, see "Two Introductions to Midrash" in G. Hartman and S. Budick (eds.), *Midrash and Literature:* esp. p. 90.

14. Although elements of theurgy are found in Rabbinic sources, they constitute a relatively minor aspect of ritual piety. (Moreover, none of these sources are focused specifically on *miẓvot Shabbat.*).

It is worth noting that theurgy took on added significance in the period immediately preceding the emergence of Kabbalah; clear evidence is found in late midrashim and traditions preserved by Ḥasidei 'Ashkenaz. For details, see M. Idel, *Kabbalah: New Perspectives,* Chaps. 7 and 8: "Ancient Jewish Theurgy" and "Kabbalistic Theurgy."

15. For another example of how Kabbalistic ritual demands cosmic responsibility, cf. Baḥyya ben Asher to Ex. 31:16. Note his cautious language at the outset:

> "To make the Sabbath" [Ex. 31:16; cf. Mekh. ad loc.]: . . . According to the path of the Kabbalah. Whoever observes the Sabbath below, it is as if he had made it on high. The reason is that whoever observes the Sabbath attests to its supernal source and essence [ʿ*iqqar*] engraved on high. Whoever neglects the Sabbath, it is as if he negates the supernal Sabbath.

At this point the more cautious language recedes:

> Hence, Scripture says: "to make" . . . and not as one may have thought, "to observe" . . . It thereby indicates that one must complete *the supernal Shabbat,* to "make it."

16. In this sense the Sabbath is truly sacramental! For further illustration, see *Sod ha-Shabbat:* Prologue (p. 14) and the accompanying notes, esp. n. 22.

17. The more one identifies with the archetype, e.g., shares in *Shekhinah*'s sorrows and joys, the less clear the distinction between the two becomes! For discussion see pp. 165–66 (n. 171) above.

18. "Tradition and New Creation," OKS: 123.

19. A distinction may be made between pantheistic views that stressed the unity of all existence in an unbroken cosmic chain and the more conventional theistic view, which stressed the qualitative jumps between various links in the chain: between divinity and the angelic worlds, and between the angelic realm and the lower realms. For details, see G. Scholem, *Kabbalah:* 144–52.

20. The quotation is from Goethe (cited anonymously in "Tradition and New Creation," OKS: 121). The concluding phrase echoes Michel Foucault. Speaking of similar medieval cosmologies, he commented:

> Up to the end of the sixteenth century, resemblance played a constructive role in the knowledge of Western culture. It was resemblance that largely guided exegesis and the interpretation of texts; it was resemblance that organized the play of symbols, made possible knowledge of things visible and invisible, and controlled the art of representing them. The universe was folded in upon itself: earth and heaven reflecting each other, faces seeing themselves reflected in the stars, and plants holding within their stems the secrets that were of use to men. . . . (*The Order of Things* [New York, 1970]: 16)

M. Foucalt's analysis of the four types of resemblance—conventia, aemulatio, analogy, and especially, sympathy—are useful in understanding the symbolic and magical ontology of Kabbalah. For one such application, see Karen Guberman, "The Language of Love in Spanish Kabbalah: An Examination of the 'Iggeret ha-Qodesh" in D. Blumenthal (ed.), *Approaches to Judaism in Medieval Times* (Chico, 1984): 53–105.

21. In some accounts all three aspects of soul are correlated with a specific sefirotic root; elsewhere, only the lofty *neshamah*—the seat of religious-spiritual life and mystical cognition—is deemed divine.

22. Common appellations in the *Zohar* and *Sefer ha-Mishqal*. One later Kabbalist, Shabbetai Sheftel Horowitz, went so far as to say that the difference between the soul and the substance of God is quantitative only. See G. Scholem, *Kabbalah:* 148.

23. According to Neo-Platonic thought, spiritual entities have a natural tendency to ascend to their source.

24. A more extended discussion on the "soul as divine entity" may be found in my article, "Ẓelem 'Elohim: Some Thoughts on God and Person in Zoharic Kabbalah." In L. Shinn (ed.) *In Search of the Divine* (New York, 1987). Also see the discussions in G. Scholem, *Kabbalah:* 152–65 and I. Tishby, MZ 2: 3–67.

25. *Perush ʿal ha-Torah,* "Parashat Bere'shit." See the close parallel in TY 89a. Other germane sources include the *Bahir* and *Temunah*. The *Bahir*

(82) correlates the seven human limbs with the seven lower sefirot. The *Temunah* follows suit and suggests that through mystical understanding of the human body, one may attain understanding of the divine archetype. For details see fol. 25a–b and the *Perush* ad loc. A still more extensive correlation is established in Baḥyya ben Asher's *Perush* to Gen. 1:27, where all ten rungs are systematically correlated with the human body.

26. For more on the relation between body and soul, see I. Tishby, MZ 2:69–124. For further discussion on the microcosmic motif and the resemblance between God and Person, see A. Altmann, "The Delphic Maxim in Medieval Judaism and Islam" in his *Studies in Religious Philosophy and Mysticism*, esp. pp. 14–19.

27. See, e.g., Meir ibn Gabbai, *ᶜAvodat ha-Qodesh* (AQ) 2:3.

28. The Kabbalists often imaged the divine world as a texture of archetypal letters comprising a primal Torah. The 613 miẓvot contained therein were specifically correlated with different aspects of the Godhead. According to Azriel of Gerona, e.g., "the miẓvot *are* the divine Glory" (*'Aggadot:* 38). R. Ezra ben Solomon correlated the 613 miẓvot with the seven lower sefirot while the *Zohar,* Joseph of Hamadan, and the TZ cross-indexed each miẓvah with a different aspect of the mystical *corpus dei* and/or all ten rungs. For further discussion, see I. Tishby, MZ 2:431–32 and R. Joseph of Hamadan's interpretation on p. 194 above.

29. Cf., e.g., Z 1:88a, 184a, 244a; 3:44a, et al.

30. Meir ibn Gabbai drew the metaphor of the two strings from Isaac Arama's simile of the two perfectly attuned violins (*ᶜAqedat Yiẓḥaq,* "Noaḥ" Gate 12: *Niggun ᶜOlam*). On the distinction between Arama's and Meir ibn Gabbai's interpretations, see M. Idel, "The Magical and Theurgic Significance of Music in Jewish Texts from the Renaissance to Hasidism" [Hebrew] in *Yuval* Vol. 4 (1982): 35–37 and 46–49.

I have used Meir ibn Gabbai's metaphor to underscore the symbolic nexus between micro- and macrocosm. This symbolism can be turned on its head, however, to assert a most radical (and controversial) theurgy; the perfectly tuned adept then becomes the *original* or *initiating* violin string, and God the responding one. See the continuation of the AQ passage and TY 7a for illustration. For discussion, see M. Idel, "The Magical and Theurgic Significance of Music" and idem, *Kabbalah: New Perspectives:* Chap. 8 ("Kabbalistic Theurgy").

31. These speculations were pioneered in the *Shiᶜur Qomah* (Measure of the Divine Body), a highly provocative text belonging to the *Heikhalot* tradition. For details, see G. Scholem, *Major Trends:* 63–67 and *Kabbalah:* 16–18; and Martin S. Cohen, *The Shiᶜur Qomah* (Lanham, MD, 1983). *Shiᶜur Qomah*-type imagery entered Kabbalistic theosophy largely through the efforts of Moshe de Leon; see, e.g., the daring anthropomorphism in the *'Idrot*

sections of the *Zohar* (discussed on pp. 16–17 above). A version of the *'Idrot* may have influenced Joseph of Hamadan here.

32. For discussion, see M. Meier's "A Critical Edition of the *Sefer Ṭa'amey ha-Miẓwoth*": 23–26.

33. As examples of the latter, consider the English expressions "later today" or "earlier today," which simultaneously indicate presentness and some remove from the moment.

34. As an example of confirmatory ritual, see *Pel'iah* 36b on the Havdalah "blessing over fire." The Rabbinic injunction "to make use of the light" (M. Ber. 8:6) is given an esoteric reading:

> We gaze on the light and dark on our hands to demonstrate that we *have derived enjoyment* from the Light [here, denoting not the candle, but its archetype] . . . the "Hidden Light" called *Zakhor,*

the radiance that emerges from *Tif'eret* during Shabbat. The heightened spirituality of the day is thereby recalled and its last moments, savored.

Detailed illustrations of all three types of "present-tensed" myth are provided in chapters 3 and 4.

35. Thus far it has been shown how the Kabbalist becomes the symbol of divinity, able to emulate the supernal model through ritual life. However, as Wendy O'Flaherty has suggested, a basic hermeneutic question is

> whether the activities of the gods and goddesses are meant to serve as models for human behavior? Gods do many things that men do not, acts that serve many purposes: wish fulfillment, a negative moral lesson, a symbol of human potential. (*Women, Androgynes and Other Beasts* [Chicago, 1980]: 128)

At first blush, O'Flaherty's remarks may seem irrelevant to the Kabbalah. For unlike many other mythic traditions, the Kabbalah always portrays divine activity in a positive light. One might therefore think that the model *of* reality would always serve as a direct model *for* reality, guiding one's behavior. And it almost always does. Yet I have found two cases in the Sabbath literature where the desirable divine activity ought not be emulated. The first is that of kindling a fire on Shabbat; such kindling is proscribed on earth despite the fact that an archetypal fire is said to burn on high. The *Zohar* explains:

> On Sabbath all fires except one are hidden for the duration of the Sabbath. Only the holy supernal fire that is revealed and included in the holiness of Shabbat may burn. When this fire is manifest all other fires remain hidden. This is the fire of the Binding of Isaac which burns on the altar on Sabbath. (2:208a)

In other words, there is but one proper fire in the celestial cosmos on Sabbath, and that is the fire of the supernal altar, *Malkhut*. Seemingly this sacred fire rises up, unites with and consumes Isaac/*Din*, eradicating the latter's harshness. The *Zohar* goes on to say that any fire offered up by a devotee, however, would symbolize and awaken the suppressed fires of *Siṭra' 'Aḥra'*. Only the sacrificial fire in the Temple, *Malkhut*'s earthly reflection, can properly symbolize this divine burning; until its reconstruction, no symbolic act is available. Of course, the *Zohar*'s motivation for this reading is halakhic: to account for the paradoxical fact that the Torah mandates the kindling of fire in the Temple, while generally proscribing it. But the result of Moshe de Leon's mythic rationale is to temporarily sever the link between Macro- and Microcosm.

Nonetheless, it should be pointed out that at least one Kabbalist (David ben Judah he-Ḥasid) found an earthly means to reflect the divine drama—to maintain the symbolic nexus—even without the terrestial Temple. He wrote (OZ 45a/60a):

> On this day Isaac, who is *Gevurah*, the seat of harsh Justice, unites with Rebecca who is the Diadem, the seat of lenient Justice; they become one entity. To reflect this mystery, the priests were allowed to kindle a fire, even on Shabbat. They followed the supernal paradigm: for the fire of Isaac descended unto the feminine, unto Rebecca, his wife, as it is written: "A perpetual fire shall be kept burning on the altar." [Lev. 6:6]

In this day and age, the OZ implies, this paradigm may still be enacted, albeit in more figurative form: through the flaming passion of marital intercourse. He noted:

> This is the hidden meaning of having marital intercourse on Shabbat. For [at this time] the desire [*raẓon*] of the supernal world pervades the cosmos and blessing is found everywhere; divine energy flows in great abundance.

One might argue that the *Zohar* never really broke with the exemplary function of the divine myth in the case of Sabbath-fire, simply deferring its emulation till Messianic Temple times. (In W. O'Flaherty's schema this would be a myth underscoring "human potential.") Perhaps a more striking case of the divine myth that cannot be replicated is found in the SṬM of Joseph of Hamadan. Despite his elaborate Macro/Microcosmic structure and the notion of *'ever maḥaziq 'ever,* he stressed the that there are aspects of divinity which cannot (or must not) be emulated, *kedei she-lo' le-hishtammesh be-sharviṭo shel ha-melekh:* lest one make improper (theurgic) use of the King's sceptre. Not only does kindling a flame on Shabbat fall within this category, but also "carrying from the private domain [*reshut ha-yaḥid*] to the public [*reshut ha-rabbim*]" (ff. M. Shab. 1:1). He explained:

> This is prohibited lest one make use of the King's sceptre, for on Shabbat the *shefa*ᶜ flows from the domain of the *Yaḥid* [here read as the realm of Unity, the sefirotic world] unto the domain of the *Rabbim*. For *Reshut ha-Yaḥid* refers to the ten sefirot which are one. His Name is called the domain of Unity. *Reshut ha-Rabbim* is so-called because it contains the mystery of *Perud,* Multiplicity . . . The *shefa*ᶜ flows from the Domain of Unity unto the Domain of

Multiplicity, but "lest we make use of the King's sceptre" [cf. M. Sanh. 2:5; Mid. Ps. 21], we are forbidden to carry things in and out.

The cases discussed here are anamolies, to be sure, but they should caution one against making overly schematic pronouncements regarding Kabbalistic ritual.

36. For example, although ordinary Jews may engage in sexual intercourse during the week, the Torah-scholar (i.e., Kabbalist) is enjoined to do so only on Shabbat (ff. TB BQ 82a). The esoteric rationale for this teaching is that the Kabbalist thereby aligns himself with the supernal rhythms. Meir ibn Gabbai explained:

> They [the Kabbalists] await the arrival of Shabbat and prepare for the moment of celestial coupling. They choose to have sexual relations when it is the desire of their Creator—during the time of celestial coupling, the union of the Bride with Her beloved—and avoid marital relations during the profane working days. (TY 50a)

While the ordinary Jew may properly be "out of sync" with the divine rhythms on certain occasions, the Kabbalist strives to always be properly aligned (barring those exceptions detailed in the preceding note). See *Sod ha-Shabbat:* Section 12 and nn. 170 and 174 for further discussion. Also see Appendix II below.

37. This phrase was coined by the sociologist of knowledge, Alfred Schutz. Its underlying conception is a helpful one here, despite the fact that Schutz used the phrase in a somewhat different manner. He noted that reality is not experienced as a unified whole but as a series of "multiple realities" or "zones of reality." He claimed that ordinary waking consciousness was generally experienced as the most real (or most frequently most real) reality and hence, merited to be called "the paramount zone of reality." For the Kabbalist, by contrast, this ordinary consciousness represents a lower rung, a reality less than fully real; it is the extraordinary, sacred reality that is understood to be the most real or "paramount zone."

For the details of A. Schutz's argument, see "On Multiple Realities" in his *Collected Papers* (The Hague, 1962) Vol. 1: 207ff.

38. On *ᶜoNeG,* cf. Z 3:273a (RM); TZ Intro (12a), and 21 (58a); also cf. *Sefer Yeẓirah* 2:4. On Shabbetai (or Saturn) as the symbol of Evil, see TZ Ibid. (56b–57a). For discussion, see *Sod ha-Shabbat:* Section 11 and n. 160 (on *ᶜoNeG*); and Section 15 and nn. 378–82 (on Shabbetai).

39. Although the mysticism of ascent reveals the influence of neo-Platonism (see n. 23), the mysticism of descent recalls motifs, concepts, and terminology developed in the Hermetic magical tradition. See M. Idel, *Kabbalah: New Perspectives:* Chap. 3 ("Varieties of Devequt in Jewish Mysticism").

The Kabbalistic ascent of the soul may also be seen as an outgrowth of the praxis found in earlier *Merkavah* and *Heikhalot* mysticism.

40. On the image of prayer as a "ladder," see *Zohar* 1:266b, 3:306b, etc. For previous discussion of sefirotic ascent, see pp. 8 and 34–35 above.

41. The notion of prayer as a spiritual ladder may be illustrated with reference to the daily profession of divine unity: *Shemaᶜ Yisra'el YHWH 'Eloheinu YHWH 'Eḥad* (Hear O Israel, the Lord is our God, the Lord is one!) (Dt. 6:4). According to Isaac the Blind, the Naḥmanidean school, and Menaḥem Recanati, the mystic traverses the world of the sefirot as he recites this pivotal prayer. Its first five words chart an ascent through the sefirotic realm. M. Recanati explained the verse word by word:

> First one binds [a reference to *Shemaᶜ*, which may mean to "call together"] the Community of Israel [symbolized by the second word *Yisra'el* = *Malkhut*] to the Foundation of the Cosmos [*Yesod*]. From there he ascends unto the Great Name [=*YHWH, Tif'eret*], then unto *Teshuvah* [=*'Eloheinu*, a cipher for *Binah*] and finally unto *'Ein Sof* [supernal *YHWH*].

In his meditation on the final word *'Eḥad* ("one!"), the adept completes the circle of his *kavvanah*, moving from the mystical peak downward:

> He then returns, [descending] on the path on which he rose. . . . [Recanati proceeds to associate each letter in אחד (*'eḤaD*) with a specific region in the divine world:] R. Isaac the Ḥasid [the Blind], son of the Rav [RaBaD] explained: [With the א (*'Alef*), one descends from *'Ein Sof*]; with the ח (*Ḥet*) one proceeds from *Ḥokhmah* unto *Yesod;* and with ד (*Dalet*) one reaches the end [*Malkhut*]. Thus we find that all is contained in the word אחד (*Perush* to Dt. 6:4)

For a similar notion of mystical prayer, see Isaac the Blind's *Perush le-Sefer Yeẓirah*, printed as an Appendix to G. Scholem, *Ha-Qabbalah be-Provans*, p. 6; see also *Be'ur Sodot ha-RaMBaN* fol. 32d (on the *Shemaᶜ*) which noted that "this is the manner in which the great men of the generation pray." For an interesting variation on the ladder motif, see Isaac the Blind's explanation of Ps. 150. In his famous epistle to Gerona, he noted that the ten *Halelu*'s in verses 1–5 chart a progressive descent from *Ḥokhmah* to *Shekhinah*, whereas the last two phrases (in verse 6) describe an ascent back to *Binah* and *Ḥokhmah*. For the text, see G. Scholem, "Teᶜudah Ḥadashah le-Toledot ha-Qabbalah" in J. Fichman, ed., *Sefer Bialik* (Tel Aviv, 1934): 143. For discussion, see G. Scholem, *Origins of the Kabbalah:* 309.

42. In some special cases (during the Sabbath meals, e.g.), divine energy seems to cascade into the world of its own accord. Here ritual enables the devotee to become a proper vessel for the descending Glory. See p. 83 above for examples.

For further discussion of the function of mystical prayer, see the typology in *Sod ha-Shabbat:* n. 186.

43. On Mircea Eliade's description of Cosmos, see *The Sacred and the Profane:* 29–36, 44–50, et al.

44. Numerous variations on these three scenarios exist. If restricted to the case of Shabbat, one might note the ascent of *Shekhinah* unto the three Patriarchs, the descent of *Gevurah* (the divine wine, the supernal song) into *Shekhinah* in order to kindle Her love. Another common motif is the ascent of *Malkhut/ᶜAṭarah* (Diadem) unto *Binah* or even unto *Keter* (thereby "coronating" the King). On this ascent, see M. Idel, *Kabbalah: New Perspectives:* Chap. 8 ("Kabbalistic Theurgy").

45. See pp. 112–19 above.

46. For the Friday night setting, see *Sod ha-Shabbat:* Section 9, pp. 28–29 (on *Va-Yekhullu*) and Section 10, pp. 31–32; for *Shaḥarit* and *Musaf* see Ibid.: Section 13, pp. 45 and 50 (on *'El 'Adon* and *Qedushah Rabbah*).

47. For discussion see pp. 83 and 114 above; also see *Sod ha-Shabbat:* Sections 15 and 20, and the accompanying notes.

48. Ff. Z 2:84a-b; cf. also TB Ber. 62a.

49. The technical term for rituals designed to avert or turn aside evil.

50. Meir ibn Gabbai repeatedly stated that service for the sake of divinity, *ᶜavodah le-ẓorekh gavoha,* is the central human task. Still, on two occasions, during the Sabbath morning and afternoon *ᶜAmidot,* he permits a prayer to be uttered for simple human needs. This quasi-petitionary prayer can be entertained precisely because sefirotic unity is so secure and powerful at the moment:

> [Now] peace is everywhere. Neither Satan nor demonic forces are to be found. But since it is a time for lovers, a time of Grace [i.e., of sefirotic harmony], we may approach God on our own behalf and recite: "O God and God of our fathers, be pleased with *our* rest." (TY 53a; *Sod ha-Shabbat:* Section 13)

For another example of a ritual without theosophic or theurgic value, see the *Me'irat ᶜEinayim:* 108. R. Isaac of Acco explained that the Friday evening prayer *Hashkivenu* alludes to a supernal drama that has already occurred. Recitation of the prayer is thus "belated," divorced from its mythic enactment:

> A wise man, a Kabbalist, told me that it was forbidden to recite "And spread over us your Sukkah of Peace." I replied: You are speaking the truth, for I have understood your point. He replied: And what is my point? I replied: For it is *already* spread and intact. When we say "And spread," it appears as though the Sabbath and its blessing do not arrive until that moment, heaven forbid. For the Sabbath day confers its holiness and blessing upon the faithful [the adepts] while it is still day, before sundown. He agreed. I continued: If so, why did the Men of the Great Assembly establish that these words be recited? Perhaps it is for the sake of the *ᶜammei ha-'areẓ* who do not understand the mystery of Shabbat according to the Path of Truth [i.e., theosophical Kabbalah], who do not know to

> say "Come, O Bride! Come, O Bride" with proper [i.e., theurgic] intent while it is still day. [See p. 199 above.] But since it was customary for all Israel to recite this prayer, the obligation to recite it falls upon all men, even sages.

For the adept, recitation of the prayer has little mystical value. Unlike Z 1:48a, it is not taken to dramatize *Shekhinah*'s numinous presence, which is felt by the Zoharic companions time after time anew. The prayer is not even given confirmatory significance, enabling one, e.g., to "savor" the drama immediately past. It is as though *Hashkivenu* were—to use a present-day simile—a tape-delay broadcast, aired for the sake of those who could not be at the event "live." For the adept it is, alas, but a "rerun"!

51. Despite the "permitted" nature of profane thoughts, some Kabbalists attempted to self-consciously limit their frequency and direct their content. See, e.g., Joseph Giqatilia's *Sodot:* Section 9 ("Rest"), where a distinction is made between two types of profane thoughts: those that arise at random, in "accidental" fashion (and are therefore permissible) and those that are "intentional," the predictable result of certain activities. One bears responsibility for these thoughts, although there is no indication that they are assigned symbolic or theurgic power:

> On the Sabbath one must attain tranquility in one's speech, action and thoughts. But are not [profane] thoughts permitted? They are only permitted because people cannot control them fully. However, it is forbidden to consciously arouse external [profane] thoughts, for this is not Sabbath-rest. Hence, we are told to avoid reading secular documents [*sheṭarei hedyoṭut*] on Shabbat.

More far-reaching is *Me'irat ʿEinayim:* 180, where special strictures apply to adepts:

> Concerning the masses who are little concerned with divine thought, our sages said: "[Profane] speech is forbidden, but thoughts are permitted." [TB Shab. 113b] But for the select who understand the mystery of the true union [embracing the sefirotic *totality*], even thoughts are forbidden, if not with respect to intelligibles [*muskalot:* here associated with the realm of *Shekhinah*—the lowest divine logos], then at least with respect to things perceived by the senses [*murgashot*].

Finally, cf. *Peli'ah* 36b where the author explicitly narrows the Rabbinic distinction between thought and recitation. Speaking of the physical preparations for Shabbat, he commented: "In whatever one does, one should think of the Sabbath's honor, for thinking and recitation are akin [*'aḥim*]."

52. Of course, Meir ibn Gabbai used this distinction for pragmatic purposes rather than to make a theoretical statement. If profane speech is deleterious, then *a fortiori*, profane acts are. His point is to move the reader to refrain from profane acts!

53. An instructive contrast. Although Sabbath-speech has positive, ritual-like value in Zoharic Kabbalah, the author of the *Peli'ah* (fol. 36b)

accepted it only with great reluctance. Shabbat for him is, at bottom, a time of mental and verbal cleansing (cf. *Pesiqta' Rabbati* sec. 63). Meditative silence and emotional equanimity—quiet a-social joy—become the ideal expressions of *ᶜOneg Shabbat:*

> "One is forbidden to speak of business matters; however one may speak of heavenly matters." [ff. TB Shab. 113a–b] However, do not discuss matters of Torah at length, *for even words of Torah were only reluctantly permitted [be-qoshi huteru,* a radical contention indeed!]. Do not speak of any burdens or of a loved one who has died, or of any distressing matter. The essence of the matter is to "call [the Sabbath] a delight" [Isa. 58:13], a day of rest. . . . Do not bring forth a tear.

CHAPTER THREE

Rituals of Preparation

At noon the *qelippah* separates from the Holy; in the later afternoon, during ritual immersion, the holy light of Shabbat pours forth.

Isaiah Horowitz, *Shenei Luḥot ha-Berit:*
"Massekhet Shabbat" (early seventeenth century)

This late source articulates a notion whose roots lie in the classical tradition: the incremental arrival of Shabbat. For the devotee does not enter into the Sabbath at once, but progressively, building up to the moment of full-Shabbat like water heating up to the boiling. Through the mime of ritual the Kabbalist successively strips away the layers of *ḥol* and aligns himself with the dramatic changes unfolding in the penumatic world. Moreover, he comes to anticipate the Sabbath-order as he prepares for it. There is a sense that Sabbath's arrival is inevitable,[1] and this prospect fills him with joy.

In a sense, the preparatory phase of Shabbat stands "betwixt and between" modalities, belonging fully to neither the fading world of *ḥol* nor to the world of complete-Shabbat which it asymptotically approaches. It is a kind of corridor bridging two discrete realms, a period of profound change.

We have noted that Kabbalistic ritual almost always dramatizes a sacred event and is part of a larger mythic system or Story. In the Zoharic tradition,[2] the dominant mythic subtext—the underlying drama—of Friday afternoon concerns *Shekhinah* and Her Liberation/Redemption from weekday Exile. This process generally unfolds in three stages, depicting first Her separation from Her entanglement in *Siṭra' 'Aḥra'* and the setting of clear boundaries between them; then Her purification; and, finally, Her renewal as She is adorned in bridal raiment and brought to the threshhold of the King's Palace. Only after these events have occurred can the divine wedding—Shabbat—take place.

Meanwhile in the earthly realm, a related pre-Sabbath scenario is unfolding. The Jew, *Shekhinah*'s symbol, is ritually aligning himself with the cosmic changes, progressively overcoming his sense of Exile as he prepares for the seventh day. He too must be transformed; before he can enter the blessed state of Shabbat, the stain of the week must be left behind. So as the changes occur on high, the devotee reflects them below in his purified body and clean cloak, in his enlarged soul, in his newly adorned home, even in the way social space is redefined via the *ʿeruv*. Through the preparatory rituals, Sabbath progressively suffuses his world, displacing both the presence and the memory of *ḥol*. His world symbolically purged and regenerated, Shabbat comes to exist both within him and without him: an ambience projected externally, assimilated internally.

There are several striking aspects to the rituals we shall consider in this section. They are physically active—extroverted—rituals with little opportunity for the contemplative inwardness afforded by mystical prayer, for example. They evince a dualistic world-view, starkly contrasting the profane week and the holy Sabbath. It is as if by highlighting the differences between the two realms while overlooking their points of continuity, the Kabbalists wished to heighten the transformative power of Shabbat, to dramatize the profound sense of renewal they felt.

These rituals both symbolize and modulate this transformative process, enabling *Shekhinah* to again become a Bride and the Jew to regain—for a day—his Edenic lustre.[3]

PROJECTING THE SABBATH INTO THE SPATIAL REALM: THE CASE OF ONE'S HOME AND COURTYARD

The transformations of Shabbat are oft depicted in spatial terms: to enter the Sabbath is to enter the Temple, to dwell under the Sukkah of Peace, to leave behind Exile and enter "the Land of Israel." Two preparatory rituals highlight these spatial dimensions of the Sabbath-cosmos, helping to project Shabbat into one's immediate surroundings. They are the acts of cleansing and adorning one's home, and the establishment of a Courtyard-Fusion or *ʿeruv*.

The Significance of Transforming One's Abode

In the Kabbalistic tradition the Rabbinic custom of making one's home ready for Shabbat (TB Shab. 119b) takes on mythic resonance, directing the adept's attention from his immediate setting to the divine realm and the approaching Sabbath-cosmos. According to the *Zohar* and TZ/RM, as the adept prepares his home, it—like the celestial world it reflects—becomes a Wedding Canopy ready to receive the Bride who is at once Shabbat and *Shekhinah:*

> One must prepare a comfortable seat with several cushions and embroidered covers from all that is found in the house, like one who prepares for a bride. For the Sabbath is a Queen and a Bride. (Z 3:272b [RM])

And more tellingly:

> "Observe the Sabbath throughout the generations [*DoRoTaM*]." [Ex. 31:16] . . . The word *DoRoTaM* hints at the notion of dwelling [*DiRoTaM*]: When the Sabbath enters, the dwelling place must be prepared like the chamber of the bridegroom set to receive his bride. . . .[4]

In so doing the Bride is welcomed into the devotee's hearth and home, and the numinous presence of *Shekhinah*/Shabbat felt:

> The Holy Bride is ushered into Israel's abode, to be in their midst, as the Sabbath begins. (Z 3:300b–301a)

The early fifteenth century work, *Sefer ha-Qanah,* builds on this notion, likening the newly ordered home to a nuptial chamber. Each of the major furnishings mentioned in the Talmudic paradigm is taken as a symbol of the divine coupling which is to follow:

> "Your table should be set, your bed made-up, and the candles burning" [TB Shab. 119b]: The table alludes to the Community of Israel which is set in the sphere of Compassion [*Tif'eret*]; the bed alludes to the Community of Israel who is made-up, adorned for the Groom. . . . The burning candles are the Eastern Candle, an allusion to *Tif'eret* which burns with [i.e., unites with] the Western Candle, the Community of Israel.

The home, in short, becomes a microcosm, a sacred reflection of the divine world.[5] As the devotee arranges his abode, he becomes a kind of bridal attendant, setting the stage for the coming hierogamy. Unlike most Kabbalistic rituals, this act of adornment is focused not so much on that which is happening at this very moment as on that which will happen on high, in a short while. It is anticipatory.[6] As he orders the home, preparing the bed and festive table, the adept directs his thoughts to the Sabbath-cosmos and beckons it into his domestic setting.[7]

In sixteenth century Safed, this preparatory act came to take on more immediate and detailed significance; it will be considered briefly here. While the *Zohar* and *Qanah* focused on the act of adornment, Moses Cordovero and his circle imputed mythic significance to the preliminary act of cleansing the home, as well. Cordovero maintained:

> One must sweep out the cobwebs from one's house [on Sabbath eve], symbolizing the mystery of "making one's home ready [for Shabbat] by lighting candles . . . and making up the bed." [TB Shab. 119b][8]

He explained that this act symbolizes the liberation of *Shekhinah* from the *qelippot*, which "according to the Tiqqunim" (i.e., TZ) may be likened to a cobweb. Although the Zoharic sources cited above likened the home to *Shekhinah*'s bridal chamber, here, however, it is implicitly homologized to the Bride Herself. Isaiah Horowitz explicated further:

> For in the Kabbalistic literature *Malkhut* is called *Bayit*, the Home, the Wife.[9] She is the "rose among the thorns" [Cant. 2:2]; "around [Her] the evil ones roam." [Ps. 12:9] They are the *qelippot* who wish to prevent *shelom bayit* [conventionally, domestic tranquility or harmony]. They are the spider whose web we must sweep out of the house. This is the inner meaning of the [liturgical] verse "abominations will be removed from the land"[10]—from the supernal Land [*Malkhut*]. They should especially be removed for the holy Sabbath, the mystery of *Malkhut*.

Only after *Shekhinah* is purified and separated from the defiling forces of the week, can the sacred marriage take place. This union occurs at the very inception of Shabbat, at candlelighting:

> The Sabbath candles intimate this for they correspond to "Remember" and "Keep," as stated in the *Bahir* [182]. The candles represent the union of the supernal lights, as in "I will grant peace [*Yesod*] to the land [*Malkhut*]." [Lev. 26:6] . . . For this reason, the candles are called *shelom bayit* [TB Shab. 23b],

the union of *Shalom*—*Yesod*—and *Bayit*, the *Shekhinah*.[11] Hence, in this tradition strand, the ordering of the home dramatizes the stages of *Shekhinah*'s transformation: its cleansing dramatizes Her Liberation/Purification, whereas its adornment intimates Her ultimate reintegration into the divine sphere.

The Establishment of Courtyard-Fusions: ᶜEruvei Ḥaẓerot

If cleaning the home serves to project the Sabbath-cosmos into the domestic sphere, several halakhot accomplish much the same in the social sphere. Brief mention should be made of the Kabbalistic re-interpretation of *teḥum Shabbat:* the restricted area in which one is permitted to travel during the seventh day.[12] In the *Zohar* the physical *teḥum Shabbat* is homologized to the divine Sabbath, or the sefirotic realm, whereas the area beyond is correlated with Sabbath's antipode, *Siṭra' 'Aḥra'*. Consider, e.g., *Zohar* 2:64a:

> "Let no man go out from his place" (Ex. 16:29) [i.e., outside *teḥum Shabbat*] . . . For this Place is precious and holy, but beyond it lies "other gods" . . .

Kabbalistically, the outer limit of one's "Place" is *Shekhinah,* the divine limen:

> "His Place" refers to the lower Glory [*Shekhinah*], the mystery of the Diadem of Shabbat.

According to another passage (2:207a), by remaining within his Sabbath-Place, the Jew dramatizes *Shekhinah*'s integration within the sefirotic realm; for on Shabbat *Shekhinah* has come home: "She does not rest anywhere outside the boundaries assigned to Her."[13]

A second example of symbolically projecting the Sabbath into the social sphere is the preparatory rite of "establishing a courtyard-*ᶜeruv.*" This *ᶜeruv* is a Rabbinically instituted device which originally had purely functional significance. Ẓvi Kaplan (EJ 6:849) explains:

> While carrying between private and public domains [*Reshut ha-Yaḥid* and *Reshut ha-Rabbim*] is forbidden on the Sabbath, the rabbis also forbade carrying between two private domains. For example, if several houses opened into one courtyard [as was generally the case in urban Jewish communities in the Middle Ages], an object could not be removed from one house to another, nor from a house to the courtyard [which was also considered a private domain]. . . . To facilitate such carrying, a loaf of bread (called *ᶜeruv ḥaẓerot*) owned by all the residents is placed in one of the houses [each Friday afternoon], thereby symbolically creating mutual ownership of all the dwellings. The houses and courtyard are thereby "mixed" [*meᶜuravim*] into one private domain.

In the SṬM, TZ, and TY this legal fiction was given a mythic rationale, transposing the halakhah into a cosmic key. Their reading exemplifies what may be called the "hypernomian" aspect of Kabbalistic ritual. That which was functional is shown to be cosmically necessary, rooted in the ontological structure of the universe. Employing a hermeneutic at once hyperliteral and mystical, the three Kabbalists correlated the private domain (*Reshut ha-Yaḥid*) with the "Realm of (Divine) Unity," while the public domain (*Reshut ha-Rabbim*) was taken to denote the "Realm of Multiplicity" and Evil outside the Sabbath Cosmos. Joseph of Hamadan wrote:

> *Reshut ha-Yaḥid* refers to the ten sefirot which are one. His Name is called the Domain of Unity. *Reshut ha-Rabbim* is so named because it contains the mystery of *Perud,* Multiplicity . . . (SṬM, Meier ed.: 293)[14]

In both the TZ and TY, preparation of the courtyard *ᶜeruv* dramatizes the integration of *Shekhinah* into divinity and more generally, the complete sefirotic fusion that takes place on Shabbat. For as the *ᶜeruv* is established, the formerly disparate private domains become one unified *Reshut ha-Yaḥid,* symbolizing the restoration of divine harmony. Moreover, the establishment of this *ᶜeruv* symbolically demarcates between the two opposing modalities, *Reshut ha-Yaḥid* and *Reshut ha-Rabbim,* redrawing the cosmic boundaries. Hence, one who carries an article outside the private domain, spiritually leaves the realm of Shabbat and enters the domain of *Siṭra' 'Aḥra'.* This profaning act has theurgic valence as well, sullying Shabbat/*Shekhinah,* which according to the TY, is the *ᶜeruv* (here, in the sense of boundary marker) par excellence. In Meir ibn Gạbbai's words,

> The *ᶜeruv* is the symbol of the crowned Bride, the locus at which the [sacred and profane] domains meet.[15]

Dwelling at the limen, She remains vulnerable to the encroachment of *Siṭra' 'Aḥra'.* The TZ explains:

> Whoever carries from *Reshut ha-Yaḥid* to *Reshut ha-Rabbim* brings *Shekhinah* into "confusion and chaos, darkness and the abyss" (Gen. 1:2),

reversing the order of Creation, polluting the Sacred with the Profane.

> Such a person causes Her to be cloaked in the *qelippot* of the four Exiles. (TZ 30 [73a])[16]

According to another passage, TZ 48 (85a), improper carrying may also dis-order higher rungs, including *Tif'eret/Yesod:*

> One who removes an article from its Place, taking it outside its domain, is considered as one who uprooted the Tree of Life and placed it in the "Alien Realm" . . . the Realm of Multiplicity . . . the realm of Shabbetai [the saturnine *Siṭra' 'Aḥra'*].

Perhaps the richest symbolization of the courtyard *ᶜeruv* is from TZ 24 (69a):

> Just as one needs the protection of the covenant lest one pass under the rule of the Foreign One [*Siṭra' 'Aḥra'*], so one needs the protection of Shabbat lest one leave the Realm of Unity [*Reshut ha-Yaḥid*] and enter the Realm of Multiplicity [*Reshut ha-Rabbim*].

According to Rabbinic definition (TB Shab. 6a), a private domain is an enclosed space not less than four handbreadths square bounded by walls not less than ten handbreadths high. In the TZ's understanding, there is nothing arbitrary about these dimensions. Rather, they have symbolic resonance, pointing to *Shekhinah*'s re-integration into the divine realm:

> The Realm of Unity is *Shekhinah;* Her "width is four" [encompassing] the Tetragrammaton, YHWH.[17] "Its height is ten" refers to [the sefirotic totality]. *Reshut ha-Rabbim* is the serpent, the harlot [i.e., Lilith], the poison of the 'Other God' who is Sammael. . . . Her husband is the profanation of the Sabbath [*Malkhut*].
>
> For this reason, whoever carries from *Reshut ha-Yaḥid* unto *Reshut ha-Rabbim* is liable to be stoned [ff. Ex. 31:14]. The *ᶜeruv* delineates the Middle Column and within it, *one may carry from home to home,* between the supernal *Shekhinah [Binah]* and the lower one [*Malkhut*].

Here we see the clearest example of how one's immediate social world may serve as a microcosm, a reflection of the supernal realm.[18]

Too much significance should not be claimed for the actual establishment of the *ᶜeruv,* however; like the Zoharic treatment of adorning the home, it has primarily anticipatory significance, becoming fully functional only when the Sabbath begins. Nonetheless, preparing the *ᶜeruv* directs the devotee's attention to the altered cosmos of Shabbat, while enabling him to project this new order into his immediate environs.

INTERNALIZING SHABBAT: THE BODY AS MICROCOSM

> In order to receive the holiness [of Shabbat] that flows into our world, we must prepare and perfect the body, for the body is the throne for the spiritual. . . . Like the house, the body must be restored.
>
> M. Cordovero, *Tefillah le-Mosheh* 10:2

If the preceding rituals tended to externalize the Sabbath-cosmos, projecting it into the devotee's surroundings, the ensuing series of rites—nail-paring, bathing or ritual immersion, and dressing in fresh clothes—dramatize the progressive internalization of Sabbath-order. The devotee himself now becomes the locus of symbolic activity, his body a microcosm of the changes occurring on high. While the preceding rituals were largely anticipatory in nature, these three are immediately transformative, representing and effecting changes in both the devotee's status and that of divinity. Together they form a kind of ritual triptych whereby the Kabbalist formally leaves behind *ḥol* and existentially enters Shabbat.

Nail-Paring

The first act of bodily preparation that we shall consider is that of nail-paring.[19] This rite—whose origins seemingly lie in Ashkenazic magical concerns—was adopted by certain Kabbalists for expressly mythic reasons. It is a striking illustration of Mary Douglas' remark that "no experience is too lowly to be taken up into ritual and given a lofty meaning."[20] Kabbalistic rationales for nail-trimming "in honor of Shabbat" are all relatively late, appearing first in the *Peli'ah* (36b), and later in the TY and *Shoshan Sodot*.[21] However, a mythic subtext for nail-pairing, in general, had been presented much earlier, in the *Zohar*. Basing himself on a midrashic tradition,[22] Moshe de Leon wrote that the finger- and toenails are the last vestige of humanity's Edenic garb:

> The primordial garment that Adam wore in the Garden was composed of those [protective] Chariots called the Backside; they were . . . garments of nail.

Here the *Zohar* is imaging Adam as a microcosm of the divine world. According to several Zohar sources, *Shekhinah* Herself is surrounded by *qelippot* or shells, quasi-angelic entities portrayed in a wide array of images: as Chariots of Light, as a coarse garment or outer shell, as a kind of divine Backside shielding the Face within, or most importantly here, as "nails" covering the divine corpus.[23] The function of these nails is to separate and protect the divine world from defiling forces without. They constitute a kind of buffer zone between the two realms. Moshe de Leon explained that a similar protective garb enfolded Adam prior to the Sin. He was in perfect symbolic alignment with the divine archetype, and so, protected from all evil:

> As long as Adam was in the Garden all these Chariots surrounded him and no evil thing could draw near him. However, when he sinned he was divested of that garment and clothed in profane ones. . . . Nothing of that primordial garment remains except for the nails at the tips of the fingers and toes. And these nails contain an alien impurity at their outer edges. (Z 2:208b)

His womb-like *qelippah* now broken and diminished, Adam (and all persons after him) became susceptible to pollution; the mundane dirt trapped under the nails becomes a symbol for humanity's post-Edenic diminution, and their vulnerability before the forces of *Siṭra' 'Aḥra'*.[24]

In his TY (46a) Meir ibn Gabbai drew upon this very myth and on Moshe de Leon's subsequent warning that "we should not allow the nails with their impurity to grow" (Z 2:208b) and included nail-paring in the preparatory rites. By implication, this act reverses humanity's post-Edenic (and post-Sabbath) diminution. Through nail-paring the adept ritually purges himself of the stain of the week and divests himself of its demonic forces; he thereby re-sacralizes his vulnerable border. As we shall see, nail-paring serves as a necessary prelude to the most crucial transformation, the reception of the Sabbath-soul, the new "Edenic garb."

On an explicit level, however, Meir ibn Gabbai provided not an Edenic rationale for this rite but one that drew on the homology between Sabbath, *Shekhinah* and the Temple. For the Sabbath, like the *miqdash*, may only be entered in a state of ritual purity:

> And since one must not bring an impurity into the Sanctuary, one must pare them on Sabbath eve, so that the Sacred [the Sabbath and kabbalistically, *Shekhinah*] is not profaned on account of this impurity.[25]

Nail-paring seems to function as a rite of boundary-definition, a means of separating the Sacred and the Profane as Sacred Time draws near. It protects the sacred at its most vulnerable point, the margin, and prevents further conflation of the two modalities. Mary Douglas has shed light on this phenomenon:

> All margins are dangerous. If they are pulled this way or that the shape of fundamental existence is altered. Any structure of ideas is vulnerable at the margins. We should expect the orifices of the body to symbolize its specially vulnerable points . . . e.g., bodily parings, skin, nails, hair clippings, etc. (*Purity and Danger:* 121)

In a sense, nail-paring protects several margins: occurring at Sabbath's limen, it aims to properly establish the sacred boundaries of Shabbat and of the devotee. By implication, it reflects the securing of proper boundaries in the divine world, as well.

The full protection of sacred boundaries entails not only an act of separation, but proper placement of the profane. Given the dangerous quality afforded the filthy edge of the nails, it is not surprising that their parings must be disposed of with great care. If the act of paring represents the separation of the sacred and demonic realms (the first stage of purification), proper disposal symbolizes the elimination or destruction of the demonic for the duration of Shabbat.[26] Meir ibn Gabbai underscored the importance of proper disposal, building upon a Talmudic teaching on the same theme:

> We read in *Moʿed Qaṭan,* Chapter "These are Permitted to Shave" [18a]: "Three things were said in reference to nails: One who burns them is pious [*ḥasid*]; one who buries them is just [*ẓaddiq*]; and one who throws them away is a villain [*rashaʿ*]."
>
> The reason for this is that nails intimate *Din* [here, *Siṭra' 'Aḥra*]. One who removes it by burning the parings promotes Peace and Compassion [the beneficent forces of divinity] in the world . . . "One who buries them is just": Even though he did not remove *Din* from the world totally, still he impedes *Din* and quiets it. However, this falls short of the deed of the pious one. "One who throws them away is a villain": for he causes *Din* to flow into the world. (TY 46b)

This is a good example of an apotropaic rite. By following the example of the *ḥasid,* the mystic helps obliterate *Din* for the duration of the Sabbath. Improper disposal of the nails, however, may effect the "de-creation of the world," to use Bruce Lincoln's phrase,[27] disrupting the newly harmonious Cosmos.

The complex symbolization of nails has only been touched on here. We shall return to this theme later, in the discussion of *Havdalah*.[28]

Bathing and Ablution

> In order to honor the Sabbath one should, as a matter of religious duty, wash his face, hands, and feet with hot water on Friday.
>
> RaMBaM, *Mishneh Torah* (Shabbat 30:2)

The Rabbinic rite of bathing before the Sabbath is turned into a transformative act par excellence in the Zoharic tradition; indeed, in the TY, it serves as the liminal moment between *ḥol* and existential Shabbat,[29] forming a kind of initiatory rite into the Sabbath-cosmos. In the *Zohar* itself, this act retains a somewhat more modest function. Let us analyze its significance there first. Bathing serves to spiritually purify the devotee, to cleanse him of the polluting stain of the week and to separate him from the influence of its archetype, *Siṭra' 'Aḥra'*, so that he may fully enter into the Sabbath. Read psychologically, this rite absolves (or more literally, dissolves) the guilt accrued over the week, affording the adept spiritual liberation, a new beginning. It should be noted, however, that this theme of expiation reached conscious articulation only later, in the Safed Kabbalah.[30] The *Zohar* itself describes the underlying dynamic of bathing more in metaphysical than in psycho-ethical terms. The polluting aspects of the weekday cosmos are placed in the foreground, thereby heightening the sense of purification:

> When the Sabbath arrives, the holy People must wash their bodies from the stain of the week. What is the reason? Because during the week Another Spirit [*Siṭra' 'Aḥra'*] sets forth and holds sway over the People. When one needs to get out from under that spirit and enter into the other, holy spirit, he must bathe so that he might receive the supernal holy Spirit. (2:204a)

The act of bathing, in other words, symbolically effects a change in personal status, enabling the devotee to move from one realm—one spiritual ambience—to another. In the most visceral way, a whole environment is stripped off, dissolved. Indeed, Moshe de Leon elsewhere likened this evil realm to a defiling garment:

> When the Evil Inclination holds sway over a person, it fashions a garment for him . . . as it is said, "She caught him in a garment." [Gen. 39:12] (Z 1:190b)

But as the Jew bathes, he leaves the enveloping presence of the profane week, "gets out from under that Spirit" and so "enters the other, holy spirit," an intriguingly vague term, evoking both Shabbat and the now imminent realm of divinity. Bathing is a preparatory act, as well, setting the stage for what I have termed the "existential Shabbat," or, the reception of the Sabbath-soul.

The power of the ritual lies in its physical immediacy: in all likelihood, this bath was the sole one for the entire week; in a literal as well as figurative sense, the stain of the week was being removed! The ritual works by integrating a gross physiological or sensory experience with powerful but abstract ideational motifs or myths. Put in Turnerian language[31] it might be said that as the Kabbalist bathes and focuses on the underlying mythos of Shabbat, the ideational and sensory poles of meaning interprenetrate so that the physical aspects of bathing are ennobled—symbolized—and the attendant Kabbalistic myth vitalized, "made real." Physically cleansed and refreshed, the Kabbalist is also spiritually renewed, purified of the pollution of the week.

Later mystics heightened the transformative impact of bathing by suggesting that one not only wash his limbs but actually immerse his entire body in a *miqveh* or body of "living water." This action carries with it a wealth of other associations which, even if not explicitly discussed, provide a kind of backdrop for the rite. Unlike bathing, ablution (Hebrew: *ṭevilah*) is traditionally associated with significant changes in ontological status. In the Rabbinic tradition, e.g., it was utilized by women to mark the formal conclusion of *niddah,* their periods of menstrual "impurity"; by men after the pollution of a seminal emission; by converts as they entered Judaism; and by women about to enter marriage.[32] In fine, *ṭevilah* functioned as a sacred means of transforming the impure into the pure, the uncanny into the orderly—and by implication, for leaving behind a lesser stage of existence and entering a higher one. In analyzing *ṭevilah* in Sabbath-preparation, two broad questions must be asked: first, when did this ritual become part of Sabbath preparation, and second, how might its symbolic significance be interpreted, in light of a) the mystics' own explanations, b) certain observable characteristics, and c) other contextual clues?

Historically, the emphasis on pre-Sabbath ritual immersion is relatively late. The literature from before the fifteenth century contains but two or three passing references to this custom, in exoteric sources of Middle Eastern provenance.[33] The *Zohar* and TZ/RM, e.g., never explicitly mention ablution or *ṭevilah,* instead using the terms *reḥizah* and *'asḥa'ah,* both meaning simply to "wash" or "bathe."[34] The first explicit mention of *ṭevilah* in Kabbalistic sources is found in the Byzantine works, the *Qanah* and *Peli'ah* (early fifteenth century). Their author viewed immersion as the most efficacious form of purification:

> Let him wash his face, hands, and feet so that the course of the profane week may be lifted from him, as it is said: From the *sweat* of your brow [reference to the polluting stain of the week] shall you get bread to eat." [Gen. 3:19]. How much more so is this true of one who immerses himself on Sabbath eve. . . . (*Qanah* 65a)

Similarly, the *Peli'ah* (36b) states:

> One then washes his face, hands, and legs near evening upon completing his preparations. And if he does so through ablution, nothing could be finer [*'ein ke-maᶜalatah*]![35]

The first source to prescribe *ṭevilah* as the sole method of purification is the TY; in this sense it foreshadowed the heightened concern with *ṭevilah* found in the Safed Kabbalah. In Meir ibn Gabbai's schema, ablution is a ritual of pivotal importance: marking not only the entry into a new ambience, but the internalization of that ambience via reception of the Sabbath-soul. To appreciate the dynamic of the ritual, it is important to recall its performance context: according to the TY, the devotee has already performed the initial act of spiritual separation through nail-paring and has affirmed the redrawn cosmic-boundaries of Shabbat via the *ᶜeruv.* The devotee now divests himself of the defiling garb of the week, and in the waning light of the day, immerses himself in the river. Ibn Gabbai's description reveals the influence of the *Zohar,* even as he went beyond it:

> During the week Another Spirit holds sway over the world and on Sabbath eve the holy people must cleanse themselves of this [impurity] to enter into the mystery of the Holy Faith [Shabbat/the sefirotic world] . . . they do so by immersing themselves in the river. (TY 46b)

As the devotee emerges, he feels the numinous presence of the Supernal Mother, *Shekhinah*, the womb-like "Shelter of Peace." She spreads Her wings and "crowns [him] with a Sabbath-soul." So begins the existential Shabbat.

In its underlying structure this ritual comes to serve as a kind of rite of passage, with the three distinct phases noted by A. van Gennep and V. Turner: 1) separation, as the devotee strips himself of his ordinary garb. This is followed by 2) a moment of liminality as the naked devotee immerses himself in the river. For an instant, he is structurally invisible, without defining garb, dissolved, as it were, in the enveloping waters. His old status no longer holds, while his new identity is not yet manifest. As he emerges from the water, he enters a new spiritual ambience: Shabbat, the realm of divinity, of *Shekhinah*. With regard to his personal identity, 3) as he is wreathed with his Sabbath-soul, he is re-aggregated or re-structured; the devotee re-enters the social sphere on a higher level of being.[36]

But if *ṭevilah* constitutes a rite of passage—a corridor between two radically distinct worlds and two somewhat less distinct personal identities—it does so in an unusual way. For classically, the term connotes one-time (or at least, infrequent) changes in ontological status of enduring impact. In the case of Shabbat, however, there is a *weekly* act of transformation whose impact begins to wane after Shabbat ends, and which by definition requires weekly renewal. Examination of the Kabbalistic evidence suggests the need to develop a new theoretical category embracing such regularly recurring (and reversible) transformations.

Finally, a hypothesis for further testing. In this section, discussion has centered on nail-paring and *ṭevilah*, two relatively obscure rites that were adopted and mythically recast by Kabbalists (notably by adepts of Byzantine-Turkish provenance)[37] and ultimately popularized due to the efforts of their spiritual heirs, the mystics of Safed.[38] Although these two rituals are employed in multiple settings in the tradition, it is striking that both acts were an integral part of women's rituals of purification upon leaving *niddah*. According to *Zohar* 3:79a, complete purification entails not only *ṭevilah* but also paring one's nails and hair, those extremities especially susceptible to pollution:

> The nails and hair grow, and therefore when a woman comes to purify herself she must cut off the hair which grew in the days of her pollution and pare her nails along with the filth that clings to them. For, as we have learned concerning the mystery of pollution,

> the filth of nails awakens Another Filth [*Sitra' 'Aḥra'*], and therefore they must be completely hidden away. Whoever does so, awakens *Ḥesed* in the cosmos.

It seems possible that in their desire to develop rituals of purification and regeneration, certain Kabbalists drew on those models long available for women. This may simply be a matter of adapting rituals for similar strategic purposes (i.e., purification and renewal), but one cannot help but wonder whether the identification formed between the mystic and the divine Female was a subliminal factor encouraging such adaptation. For the Zoharic tradition had commonly described *Shekhinah*'s passage into Shabbat in terms of Her purification from *niddah*. Indeed, Meir ibn Gabbai himself did so on at least two occasions in the TY.[39] In this study, however, no classical sources have been found which correlate the myth of *Shekhinah*'s purification from *niddah* with *ṭevilah* and nail-paring on Sabbath eve.[40] So far as is known such associations were first made in the Safed Kabbalah. One later source, the *Shenei Luḥot ha-Berit*, drew upon the obvious menstrual associations in these rites and imaged the devotee himself as "a woman in *niddah*." According to I. Horowitz, on Friday afternoons:

> One should investigate his deeds and awaken in repentance, repairing that which is flawed. . . . Thereafter he should cut his nails and immerse himself in water, *like a woman purifying herself after niddah*. ("Massekhet Shabbat")[41]

This general topic merits further investigation.[42]

The Rite of Dressing:
The Tolaᶜat Yaᶜaqov*'s Account*

If immersion is a rite of transformation in the TY, the contiguous act of dressing is one of confirmation, visibly affirming the devotee's new ontological status. The act takes on mythic resonance as well. By putting on clean clothes the devotee is said to represent the changes occurring in the supernal realm. Loosely basing himself on a TZ passage (69 [108b–109a]), Meir ibn Gabbai explained that divinity is garbed in "ten lower crowns during the week." These crowns (issuing from the world below divinity) dim the divine light and serve as a barrier between God and humankind: "But on Shabbat, He is divested of them and dressed in several garments of light," issuing from the divine world itself. Accordingly, Meir ibn Gabbai bade the devotee to don "fresh clothes so as to emulate the Creator," newly adorned in royal vestment. Through dressing "in accord with one's means," the devotee is afforded intimate access to the divine realm: now "he may be seen before the King dressed in accord with the celestial paradigm." (TY 46b)[43]

In this way the Kabbalist adds a distinctively mythic rationale to the Talmudic teaching that "one's Sabbath garments should not be like one's weekday garb." (TB Shab. 113a) The nature of the mystical re-reading may be brought into sharper relief when juxtaposed with Moses Maimonides' explanation of the custom (*Mishneh Torah,* "Shabbat" 30:2). Basing himself on Rabbinic sources, Maimonides simply averred that changing one's garb is a way of honoring Shabbat. For him, the act of dressing is primarily of metaphorical significance: one dresses on Shabbat as one does to meet a king:

> The sages of old used to assemble their disciples on Friday night, put on their best clothes, and say: "Come, let us go forth, to meet the Sabbath, the king." Honoring the Sabbath involves putting on clean clothes. . . .

By contrast, the act takes on precise symbolic and cosmic significance in the Zoharic tradition. Putting on new clothes honors not only the Sabbath, but God. More to the point, it becomes an exemplary gesture, whereby the person mirrors the divine archetype and partakes of its splendor.

The Significance of "Dress" in the Zohar *and* Tiqqunei ha-Zohar/Ra

But what does the Kabbalist mean when he speaks of the re-garbing of divinity? To more fully grasp this notion and its implications for Sabbath-dress, it is helpful to turn to the *Zohar* and its ancillary sources. Of particular interest is the TZ/RM, which developed the garbing of divinity into a primary mythic motif.

The Zohar and TZ/RM both speak of the cloaking of divinity in an array of worlds, potencies, and attributes, all suggestively symbolized as *levushin,* or garments. This symbolism implicitly rests on a neo-Platonic view of reality; the cosmos is envisioned as a series of concentric spheres, with divinity at its innermost core. Each consecutive sphere constitutes a mediating principle, a *levush* (garment) or *qelippah* (shell) from the perspective of what lies inside, but a body or *moḥa'* (kernel) from the perspective of what lies outside. Taken as a whole, the manifold spheres between divinity and the terrestrial world are imaged as layers of God's *levush*.[44] In a sense, the entire world is God's garb. This pantheistic notion is aptly described in TZ 22 (65a):

> *Shekhinah* has many garments, from which the Holy One created the divine Throne and the angels, the *ḥayyot* and the seraphim, heaven and earth and all the creatures therein.

In most cases, however, only certain aspects of the cosmos—e.g., the angelic worlds, and in the more dualistic accounts, *Siṭra' 'Aḥra'* as well—serve this cloaking function. Full-blown pantheism is thereby deflected. The following passage is exemplary (Z 3: 273a [RM]):

> *Shekhinah*'s garments consist of the holy angels from on high and Israel from below.

Alongside this model of cosmic garbing stands a second one, according to which divinity may be garbed by the descent of *shefa*ᶜ from on high, or by the ascent of the sacred energy released through performance of the miẓvot below.[45] In contrast to the first model, garbing here serves to adorn divinity with more refined light rather than cloaking it in coarser stuff. Here the implicit cosmological model is not one of concentric spheres, but of a great Chain of Being. The movement is not so much in-out, as up-down. The focal point of this garbing is the lower sefirot, especially the Holy One and *Shekhinah,* primary recipients of the divine flow. To cite one example from the *Qanah:*

> Know, my son, that the Sabbath garments are the divine blessing [*shefa*ᶜ] that She [*Shekhinah*] receives from the upper sefirot. . . . (65a)

The symbolism of *levushin* is an apt one for the Kabbalist, because these cosmic entities—be they outer worlds or *shefa*ᶜ from on high—serve much the same expressive role that clothing does in the social sphere. Clothing may hide, reveal, frame, adorn, constrain—in short, make a symbolic statement about its wearer's status and personality;[46] so too, the type of clothing divinity is said to put on is always a theological statement. As shall be seen, God's garbing generally serves multiple roles.

Revealment Versus Concealment

The garments may express or reveal the hidden divine personality and its attributes of action. Thus, *Shekhinah*'s harsh weekday garb expresses rigorous divine Justice in the world, the quality of *Din*. According to one Zoharic account, She garbs Herself in these harsh *qelippot* during the week—and takes on a rather fierce appearance—so as to direct the world in its current imperfect state. By contrast, on Shabbat, when *Ḥesed* pervades the cosmos, such external garments—armor of sorts—are not needed; and so at this hour divinity is arrayed in garments of *Ḥesed*, pure Love, which the *Zohar* terms "the garment of Glory of the Sabbath." (2:204a)

If the garments of divinity may serve to reveal or express aspects of the divine personality, they may also serve as barriers between God and humanity, as masks concealing the divine light.

The multiple garments in which divinity is cloaked are often a way of symbolizing the mystery of the divine-human encounter, of capturing the paradox of mystical experience. For each revealment—each stripping away of a layer—is followed immediately by a concealment, a sense of heightened mystery. There are always deeper layers within.

At other times, these garments seem to protect the adept from the blinding intensity of divine light: there is a sense in which divinity must be cloaked, mediated, to be withstood. As the Zoharic Comrades often recalled: "No man shall see Me and live." (Ex. 33:20) This imagery conveys the dangerous, awesome aspect of religious experience, and the ambivalent reactions of attraction and repulsion that such powerful encounters often elicit.[47]

If the divine garments come to protect or shield the person, they are sometimes understood to protect divinity as well. In several accounts, those *qelippot* nearest *Shekhinah* are understood to protect Her from the harsher aspects of undiluted Evil, the more external *qelippot*.

But if masking may serve a beneficent function, more frequently it is seen as a tragic distancing, the erection of a thick barrier between person and God. Thus, the *qelippot* that protect *Shekhinah* also conceal Her: their function is dual, ambivalent.

Several sources portray this distancing or concealment in a more unequivocally negative light. Consider TZ 69 (109a), where the *qelippot* are seen as the consequence or outgrowth of human sin:

> "[There is] an unclean spirit over the Land" [ff. Zech. 13:2], namely those *qelippot* which cause a separation between the Holy One and

> Israel. This is the hidden meaning of "But your *iniquities* have been a barrier between you and your God." [Isa. 59:2]

This barrier that occludes the divine light is breached through devotional life and temporarily removed on Shabbat, as God takes off the harsh clothes needed for the weekly rule and dons holy garb, luminiscent, gossamer:

> On high [i.e., on Shabbat] the Holy One wears *qelippot* as well. But they are cloaks made of many shades of beautiful light.

These are garments of pure *Ḥesed* which transmit, refract the divine light. As they are donned the world is lit up, warmed.

Divestment Versus Adornment as Ideals

According to the TZ/RM even this re-garbing falls short of the ultimate state. Its author envisions the eschaton as a world wherein all the mediating garments will be stripped off, where full revelation, face-to-Face beholding, will be possible. TZ 69 continues:

> In the time to come the Holy One will remove these *qelippot* entirely and be disclosed before Israel like the kernel of a nut, as it says: "Then shall your Guide no longer be hidden away, and your eyes shall behold your Guide." [Isa. 30:20]

In that age of complete Shabbat divinity will be fully disclosed to itself, as well:

> There will no longer be any barriers between the Holy One and *Shekhinah* and Israel.

The garb of Exile, which separates as it protects, will no longer be needed.

An even more striking account of cosmic divestment may be found in Z 2:116a [RM]. At the present time, due to human sin, both humanity and divinity are garbed in *qelippot;* a double-barrier stands between them:

> Whoever is garbed in the *qelippot* of the "terrestrial" body . . . skin, flesh, bones and sinews, is not fully alive. His spirit within is dead. He does not truly see, he does not hear or speak; his limbs have no vitality. . . . Within this body . . . one cannot perceive

> the angels, much less *Shekhinah* or *a fortiori,* the Holy One above Her. . . . Because of their sins they are garbed in these *qelippot* and because of these *qelippot* Scripture says, "But your iniquities have been a barrier between you and your God." [Isa. 59:2]

In a startling re-reading of Isa. 6:2, God Himself is said to put on the four *qelippot* as a response to human sin:

> Because of these *qelippot* the Holy One is covered over with wings, as it says: "With two He covered His face, and with two He covered His legs."

Through the life of miẓvot one can transcend the terrestrial *qelippah,* but a partial barrier remains around divinity. In the time to come, however, divinity will no longer be kept under wraps: the concealing wings will be lifted and God fully revealed:

> But in the time to come "your Guide will no longer be hidden under wings and your eyes will truly see your Guide." [Isa. 30:20]

Alongside this ideal of stripping away the barriers, of piercing to the core, is the ideal of adornment, itself an expression of divine-human intimacy and cosmic vitality. Through the life of miẓvot divinity is crowned, the Bride bedecked, the Lovers enrobed in sefirotic light. Accordingly, prayer is oft symbolized as an act of mystical coronation, each word a point of ascending light. The *Zohar* (2:207b), for instance, explains that each of the seventy words of the Sabbath *Qiddush* mounts upward to grace *Malkhut,* "wreathing [Her] with seventy crowns." Speaking more generally, the *Zohar* (3:160b) avers:

> When prayer is being offered, all the words that a person utters ascend on high, cleaving their way through ethers and firmaments until they reach their destination. There they are woven into a crown to adorn the King's head.

The coronation from below is said to stimulate a coronation from on high. As Israel adorns the King, the supernal Mother blesses Him from above. Mixing regal and nuptial imagery Moshe de Leon added:

> It is the Jubilee's desire to crown the Witness [*Tif'eret*] and shower Him with blessing, to cause the sweet springs [*shefa'*] to flow over Him, as it is written, "Go forth, daughters of Zion, and gaze upon

King Solomon, upon the crown with which His Mother adorned Him on this his wedding day." [Cant. 3:11]

Even more common is the dual adornment of *Shekhinah*, from above and below, "from all sides" (Z 2:207b).[48] As we have already seen, Sabbath observance helps garb *Shekhinah* in raiment of glory, divesting Her of the profane weekly garb that is said to sully and constrain Her, while decorating Her in bridal garments and regal apparel. (See pp. 113–14, 118 and 120 above for details.) Speaking more generally, the TZ/RM's author enthusiastically proclaimed that each consequential act that the Jew undertakes may be understood as a garbing of *Shekhinah:*

> She wears garments of light whenever Israel gives forth light through the performance of good deeds. . . . But when Israel does evil, [*Shekhinah*] is garbed in black garments . . . in Lilith; at such time, She says, "Do not gaze upon me for I am swarthy." [Cant. 1:6] (TZ 22 [65a])

Summarizing the Zoharic literature, it might be said that the Kabbalist is the one who knows best how to adorn the Bride, the one who—in his sacred activity—becomes Her *shoshevin* or bridal attendant.[49]

Sabbath-Dress in the Tiqqunei ha-Zohar/Raʿaya' Meheimna'

The mythic images presented above are but a small portion of an extensive Zoharic literature, yet even this sampling should alert us to the complex significance garments have for the Kabbalist, and the symbolic resonance that donning fresh garb for Shabbat may have. If the broad array of *levush* imagery creates a web of remote influences that subliminally color the experience of dressing for Shabbat, a more limited cluster of myths form the immediate subtext, those proximate influences which explicitly undergird and give shape to the devotee's experience.[50] These myths dramatize the re-garbing of divinity on Sabbath eve; many are self-consciously correlated with the Kabbalist's own regarbing. Concentrated in the TZ/RM, they symbolize the transformation of divinity and cosmos on Shabbat, much as the marital motif does elsewhere in the tradition.

Although the degree of transformation varies from myth to myth, all entail the removal of the lesser garments of the week and the donning of holier garments for Shabbat. On occasion, this transformation is but a matter of degree, suggesting a harmonistic view of the relations between Sabbath and *ḥol*. During the week, it is said, the Holy One is also dressed in holy raiment; but on Sabbath, He is cloaked in yet holier—more refined and inward—garb:

> On Sabbath . . . He is dressed in royal garb, the ten sefirot of *Beri'ah* [the world just below divinity], but on weekdays, He is cloaked with ten bands of angels [i.e., from the third world, *Yeẓirah*] who minister to the ten sefirot in *Beri'ah*. (TZ Intro: 3b)

A similar notion is expressed throughout the *Zohar* itself. Moshe de Leon wrote that *Shekhinah* is garbed in the angelic realm during the week; on Shabbat, however, She is adorned in divine light alone, the effulgence of the sefirotic realm.[51]

But more frequently the TZ/RM depicts a more radical transformation, a fundamental shift in modalities. In this schema divinity is garbed in the *qelippot* of *Siṭra' 'Aḥra'* during the week, only to divest them on Shabbat. In several accounts this weekday garbing is not seen in a wholly negative light: indeed, by 'wearing' Evil divinity maintains control over it, neutralizing its excesses and directing its energy for positive ends. Consider TZ 69 (108b–09a):

> As there is a holy kingdom so is there a sinful one. [The author goes on to show how *Siṭra' 'Aḥra'* forms a counter-sefirotic world, opposite divinity]. . . . These are the ten Lower Crowns, which are the *qelippot* for the ten sefirot [of divinity]. The sefirot are the fruit [*moḥa'*] within. These *qelippot* form a barrier between Israel and their Father in heaven. The Holy One and *Shekhinah* are cloaked in these *qelippot*, that *Shekhinah* may uphold the dicta, "His Kingdom [*Malkhut*] rules over all" [Ps. 103:19] and "For *'Elohim* is King over all the earth. . . ." [Ps. 47:8],

including the realm of evil. This harsh framing of divinity is not without its loving aspect. The TZ explains that the coarse garb that *Shekhinah* wears while in Her weekly Exile is an expression of Her solidarity with suffering Israel, and ultimately has a protective function:

> In Exile . . . She dons [harsh] garments so as to protect Israel, who are themselves garbed in the *qelippot* [surrounded by their enemies] below. Hence, the verse: "In all their troubles [kabbalistically, the *qelippot*], He is troubled." [Ps. 91:15]

In Her divinity, *Shekhinah* is not sullied by donning these garments nor is She subject to them; rather, She uses them "like a woodcutter uses an axe." Nonetheless, on Shabbat, Exile ends and harshness departs from the world. Divinity is thus able to take off these *qelippot*. On Shabbat,

> the Holy One wears *qelippot* as well. But they are cloaks made of many shades of beautiful light. [I.e., unlike the ordinary *qelippot* they do not filter out the divine light]. . . . The Holy One is garbed in *qelippot* during the week. But on Shabbat, He is divested of them and arrayed in holy garments.

There is a radical shift in modalities:

> Of these ten holy garments, it is said: "The Lord *BaDaD yanḥennu*,"

conventionally read: "alone led him," but here:

> wears Ten; no 'alien god' at His side." [Dt. 32:12] For *BaDaD* [*Beit Dalet Dalet*] in gematria is ten, [ten holy garments] corresponding to the ten *qelippot* worn during the week. When He wears the holy garb, it is said: "*BaDaD*, these other ten, sit outside; they dwell beyond the Camp" [Lev. 13:46],

far from divinity, in the now quiescent realm of Sammael or radical Evil.

There are two texts which provide an explicit mythic commentary to ritual dressing. Both are focused on the liminal sefirah, *Shekhinah*, whose fate may be seen as a cosmic cipher for (or from a critical point of view, as the projection of) the fate of Israel. Again a kind of dualistic model of transformation is employed. First, TZ 24 (69a–b):

> *Shekhinah* is like an orchard in Exile: She is the fruit within. She is called "the nut" [within the shell], as King Solomon stated: "I went down to the nut garden." [Cant. 6:11]. *Shekhinah* is the kernel within, as it is written: "The glory of the Princess is within . . ." [Ps. 45:14] The outer *qelippah* [shell] connotes the alien domains which clothe Her. But on Shabbat, the Queen divests Herself of this garb and puts on beautiful raiment.

In accord with the divine paradigm:

> Israel below must renew itself each Shabbat, by putting on beautiful raiment, as well.

This symbolic act is given theurgic import, arousing supernal blessing:

> This will cause Her to be bound to the [sefirot]—enabling Her to be filled with divine blessing, to be irrigated from on high.

The second text is the most dualistic of all and may be contrasted with the earlier sources. In virtually all of them some positive purpose was served by *Shekhinah*'s donning of the *qelippot;* moreover, She was in control of them, and impervious to their defiling qualities. In this radical myth, however, *Shekhinah* is the prisoner of *Siṭra' 'Aḥra'* and its feminine personification, Lilith. They form a kind of straitjacket that both constrains and defiles Her. Indeed, they are likened to "the shells of Death" (cf. Z 3:243b [RM]). Each Sabbath eve, She must be divested of this garb or liberated; then purified; and, finally, adorned in holy raiment. This three-fold process provides a mythic subtext for the devotee's actions below: his stripping off of the garment of the week, his bathing, and his re-garbing for Shabbat. The sharply dualistic view articulated by the myth serves to heighten the sense of transformation and renewal conferred by the Sabbath. The TZ passage (48 [85a–b]) reads:

> Regarding the Splenetic One [Shabbetai/Lilith] it is written: "Take that which imprisons you [*neᶜalekha*] off of your feet" [Ex. 3:5], the soiled shoe, the fetid drop, "for the ground on which you stand is holy ground," namely Shabbat. Concerning Lilith, *Shekhinah* says: "I had taken off my robe—was I to don it again? I had bathed my feet—was I to soil them again?" [Cant. 5:3]

As the devotee engages in the three-fold process of purification and renewal, he aligns himself with the transformations on high and becomes *Shekhinah*'s symbol. The TZ adds:

> For this reason one must change his clothes [on Sabbath eve] . . . and must add to the holy by taking from the profane.

Mircea Eliade has shed light on this ritual process, whereby the person becomes a cosmic symbol:

> By consciously establishing himself in the paradigmatic situation to which he is pre-destined, man cosmicizes himself. . . . He repro-

> duces on the human scale the system of rhythmic influences . . . that characterize and constitute a world, that . . . define any universe. (*The Sacred and the Profane:* 172)

But Sabbath-dress is not without magical valence, as well; indeed, the two modalities of Kabbalistic ritual freely mix here. By dressing in clean, preferrably light-colored clothing (black being the color of Lilith/Shabbetai[52]), the Jew—like *Shekhinah,* his archetype—escapes from the clutches of Lilith, that "snake-filled pit, which is Israel's Exile." The devotee ascends unto the divine realm, unto Shabbat:

> Whoever honors the Sabbath escapes from this pit. Whoever sins, remains ensnared. . . . He who observes the Sabbath ascends unto *Malkhut,* who is the Sabbath. . . .

The aesthetic delight that wearing beautiful clothing confers also has apotropaic value, warding off the doleful presence of Lilith, the antithesis of Shabbat. Based on a complex web of associations drawn from Kabbalah and medieval astrology alike, Lilith is associated with the melancholic planet Saturn (Heb.: *Shabbeta'i*) which, in the Gentile world, was commonly thought to hold sway over the seventh day.[53] Engaging in Sabbath-delight banishes Lilith/Saturday while strengthening *Shekhinah*/Shabbat:

> On Saturn's day it behooves Israel to make certain changes: to eat and drink sumptuously, to wear fine raiment, to enjoy themselves . . . to display abundant mirth. When [Saturn/Lilith] realizes there is no resting place for her, she flees. (TY 55a)

And:

> On the Sabbath, one must . . . exhibit joy in contrast to the maidservant Lilith, that bitter presence

who according to Z 3:272b [RM], "remains in darkness, wearing black garments like a widow." The devotee must model himself after *Shekhinah.* Accordingly,

> one must adorn oneself in beautiful clothing. If one does so he is the child of Shabbat, the child of the Queen. But if not, he is the child of Lilith. (ZḤ "Yitro": 33d–34a, written by TZ's author)[54]

Clothing, in short, reveals one's spiritual parentage, indicating just "who" one is.

Hence, within the context of the Kabbalistic Shabbat, *levush* becomes a deceptively complex symbol of purification and regeneration, both human and divine; dressing becomes yet another means of aligning oneself with the changes on high, a way of expressing "Shabbat."

CONCLUSION

The phases of Sabbath-preparation which have just been examined may be viewed in a slightly different light. In a sense these rituals detail the progressive rapprochement of the Sabbath and Jew, their meeting and interpenetration. As the Jew enters the Sabbath, the Sabbath enters the Jew. This dual process is evoked in the imagery employed on Sabbath eve. The Jew is said to dwell within Shabbat—"under the *Sukkah* of Peace," within the Temple, at the Edenic center—while the Sabbath is said to dwell within the devotee's abode and within the chambers of his soul. Externalized, the Sabbath envelops him; internalized, the Jew becomes its honored host.

Through preparation and joyful anticipation, the devotee's world has been scoured clean, purified, in a sense, reborn. Having divested his home of all polluting influences, then freshly adorning it, the Jew prepares a nuptial chamber for the Bride. Having divested himself of the profane through the acts of nail-paring, disrobing, and ablution, the devotee has become temporarily empty, spiritually ready to receive and be filled with Shabbat.

As the devotee begins the Sabbath prayers, the forces of *Din* are fully vanquished. The "world that is fully Shabbat" has arrived. *Shekhinah* and devotee have now entered the Palace[55] and a different modality holds sway, a different music, heard. The world is protected, quietly joyous; borders secured, the mythic focus shifts from the limen between the sefirotic and lesser worlds to the intradivine pleroma, the Sabbath-cosmos par excellence. As the mythic focus shifts, so does the function of Kabbalistic ritual. Themes of liberation and separation give way to coronation and *hieros gamos.* Those apotropaic rituals that punctuate the week are no longer needed, for in Meir ibn Gabbai's words, "the Sabbath protects the cosmos." (TY 48a and 58b) Quite the contrary, such rituals sound a jarringly dissonant note in the Sabbath-music: they are counter-transformative, waking the slumbering forces of *Din.* The Sabbath-observer focuses on the joyous events unfolding in the divine world and knows "rest, quietude and safety." (TY 47b) He completes his prayers and walks home from the synagogue to greet his family and "receive his Guest in joy." As he does so, he feels the numinous presence of angels and the divine Mother:

> He is accompanied by angels on either side, with *Shekhinah* arching over all, like a mother [bird] hovering over her fledglings. At that moment, "a thousand arrows may fall at your side and ten thousand at your right hand but it shall not reach you . . . no harm shall befall you." [Ps. 91:7] (ZḤ, " 'Aḥarei Mot": 48d)

The vulnerability of Exile has given way to security; tension to a certain ease. Sabbath peace reigns. In a profound sense, the Jew has come "home."

In this fashion do the Zoharic Kabbalists describe the entry into Shabbat.[56]

Rel-Cl. quote

NOTES TO CHAPTER THREE

1. See the discussion in chapter 4, pp. 269–70 and the accompanying note, n. 24, on page 280 below.

2. I shall deal mainly with Zoharic sources in this chapter: the *Zohar* itself (including the ZḤ), the TZ/RM, and the TY. I shall also refer to the *Qanah* with some frequency and will occasionally bring in other sources for purposes of clarification.

3. The rituals considered here are drawn both from *minhag* (custom) and from the miẓvot proper. In the Zoharic tradition both are equally efficacious, as Jacob Katz has pointed out in his pioneering study, *Halakhah ve-Qabbalah* (Jerusalem, 1984). See esp. pp. 34–51 ("Hakhraᶜot ha-Zohar bi-Dvar Halakhah").

4. In Ex. 31:16, the word *DoRoTaM* is written *ketiv ḥaser*, with the vocallic *Waw* missing. In the *Zohar* this unusual spelling becomes the occasion for a mystical midrash. Moshe de Leon has reread the extended verse to mean: "The Children of Israel shall keep the Sabbath, preparing their dwelling places for the [divine] Sabbath [*la-ᶜasot 'et ha-Shabbat le-dirotam*]."

5. The home as microcosm is a recurring motif in many religious traditions. See Mircea Eliade, *The Sacred and the Profane*: 45–47 and esp. 172–79 ("Body-House-Cosmos").

6. See the discussion on p. 195 above.

7. *Peli'ah* 36b stresses the mental refocusing that accompanies these domestic preparations: "In whatever one does, he should think of the

Sabbath's honor, for thinking and recitation are akin," having transformative powers!

8. Quoted in his disciple E. de Vidas' *Toẓe'ot Ḥayyim* sec. 90; replicated (and explicated) in I. Horowitz, *Shenei Luḥot ha-Berit,* "Massekhet Shabbat." Also cf. the versions preserved in M. Cordovero's own *Tefillah le-Mosheh,* Gate 10:2 and *'Or Yaqar,* Part 8:13.

9. Ff. TB Yoma' 13a and Shabbat 118b, et al. The former reads: "His house—that means his wife!"

10. From the *ʿAleinu* Prayer.

11. *Shenei Luḥot ha-Berit:* Ibid. On candlelighting as the mystical *shelom bayit* or sefirotic coupling, see the many examples provided in my discussion of *hieros gamos,* Chap. 1.

12. The Rabbis interpreted the Biblical injunction "Let no man go out of *his place* on the seventh day" (Ex. 16:29) to mean that a person should not travel long distances—i.e., more than 2,000 cubits—outside his town or "place of residence." Cf. TB ʿEruv. 51a. For elaboration on this law, see MT, "Shabbat": Chap. 27; Ṭur OḤ 398; and the synopsis in EJ 6:849 ("Eruv").

13. For a more complex example of this homology, see *Zohar* 2:63b–64a, where the Sabbath-Place variously connotes the physical *teḥum Shabbat;* a stage of mystical awareness; and the sefirotic realm from *Binah* to *Malkhut.*

Also see the somewhat different connotation of *teḥum Shabbat* in Z 1:5a. On the one hand, the *teḥum Shabbat* delimits and restricts, establishing firm boundaries between permitted and forbidden, sacred and profane. However, it also expands the notion of one's place by allowing one to travel "2,000 cubits *beyond* the town limits." Z 1:5a emphasizes this expansive sense of the *teḥum* and so too, the increased holiness of Shabbat. Discoursing on the mystery of the sefirotic Sabbaths, the *Zohar* begins:

> " 'Et Shabbetotai" (Lev. 19:30): The particle *'et* is added to *include* [within the divine Sabbath] the *teḥum Shabbat* which extends an additional 2,000 'cubits' in all directions.

The divine Sabbath is thereby enlarged, coursing beyond "Her Place" (*Shekhinah*) into the realm below.

For more on the mystical symbolization of *teḥum Shabbat,* see Z 2:207a; *Rimmon* (MS Brit. Museum) 98a–b; TZ Intro (12a) and 21 (55b); and TZḤ 103a.

14. For the full text, see pp. 211–12 n. 35 above.

15. TY 46b. For the entire TY passage see *Sod ha-Shabbat:* Section 4.

16. Also Cf. TZ 21(60a).

17. Kabbalistically, the entire sefirotic world. See p. 30 above.

18. For another mystical interpretation of the Sabbath domains, see OK to Shab. 2a. Its author, Ṭodros Abulafia, associated the various domains not only with rungs in the supernal world but with stages of mystical cognition.

For a fascinating interpretation of the *ᶜeruv* used to symbolically unify an entire town, see Joseph ben Shalom Ashkenazi, *Perush le-Farashat Bere'shit:* 192. Here it is Diadem/*Malkhut* that is *Reshut ha-Rabbim:*

> Know that Diadem receives energy from all the sefirot. Hence, She is called [*Reshut*] *ha-Rabbim,* [here meaning] the "Realm of Plenty."

By means of the supernal *ᶜeruv*—the integration of sefirotic domains on Shabbat—"carrying" from *Reshut ha-Yaḥid* unto *Reshut ha-Rabbim* is made possible: i.e., *shefaᶜ* flows from the upper sefirot unto *Malkhut.* The full text reads:

> " 'And God blessed the seventh day' [Gen. 2:2]: He blessed it *be-hoẓa'ah* [conventionally, by providing for additional expenditure, but here: by carrying]." (Gen. R 11:3) For [normally] it is forbidden to carry [*le-hoẓi'*] from *Reshut ha-Yaḥid* to *Reshut ha-Rabbim.* Know that Diadem receives energy from all the sefirot. Hence, She is called *Reshut ha-Rabbim,* the Realm of Plenty. [Carrying from] *Reshut ha-Yaḥid* [to another domain] is one of the categories [of prohibited labor]. Therefore, our Rabbis of blessed memory established *ᶜeruvin, the fusion of the rungs and their union on Shabbat* [emph. mine]. Were not the rungs unified, one could not carry from *Reshut ha-Yaḥid* to *Reshut ha-Rabbim* or vice versa.

From the standpoint of the devotee, the humanly constructed *ᶜeruvin* are here purely symbolic, a means of reflecting the divine harmony of Shabbat.

19. This is the first act of bodily preparation in the TY. Curiously, I have found no Zoharic sources which incorporate the well-known custom of fasting on Friday afternoon—"so as to eat with heightened appetite on Friday night." (On this practice, see TJ Taᶜan. 2:12, s.v. "R. Abin"; TB Pes. 99b–100a and ᶜEruvin 40b; Isaac b. Moshe of Vienna's *'Or Zaruᶜa* "ᶜErev Shabbat" sec. 21; and Ṭur OḤ 249.) By contrast, the custom of preparatory fasting was of concern to some Byzantine Kabbalists. The *Pel'iah* (36b), e.g., considers it part of a mystical "rite of passage":

> On Sabbath eve, one should not eat from *Minḥah* onward, so that he may enter the Sabbath with appetite [*ta'avah*/desire] for the groom neither eats nor drinks [on the day of the Wedding] but enters the Bride's home [i.e., Shabbat] with appetite."

By fasting, the adept separates himself from his profane weekday status and prepares to become a groom unto Shabbat/*Shekhinah*! (For further comment, see Appendix I below.)

Shoshan Sodot (77b) appends a sefirotic rationale to the traditional reason for fasting. Although the Sabbath day is under the sway of the divine Sabbath (*Yesod*), Friday is correlated with *Hod,* a rung on the Left with close ties to *Din.* Hence, on Friday:

> It is the custom of *ḥasidim* to fast all day. . . . The reason is that *Ẓaddiq*, the Foundation of the World, [holds sway on] Shabbat, while the eve of the Sabbath [belongs to] *Hod*, a "day" of *Din*/Judgment. Therefore, one is not to provide the soul with [gustatory] delights, but should starve it; this enables one to come to the King's table with great appetite [i.e., increasing *ᶜOneg Shabbat*] . . .

The subsequent popularity of fasting on Friday—for Kabbalistic reasons—owes much to the Safed Renaissance. For one influential example, see *Re'shit Ḥokhmah*, "Gate of Holiness" 7:98, where E. de Vidas gives fasting a mystico-ethical coloration.

20. *Purity and Danger* (London, 1966): 114

21. Zohar 2:208b does counsel one to pare the nails daily, but makes no special provisions for entering Shabbat:

> Therefore a person must not let his fingernails of impurity grow, for as they grow so does the impurity of that Camp [*Siṭra' 'Aḥra'*]. One should attend to them daily and cut them. . . .

Non-Kabbalistic enjoinders to trim the nails before Shabbat are fairly numerous, however. Although the evolution of this rite is still inadequately understood, a fuller sense of its early history would allow a better assessment of its Kabbalistic recasting. According to the mid-sixteenth Kabbalist Naftali Hirz Treves, preparatory nail-paring was practiced among Ḥasidei 'Ashkenaz. He attributed the following parable to the Roqeaḥ:

> Once a rabbi died and appeared before his disciple in a dream. He had a stain on his forehead. The disciple asked why this happened. He replied: Because I was not careful to refrain from talking during the benediction of *meᶜein shevaᶜ* [on Friday evening] and when the Ḥazzan recited *Qiddush, nor was I careful to trim my nails on Sabbath eve.* [emph. added] Thus far, the words of [the Roqeaḥ].
>
> Moreover, *Sefer ha-Gan* [early thirteenth century, only fragments extant] enjoins not trimming them on Thursday for they will have already grown by Shabbat. Thus far, the words of the Roqeaḥ. (*Siddur Mal'ah ha-'Areẓ Deᶜah:* "Maᶜariv le-Shabbat," s.v. "Va-Yekhullu")

Although I suspect that these are genuine early thirteenth century Ḥasidic teachings, I have been unable to locate them in extant sources. The earliest established sources to incorporate nail-pairing into Sabbath preparation are the Provençal halakhic anthologies *Kol Bo* (section 35) and *'Orḥot Ḥayyim* ("ᶜErev Shabbat," sec. 12). Both of these sources, dating from the turn of the fourteenth century, recast the dream parable related above. A brief mention of nail-paring is also found in the early fourteenth century *Sefer ha-Minhagim* from the school of Meir b. Baruch of Rothenburg:

> On [Friday afternoon] one should not eat from *Minḥah* onwards. He should be scrupulous concerning wine for *Qiddush* and in paring one's nails, sharpening his knife, etc. (Elfenbein ed., p. 7)

The Spanish work *Sefer Abudraham*, ca. 1340, holds that one may pare one's nails "in honor of Shabbat from Wednesday on" (pp. 368–69) whereas the *Shevilei 'Emunah* (1360) is the first source to call it a miẓvah. This Spanish source betrays certain magical concerns (similar to those found in Abudraham):

> It is a miẓvah to pare one's nails on Sabbath eve, beginning with the third finger on the left and concluding with the thumb; with the right hand begin with the thumb and conclude with the third finger. Do not alter this order and do not pare two that are adjacent to each other because this causes forgetfulness. . . . (Warsaw 1887 ed., p. 157a)

Only in *Sefer ha-Peli'ah* (ca. 1410) does one find an explicit Kabbalistic rationale for trimming the nails in preparation for Shabbat. See n. 28 below for details.

22. Cf. Gen. R 20:12; *Targum Yerushalmi* [Pseudo-Jon.] to Gen. 3:7 and 3:21; and PRE 14. For discussion see *Sod ha-Shabbat* n. 51.

23. E.g., the sefirotic world is commonly likened to the ten fingers and the grades immediately below, to the nails. For further discussion of these and other related images, see the analysis of the Havdalah blessing over the fire in chap. 4.

24. Cf. the similar notion expressed in *Peli'ah* 36b:

> See and understand what our Rabbis of blessed memory said. Adam was created without any *Din* for he was entirely nail. When he sinned, *Din* entered into him.

25. See *Sod ha-Shabbat:* Section 3 for a complete rendering.

26. In the popular imagination, demons were thought to reside in the nail-parings. See Z 2:208b and 3:79a, et al. Also see the Talmudic source (MQ 18a) quoted in the ensuing TY text.

27. See his article "The Treatment of Hair and Fingernails Among the Indo-Europeans," in *History of Religions* 16: 351–62 (1977). The quoted phrase is found on p. 360.

28. The TY's interpretation of nail-paring had an important effect on later observance. It was quoted in such influential sources as the *Shenei Luḥot ha-Berit* ("Massekhet Shabbat"); *Be'er Heiṭev* to Sh.A OḤ 260; *Maṭṭeh Mosheh* 4:211; and the more recent *Ṭa*ᶜ*amei ha-Minhagim ve-'Oẓar ha-Dinim* of Sperling (sec. 254–55).

The TY's multi-layered rationale for nail-paring and disposal may be compared with the more monochromatic *ṭe*ᶜ*amim* found in *Sefer ha-Peli'ah* and *Shoshan Sodot*. The *Peli'ah* focuses primarily on the magical-apotropaic aspects of the *paring* and its beneficial effects on the devotee:

> [On Sabbath-eve] one should pare his nails for "every addition is deemed equal to a loss" [TB Ḥullin 58b, Bekh. 40a], affecting the

[neighboring] limb too. The force of impurity derives nourishment from *Pardes* [the sefirotic world]. Therefore, remove from yourself that which causes injury to the People. . . . (fol. 36b)

The Talmudic reference is to a basic law of *kashrut:* the abnormal addition of a limb or organ causes the animal to be treated as though both the normal and the abnormal limb were missing, rendering the creature unfit for consumption. Kabbalistically, the 'abnormal' growth of the dirty nails sullies the Sabbath-cosmos, causing *Siṭra' 'Aḥra'* to be nourished instead of the terrestrial world. The addition of dirt under the nails, in other words, represents a loss for us. Conversely, to pare the nails is to starve or eliminate Evil for the duration of Shabbat, enabling us to receive blessing from on high.

Shoshan Sodot (78b), by contrast, stresses the theurgic or intra-divine consequences of nail-paring: it symbolizes and effects "the removal of the external *qelippot,* the Ten Bands of Impurity that adhere to *Malkhut.*"

29. On this term, see p. 130 above.

30. Cf. e.g., *Re'shit Ḥokhmah* ("Shaʿar ha-Qedushah": Chap. 2) and esp. the *Shenei Luḥot ha-Berit* cited on p. 231 above.

31. See V. Turner's *Forest of Symbols* (Ithaca, 1967): Chap. 1 (esp. 28ff.) and *Dreams, Fields and Metaphors* (Ithaca, 1974): 55–57.

32. It had previously been associated with the entry into sacred space, as well—prescribed, e.g., for *kohanim* about to perform their priestly service and for pilgrims about to enter the Temple Mount. A Geonic tradition also associated it with the entry into *Yom Kippur,* the most solemn of days. See n. 37 below for further discussion.

33. On the evolution of this custom, see n. 37 below.

34. The only conceivable allusion to *ṭevilah* is in Z 2:136b: "When Rav Hamnuna Sava used to come out of the river on Friday afternoon he would rest a little on the bank . . ." Although Safed Kabbalists interpreted Rav Hamnuna's act as *ṭevilah* (cf. *Toẓe'ot Ḥayyim* sec. 91 and *'Or Yaqar* vol. 9: 64), they may well be reading contemporary practice back into the *Zohar.* The Zohar source contains no explicit evidence that anything more than *reḥiẓah* is taking place.

35. For another reference to ablution in the *Peli'ah,* see the vignette on fol. 7d, which begins: "One time I went to immerse myself [*li-ṭbol*] in the water; it was Sabbath eve, and as I went out from the water. . . ."

36. One of the richest discussions of aquatic symbolism may be found in the writings of Mircea Eliade. (See *The Sacred and the Profane:* 129–36 and *Patterns in Comparative Religion:* 188–215.) Although his theories cannot be applied wholesale to the material at hand, I have been informed by

several of his insights regarding immersion and emersion. His claims regarding death-birth symbolism seem less applicable here.

On the three stages in rites of passage, see A. van Gennep, *The Rites of Passage* (Chicago, 1960), esp. pp. 10–11 and 21; and V. Turner, *The Forest of Symbols:* 93ff.

37. On the evolution of the custom of nail-paring, see n. 21 above. The historical development of *ṭevilah* in preparation for Shabbat is not yet sufficiently understood. It seems that it was sporadically practiced in certain Middle Eastern locales long before its appearance in the *Qanah* and *Peli'ah.* The first mention of pre-Sabbath ablution is in 2 *Maccabees* 12:38. It is told that upon returning to the town of Adullam on Sabbath eve, Judah and his men "purified themselves as was their custom and celebrated the Sabbath." It is not certain, however, whether this ablution was for the "honor of Shabbat," as suggested by G. Alon and H. Albeck (see, e.g., the former's *Meḥqarim be-Toledot Yisra'el* [Tel Aviv, 1957] 1:156–57) or a means of purifying the soldiers from the blood on their hands prior to their entering the town (ff. Num. 31:19). This latter reading, which was first suggested by Ralph Marcus (*Law in the Apocrypha* [New York, 1927]: 80), seems more likely in my estimation. For further discussion, see L. Schiffman, *The Halakhah at Qumran:* 107.

A second piece of evidence is preserved in the responsa of the mid-eighth century Gaon of Sura, R. Yehudai (in B. Lewin, *'Oẓar ha-Ge'onim,* "Rosh ha-Shanah" [Jerusalem, 1928], *teshuvah* 14). R. Yehudai was asked whether "one needs to recite the blessing over *ṭevilah* on Sabbath eve, the eve of festivals [cf. *Sifra'* "Shemini" 4:9 and TB RH 16b] and the eve of Yom Kippur." Despite the fact that he responded in the negative—noting that one was not *obligated* to perform these ablutions—the *she'elah* demonstrates that pre-Sabbath immersion was practiced in at least some circles in Babylonia.

A third attestation is found in the *'Eshkol ha-Kofer* (sec. 150) of Judah Hadassi, the twelfth century Karaite sage from Constantinople. He noted that on the eve of Shabbat one "should bathe and sanctify himself in purity [*le-hitqaddesh be-ṭaharah*—apparently, through ablution] in order to pray to his Maker." As Żvi Ankori has noted, Hadassi's work was not original but anthological, reflecting current beliefs and practices of Byzantine Jews. Unfortunately, no other references to pre-Sabbath ablution are found in the Byzantine literature of that period. As a result, it is unclear whether the *Qanah* and *Peli'ah*'s emphasis on *ṭevilah* was an outgrowth (and kabbalization) of an enduring Byzantine practice or a renovation—for mystical reasons—of a custom that had fallen into desuetude.

A final point. The Byzantine-Turkish Kabbalistic emphasis on pre-Sabbath ablution may conceivably be related to a broader phenomenon: the new stress on ritual purification that began with Hai Gaon's renewal of *ṭevilah* for men who had nocturnal emissions (*ba^calei qeri*). This eventuated in a growing tendency in certain High Medieval communities to do ablution before the performance of highly significant miẓvot, e.g., before blowing the shofar; before reciting the priestly benediction and performing *nesi'at kappayim* (the priestly lifting of hands); before leading the prayers; and most commonly of all, before entering Yom Kippur, the "Sabbath of Sabbaths." Still, direct historical linkage is hard to establish; indeed, with the exception of the last example, these ritual ablutions were limited to the Ashkenazic setting (where references to pre-Sabbath *ṭevilah* have not been found). So the question of influence remains moot.

On the requirement of ablution before *nesi'at kappayim* and before leading prayers, see Y. Zimmer's recent article "Moᶜadei Nesi'at Kappayim," *Sinai* 100 (1987): 452–70. On the more widely disseminated custom of performing *ṭevilah* on Yom Kippur eve, see the aforementioned responsum of Yehudai Gaon; *hilkhot Yom ha-Kippurim* in *Siddur Rav ᶜAmram, Siddur Rav Saᶜadiah Ga'on, Siddur RaSHI, Sefer ha-Manhig,* and the *Kol Bo;* Jacob of Marveges' *She'elot u-Teshuvot min ha-Shamayim* (sec. 83), *Sefer ha-Minhagot* in S. Assaf, *Sifran shel Ri'shonim:* 151, and Ṭur OḤ 606. Of special Kabbalistic interest is Z 3:100b and 3:214b. This entire issue requires further investigation.

38. The possible connection between the ritual adaptations of Byzantine-Turkish provenance and the full-blown ritual creativity of Safed Kabbalah needs to be investigated. Many of the Safed adepts had previously spent time in the Turkish-Balkan setting, where they were exposed to a wide array of *minhagim,* not to mention the *Qanah, Peliah,* and TY.

39. See, e.g., TY 43b and 49b; and *Sod ha-Shabbat:* Section 12.

40. Perhaps the closest parallel is Z 3:100b which correlates the adept's ablution on the eve of Yom Kippur with *Shekhinah*'s ritual purification prior to Her marriage and union with the Holy One. See n. 37 and p. 174 n. 223 above for further discussion. Another intriguing source is de Leon's *Sodot,* MS Schocken fol. 91a, wherein the newly liberated *Shekhinah* ritually immerses Herself on *Sabbath eve* in preparation for Her union with "Joseph the Ẓaddiq" (*Yesod*):

> On the sixth day . . . as He is aroused [*be-hitᶜoreruto*], the Bride immerses Herself [*ṭovelet*] in the water which "flows from Lebanon [a cipher for the upper sefirotic world]." [Cant. 4:15]

There is, however, no mention of a parallel *ṭevilah* on part of the adept here.

41. For similar imagery, see Ḥayyim of Chernovitz, *Sidduro shel Shabbat* (reprint, Jerusalem, 1960): Root 1, Branch 3, Section 5.

42. It should be noted that ritual ablution was given added layers of meaning by various Safed Kabbalists in the sixteenth century. To cite but two examples: Moshe ibn Makhir, the *ro'sh yeshivah* of the neighboring town of ᶜEin Zeiton, recorded many of the new Sabbath rituals developed in the Safed milieu. In his *Sefer Seder ha-Yom* (41b), he wrote that:

> The pietists of old used to go down to the river to immerse themselves. Afterwards they went out to greet the Bride and received their Sabbath-soul in purity and holiness.

This seems straightforward enough, but then he adds a surprising and somewhat cryptic remark:

> They used to immerse themselves with their wives in order to direct their hearts to one Place.

This passage portrays ablution as a mystery rite, apparently symbolizing the union of the supernal Bride and Groom. This rite also has magical significance for the adept and his wife. One plausible reading: The joint ritual purification transforms and elevates them as a couple, enabling them to "direct their hearts to one Place"—to have singularly elevated thoughts during marital union—so that they may draw a high soul into conception.

Another striking description of ablution is found in the *Kanfei Yonah* (3:45). Here the act of *ṭevilah* self-consciously assumes three distinct stages: (1) separation from weekday status; (2) alignment with the divine transformations, and (3) re-integration into a higher ontological order. According to its author there are three separate immersions. The first is to remove the polluting presence of sins and the spirit of *ḥol:*

> One should immerse oneself on Sabbath eve, either before *Minḥah* or thereafter, at any event, after noon. . . . When in the water, he should bow towards the West [kabbalistically, *Shekhinah*] and recite for the first dip, "I hereby immerse myself stripped of the garments of the profane week."

As he immerses himself a second time, he focuses on the transformations occurring in the supernal world and aligns himself with it:

> He should enter a second time, saying: "I hereby immerse myself to receive the luminescence of Shabbat, Remember [*Tif'eret*] and Keep [*Shekhinah*] in union."

As he concentrates on various divine Names,

> Clouds of Glory encompass the person in the water.

Only at this juncture may he receive his additional soul:

> Thereafter, he immerses himself a third time, saying: "I hereby immerse myself in order to receive a Sabbath-soul." When he emerges, let him walk backwards *like one departing from the Temple.*

Through the later popularization of the Safed Kabbalah, *ṭevilah* became a standard feature of Sabbath-preparation in many communities. For recent examples see A. Sperling's *Ṭaʿamei ha-Miẓvot:* 119ff.; M. Zborowski and E. Herzog, *Life Is With People* (New York, 1952): 41; and B-Z Muẓapi (ed.), *ʿOlamo shel Ẓaddiq* (Jerusalem, 1985/86): 145–46. Also see EJ 11:1534 ("Miqveh").

43. On the royal nature of Sabbath-garments, also see J. Giqatilia, *Sodot,* section 10, "Garments":

> To wear garments that are appropriate for royalty, holy vestment. For it is fitting that one who stands in the king's palace should

> wear royal garments. For this reason, our Sages of blessed memory said: "The clothing that one wore when cooking a dish for one's master [here, connoting the profane week] should not be worn when offering him a cup of wine [i.e., on Shabbat]." [TB Yoma' 23b] The mystery is "You shall make holy vestments [to wear in the Sanctuary]" [Ex. 28:2], truly.

The symbolism developed in *Shoshan Sodot* should also be noted. The custom of washing one's clothing on Thursday is given Kabbalistic meaning:

> Thursday corresponds to the rung of *Ḥesed,* which removes all impurity. Hence, it is proper to cleanse one's garments on this day, in order to be purely attired when greeting the King and Queen. (77b)

Later (fol. 78a), R. Moshe ben Jacob noted that the change of clothes parallels *Shekhinah*'s re-garbing:

> The reason for washing the body and donning new clothes: During the week *Malkhut* functions [in the lower world] through the aspects of *Din,* strict Judgment, and *Raḥamim,* Compassion: they are Her garments [cf. Z 2:204a and *Qanaḥ* 65a]. . . . But on Shabbat *Malkhut* wears Sabbath-finery, royal vestment, pure Compassion. To emulate this paradigm, it is proper to remove one's weekday garments, which suggest *Din,* and don Sabbath vestment, which intimates Compassion.

44. This structure is sometimes extended to the divine world as well. That is, the lower (or more outward) sefirot serve as the garment to the potencies above (or within). See Z 3:283a (RM): "*Shekhinah* is the cloak covering all Three [*Ḥesed, Gevurah, Tiferet*]."

The image of divinity cloaked in layered garments appears in older Greek, Iranian, and Jewish sources, as well. See R. Eisler, *Weltenmantel und Himmelszelt* (Munich, 1910); R. C. Zaehner, *Zurvan: A Zoroastrian Dilemma* (Oxford, 1955); A. Altmann, "A Note on the Rabbinic Doctrine of Creation" in his *Studies in Religious Philosophy and Mysticism:* 128–39; and G. Scholem, *Jewish Gnosticism:* 57–62. The older imagery lacks the pantheistic sweep found in much of the Kabbalistic imagery, however. See the ensuing TZ text for illustration.

45. See discussion on p. 200 above.

46. See T. Polhemus' anthropological study, *Fashion and Anti-Fashion* (London, 1978).

47. On the often ambivalent responses to the sacred, see Mircea Eliade, *Patterns in Comparative Religion:* 14, 17–18, 417–20, and 460. On Zoharic use of Ex. 33:20, see Z 1:98a, 211b, 226a and 3:147a. On the awesome "Face of God," also see ZḤ 22c–23a (MN). This motif was well-developed (indeed, more frequently and powerfully expressed) in earlier Jewish Mysticism. Cf. G. Scholem, *Jewish Gnosticism:* Chap. 8 and the numinous hymn

from *Heikhalot Rabbati,* reprinted in T. Carmi, *Penguin Book of Hebrew Verse* (New York, 1981): 196–97.

48. Cf., e.g., Z 1:2a:

When the males of Israel perform the miẓvot of the Three Festivals [adorning Her from below], Her Mother lends the Daughter Her garments and decorates Her with Her own adornments.

49. Perhaps the most striking example of the mystical adorning of the Bride is the *Zohar's Tiqqun Leil Shavuᶜot.* See 1:8a and 3:98a–b; also see Moshe de Leon's *Sodot,* MS Schocken 14 fol. 86a–b. For discussion, see G. Scholem, OKS: 138 and Y. Wilhelm, "Sidrei Tiqqunim" in *ᶜAlei ᶜAyin* (Jerusalem, 1948–52): 125–30.

50. On the distinction between remote and proximate influences in mystical experience, see Robert Ellwood, *Mysticism and Religion* (Englewood Cliffs, NJ, 1980): 70.

51. Cf. Z 2:204a.

52. On wearing light and gaily colored garments on Shabbat, see ZḤ "Yitro" 34a and 37a (TZ?). (The injunction to wear white garments is a later insertion, introduced into the 1663 Venice ed. of ZḤ [fol. 59b]).

On Lilith and her spiritual children wearing black, see Ibid. 37a and Z 3:272b (RM).

For broader discussion, see *Sod ha-Shabbat* nn. 380–82.

53. See R. Klibansky, F. Saxl, and E. Panofsky, *Saturn and Melancholy* (London, 1964) for discussion. For Jewish parallels see *Sod ha-Shabbat,* nn. 378–79 and R. Kiener, "The Status of Astrology in the Early Kabbalah," *Meḥqerei Yerushalayim be-Maḥshevet Yisra'el* 6:3–4 (1987): 28, English section.

54. There is a highly complex historical backdrop for this symbolization of Lilith/Shabbetai which I hope to address in a future article. For some initial thoughts, see my dissertation "The Sabbath in the Classical Kabbalah" (Ph.D. thesis, University of Pennsylvania, 1984), pp. 531–38. A condensed version may be found in my comments to *Sod ha-Shabbat,* nn. 378–83.

55. On *Shekhinah* entering the Palace as Sabbath begins, see Z 2:135a–b ("Raza' de-Shabbat") and pp. 113–14 above.

56. It should be noted that there are a few Byzantine sources that hold a somewhat different view of the Sabbath mythos and its underlying rhythms. Perhaps the most prominent example is *Sefer ha-Qanah.* Its author, a highly creative adept, had strong dualist tendencies which he here extended into Sabbath proper. That is, he prolonged the anti-demonic rituals of "separation" far beyond the halakhic boundary of candlelighting, well into the Sabbath day. (Curiously, these 'radical' views are not evident in the same author's *Peli'ah.* They are, however, intermittently evident in the

anthology *Shoshan Sodot* [completed 1498], where uncited teachings from the *Qanah* appear.) It is worthwhile noting the broad outlines of the *Qanah*'s distinctive vision.

The preparatory rituals mentioned in the text are few in number and concerned primarily with the time just prior to Shabbat. The first ritual mentioned is that of changing garments:

> And how does one honor the Sabbath? With special garments not worn during the week. Know, my son, that the Sabbath garments are the divine blessing [*shefa*ᶜ] that She [*Shekhinah*] receives from the upper sefirot. For during the week She receives both *Din* and Compassion, and acts through them. But on Shabbat all the *shefa*ᶜ is of Compassion. So one is bidden to change his clothes . . . in accord with this [transformation on high].

One thereby exemplifies the flow of divine blessing into the world. In contrast to the other sources (including the *Peli'ah*), bathing *follows* the act of dressing. The text reads:

> After he has changed, let him wash his face, hands and feet so that the path of the profane week may be lifted from him. . . . (65a)

This is a glimpse of a trait that courses through *miẓvat Shabbat* in the *Qanah:* that is, the beneficent Sabbath-cosmos must repeatedly be re-won, for it is not stable or secure. Despite the devotee's and *Shekhinah*'s transformation on Sabbath eve, *Din* is a force to be reckoned with throughout the day. Whereas the *Zohar* depicts *Din* as a kind of slumbering demon that is best left alone and forgotten, the *Qanah* devotes a good deal of energy to actively warding it off. For example, the act of candlelighting must be done so as to confuse the demonic powers:

> It would be proper to light two candles corresponding to the East [*Tif'eret*] and West [*Malkhut*]. . . . However, one should light three, for Satan and the demonic powers do not see threes and they will not cause any harm. (65b)

The Friday night *Qiddush* has a dual function: it is both an anti-demonic ritual and the occasion for the divine marriage. The author explained:

> Through reciting the *Qiddush* on Friday night, one sanctifies (or betroths) the [Queen] unto the King and banishes the profane ways.

Drawing on the sefirotic association of wine with *Gevurah,* he avers:

> One makes a blessing over the wine to appease [and hence neutralize] *Din.* . . .

The ultimate purpose of the final *Qiddush* blessing—*Qiddush ha-Yom*—is to bring divine blessing down from *Ḥokhmah* unto *Malkhut;* but to do that the demonic realm must first be "attacked":

> We then say that Shabbat is "first among the holy convocations" meaning that Shabbat alludes to *Binah,* called the Great Sabbath, the first of the [active sefirot]. Therefore, we say "in commemoration of the Exodus from Egypt," because *Binah* lets *Tif'eret* ride on the

> Arms [*Ḥesed* and *Gevurah*] and makes war with Egypt [*Siṭra' 'Aḥra'*] and brings us [the Community of Israel/*Malkhut*] from slavery to freedom.

For those who did not prepare for Shabbat beforehand, the *Qiddush* serves as the rite of separation, a kind of *Havdalah.* Paraphrasing a halakhic discussion to TB Pes. 99b–100a (cf. Tos. ad loc.), the *Qanah* notes:

> If one were eating a meal on Friday afternoon and Shabbat drew near, one should stop the meal, recite the weekday Grace after the meal, and thereafter, *recite the Qiddush and separate the Profane from the Holy.*

The first two sacramental meals, which are occasions for *hieros gamos* in the Zoharic tradition take on anti-demonic valences in the *Qanah.* The first meal, corresponding to *Shekhinah,* facilitates Her liberation from the realm of harsh *Din,* while ushering Her into the Realm of Compassion. Evidently, *Shekhinah*'s status in the divine realm is not secure until well into Friday evening. The second meal, corresponding to *Tif'eret,* has even stronger anti-demonic overtones, alluding to *Tif'eret*'s "war against Sammael" which will come to a head in the future.

Only the third Meal, parallel to *Keter,* is devoid of apotropaic significance. For this Meal points to the "supernal Source . . . a rung without *Din.*" Finally, on Saturday afternoon, complete Shabbat is attained, and "All is Compassion." The author explained the rabbinic custom of using only one *ḥallah* for the third meal in mystical terms. During the first two meals two *ḥallot* are required since the divine world is not yet integrated: by holding two *ḥallot* together, *qeruv* [union] is promoted. However, at *Seuᶜdah Shelishit* only one loaf is required for "all is in union" already: that which was two is now one! (66a–b)

For parallels in the *Shoshan Sodot,* see fol. 76b (on *Qiddush*); 76b–77a (on the sacramental meals); 78a (on dressing); and 78a–b (on candlelighting). Also noteworthy is the apotropaic significance accorded the *berakhah meᶜein shevaᶜ* on Friday night (79a). Through proper recitation, the supernal entities unite "so that [finally!] the Opposing Forces are snuffed out and gone." Nonetheless, this anthological work is hardly systematic or univocal in its symbolism; it also incorporates views that are akin to those found in Gerona and Zoharic sources.

CHAPTER FOUR

Rituals of Separation: The Drama of Sabbath's Departure in Zoharic Kabbalah

The Kabbalist seeks to prolong the Sabbath-cosmos both before and aft, welcoming the Sabbath-Bride while it is still Friday (from the vantage point of "profane—solar—time") and not letting Her go until well into Saturday night. Following the Rabbinic tradition "of adding to the sacred by taking from the profane"[1], Sacred Time is stretched. As seventh day draws to a close, it is to be lingered over and savored, for the Sabbath is truly a beloved guest. Meir ibn Gabbai spoke of the bittersweet mood of Saturday night:

> We prolong the Sabbath by extending it into Saturday night, thereby showing that we do not like to see the departure of the holy guest; indeed, its parting evokes a feeling of deep regret. So we detain it and, in our great affection, escort it with song and choruses of praise, as in the teaching, "We will send you off with joyous song." (TY 58a)[2]

The liturgy of *Moẓa'ei Shabbat* (Sabbath's departure), marks the slow tuneful "escorting of the Queen and Bride." But as occurs so frequently in the Kabbalah, it dramatizes other scenarios as well. Drawing on a variety of sometimes complementary, sometimes clashing mythic subtexts, a dense weave of meaning is fashioned in the closing rites. For Saturday night is a period of multiform transformation: of time, of divinity, of the upper worlds, of the devotee. Sabbath gives way to *ḥol*, divine integration is lessened, the devotee gives back his Sabbath-soul and once again (according to several suggestive myths) leaves Eden. Saturday night is a time marked by "the Changing of the Cosmic Guard," to use the *'Or Zaruᶜa*'s apt phrase. In many accounts, direct Providential authority is transferred from *Shekhinah* to the benevolent angelic realm below.[3] More ominously, harsh *Din, Siṭra' 'Aḥra'*, re-emerges after its suppression on Shabbat.

The ritual strategies of *Moẓa'ei Shabbat* are accordingly multiple: to acknowledge and attune oneself to these changes, which are seen as an inevitable part of the pre-Messianic world; to ensure the proper transfer of Providential authority; to set firm boundaries between the Holy and the Profane, lest they mix and divinity be garbed in 'confused' attire or *sha^caṭnez* (ff. Lev. 19:19); or again, to neutralize (*lehamtiq*, lit. "to sweeten") *Siṭra' 'Aḥra'* or even to suppress it for a while longer; to afford the newly vulnerable devotee protection against the demons of the week;[4] and to heal his diminished soul. There is a two-fold movement in many of these rituals: to help create proper change, but also to limit it, to assert continuity. Through these rites the devotee aims to extend the Sabbath-cosmos into the week, to bask in its warm afterglow. The multiform tonality of these rituals attests to the ambivalence, the truly mixed emotions with which the Kabbalist escorts the Bride and enters the new week.

THE CONCLUDING PRAYERS: THE NEED FOR APOTROPAICS

> Why do we recite "May the Pleasantness"? As we have seen, *Din* is banished on Sabbath eve, departing from even the sinners in Gehinnom. For Shabbat protects the cosmos. But on Saturday night, *Din* is restored to its station. A herald cries out: "Return, o you wicked to She'ol!" [Ps. 9:18], for *Din* is aroused at this hour. (TY 58b)

> "Blessed shall you be in your comings and blessed shall you be in your goings." [Dt. 28:6]
>
> (recited in the *Moẓa'ei Shabbat* liturgy)

Mircea Eliade has noted that threshholds and transitional zones are oft fraught with danger (*Sacred and Profane:* 181). This notion is richly illustrated in the Zoharic literature on *Moẓa'ei Shabbat.* As the devotee leaves the blessed state of Shabbat, he is newly vulnerable to the revived demonic forces. The concluding prayers serve to deflect those forces, to build up a store of Sabbath-protection to shield one in the profane week. The TY explains:

> We recite the verse: "May the Pleasantness [*No^cam*] of YHWH our God come unto us" [Ps. 90:17], alluding to the pleasing [radiance] that is *No^cam*. It is the Great Light which perpetually shines upon us, streaming forth from Naomi [*Binah*] without end.

Recitation of the verse draws down this supernal light unto the devotee; moreover,

> it delivers us from the dread of Gehinnom and the harshness of unmitigated *Din,*

which according to midrashic tradition befall the wicked in Hell upon the conclusion of each Shabbat.[5] The TY continues:

> As Scripture says: "Gaze upon the Pleasantness of YHWH, and you shall frequent His Sanctuary." [Ps. 27:4]

Apparently, Meir ibn Gabbai read the last verse as if there were a causal connection between its two phrases: *If* one partakes of the divine *No^cam* on Saturday night, *then* he is protected from the ascending rigor of *Din* and able to remain in the realm of holiness a bit longer. This prayer, in short, helps to cushion the potentially traumatic re-entry into the profane, post-Sabbath cosmos.

The protective qualities of this prayer are amplified in the *Zohar.* As the devotee recites it, he is bathed in a supernal light which

> issues from the World-to-Come [*Binah*], from which all light streams forth, radiating in every direction. . . . For when the Sabbath departs, we must beckon the supernal Joy unto us, and be delivered from the punishment that the wicked undergo from that hour forward. We do this by reciting "May the Lord's Pleasantness [shine] on us," referring to that Pleasing Radiance which brings us pervasive joy. (1:197b)

Other closing prayers serve a similar function. Consider the next Psalm—the 91st—the so-called "Song against the Demons."[6] *Zohar* 1:14b elaborates:

> When the Sabbath enters, holiness reigns over the cosmos. *Siṭra' 'Aḥra'* is weakened and goes into hiding for the rest of Shabbat. . . . When the Sabbath departs, innumerable bands of evil spirits roam the world. The recitation of the Song against Demons was instituted to ward them off, lest Israel come under their control.
>
> Where do these spirits roam on Saturday night? They set out hastily, intending to gain rule over the holy People. But when they see [Israel] immersed in prayer, reciting this Song and making *Havdalah* . . . these spirits flee. They wander to and fro till they reach the wilderness,

far from the "holy Camp."

THE "HAVDALAH OVER WINE"

This renewed concern with the extra-divine world, and with *Din* in particular, telegraphs the arrival of a transitional period, a kind of limen between full Shabbat and the approaching world of *ḥol.* The mythic heart of this period is the *Havdalah,* the formal rite of Separation. Following Rabbinic tradition (TB Ber. 33a), two *Havdalot* are performed, a private one offered in the Standing Prayer, and the more dramatic "Havdalah over wine" performed subsequently in public. In some Kabbalistic sources, e.g., the *'Or Zaruᶜa,* it is the first *Havdalah* that demarcates between Sabbath and *ḥol:*

> One should prolong Shabbat lest the Guards change too soon. When *Havdalah* is recited in the Standing Prayer, the [legitimate Changing of the Guard] occurs. (53b/68b)[7]

But in the *Zohar* and TY, the fundamental transition occurs during the *Havdalah* over wine. *Zohar* 1:14b, e.g., maintains that the "camps in charge of the weekdays return to their appointed stations" at the first *Havdalah,* but are not "granted dominion" till the blessing over the fire in the public ceremony. Indeed,

> until the last moment it is still Shabbat; its holiness is sovereign.

In these Zoharic sources the *Havdalah* over wine takes on a complex mythic significance unmatched by any single Sabbath ritual. It serves as a kind of magnet for sundry mythic motifs coursing through the day and for the conflicting emotions the devotee experiences at its end. Nonetheless, if the mythic subtext is complex, the visible rite is one of simplicity. Performed in a numinous darkness punctuated only by a multiwicked torch or flaming candle—a play of shadow and light—the Jew recites a series of three blessings: over wine, fragrant herbs, and the fire. He then concludes with a benediction of formal *Havdalah,* distinguishing between the holy and the profane, light and darkness, Israel and the nations, the Sabbath and the six working days. The ritual is accompanied by three gestures which capture the Kabbalistic imagination: the herbs are smelled, the fire's light reflected off the fingernails, and the wine drunk.

The first act of this *Havdalah*—preceding any sacred or transformative utterance—is candlelighting, a *mela'khah* (active labor) that halakhically signals Sabbath's end, and for the Zoharic Kabbalist, the end of the Sabbath-cosmos. It is crucial that this act not be performed too soon, Meir ibn Gabbai told his readers,

> for such an act causes the flames of Hell to be kindled prematurely,

causing a Changing of the Guard before its appointed time.[8] Properly performed, however, this act provides symmetry and closure to Shabbat. For as candlelighting marked Sabbath's inception, so too, it dramatizes its departure. The mythic meanings accorded this Havdalah flame are numerous. They will be treated below, in the analysis of the blessing over the fire.

The Havdalah *Blessings as Rites of Healing*

> On Sabbath eve the Holy One gives the human being an extra soul and on Saturday night He takes it away. (TB Beiẓah 16a)
>
> But it was explained: a person's soul *[nefesh]* takes in this spirit *[ruaḥ]* on Sabbath eve and houses it. The spirit resides there all Sabbath long, and the soul is elevated and enlarged, greater than before.
>
> For this reason we learn: All souls of Israel are crowned on the Sabbath, adorned by this indwelling spirit. When the soul departs, woe to the soul, for it has lost its crown! (TY 59a ff. *Zohar* 2:204b)

Havdalah marks the departure of the devotee's Sabbath-soul and consequently, his spiritual diminution. As Meir ibn Gabbai attested:

> For at this hour a person's Sabbath-soul takes its leave and one enters the days of toil and privation, diminished and saddened. (TY 58b)

The *Zohar* graphically measures this loss, noting that one is left with but two-thirds of a soul:

> When the Sabbath departs, the bond [uniting the three aspects of soul] is severed; the *neshamah* ascends and the *nefesh* and *ruaḥ* [the two lower parts of the soul] are left estranged and saddened. (Z 3:35b)

Yet if *Havdalah* is the occasion for marking this loss, it dialectically serves as the therapeutic moment, wherein the ordinary soul may be healed, and the emotional let-down attenuated. In the pre-Zoharic literature the fragrant herbs (*besamim*) were thought to symbolically afford such healing.[9] Although the *besamim* retained a pre-eminent position in the Kabbalistic tradition, it is interesting to note that all three ritual objects—wine, herbs, and flaming candle—were given therapeutic valence. Essentially the Kabbalists took what was a minor point in the earlier tradition—widely acknowledged but little discussed—and developed it into a multi-faceted mythic motif.

It was Meir ibn Gabbai who first imputed to wine some of the soul-quickening qualities most commonly associated with *besamim*. Finding a Kabbalistic rationale for the seemingly repetitive *Havdalah* over wine, he noted:

> So one makes a *Havdalah* over wine, for it rejuvenates [the soul]; it brings down strength from *Gevurah* and stimulates good cheer. (TY 58b)

For the initiated Kabbalistic reader, the association is clear. Wine, with its red hue and transformative (i.e., intoxicating, exhilarating) power, is a common appellation for *Gevurah*, the supernal source of strength and in the Sabbath-context, of joy, as well: "the mystery of 'the wine that cheers *'Elohim* and humankind.' " (Jud. 9:13)[10] The sacramental wine both represents and calls forth its archetype, drawing down *Gevurah*'s abundant vigor. One might say that the devotee literally incorporates its qualities as he later partakes of the Havdalah wine. In this way he is able to retain part of the Sabbath-cosmos even as the additional soul departs and the world about him is transformed.[11]

TZ Addition 6 (143b) ascribes a similar rejuvenating power to the candlelight. This text is more complex, owing to its ambiguous language. According to the TZ, there is a dual loss at Sabbath's end; like the ordinary soul, *Shekhinah*, the archetypal Soul, has been divested of Her Sabbath-crown. Again, the fate of the Jew and *Shekhinah*, symbol and archetype, are intertwined. The author addresses the reader on two levels, referring to the cosmic situation explicitly, and to the microcosmic plight on a subliminal level, as a kind of subtext:

> On Friday night there are two flames and so too, on Saturday night. Thus, the blessing: "Who creates the lights [in the plural] of fire." Concerning this it is written: "Sustain me with *'ashishot*" [Cant. 2:5],

normally rendered, "with raisin cakes," but here:

> with two fires [*'ishot*].[12]
> Why does it say "Sustain me?" On Friday night, a Sabbath-soul descends to sustain the lower *Shekhinah* in Her Exile. . . . When Sabbath departs, Her Sabbath-soul departs, *"va-yinnafash"* [ff. Ex. 31:17 and TB Beiẓ. 16a]: As soon as it leaves, woe to the Soul, for there is none to support it! At this hour the Soul calls to Israel, "Sustain me with *'ashishot*, namely the "lights of the Fire." What are they? The two *Torot* hewn from Fire [*Neẓaḥ* and *Hod*], from the aspect of *Gevurah.*

Later the TZ explains the rejuvenation of the Soul/soul in more conventional terms, in relation to the fragrant herbs. Here the mythic referents blur further, as the "Soul's husband" may connote either *Tiferet* (following the *hieros gamos* motif) or the special Sabbath-soul:

> [The Soul] may be compared to a princess on her sickbed. Out of love for her husband who has left, she swoons onto her bed, and cries out: "Sustain me!" With what? "With apples!" [Cant. Ibid.], the apples growing abundantly "on the trees of the forest" [Ibid. 2:3]. This refers to the spice trees . . . to myrtle [sefirotically, *Tiferet*]. . . . Thus it says: "Stay me . . . for I am faint with love." [Cant. 2:5] (TZ Ibid.)

This last passage has introduced us to the most frequent and well-articulated therapeutic strategy: the blessing over (and smelling of) the fragrant herbs. The nexus between soul and fragrance was already firmly established in the Talmudic literature, providing the Kabbalists with several inchoate associations. In a passage the mystics were fond of quoting, it was explained:

> How do we learn that a blessing should be said over fragrant smells? Because Scripture says: "Let every *neshamah* [meaning both 'every soul' and 'all that breathes'] praise the Lord." [Ps. 150:6] What is it that gives enjoyment to the soul but not the body? Fragrant smells! (TB Ber. 43b)

The *Zohar* itself developed a sophisticated web of what may be called olfactory symbolism, embracing such diverse phenomena as roses, burnt offerings, incense, the scent of Eden and the scent of souls. In one lyrical passage (Z 2:20a) that calls to mind the nature imagery of the Franciscan Spirituals,[13] Moshe de Leon imputed the power of cosmic sustenance to fragrant scents, and singled out myrtle, the Havdalah herb par excellence:

> R. Abba was walking along the road with R. Isaac. In the course of their journey they came upon some roses. R. Abba picked one and resumed walking. R. Yose came upon them and said: "Surely the *Shekhinah* is here! I can see from the rose in R. Abba's hand that one can learn great wisdom from this. I know that R. Abba picked the rose to teach us something."
>
> R. Abba said: "Sit, my children!" They sat. R. Abba smelled that rose and said: "Surely the world is only sustained through fragrant smells. . . . For I have come to understand that the soul is only sustained through smell; thus, we smell myrtle at the conclusion of Shabbat."

In another passage (Z 3:35b), de Leon underscored the power of fragrant herbs to heal and re-integrate the soul:

> The world [another version: vital soul] is only sustained through smell. From this earthly fragrance we come to know of another [supernal] fragrance. At the conclusion of Shabbat, the bond [between the three aspects of soul] is severed. The Sabbath-soul ascends and the *nefesh* and *ruaḥ* grow apart from each other and are sad. But through the fragrance these two aspects of soul again draw near and rejoice. . . . This is like the fragrance of the *QoRBaN* [sacrifice]; through it, all the entities are drawn together [*mitQaRBiN*].

According to Meir ibn Gabbai, the Havdalah blessing over the spices dramatizes a two-fold integration. The renewal of the terrestrial soul mirrors the re-integration of the *neshamah yeterah* into its divine abode and its resulting vivification:

> From the earthly fragrance we come to fathom the heavenly Covenant. On Saturday night when the Sabbath-soul [*neshamah*] departs, one is diminished; his *nefesh* and *ruaḥ* grieve over their loss. He smells the fragrant spices to gladden and strengthen [these two] and to draw them together. Through this fragrance the [departed] *neshamah* is strengthened in the supernal Faith [the sefirotic world]. She is energized in the presence of these supernal spirits. (TY 89b)

The Symbolism of Myrtle

In virtually all streams of the Medieval literature, myrtle was singled out as *miẓvah min ha-muvḥar*, the choicest way of fulfilling the Havdalah blessing. While the pre-Kabbalistic rationales remain somewhat opaque to scholars,[14] the Zoharic adepts explicitly correlated the use of myrtle with two mythic scenarios.

The first one is based on another symbol-archetype relationship: The *Zohar* sometimes calls *Tif'eret*—the matrix for the Sabbath-soul—the Supernal "Myrtle Tree." As the mythic scenario goes, each Sabbath eve, souls bloom forth into the world and each Saturday night they return to their Root. Smelling the myrtle sprig dramatizes this return. The TY (59a) elaborates:

> One must smell the fragrant spices as Sabbath departs and the choicest way of fulfilling this miẓvah is with myrtle. For *myrtle brings to mind the soul's abode* [emph. mine]: from it souls depart to sojourn with us each Shabbat and to it they return; from it they draw sustenance. The Tree from which these souls flower forth is called *Hadas,* Myrtle. Thus, Scripture says: "It [the soul] was standing among the myrtles." [Zech. 1:8]

As the italicized prints suggests, myrtle leaves are literally redolent of the supernal Myrtle from which the souls derive. The ZḤ (Cant. 64d) underscores this notion while adding another layer of significance to the ritual act:

> The scent of myrtle is a fragrance wafting down from the Supernal Myrtle. It is a divine point which goes forth into the world . . . to strengthen [the ordinary soul].

In sum, by smelling myrtle the adept participates in two core ritual-processes:

(1) His focus is directed from the local to the cosmic, as he concentrates on the ascent of the Sabbath-soul to its home—the attestation of the *Tolaʿat Yaʿaqov.*

(2) Through the symbolico-magical valence of ritual action, an infusion of supernal energy is said to be drawn down from the cosmic Myrtle unto the devotee's ordinary soul—the attestation of the ZḤ.

The second mythic motif (found in Z 2:208b–209a) moves on two mythic planes at once, directing the Kabbalist's attention not only to events unfolding in the supernal realm, but also those in *illo tempore,* in pristine Eden. At the heart of this myth is the symbolization of the *neshamah yeterah* as the lost Edenic garb which is returned to the Jew each Sabbath. The text opens:

> Upon the conclusion of Shabbat we must smell aromatic spices for the [additional] spirit has now departed, and our souls are left naked.

At this point the *Zohar* begins a homily on the *besamim* by way of Gen. 27:27, i.e., Isaac's blessing of Jacob disguised in Esau's mantle. The verse contains two acts central to the *Havdalah* ceremony, smelling and blessing:

> It is written: "And he [Isaac] smelled the smell of his clothes and blessed him." This verse has been interpreted [*Zohar* 1:142b, 24b; 2:39b]. But come and see! It is the scent that sustains the soul; for scents enter the soul, but not the body [cf. TB Ber. 43b, etc.].

The *Zohar* now skillfully weaves an Edenic motif into the homily. It alludes to PRE 24 and Gen. R 65:22, where Jacob's garments are said to be redolent of Eden. In the former, it is told that Esau stole the fragrant cloak that God had fashioned for Adam and Eve. Isaac smelled these garments, which Rebecca had subsequently given to Jacob. The Gen. R passage merits quoting here:

> "And Isaac went up and kissed him. And he smelled the smell of his clothes." Said R. Yoḥanan: "there is nothing with a more pungent odor than goat-skin and yet it is said: 'He smelled the smell . . . and he blessed him.' For when Jacob our father came before his father, the [scent of] the Garden of Eden entered with him. Thus, Isaac said: 'See, the smell of my son is as the smell of the field that the Lord has blessed.' [Gen. 27:27]

With this source in mind, we may now return to the *Zohar:*

> It is written, "And he smelled the smell of his clothes and blessed him." As has been explained these are the garments in which the Holy One adorned the first human being. When he sinned, these precious garments were removed from him . . . and he was dressed in other garments [cf. pp. 224–25 above] . . . The Holy One fashioned this garment from the leaves of the trees in the terrestrial Garden of Eden. . . . His new garment was redolent of the perfumes and spices of the Garden, scents that calm the soul and give it joy. Thus, Scripture says: "And he smelled the scent of his clothes and blessed him." For Isaac's soul was soothed by this scent.
>
> And so, when the Sabbath departs we must inhale the fragrance of spices to soothe the soul; for its fragrance comes from the holy supernal scent [see Z 2:20a; 3:35a; TZ Add. 6, 143b]. The choicest of all the scents is surely myrtle, for it is Myrtle[15] that

> sustains that holy Place [*Malkhut*] whence the souls come. And it is myrtle that sustains the human soul that has been left naked.
>
> It was at the Sabbath's conclusion that Adam was dressed in these garments of earthly Eden. Their fragrance wafted forth and fortified his soul which had lost its holy spirit. And it is surely myrtle that sustains the soul, just as it [*Tiferet*] sustains the Soul [*Malkhut*] on high.

A mythic paradigm for *Havdalah* has been deftly drawn in this passage. Part of its power lies in its dreamy, fluid quality that evokes rather than explains. Both Isaac and Adam serve as the devotee's archetype or role model. The implicit message of the Isaac story: as Isaac's soul was soothed by the Edenic scent, so is one's own comforted and delighted by the Havdalah herbs. The Adamic imagery is more intricate and bears closer scrutiny.

Of particular interest is the final section of the text where an interesting web of Edenic associations has been fashioned. As entering the Sabbath is homologized to re-entering Eden, leaving it may be likened to Adam's exile from it. To clothe and sustain the newly vulnerable Adam and to remind him of his Edenic origin, he is fashioned a garment literally redolent of the Lower Garden. By analogy, the Jew is newly naked as he leaves the Shabbat, stripped of his extra-soul. To sustain him in the post-Edenic week, he is afforded a final whiff of Eden/Shabbat, as he smells the myrtle. In so doing, his naked soul is re-garbed, renewed.

By subtly, perhaps only semi-consciously, drawing upon Edenic imagery at Sabbath's end as well as at its inception, the *Zohar* provides symmetry and mythic closure to the Sabbath celebration.

Thus far our discussion has relied on the Kabbalists' own rich phenomenology of the blessing over myrtle. But perhaps we can derive additional insight into the inner workings of this ritual by considering certain contextual, informal[16], and subliminal factors that, perforce, remain outside the Kabbalist's own ken.

In effective ritual, Victor Turner has suggested,[17] the physiological and cognitive poles of meaning—stored in the ritual symbol—interpenetrate, so that the grossly physical is ennobled, made meaningful, and the purely ideational vitalized, made real. In this case, the actual fragrance of myrtle gives the Havdalah mythos a visceral reality it might not otherwise have; conversely, the Zoharic narrative quite obviously accredits myrtle with a symbolic significance far beyond its inherent value, i.e., the aesthetic pleasure it naturally imparts. Let us consider the second point first.

In the fertile kabbalistic imagination, the simple myrtle sprig has become a cipher for—and ladder to—the sacred mystery of Sabbath's departure. Its leafy branch symbolizes the Soul's home in the sefirotic Tree even as its fragrance intimates—and calls forth—the *shefa*ᶜ that quickens the ordinary soul. Or again, it may reflect one's Edenic garb and pristine origins, one's ideal self. Myrtle, symbolized, becomes the bridge linking macro- and microcosm, Soul and soul, this moment and *illud tempus.* It points beyond itself, to the ultimate frame of reference and meaning.

But this is only part of the story. Ultimate meaning is embodied and more richly experienced as the myth of *Havdalah* is infused—if for a fleeting second—with the spontaneous associations unlocked by inhaling. Abstract symbolism and gross physicality, intended and unintended significations, all interweave to form a rich Gestalt that defies easy unpacking.

Moreover, the physiological basis for the sustaining power of fragrance should not be overlooked. Certain scents, like smelling salts, literally refresh, stimulate, awaken. Others delight. As experimental psychologists have demonstrated, smell is uniquely able to revive and, so sustain buried memories, to trigger and unlock webs of association. On many levels, fragrance can inspire.[18]

Finally, the larger physical and psychological setting must not be ignored. The numinous darkness of *Havdalah,* the devotee's anxiety over leaving Shabbat, expectation borne from memories of *Havdalot* past[19]—all these serve, as well, to intensify the drama of *besamim.*

In a sense, this ritual enables the devotee to perform two crucial acts of closure at Sabbath's end: first to acknowledge the passing of the blessed state of Shabbat, to mourn one's lost pneuma, and dialectically, to be healed and soothed, regarbed, so that one can enter the week with renewed strength. One is reminded of the ancient Confucian philosopher, Hsun-Tzu, who noted that the power of ritual lies in its ability to express emotion, yet to contain the chaos of emotion, to shape and modulate the devotee's inner life.[20]

The Blessing over the Fire

At this point in the ceremony, attention shifts to the flickering flame which punctuates the darkened room, creating a dramatic interplay of shadow and light. Turning towards the multi-wicked candle, the Kabbalist recites the traditional blessing, *bore' me'orei ha-'esh,* "Creator of the lights of fire," and holds his right hand before the flame so that its light shines on his nails. As he does so, the mystic directs his mind's eye to the mysterious events unfolding in the supernal worlds. If the blessing over spices highlights the transformation of the person, the one over fire emphasizes a series of celestial transformations which together signal the end of the Sabbath-cosmos. Two transformations stand out:

(a) The re-emergence of *Siṭra' 'Aḥra'* and hence, the world of duality, and

(b) the Changing of the Cosmic Guard, as direct Providential authority passes from *Shekhinah* to the angelic realm below Her.[21]

The Re-Emergence of Siṭra' 'Aḥra'

As Sabbath ends, the forces of *Din* are roused and return to their stations. Meir ibn Gabbai wrote:

> We then recite the blessing over the fire. Know that on Sabbath eve the Fire of the North [*Siṭra' 'Aḥra'*] is hidden away and concealed. Lest we rouse it in the slightest, it is written, "You shall not kindle a fire." [Ex. 35:3] As Israel recites the blessing over the fire on Saturday night, this [Fire] goes out to stand guard as before. (TY 59a)

In the post-Sabbath world, ibn Gabbai seems to say, harsh *Din* has a legitimate place and function. By reciting the blessing over the fire, the adept is acknowledging the inevitable return of the quotidian order while ensuring that *Din*'s restoration occur within proper limits, in orderly and timely fashion. This notion is elaborated in the *Zohar* (2:203b):

> Come and see. When the Sabbath arrives, the [blaze of the Left Side] is hidden in the Great Abyss, and all the harsh fires are concealed and suppressed. . . . *When the Sabbath departs* and Israel blesses the fire, all the fires that were in hiding emerge, each going to its *appointed place.* [emph. added]

But alongside this acceptance of *Din*'s restoration runs an antithetical emotional current. *Zohar* 2:203a–b, the immediately preceding passage, attests to the profound desire to extend the Sabbath-cosmos, and hence, to suppress and hem in *Din.* Although the demonic fires are perforce re-kindled on Saturday night, the blessing over the fire serves to keep them under wraps:

> As Israel prepares for Shabbat a flame of [holy fire] emerges and batters the Fire [of the North] so that both of them are hurled down into the Cavern of the Great Abyss. The flame belongs to the Right Side and can sweep away the fire of the Left, confining it to this Cavern. . . . There it remains until the end of the Sabbath. When the Sabbath departs Israel must make a blessing over the fire. Through this blessing the flame [of holiness] goes forth and keeps the blazing fire in check all night. Hence, the blazing fire remains in subjugation. (2: 203b)

Here, the Havdalah flame represents not the Fire of the North but its cosmic adversary, the flame of holiness, of *Ḥesed,* the Right Side. Recitation of the blessing has magical valence: re-activating the divine flame needed to suppress *Din.* The ritual has become an apotropaic, a means of affording Israel and cosmos renewed protection.

There is an urgency underlying the devotee's actions here which contrasts with the sense of inevitable cosmic harmony expressed in some of the preparatory rituals. This contrast is dramatized in this particular section of the *Zohar.* The sources cited above are part of an extended mythic narrative (2:203a–04a) detailing the cosmic battles between divinity and evil which take place before and after Shabbat:

> On Friday as evening approaches, a brilliant Star from the North [*ruaḥ seʿarah,* the outermost and harshest of the four *qelippot* surrounding divinity[22]] shines forth, accompanied by seventy others [holding sway over the seventy nations].

Wishing to attach itself to *Shekhinah* and parasitically derive nourishment from Her, the North Star consolidates its forces:

> This [great] star smites the others, absorbing them so that the seventy are made into one. This star expands, becoming an inferno blazing from all sides. The flaming mass then extends itself around one hundred thousand mountains [the angelic world], surrounding them like a rope. . . .

Then this evil Star turns inward to the three more refined *qelippot* which surround *Shekhinah:*

> Then the blazing fire draws out different hues, from [the *qelippot*] inside it. The first hue is greenish [the *qelippah* called *'esh mitlaqqaḥat,* the Flashing Fire]. When this hue is drawn out, the blazing fire pounces upon it and makes its way deeper inside, casting the

> green hue outside in the process. . . . Next the [fire] draws out a white hue [the *qelippah* called *ʿanan gadol,* the Great Cloud]. As this occurs, the blazing fire pounces on it, as well; it casts the white hue outside, and proceeds inward yet again. So it makes its way past all the other hues [belonging to the innermost *qelippah, Nogah,* or Brightness] till it reaches the hidden Point [*Shekhinah*], to take its light. . . .
>
> On Friday as evening approaches, this blazing fire. . . presses ever inward, making its way past all the hues. It is at this time that Israel below prepare themselves [for Shabbat], arranging their meals, setting their tables, each one according to his means.

The preparatory rites, however, merely indicate the temporal setting of these mythic events. There is no attempt to specifically correlate these preparations with the battle on high, to give them theurgic valence. Rather, with no ritual prompt:[23]

> At this hour, a flame [from divinity] issues forth and attacks the blazing fire. As they clash, they both are hurled down to the Cavern of the Great Abyss, where they are shut in. This flame is from the Right Side; it is its task to sweep away the blazing fire and confine it to the Great Abyss, where it remains for the duration of Shabbat.

Though one cannot generalize absolutely from any given *Zohar* source, one can note a tendency which this passage exemplifies: Havdalah ritual tends to stress the magical component of ritual, whereas many of the preparatory rituals are primarily symbolic in nature: a means of aligning oneself with the blessed transformations unfolding on high. Shabbat, it might be said, seems to begin naturally; by contrast, its extension is not natural: it must be effected, theurgically won.[24]

In addition to suppressing *Sitra' 'Ahra',* there are two other ritual strategies for gaining protection at *Havdalah.* The first seeks to separate the demonic realm from divinity and devotee, to keep evil at a distance. The *Havdalah* as a whole does this, much like the prayers of *Moza'ei Shabbat:*

> The *Havdalah* is directed against the Left. . . . When Israel performs this ritual . . . the Left Side withdraws from them and goes down to its place in She'ol. (Z 1:17b)

In contrast to the previous source, there is no sense of struggle, of cosmic battle here.

The final ritual strategy is one which seeks to sweeten or neutralize *Din;* hence, to limit its deleterious aspects. This strategy seems to complement the ritualized acceptance of *Din* mentioned earlier. Here, however, it is the ritual gesture (rather than the candlelighting) that is seen as efficacious. Basing himself on an uncited source from the *'Or Zaruʿa,* Meir ibn Gabbai explained:[25]

> There is another reason that we gaze upon the fingernails. For they allude to Another Causality, as we mentioned above [in the rite of nail-paring].

The *qelippah*-like nails are homologized to *Siṭra' 'Aḥra',* whereas the flesh within represents the divine world:

> This is the mystery of "the wicked encircling the righteous." [Hab. 1:4] Because this realm expands as the Sabbath departs, we gaze upon the fingernails to sap its strength and be spared harm during the coming week. One should make sure, however, that use is made of the candle's light. (TY 59a)[26]

That is, the act of gazing upon the nails and specifically, of seeing them illumined is a way of neutralizing *Din,* freezing its expansion. The act of symbolically filling them with divine light robs them of their ruinous power. The Rabbinic injunction to "make use of the Havdalah light" (M. Ber. 8:6)[27] is given mythic valence.

Several other sources speak of the protective influence of the Havdalah flame in Edenic terms, adding another layer of mythic significance to their more expressly sefirotic readings. Two such examples are David ben Judah he-Ḥasid (OZ 53a) and Meir ibn Gabbai (TY 59a). Both homologize the departure from Shabbat to the departure from Eden. Perhaps something akin to a post-partum syndrome is present here, rapture giving way to sadness and a keen sense of loss. Each Jew is likened to Adam on that first Saturday night: having left the blessed state of Eden/Shabbat, confronting the thick darkness, he is now downcast and depleted, vulnerable to the jealous forces that are out to "get him." Lighting the Havdalah fire and invoking God's name in blessing is a means of attaining divine protection for the profane week. The TY retells the paradigmatic midrash:

> At twilight [on Saturday night] Adam sat down and pondered his situation. "Woe is me", he said. "I fear that the snake that led me

> astray will come and 'strike my heel.'" [ff. Gen. 3:5] [At that moment] he was sent a pillar of fire to light up [the way] and protect him from evil. When Adam saw the pillar of fire, he rejoiced and said: "Blessed are You, Adonai, Creator of the lights of the fire." (PRE 20)

By stressing the apotropaic influence of the Havdalah flame, whether via esoteric symbolism or midrashic parable, the Kabbalists are reflecting the popular wishes and fears that rise to the surface as the Jew leaves the Sabbath and enters the new week.[28] Isaiah Tishby finds this desire for protection to be at the core of the Kabbalistic blessing over the fire:

> The flame of the Havdalah candle lights the way for Israel amid the darkness of the week. It helps them escape the terrors of the dark powers that lurk everywhere and seek to lay Israel low. The flame helps the Jews stand firm till the hidden light of the Sabbath [*ha-'or ha-ganuz shel Shabbat*] returns and shines brightly, again enabling them to enter the divine realm. (MZ 2:507)[29]

From the examples presented thus far it is quite clear that the symbolic structure of this benediction is fluid and dense. That is, the candlelight may represent *Din* or its opposite, the sweet light of *Ḥesed*, the protective light of divinity. The transforming agent may be the recitation of sacred words, the kindling of the flame, or the reflection of that flame on the nails. This symbolic index takes on added complexity as we consider the second major mythic subtext:

The Changing of the Cosmic Guards: The Empowerment of the Angelic Realm

According to one Zoharic tradition, the angelic realms are re-absorbed into divinity on the Sabbath:

> The four [angelic camps] . . . were incorporated into the Diadem [*Shekhinah*] on Sabbath eve, and entered with Her into the King's Palace. For they are Her Chariot, and on Sabbath they are incorporated into the Supernal Lights. (*Ketem Paz* to Z 1:20b)

But on Saturday night as the lights are kindled below, they emerge newly individuated. The cosmic unity of Sabbath fades and multiplicity resumes. It is as if *Shekhinah*, the Supernal Fire and Matrix, gives birth to the angelic world, creating these angelic flames out of Her recesses:

> Why does [the benediction] say "*Creator* of the Lights of the Fire" and not "Illuminator of the Lights"?. . . . When the Sabbath arrives all the lower [angelic] rungs . . . ascend and are absorbed in this supernal Flame [*Shekhinah*]; they are concealed within and protected; they are rendered invisible, included within this Point. But when the Sabbath ends, [*Shekhinah*] brings them forth, as though creating them anew. . . . Then the Flame is blessed. (Z 2:208a)

For the Zoharic Kabbalist, the blessing over the fire tells several stories at once. Different mythic strands, ranging from the popular to the esoteric, weave in and out of the ritual performance. Here the devotee's attention is directed to that second cosmic change, the re-emergence of the angelic realm and more significantly, the transfer of direct Providential authority from *Shekhinah* to that realm. The TY elaborates:

> Four Camps [the angelic world] are illumined by the candlelight. They are called the "lights of the fire." We bend the four fingers of our right hand and hold them up to the candle. The fingers symbolize these Camps, the Mystery of the Lower Chariots, which are illumined by the [supernal] Candle, the Bride. She, the Community of Israel, holds sway over them. She lights them up and sustains them. (TY 59a ff. Z 2:208a–b and 1:20a)

In this schema, the four fingers (especially the nails) symbolize the angelic realm. The specific use of the right hand—found in certain Zoharic sources alone—indicates their intimate relation to the beneficent divine realm.[30] The illumination of the nails by the Havdalah candle suggests the angelic reception of the *shefa*ᶜ from *Shekhinah* and the transfer of authority to the lower realm. Even the precise positioning of the hand vis-a-vis the light is given symbolic significance:

> One may only gaze upon the backs of the fingers, which symbolize the Lower Lights [the angelic world]. As it is said, "You shall see My back." [Ex. 33:23] But one may not gaze upon the inner side which symbolizes the Supernal Lights [the sefirot]. Of them it is written, "But My Face must not be seen." [Ibid.] So we never let the inner part of the fingers catch the light, for they are inward and not illumined by the Lower Candle; rather, they are illumined by the Supernal Lamp on high [*Keter*]. But since the "Backside" [*'Aḥorayim*] is lit up by the Lower Candle, we bend down the outer part of the fingers and hold them up to the flame. Thus we dramatize whence they derive their light. (TY Ibid.)

Utilizing Scripture, word play and hand-structure, a striking web of correspondences has been fashioned. The backs [*'aḥorei*] of the fingers are homologized to the *'Aḥorayim,* or the divine Backside, as the angelic Camps are often called; the inner side [*penimi*] of the fingers represent the *panim,* the divine Face or Countenance, which is to say, the sefirotic world. Although in the non-mystical tradition it is customary to gaze at the palms, as well, the *Zohar* and TY specify: the nails only.[31] The gesture is re-shaped for patently mythical reasons. A theological insight is manually signed: As the Sabbath departs, only the angelic presence can be perceived; the divine Face is beyond one's lowered ken. The radical immanence of Shabbat has given way to renewed transcendence. Now "[*Keter*] is utterly concealed and hidden, on high, on high." (Z 1:21a)

The spiritual descent entailed in the transfer of Providential authority is also indicated in the downward inclination of the cupped fingers. For in the Zoharic tradition, the ten fingers may symbolize the ten sefirot, as well. Their positioning determines their meaning. The *Zohar* explains:

> When we offer other blessings we raise our [ten] fingers [cf. Z 2:67a and 76a] to show the high sanctity of the supernal rungs [the sefirot] that rule over all. . . . All these rungs are blessed together and illumined by the Supreme Lamp [*Keter*]. . . . But [at *Havdalah*] we must bend down the fingers before the flame to indicate those lower rungs that are illumined by the Light on high [*Shekhinah*]. Thus, they are called "the lights of the Fire." (2:208a)

In this reading the Zoharic tradition has made detailed use of the body, specifically, the right hand, to symbolize the divine world and its margins. As in the preparatory rituals, the devotee, in his very flesh and bone, comes to represent and participate in the cosmic drama. The focus on the hand's margins, the nails, is especially apt for the rite of *Havdalah.* At Sabbath's limen, the boundaries between sacred and profane, between sefirotic and angelic realms, are redrawn. Through the ritual, Cosmos, and by implication society, are re-ordered, preserved.[32] More will be said about the social implications of *Havdalah,* below.

It is also interesting to note that the blessing over the lights facilitates two processes which are superficially at odds with each other, but which dramatize the mixed emotions of leaving Shabbat:

(1) Bending down the nails and hiding the palm highlights the *distinction* between the hidden sefirotic world and the newly illumined

angelic realms. The message telegraphed: the cosmic unity of Shabbat is lost.

(2) The illumination of the nails via the Candle stresses the *connection* between the sefirotic world and the angelic camps which now hold sway.

This may be stated in more experiential language. The first process intimates the end of the Sabbath-ethos while the second evokes its continuation, or afterglow. Nails are especially well-suited to express these dual emotions. Located at the body's margin, they seem to be both part of the body and independent of it (growing after death; able to be cut without causing pain; etc.) They evoke both worlds at once.[33]

CONCLUDING BLESSING, CONCLUDING THOUGHTS

Evil having been warded off or neutralized, the soul healed and gladdened, the Changing of the Guard properly marked, the devotee now rehearses those distinctions upon which the post-Sabbath, pre-Redemptive world is based. The final benediction of *Havdalah* is comparatively straightforward in the literature, without the dense symbolic chording found in the blessings over spices and fire.

In the Zoharic tradition the blessing distinguishing "between the Sacred and the Profane" dramatizes the proper ordering of the weekday cosmos, much as *ᶜeruv* did for Shabbat. One stream of thought emphasizes the distinction between the divine world—the so-called garments of holiness—and the profane worlds—the impure garments. *Havdalah* ensures that the two realms are not improperly mixed together lest the world be garbed in a "confused" garment, in *shaᶜaṭnez* (ff. Lev. 19:19). Alternatively, the TZ (69 [108b–09b] claims that the purpose of *Havdalah* is to separate good and evil in the world of *Beri'ah* (below divinity) so that *Shekhinah* may be properly garbed.[34] These separations on high reflect—and give mythic legitimation to—the fundamental social division between "Israel and the [idolatrous] Nations," reminding the Jew of his cosmic address. Meir ibn Gabbai wrote:

> "Between light and darkness": the former referring to the supernal lights and the latter to the four *qelippot*. Between Israel and the Nations": Israel laid claim to the summit of the Tree, the holy Place, and the idolatrous nations, to the four "shells." (TY 59b)[35]

Finally, the distinction between sacred and profane Time is highlighted, as the devotee intones the separation "between the seventh day and the six working days." The benediction now complete, the wine is drunk, the candle extinguished; a new week begun.[36]

The *Havdalah* is undoubtedly the most complex ritual of the Kabbalistic Shabbat. Ambivalent impulses suffuse its performance, like tide and undertow. On one level, the *Havdalah* is a ceremony marking the inevitable distinction between sacred and profane that exists in the unredeemed world. It dramatizes the cosmic Changing of the Guards and insures that it be done in the proper way, lest good and evil become confused, *shaʿaṭnez*. It serves to re-affirm social distinctions, transposing them into a cosmic key.

But alongside this dualistic impulse is a more harmonistic one, asserting some modicum of continuity between worlds, between Sabbath and the week. In short, it might be said that the Zoharic *Havdalah* oscillates between *ha-mavdil ve-ha-megasher bein qodesh le-ḥol,* revealing both the abyss and the bridge between the two realms. Here the tone of *Havdalah* stands in stark contrast to that of the preparatory rituals. In a sense, it is the latter which is the unequivocal *Havdalah* in the etymological sense of the word. There a more purely dualist mythos is highlighted, enabling the devotee to make a clean break with the week. But the spiritual renewal of *Havdalah* is attained in more complex fashion: one leaves Shabbat but takes it with him.

Viewed from one angle, the very separations that *Havdalah* proclaims enable the devotee to align himself with that current of holiness that courses through the profane week. Or to look at it another way, the ritual gestures of *Havdalah* project a Sabbath beachhead into the week: by strengthening the soul with wine, by incorporating a last whiff of Shabbat through the *besamim,* by reflecting the beneficent glow of Shabbat on the body—in short, by formally allowing the devotee to take some of the Sabbath-cosmos with him.

AN EPILOGUE
(From the *Zohar*)

What does the Sabbath mean? It is the Name of the Holy One, perfected on all sides. . . .

On this day, the patriarchs are crowned and all their children[37] imbibe[38] [the splendor], such as is unknown on other festivals and holy days. On this day, sinners in Gehinnom find rest. On this day punishment lies inert, never stirring. On this day the Torah is wreathed in perfect crowns. On this day, [the sound of] rejoicing and delectation is heard in 250 worlds[39]. . . .

On this day in which the Torah is crowned, she is crowned with All, with all the miẓvot and decrees, with seventy branches of light[40] which shine from every side. Who can behold these branches [of light], branches upon branches . . . ? Who can behold the luminous gates[41] which open at all sides? They are all shimmering and radiant, bringing forth streaming, inexhaustible light! (*Zohar* 2:88b–89a)

NOTES TO CHAPTER FOUR AND EPILOGUE

1. Ff. TB Ber. 52a and Shab. 118b.

2. On parallels to the TY here, cf. *Siddur RaSHI:* 267; MV: 116; *Shibbolei ha-Leqeṭ:* 428–29; *Sefer ha-Manhig:* 198; and *Sefer 'Abudraham:* 182. For an early Kabbalistic interpetation, see *Perush ha-Tefillot ve-ha-Berakhot* of Judah ben Yaqar, 1:124–25.

The Saturday evening prayers and the subsequent *Havdalah* over wine are the primary ritual means used to detain Shabbat, and to escort it properly. Several classical Kabbalists—e.g., the authors of the *Peli'ah* (36b) and the *Maʿarekhet ha-'Elohut* (185b)—also adopted the custom of making a fourth symbolic meal at Sabbath's end (cf. TB Shabbat 119b; *Shibbolei ha-Leqeṭ:* 429–30; and Ṭur OḤ 300). This farewell meal—with meagre fare but filled with song—provides regal symmetry to Sabbath-celebration. To use *Shibbolei ha-Leqeṭ*'s analogy: "Just as one welcomes a king at his arrival, so one escorts him at his departure." Kabbalistically, it is a means of extending

> the [supernal] union, so as to strengthen Diadem as She returns to function during the six days of the week, called "this world." For She is active there and watches over it. (*Maʿarekhet ha-'Elohut*)

The goal of the meal, in short, is theurgic: to fortify *Shekhinah* as She embarks on Her weekly journey, to enable Her to take the blessings of Shabbat into the profane week.

3. This framing predominates in the Zoharic sources. In my notes, I shall occasionally refer to other scenarios. See, e.g., n. 36 below.

4. The tradition of beginning the new week by reciting prayers against demons is very old and has surely influenced the Zoharic tradition. Such prayers, as well as incantations for gaining divine and angelic protection, are found in the "magical Havdalah" literature. G. Scholem has traced its origins in the Geonic period and its subsequent development in the Ashkenazic setting. See his edition of the "Havdalah de-R. Aqiva" in *Tarbiẓ* 50 (1981): 243–81 as well as n. 6 below.

5. This notion was a commonplace in the medieval literature. See Gen. R 11:5; Tanḥ. "Tissa'" 33; *Yalquṭ Shimᶜoni* Job 906; *Siddur Rav ᶜAmram* (Goldschmidt ed.): 81; MV: 115; and *Sefer ha-Manhig:* 189.

6. Psalm 91 had long had magical significance, and was already designated as "the Song against the Demons" in Talmudic literature. See *Sod ha-Shabbat* n. 545 for sources. On this psalm's special significance in the Havdalah setting, see also G. Scholem's edition of "Havdalah de-R. Aqiva": 248 and 251. The worshipper was enjoined to recite Ps. 91 as an incantation, invoking the names of safeguarding angels at the end of each verset.

7. For a parallel, see Joseph Giqatilia's *Shaᶜarei 'Orah* 2: 47–48. These Kabbalistic sources do not distinguish between the symbolism of the two *Havdalot,* treating them as identical. It is as though nothing happens between the two ceremonies; the underlying mythos lacks the dynamism found in the Zoharic tradition.

8. TY 58b ff. Z 1:14b.

The question of when, precisely, the Havdalah candle could be lit was never resolved in Moshe de Leon's writings. Three distinct views have been preserved: according to *Sodot* (MS Schocken 14 fol. 90a), candlelighting could occur "after Israel has made the *Havdalah* in the Standing Prayer." By contrast, a view in Z 1:14b held that one must wait until after the completion of the *Qedushah de-Sidra',* i.e., somewhat after the Prayer. Another view recorded in Z 1:14b held that candlelighting must be postponed until "Israel arrives at the *Qedushah de-Sidra'.*"

Subsequent Zoharic adepts tended to accept the latter two views; see, e.g., TY 58b (*Sod ha-Shabbat:* Section 22) and RM (Z 3:246a) which stated that candlelighting be postponed until one "comes to the *Qedushah de-Sidra'.*"

9. As I note in *Sod ha-Shabbat* n. 565, non-Kabbalists interpreted this ceremony in a somewhat different light. See there for elaboration.

10. From TY 49a. In special ritual settings—*Havdalah,* the Friday night *Qiddush,* the Sabbath morning Psalms, the wedding ceremony—*Gevurah* is granted unique gladdening powers. For examples, see *Rimmon* (MS Brit. Mus.) 29b–30a and *Sod ha-Shabbat:* Section 10; as well as pp. 114 and 176–77 (n. 234) above.

11. Curiously, the significance of this benediction is rarely highlighted in other Zoharic sources. Consider, e.g., Z 1:17b, the sole Zohar source to mention the blessing over wine:

> The *Havdalah* is directed against the forces of the Left [*Sitra' 'Aḥra'*]. . . . When Israel performs this rite over myrtle and wine and recites the *Havdalah*, the Left Side withdraws and goes down to its place in She'ol.

The apotropaic significance of wine is evident here, yet wine has no distinctive symbolic role; it is dissolved in the aggregate.

A more pointed treatment is found in *Rimmon* 32b which calls attention to the special apotropaic value of wine:

> This wine comes from the side of *Gevurah;* it is "preserved in its grapes from the six days of Creation" [TB Ber. 34b],

i.e., with origins in *Binah,* the supernal "grape cluster" (cf. Z 1:135b, 3:40b, ZḤ Ruth 76a). Apparently, by reciting the blessing over the wine, one draws down *shefa*ᶜ from *Gevurah—Din* from the Holy realm—to counteract harsh *Din*—from the Side of Impurity—that awakens at this hour. For another interpretation of the blessing over wine, developed in Naḥmanidean circles, see *Keter Shem Ṭov* (Coriat ed.) fol. 37b.

12. The doubling of the *Shin* in *'ashishot* may be read to connote a quality of fieriness. More colloquially, the term may be rendered as *flames.* For the midrashic precursor for this interpretation, see PRK 101b:

> "Sustain me with *'ashishot*": with the two fires, the fire on high and the fire below, the Written Torah and the Oral Torah. . . .

13. For discussion, see Y. Baer, *A History of the Jews in Christian Spain,* Vol. 1: 268–69; and pp. 38 and 58 (n. 105) above.

14. See the discussion in my dissertation "The Sabbath in the Classical Kabbalah": 599–600. Only in the esoteric writings of Eleazar of Worms (before 1230) have I found a rationale for using myrtle. His *Perush ha-Tefillot* (MS Oxf. Bodl. 1204), fol. 135b, reads:

> We smell myrtle sprigs in order to restore the soul. For the soul smells all, including the stench of sulfur from Gehinnom with which the sinners of Israel are punished when the Sabbath departs. And so, one should smell myrtle sprigs.

15. Sefirotically, *Ḥesed, Gevurah,* and *Tif'eret.*

16. By this I mean certain accidental or spontaneous features that occur in the course of ritual performance, but which are not part of its acknowledged structure.

17. See p. 248 n. 31.

18. Cf., e.g., H. Lawless and T. Engen, "Association to Odors: Interference, Mnemonics and Verbal Labelling" in *Journal of Experimental Psychology: Human Learning and Memory:* 1977, Vol. 3:1, 52–59. They write that

"odors have a striking tendency to revive memories from the past with emotional impact" and put forward a theory to explain why familiar odors have the ability to trigger a wealth of associations drawn from several sense-modalities. On the emotional reactions produced by personally meaningful odors, also see D. A. Laird, "What Can You Do With Your Nose?" [!] in *Scientific Monthly*, 1935, No. 41, 126–30.

19. As Barbara Myerhoff has noted, sacred rituals provide the occasion for bringing one's past into the present. She writes:

> Originating in the most basic layers of childhood, rooted there with the earliest emotions and associations, . . .[certain familiar rituals have] Proustian powers for arousing deep involuntary memories, those surges of remembrance that are not merely accurate and extensive but bring with them the essences and textures of their original context, transcending time and change. (*Number Our Days* [N.Y., 1978]: 225)

20. Cited in R. Ellwood, *Mysticism and Religion:* 126.

21. For a third, less common theme, see n. 33 below.

22. This imagery is derived from Ezek. 1:4. On its Kabbalistic usage, see *Sod ha-Shabbat* n. 591.

23. The absence of a ritual prompt is striking, for myth and ritual are generally fixed correlates in the Zoharic literature.

24. The notion that Sabbath blessing flows into the world without human prompt has its ultimate roots in the Rabbinic literature. In Tos. Beiẓ. 2:2, TB Beiẓ. 17a, and TB Ber. 49a, a distinction is drawn between the holiness of the Ṣabbath, which stems entirely from God (cf. Gen. 2:1–3), and the sanctification of the festivals and new moons, which is also dependent on human activity, viz., the calendrical determinations of the rabbinic court. (See the TB sources and RaSHI ad loc. for explanation.) The mystical recasting of this distinction, implicit in the Zoharic sources discussed here and in Z 3:94a–b (pp. 155–56 n. 114 above), is more fully realized in later Kabbalistic literature. See, e.g., the Spanish-Italian adept Joseph ibn Shraga's *Sod Qiddush le-Maᶜalei Shabbeta'* (ca. 1500), printed in Abraham Elmalik, *Liqquṭei Shikhe-ḥah u-Fe'ah* (Ferrara, 1556) fol. 39b; *Shaᶜarei Gan ᶜEden* of Jacob Koppel Lifshitz (Korzec, 1803); and esp. *Sidduro shel Shabbat* of Ḥayyim of Chernovitz (Jerusalem, 1960) fol. 9a-b. The last adept explained:

> At other times [during the festivals and new moons], the influx of supernal love, the revelation of light and the restoration of worlds all depend on our activities, in accord with the principle *'itᶜaruta' di-le-tatta'* [a rousing below produces a similar rousing on high; ff. Z 1:88a et al.]. . . . On the Sabbath, however, the holy divine light suffuses all worlds on high and below by virtue of divine grace, without any rousing from those below [*be-ḥasdei ha-Maqom barukh*

> *hu', beli shum 'itᶜaruta' didan*]. . . . All occurs of its own accord [*naᶜaseh me-'elav*].

25. It should be noted that David ben Judah he-Ḥasid, author of the OZ, was also relying on an uncited source, Moshe de Leon's *Sodot*, MS Schocken 14 fol. 90a-b. Compare!

26. The OZ source (fol. 53b) which inspired ibn Gabbai reads:

> Whoever gazes upon his nails in the candlelight as the Sabbath departs, saps the strength [*matish koaḥ*] of Another Causality which expands throughout the cosmos on Saturday night. [Whoever does so] will be spared harm during the week. One should make sure, however, that use is made of the candle's light. . . .

Cf. also the ultimate source, Moshe de Leon's *Sodot* (n. 25 above).

27. One must "make use of the candle's light" lest the blessing be "wasted," a *berakhah le-vaṭṭalah.* On the Rabbinic and medieval interpretations of this injunction see my dissertation, pp. 605–08; and the condensed discussion in *Sod ha-Shabbat*, n. 582.

28. See, e.g., Th. Gaster, *Festivals of the Jewish Year* (New York, 1953): 276–77.

29. Two Byzantine sources, the *Peli'ah* and *Shoshan Sodot*, also associate the benediction over the fire with Edenic myth. However, while the OZ and TY focus on the apotropaic value of the Edenic fire—its ability to confer protection for the coming week—the Byzantine texts use the ritual for retrospective purposes: to reflect on and savor (for one final moment) the Edenic blessings of Shabbat. According to *Peli'ah* (36b), the Havdalah flame calls to mind the Edenic light of pneumatic insight:

> We gaze on the light and dark on our hands to demonstrate that we have derived enjoyment from the Light [re-reading M. Ber. 8:6] that Adam enjoyed before the Sin, the [supernal] Light [i.e., *'or ha-ganuz*] called *Zakhor*/Remember. . . .

For *Shoshan Sodot* (77a), the illumined fingernails recall the radiant Edenic garment whose splendor is experienced each Shabbat. The adept tries to extend this experience for an additional moment:

> One gazes on the nails to arouse Compassion [*Raḥamim*], for prior to Adam's sin, his garment was made [of nail]; he was pure Compassion. As we gaze on the nails, let it be our intention to praise our God who gave us the Sabbath, *the day of pure Compassion*, and to indicate that we have derived enjoyment from this Compassion.

Inevitably, however, one must leave this exalted Edenic state to re-enter the weekday world:

> Now from the nail that is Compassion, we again become flesh, which is [the aspect of] *Din*.

For a TZ precursor of this text, see n. 33 below.

30. All non-Kabbalistic sources speak of gazing at both hands. Many Kabbalists—holding a different rationale for "using the light"—persisted in gazing on both hands. See, e.g., the *Peli'ah* source cited in n. 29 and OZ (MS Brit. Mus. 771 fol. 54a-b). Although he was clearly familiar with the view that one must gaze on the nails of the right hand, David ben Judah proceeded to uphold the tradition of gazing on all ten nails:

> According to the Path of Wisdom, we must gaze on [all] ten nails to evoke *'Adam ᶜElyon,* the Supernal Person, the mystery of *Tif'eret* and the mystery of "the beauty of Jacob is like the beauty of Adam." [TB BM 84a] . . . [We also gaze on all ten nails] to show the unity of our God who created the ten lights [sefirot] . . . and who created us in His great light.

31. On gazing on the palms see, e.g., Ṭur OḤ 298 and *Sefer 'Abudraham:* 188–90.

For a scathing Kabbalistic critique of gazing on the palms, see OZ 54a–b, which clearly follows the teaching in the Zohar and in Moshe de Leon's *Sodot* (90a-b). The OZ states:

> Following the ancient secret teaching [which de Leon ascribed to the Rabbis], one should look only upon the nails at *Havdalah* and not upon the inner fingers or palm as many do out of perverse stupidity when they do not grasp the essence. . . . I have seen many men stretch out their palms [to the light] and recite the blessing. They do so out of madness [*shiggaᶜon*] and folly [*ṭippeshutam*]. . . . The heart of the matter is that we must gaze only upon the nails, for they are the cloak [of divinity].

32. On the nexus between bodily manipulation and the symbolic imaging of society, see Mary Douglas, *Purity and Danger:* Chapter 7, "External Boundaries." For further discussion on the custom of gazing on the nails at Sabbath's end, see *Sod ha-Shabbat* n. 582 and the sources therein. See also S. Finesinger, "The Custom of Looking at the Nails at the Outgoing of the Sabbath" in HUCA 12–13 (1937–38): 347–65 and D. Noy, "Histakkelut ba-Ẓippornayim bi-Shᶜat ha-Havdalah" in *Maḥanayim* 85–86 (1963): 166–73.

33. I have concentrated on the major Zoharic rationales for gazing on the nails: as an apotropaic against *Din* and its tribulations; and as a means of properly modulating and/or acknowledging the Changing of the Cosmic Guard.

A third, more unusual rationale may be found in TZ Intro (10b–11a) where attention is again drawn to the Edenic subtext of Shabbat. The author subtly cross-indexes Adam's first Saturday night with the devotee's own experience of leaving Shabbat. To gaze on one's nails is to recall Adam's loss of "his precious multi-colored garment of nails." This garment was called *me'orei ha-'esh* (the "lights of the fire") and they "shone like the Cloud of Glory." Now each Shabbat the Jew's soul is garbed in an Edenic garment of light—the additional soul—but each Saturday night he too is divested of it. Adamic vignette and personal story momentarily fuse as the devotee considers the physical vestige of the "glorious garment," his illumined nails.

34. See the translation and discussion in *Sod ha-Shabbat,* n. 605.

35. It should be noted that the TY (60a) incorporates a further social-cosmic distinction into this ceremony, one entailing gender. The specific point of contention concerns the consumption of the Havdalah wine. Meir ibn Gabbai explained the custom whereby women are barred from partaking of this wine on patently mythic/Edenic grounds. For explanation, see *Sod ha-Shabbat:* Section 22 (p. 73) and nn. 627–33.

For an interesting parallel to this TY passage, cf. *Shaᶜarei 'Orah* 2:46–47.

36. At least one Zoharically influenced Kabbalist, David ben Judah he-Ḥasid, depicted the transformations of *Havdalah* in less dramatic terms than the *Zohar,* TZ or TY. Although R. David spoke of the restoration of *Din* at this hour, he saw the shift in Providential authority more as an intra-sefirotic matter than as a radical shift in cosmic modalities. Like Moshe de Leon (and TY) he enjoined the devotee to gaze upon the fingernails only, citing expressly mythic reasons for so doing. But as shall be seen, R. David reframed the underlying myth. Interestingly, the OZ opens with an uncited quotation from de Leon's *Sodot* (MS Schocken 14 fol. 90a-b):

> "Nails are the outer garment for the inner organs; they are called the 'Backside,' and may be likened to a shell covering the fruit. They are alluded to in the benediction made over 'the lights of the fire.' " [Upon this, R. David commented:] Now *Keter ᶜElyon, Ḥokhmah* and *Binah* are the Fire. [The upper Triad is the province of Shabbat in the OZ; cf. also OZ, MS Brit. Mus. 771 fol. 62a.]

R. David has here, in effect, fashioned a counter-commentary to de Leon's own views. The OZ continues, again building on the *Sodot:*

> "We gaze upon their lights [for R. David, the lower sefirot!] and impart *shefaᶜ* unto them. The mnemonic for this is 'You may see My Back, but My Face may not be seen.' [Ex. 33:23 . . ." [R. David commented, again diverging from de Leon's views:] The essence is to gaze upon the nails which symbolize the outer garment, namely *Gedullah, Gevurah, Tif'eret, Neẓaḥ, Hod, Yesod* and *Malkhut.* They are the garment for what lies beyond, namely, *Keter, Ḥokhmah,* and *Binah.* Understand this fully! (OZ, MS JTSA fol. 54b)

In the post-Sabbath world, the OZ suggests, it is the upper triad alone that is beyond human ken. (In the Zohar-TY, by contrast, the transcendence of the entire sefirotic realm is stressed.) By focusing his gaze on the seven lower sefirot instead of on the angelic world of Meṭaṭron, R. David has seemingly fashioned a harmonistic *Havdalah,* one which brings to mind the claims of the *Me'irat ᶜEinayim.* R. Isaac of Acco distinguished between the sefirotic union attained during the week—involving the seven active rungs—and the more inclusive union of Shabbat, in which the lower grades ascend into the upper Triad.

Interestingly, R. David's interpretation of the final blessing of *Havdalah* is less harmonistic in tenor. Although it opens with a relatively measured distinction between "Sacred and Profane," it proceeds to take on a progressively more dualistic tone. The passage reads:

> "Who makes a separation between Sacred and Profane": between the upper world, the Holy of Holies, and Diadem [*Malkhut,* exemplar of the seven lower rungs] called "Profane" [!]. "Between light and darkness": between *Ḥesed* and *Gevurah,* for there is separation between them, the latter being *Din* and the former, Compassion. "And between Israel and the Nations": the former being holy from the Side of Holiness, and the latter, impure, from the Side of Impurity.

R. David concludes his discussion by returning to the benediction over the flame:

> "Lights of the Fire": for through the mystery of the efflux of the elemental Fire [the upper Triad] . . . all [these lights from the lower seven] stream forth and hold sway over the world. (OZ 54a)

37. Kabbalistically, the patriarchs denote *Ḥesed, Gevurah,* and *Tif'eret,* which are nourished by the rungs above. The children are *Neẓah, Hod,* and *Yesod.*

38. Aramaic: *yanqin,* lit., suck.

39. A reference to *Shekhinah* in mystical union. I. Tishby, MZ 2: 533, explains: As She unites with Her lover, Her 248 limbs or aspects are embraced by the two Arms, *Ḥesed* and *Gevurah.*

The full complement of 250 indicates that the entire pleroma is now brimming with joy.

40. The branches stream forth from the seven lower sefirot. Each branch corresponds to one of the "seventy faces" of Torah, which are disclosed on Shabbat.

41. A reference to the fifty gates of *Binah* which open on Shabbat to illumine the divine realm and the worlds below.

Appendix I

Some Further Thoughts on the Transformation of the Person during Shabbat

In chapter 1, I analyzed accounts of the devotee's transformation by focusing on the motif of the Sabbath-soul. (See pp. 121–36.) At the same time, I noted that some Kabbalists (e.g., Baḥyya ben Asher) virtually ignored this rich motif and/or developed alternate imagery to articulate the momentous changes which they experienced on this day. Here I shall briefly limn three of the these additional motifs:

(1) Transformation through reception of *shefa*ᶜ from on high. Shabbat, it has been shown, is a day of overflowing divine blessing, its bounty sustaining the entire week. The devotee is able to internalize this bounty through:

(a) *Devequt,* mystically *ascending* and cleaving unto the divine Source. E.g.:

> On Sabbath night, when *Shekhinah* is sanctified and blessed [on high], those who cleave unto Her are also blessed and strengthened. (*Me'irat ᶜEinayim:* 21)

(b) Through making oneself into a receptacle for the *descending* divine energy. Consider the following where the *shefa*ᶜ is imaged as light:

> "God blessed [the Sabbath] with the light of a person's face; [for the light of a person's face during the week is not the same as on Shabbat.]" (Gen. R 11:2) Each Sabbath the hidden *shefa*ᶜ from *Keter ᶜElyon* comes unto *Tif'eret* and each Jew 'sees' with it. (Joseph ben Shalom Ashkenazi, *Perush le-Farashat Bere'shit:* 191)

Frequently it is the ordinary soul that serves as the receptacle for the divine outflow. According to Baḥyya ben Asher, each Shabbat, *Yesod,* the supernal Sabbath, pours blessing into the devotee's soul. The soul ceases being a stranger, a wanderer on earth. Infused with Shabbat, it (and by extension, the Jew) comes home; the weeklong spiritual Exile is overcome. (See p. 125 for details.) Judah Ḥayyaṭ (to *Maʿarekhet ha-'Elohut* 73b) fashioned a more elaborate scenario, speaking of the triune soul's progressive enrichment during the sacramental meals. Following a common symbolic pattern, the three meals are said to correspond to Diadem, *Tif'eret,* and *Keter,* respectively. Each of these meals/rungs nourishes a different aspect of soul. The third meal, e.g., corresponds to *Keter,* which provides the week's supply of *shefaʿ* for the *neshamah,* the loftiest pneumatic aspect:

> It is fitting that the *neshamah* receive its nourishment on Shabbat which is the time of its rule, as it is said: *Shabat va-yinnafash* [Ex. 31:17], meaning "on the Sabbath, the soul was refreshed", i.e., in all three aspects.

On Shabbat—on this day alone—the soul is fully realized.

(2) Transformation through the experience of divine immanence. In the first motif, one is transformed by receiving divine energy from above; God is still generally depicted as a transcendent being. In other scenarios however, one is transformed by entering into intimate contact with divinity itself, now experienced as an immanent Presence. Through Sabbath-observance one may become a throne upon which God rests. Joseph Giqatilia wrote:

> Know that whoever keeps the Sabbath properly becomes like a throne for the divine Chariot; therefore, the Sabbath is called "Rest." It is written: "This is my resting place for all time," [Ps. 132:14] as if the Holy One were resting upon the person, abiding with him as the king sits upon his throne. . . . (*Shaʿarei 'Orah* 1:106)

In a more radical image, divinity may actually enter into the devotee on Shabbat, initiating mystical union. This is intimated in TZ 6 (22b) (cf. MZ 2:493):

> *'Et ha-Shabbat le-DoRoTaM:* "Make for the Sabbath a dwelling place" [rereading Ex. 31:14; cf. p. 113 above]. . . . Happy is the one who prepares for Her [*Shekhinah*] a lovely place in his heart and good vessels in his limbs, and a lovely woman who is the soul."

(3) Finally, the exaltation that the devotee experiences on Shabbat is indicated in relational symbolism: as spiritual marriage. Not only can he become the *shoshevin,* or bridal attendant of *Shekhinah,* but he may—in some scenarios—become the spouse of divinity. He may be a groom unto the Bride (as in *Peli'ah* 36b; see p. 245 n. 19

above) or more traditionally, a bride betrothed unto God. See, e.g., *Sod ha-Shabbat:* Prologue, p. 14 and n. 22. A more thoroughgoing use of marital symbolism is found in the *Sodot* of Joseph Giqatilia, where it becomes the leitmotif for the Jew's Sabbath-transformation. While the *Peli'ah* and TY restrict themselves to warm nuptial imagery, Joseph Giqatilia spoke more broadly—and in hierarchically more pronounced fashion—about spiritual marriage (qua institution). In section 3, he wrote:

> On Shabbat one leaves the realm of the Profane and enters the Holy Palace to stand before the blessed Name. For his soul is wed unto God.

This marriage carries with it not only heightened joy, but heightened obligations; one is to honor it scrupulously:

> Hence, [on Shabbat] one must perform only sacred deeds. Should he perform a profane act, desecrating the Sabbath, he is like an unfaithful wife. . . . For the soul is consecrated to God like a woman unto her husband. Should [the soul] commit adultery she shall . . . drink the "cursed water of bitterness" [ff. Num. 5:11–31]. For this reason, the Sabbath was given at Marah (meaning "bitterness") [cf. TB Sanh. 56b and RaSHI to Ex. 15:25]. Whoever profanes the Sabbath secretly will some day have to drink this bitter water.

In a striking turn, the Havdalah ceremony (section 9) becomes the moment of counter-transformation, wherein the soul must again take leave of the "divine Palace." Before departing, she is granted a conditional divorce:

> Just as the soul is betrothed [unto God] at the Sabbath's arrival and designated for divine service on Shabbat, so at Sabbath's end is she given a *geṭ zeman,* a "temporary bill of divorce," divorcing her from the Sabbath-order. This is only done conditionally until the next Sabbath [i.e., the divorce will only be legally binding if they are not joined the next Sabbath].

Giqatilia took pains to stress that this divorce is only with respect to the higher Sabbath-order marriage. All Israel is, of course, "betrothed unto the Holy One in perpetuity." Still, it is the special Sabbath-marriage that allows for true mystical ascent:

The Sabbath is the mystery of the entire Torah. It is the mystery of Israel's cleaving unto *Yesod,* the gateway to Eternal Life [sefirotically, *Binah*]. Of [Shabbat] it is said: "This is the gateway to YHWH, the righteous shall enter it." [Ps. 118:20]

Appendix II

Sabbath-Ritual as a Means of Furthering the Divine-Human Nexus: Two Examples from Zoharic Kabbalah

In chapter 2 of this study, I sketched the basic contours of Kabbalistic ritual, noting its power to link God and Person. This portrait may be further refined by providing two additional examples of how ritual works. Before proceeding, it is useful to recall my earlier characterization: Kabbalistic ritual may be grasped as symbolically significant activity which is understood to accomplish one or more of the following:

1) to dramatize an event (or myth) in the sacred realm, especially one pertaining to the supernal world;

2) to theurgically affect the supernal world (most prominently, by helping to restore the divine Gestalt); and

3) to transform the life of the devotee, by bringing him in alignment with the divine paradigm (and/or his Paradisical self), thereby ushering him into a higher state of being.

The first category underscores the symbolic valence of ritual life, whereas the other two evince its magical import. The second category is focused on ritual's cosmic efficaciousness while the third suggests its reflexive power or "inner magic." All three levels of signification will be observed in the two exemplary (and complementary) rites: the first, that most intimate and physical act of marital intercourse; and the second, the cognitive-spiritual act of Torah-study or sacred learning.

In theosophical Kabbalah, the traditional miẓvah of marital intercourse is replete with symbolic and magical significance. It becomes a dramatic representation and realization of divine androgyny: the union of the Holy One and *Shekhinah* (categories 1 and 2). At the same time, it is a means of transforming the devotee and his wife (category 3): first, by enabling husband and wife to be more perfect symbols of the divine Androgyne and secondly, by affording them a momentary return to the primordial androgyny of Eden. In good Rabbinic fashion, this last notion will be examined first:

Invoking Gen. 5:1–2 and a few Rabbinic sources (e.g., Gen. R 8:1), the Kabbalists taught that Adam and Eve were one entity before the Sin. According to one account, Adam/Eve emerged as an androgyne, united back to back; when Eve separated from Adam's side, they immediately cleaved to each other and entered into a higher union, one which both symbolized and theurgically completed the divine androgyne. Building on Z 3:296a (IZ), Meir ibn Gabbai wrote:

> And the *Zohar* states: "They joined face to face . . . became one real body" . . . I.e., Adam and Eve were one complete *'adam*, one person. . . . Through coupling with her, Adam attained fulfillment. When they were united face to face they symbolized the completion of the divine structure. . . . Through Eve the Structure was completed and the divine union perfected, as in "they became one flesh" [Gen. 2:24] and "The Lord [kabbalistically, *Tif'eret*] was one and His Name [*Shekhinah*] one." [Zech. 14:9]

However, due to the primal sin, humanity's androgynous nature has been lost. In this bi-furcated state, the individual is but "half a person," an incomplete "image of divinity." Through the institution of marriage and the periodic union of husband and wife, primordial personhood can be recovered, renewed:

> The *Zohar* states: "[Adam and Eve] joined face to face . . . and became one body." Thus we learn that when a man is alone he is half a body, and so too, a woman. But when they unite, they are whole, one real body.

In the conclusion of the passage, this recovery of primal androgyny is said to have cosmic resonance:

> When a man and woman [truly] unite, all is one Body: the cosmos rejoices for it becomes one complete Corpus.
>
> *ᶜAvodat ha-Qodesh* Part 4:13

In some mystical sources, the Edenic motif is either absent or relegated to the background; attention is more narrowly focused on the relationship between androgynous divinity and the married couple. The following text, from the *Tolaᶜat Yaᶜaqov* of Meir ibn Gabbai, is exemplary:

> R. Eliezer said [TB. Yev. 63a]: "Anyone who does not have a wife is not a [complete] person [*'adam*] as it says: "Male and female He

> made them and blessed them, and called *their* name *'adam.*" [Gen. 5:2]
>
> For a person must symbolize the androgynous composition of the Supernal Structure, because the glory of the man is to dwell in the house [a Rabbinic idiom for marital union; kabbalistically, a reference to *hieros gamos*]. In this way [the devotee] will become a complete person and blessing will rest upon him fully.

It is the theurgic valence of the rite that helps draw down blessing, causing "the river that goes forth from Eden [sefirotically, *Binah*] to water the Garden [*Shekhinah*]." Ibn Gabbai explained:

> Through the earthly coupling, the Heavenly One is aroused. Everything is blessed from the Source because He is given the power to do valiantly. The Tree [*Tif'eret*] regenerates its fruits and passes them into the Hidden Chamber [*Shekhinah*]; from there it courses into the worlds below.

As an epiphenomenon of marital union, a high soul may be drawn forth for the devotee and his wife, the fruit of *Shekhinah* and *Tif'eret*'s coupling.

In a later section of this text, the symbolic nexus between *Shekhinah* and the woman is emphasized:

> We have stated that the woman is the cause of all these good things, for [only] with her can there be wholeness. This symbolizes the situation on high; this is the mystery of the "image" and the "likeness" [Gen. 1:26]. The supernal entities desire to pour blessing into the "House of David" [*Shekhinah*], and through Her, King Solomon [kabbalistically, *Tif'eret*] is blessed. For this reason, he said of Her: "My Sister, My Beloved." [Cant. 5:2] Thus the Rabbis, of blessed memory, said in *Midrash Ḥazita:* "My beloved who sustains me."
>
> *Tolaʿat Yaʿaqov* 92a–b

One of the most succinct accounts of the symbolic nexus between the human couple and divine androgyne was supplied by Avraham Azulai in his commentary to *Zohar* 2:11b. Speaking of the human pair, he wrote:

> Their desire, both his and hers, was to unite *Shekhinah*. He focused on *Tif'eret* [as his archetype] and she on *Malkhut*. His union was to join *Shekhinah;* she focused correspondingly on *being Shekhinah*

> and uniting with Her Husband, *Tif'eret.* [*'Or ha-Ḥammah,* cited in D. Matt, *Zohar,* pp. 236–37]

This is a revealing passage. First, it is the rare Kabbalistic text which speaks of the woman's mystical intentionality. Secondly, the text provides a glimpse into two complementary psycho-religious phenomena: the search for an archetypal model of Self and the so-called "search for polarities," the longing for the divine Other. For example: the woman represents and to some extent *becomes Shekhinah,* her archetype. At the same time she enters into relation with (and in some sense is completed by) *Tif'eret,* the divine Other. In embodied fashion, the husband and wife have become symbols of and participants in the unfolding cosmic drama.

A final observation. As in virtually all rituals, timing is of the essence here: the mystic and his wife must engage in marital intercourse at the appropriate moment. Although ordinary Jews may engage in marital intercourse during the week, the adept is bidden to wait until Shabbat, Edenic time par excellence[1], the hour when the divine *hieros gamos* occurs. The TY (49b) relates the mythic rationale:

> The prescribed time for scholars [to engage in marital intercourse] is on Sabbath nights. Our Sages expounded on this matter in Tractate *Bava' Qamma',* Chapter "There is More Frequently Occasion" [!] [82a]. . . . According to the Path of Truth this is [mandated] because "the Garden [*Shekhinah*] is locked" [Cant. 4:12] during the six days of the week, as it is said: "The gate of the inner court that faces east [i.e., outward, away from the Holy of Holies] shall be closed on the six working days; but on the Sabbath day and on the day of the new moon it shall be opened." [Ezek. 46:1] For the six days of creation are garbed in Profane Days, [those impure forces] that dwell outside the encampment.

Here ibn Gabbai, inspired by TZ 36 and especially by Z 1:75b, has depicted *Shekhinah* in the idiom of sacred geography—as paradisical garden and the inner court of the perfect Temple of Ezekiel's vision. During the week, when *Shekhinah* "faces east," i.e., is among the *qelippot* of *Siṭra' 'Aḥra',* She closes Herself off lest She be sullied. But on Shabbat, as She returns to Her husband and faces inward, She opens up and receives His love. In the words of the *Zohar,* "on Shabbat all gates are open." The TY continues:

> Therefore, during the week there should be no coupling, for the man is not in his "house" [*Tif'eret* is not in union with *Shekhinah*].

> However, on the day of the Throne [*Shekhinah*'s coronation], the mystery of the Seventh Day, the Sabbath unites with His mate, because at that time, the Profane days have passed away, the days of impurity and separation[2] are gone, and the wife is permitted to her husband.

Meir ibn Gabbai's point: by reserving sexual union for Sabbath night, the adept and his wife are synchronizing themselves with the supernal rhythms. Only thus do they become the true "image of the divine."

The second example of the nexus created by ritual life concerns Torah-study, the Rabbinic rite par excellence. As above, the primary source comes from the writings of Meir ibn Gabbai. The specific focus is on the miẓvah of "studying Torah for its own sake" on the Sabbath.

In classical Kabbalah, Torah study is placed in a special mythic context. The Torah—in its primal essence—is conceived as a corpus symbolicum, a texture of divine names and symbols whose infinite meaning can never be fully grasped, only approximately interpreted, further mined. The traditional exoteric meanings of the text are not so much denied as revealed to be the outward manifestation of a mysterious—usually sefirotic—essence. Study of the Torah generally becomes a contemplative endeavor; as in mystical prayer, the words of the text serve as a map of divine consciousness, revealing inner aspects of supernal life. At the same time, the words serve as markers or blazes for the devotee's ascent to God, charting the way to *devequt* or mystical communion.

Yet if the Torah points to the entirety of divine life, the two primary aspects of Torah, the so-called Written and Oral *Torot*, are often seen as deriving from two sefirot, *Tif'eret* and *Shekhinah*, respectively. To study these twin aspects of Torah, therefore, is to encounter the divine Lovers, the Groom and Bride. Bearing this in mind, ibn Gabbai's text may now be approached.

In the first paragraph the theurgic significance of Torah-study is stressed. Note the sustained use of erotic imagery here:

> When Israel studies these two *Torot* for their own sake, their celestial counterparts are aroused: "They are joined one to another" [Job 41:19] through a kiss and the "Tabernacle [the divine structure exemplified by *Tif'eret* and *Shekhinah*] becomes one." [Ex. 26:6] Then blessing descends from them on high and peace fills the cosmos. This is the meaning underlying that which our Rabbis of blessed memory taught in the chapter "These Are the Knots" [TB Shab. 114a]:

> What are the *banna'im*, builders? Said Rabbi Yoḥanan: They are scholars, who are engaged all their days in building up the world.

This building up refers to the union of the Torah on high [*Shekhinah*] with the Holy One; upon such activity the existence of the world depends. . . .

Now when Israel learns Torah for its own sake, their Mother on high sings unto Her lover, chanting: "Let him kiss me with the kisses of his mouth." [Cant. 1:2] For it is the way of lovers to kiss each other mouth to mouth, visibly affirming that they have one spirit [between them], so great is their love. This [supernal love] is symbolized by the two lovers in the Song of Songs who unite through a kiss. Thus, [the Bride *Shekhinah*] says: "If only he were to kiss me with the kisses of his mouth," speaking in the third person before the kiss. But once [they are united], She addresses him directly: "How good is *your* love *mi-yayin* [here read]: through the wine" [Cant. Ibid.], meaning: how sweet and good is your love to me when Israel is studying Torah, which is compared to wine [cf. TB Taᶜanit 7b].

That is, Torah-study becomes a sort of divine "aphrodisiac." It promotes the most intimate union of *Tif'eret* and *Shekhinah* or to use the grammatical metaphor, it enables *Shekhinah* to address Her lover as "You" instead of the more distant "He." The curious grammatical shift in Cant. 1:2 is thereby given mystical meaning. The text continues:

> For through [such activity] the divine structure is completed. So it is that Israel strengthens the love between the Holy One and the Community of Israel whenever its people learn Torah for its own sake.[3]

But Torah-study also transforms the devotee, working its reflexive-magic:

> Know that when the adept [*shalem:* lit., perfect one] studies Torah he becomes like an angel of the Lord of hosts. In his contemplation he resembles them, for their activity is purely contemplative. This [experience] is a taste of the World-to-Come, for the "righteous sit with crowns on their heads basking in the splendor of the *Shekhinah*." [TB Ber. 17a] . . . The Sabbath is a symbol of this world. It is devoid of bodily concerns, for it is the World of Souls. Thus, one must perfect one's soul on this day.

How different this transformation is from that described in marital intercourse! There, the person served as symbol of the divine macrocosm; here, it is the earthly Torah that is most obviously the symbol of the divine. There, the individual was necessarily "half a person"; here, the individual can become *shalem*, spiritually perfected. There, the person regained his Edenic self; here, he partakes of his eschatological essence. There, in marital intercourse, the adept's physicality was granted sacred meaning; here, his physicality is utterly transcended. Rather than becoming *'adam,* he leaves behind his humanity and becomes disembodied, angelic.

It has been noted that Zoharic Kabbalah oscillates between several models for spirituality. While one model underscores the Kabbalist's sacred physicality on the Sabbath (the preferred time for marital union),[4] the other stresses his purely pneumatic essence. Which model is placed in the foreground—and which, left unattended—depends largely on the miẓvah to be performed. For ritual tends to selectively frame one's thoughts and images; to use Erving Goffman's metaphor, as the lights are turned up in one room, they are dimmed in another. In the context of Torah-study, the Sabbath is portrayed as a day so utterly transforming that bodily concerns are superceded and the future non-corporeal world glimpsed.

The final paragraph refers to the presence of the "Sabbath-soul," the special celestial pneuma which supplements the ordinary soul on Shabbat, enabling the devotee to experience the divine in more profound fashion:

> [The way to] perfection is [through] Torah-study, engaged in for its own sake. We have already explained [our Sages'] intent in saying *li-shmah,* "for its own sake." But this phrase has an additional meaning: namely, [through Torah-study] the spirit which sojourns with us this day is made whole. (TY 56a–b)

That is, the term *li-shmah* may also be read: for *her* sake, for the sake of the Sabbath-soul, which one is enjoined to regale through Torah-learning. According to the *Zohar* (3:173a–74a passim), the Sabbath-soul takes special delight in each new meaning the devotee uncovers in the text. As it rejoices, the soul ascends on high to join with its other half (the aspect of soul remaining in divinity), thereby becoming whole.

In sum, Torah-study on Shabbat serves four major purposes in this text:

(a) a theurgic one, promoting the union of *Shekhinah* and *Tif'eret*, the Oral and Written *Torot*.

(b) a reflexive one, whereby the devotee is transformed into an angel. He is transported beyond his bodily self, becoming purely spiritual.

(c) Moreover, this transformation has a prospective meaning, affording the adept a foretaste of his ultimate reward in the World-to-Come, the realm of perpetual Shabbat. Through Sabbath Torah-study, he glimpses the splendor of *Shekhinah*. And finally,

(d) Through sacred learning he regales his Sabbath-soul, and perfects it.

This multi-leveled transformation enables the devotee to better participate in the divine mysteries and to reinforce the divine-human nexus—in Meir ibn Gabbai's words, "to perfect and unite . . . upper and lower worlds." (*ʿAvodat ha-Qodesh* Part 2:3)

NOTES

An earlier version of this piece appeared in L. Shinn (ed.), *In Search of the Divine* (NY, 1987).

1. Not only for the devotee but for divinity. Through marital union on Shabbat, the divine Garden is watered and *Shekhinah* recovers Her paradisical state. In the words of Menaḥem Recanati:

> The hidden purpose of intercourse "every seventh day" [on Sabbath night] is the mystery of the circling of the wheel to and fro [the completion of a cycle]. We intend to draw down the abundant water from the Edenic river unto the dry Garden [*Shekhinah*], irrigating Her with the waters of Repentance [*Binah*] and Compassion [*Tif'eret*].
> *Sefer Ṭaʿamei ha-Miẓvot* (Lieberman ed., p. 48)

2. Hebrew, *yemei niddah:* A reference to *Shekhinah's* 'menstrual bleeding' as She dwells amid the harsh *qelippot*. See pp. 116, 231, and 174 n. 223 above; and my comments in *Sod ha-Shabbat*, n. 171.

3. "The Holy One and the Community of Israel": Although the primary meaning is sefirotic here, this phrase also evokes the love between God and the People Israel as a subtext.

4. On sacred physicality, also see *Zohar* 2:47a: "The Sabbath is a delight to *both the body and the soul*"; and my analysis of the sacramental meals in chapter 1, pp. 135–36 above.

Bibliography

Introductory Note

The following is a list of works consulted in the preparation of this study. Standard reference works have been omitted from the list, as have basic classics of pre-modern Jewish literature, e.g., the Bible, Mishnah, Babylonian and Palestinian Talmuds, RaSHI's commentaries, etc. These works have been cited according to their standard editions.

This bibliography is divided into two categories: a) primary sources drawn from the classical (pre-modern) Jewish literature and b) secondary sources and modern works.

Classical Sources

Aaron ha-Kohen of Lunel. *'Orḥot Ḥayyim.* Jerusalem, 1956.

Abulafia, Abraham. *Sitrei Torah.* MS Paris, BN 774.

Abulafia, Ṭodros. *'Oẓar ha-Kavod.* Warsaw, 1879. Reprint. Jerusalem, 1970.

———. *Shaʿar ha-Razim.* Edited by H. Erlanger. Jerusalem, 1986. Also used, MS Munich 209.

Abudraham, David. *Sefer 'Abudraham* (also: *'Abudraham ha-Shalem*). Jerusalem, 1963.

Al-Naqawa, Israel. *Menorat ha-Ma'or.* Edited by Hyman Enelow. 4 vols. New York, 1929–32.

Albo, Joseph. *Sefer ha-ʿIqqarim.* Edited by I. Husik. 5 vols. Philadelphia, 1929–30.

Alcastiel, Joseph. *Teshuvot le-She'elot ʿal Derekh ha-Qabbalah.* Edited by G. Scholem in "Li-Ydiʿat ha-Qabbalah bi-Sfarad ʿErev ha-Gerush." *Tarbiẓ* 24 (1954): 174–206.

Aldabi, Meir ben Isaac. *Sefer Shevilei 'Emunah.* Warsaw, 1887.

Anatoli, Jacob. *Malmad ha-Talmidim.* Lyck, 1886.

Anav, Ẓedeqiah ben Abraham. *Shibbolei ha-Leqeṭ.* Edited by S. Buber. Vilna, 1886.

Angelino, Joseph. *Livnat ha-Sappir.* Jerusalem, 1913.

Arama, Isaac. *ʿAqedat Yiẓḥaq.* Venice, 1573.

Asher ben David. *Sefer ha-Yiḥud.* Edited by R. Ḥassidah. *Ha-Segullah* 4 (1937). Also in J. Dan, ed. *Ha-Qabbalah shel R. 'Asher ben David.* Jerusalem, 1979.

Asher ben Saul of Lunel. *Sefer ha-Minhagot.* Printed in S. Assaf, ed., *Sifran shel Ri'shonim,* pp. 123–82. Jerusalem, 1935.

Ashkenazi, Joseph ben Shalom. *Perush le-Farashat Bere'shit.* Edited by Moshe Ḥallamish. Jerusalem, 1985.

Avraham bar Ḥiyya. *Megillat ha-Megalleh.* Edited by A. Posnanski. Berlin, 1924.

Avraham ben Nathan of Lunel. *Sefer ha-Manhig.* Edited by I. Rafael. 2 vols. Jerusalem, 1978.

Azriel ben Menaḥem of Gerona. *Commentaire sur la liturgie quotidienne.* Translated by G. Sed-Rajna. Leiden, 1974.

———. *Perush ha-'Aggadot le-Rabbi ʿAzri'el.* Edited by Isaiah Tishby. Jerusalem, 1945.

———. *Shaʿar ha-Sho'el: Perush ʿEser Sefirot.* Printed in Meir ibn Gabbai, *Derekh 'Emunah.*

Azulai, Abraham. *'Or ha-Ḥammah.* 4 vols. Przemysl, 1896–98. Reprint (3 vols.) Benai-Beraq, 1973.

Baḥyya ben Asher. *Be'ur ʿal ha-Torah.* Edited by Ḥ. Cheval. 3 vols. Jerusalem, 1972.

———. *Kitvei Rabbenu Baḥyya ben 'Asher.* Edited by Ḥ. Cheval. Jerusalem, 1970.

Bere'shit Rabbah. Edited by J. Theodor and Ch. Albeck. 3 vols. Reprint, Jerusalem, 1965.

Cordovero, Moses. *'Or Yaqar.* Edited by I. Elbaum. Multiple volumes. Jerusalem, 1961–.

———. *Pardes Rimmonim.* Munkacz, 1906. Reprint. Jerusalem, 1962.

———. *Tefillah le-Mosheh.* Przemysl, 1892.

David ben Abraham ha-Lavan. *Masoret ha-Berit.* Edited by G. Scholem, *Qoveẓ ʿal Yad* o.s. 1 (1936): 25–42.

David ben Judah he-Ḥasid. *'Or Zaruʿa.* MS JTSA 2203 and MS British Museum 771.

———. *Sefer Mar'ot ha-Ẓove'ot*. Edited by Daniel Matt. [*The Book of Mirrors*.] Chico, 1982.

de Vidas, Elijah. *Re'shit Ḥokhmah*. Jerusalem, 1972.

———. *Toẓe'ot Ḥayyim*. Jerusalem, 1985.

Donnolo, Shabbetai. *Sefer Ḥakhmoni*. Edited by D. Castelli as *Il Commento di Sabbetai Donnolo sul libro de la Creazione*. Florence, 1880.

Eleazar ben Judah of Worms. *Perush ha-Tefillot*. MS Oxf. Bodl. 124.

———. *Sodot ha-Tefillah*. MS Oxf. Bodl. 1595/96.

Eliezer ben Joel ha-Levi of Bonn. *Sefer RaVYaH*. Edited by S. Y. Cohen and E. Prisman. 4 vols. Jerusalem, 1965.

Ezra ben Solomon of Gerona. *Perush le-Shir ha-Shirim*. In Ḥ. Cheval, ed. *Kitvei RaMBaN*. Jerusalem, 1967. Vol. 2: 473–518.

———. *TaRYaG Miẓvot ha-Yoẓe'ot me-ʿAseret ha-Dibberot*. In Ḥ. Cheval, Ibid. Vol. 2:519–548.

Giqatilia, Joseph. *Shaʿarei 'Orah*. Edited by J. Ben-Shlomo. 2 vols. Jerusalem, 1970.

———. *Sodot*. Printed in back of *Noʿam 'Elimelekh*, Lwow, 1817. Also MS JTSA 1609 fol. 117–20a; MS Vatican 214, fol. 64a.

Ḥayyaṭ, Judah. *Minḥat Yehudah* to *Maʿarekhet ha-'Elohut*. See *Maʿarekhet ha-'Elohut*.

Ḥayyim ben Solomon of Chernovitz. *Sidduro shel Shabbat*. Jerusalem, 1960.

Horowitz, Isaiah. *Shenei Luḥot ha-Berit*. 4 vols. Josefov, 1878. Reprint. 2 vols. Zikhron Yaʿaqov, n.d.

Ibn Ezra, Abraham. *Sefer Re'shit Ḥokhmah*. Baltimore, 1939.

———. *Sefer Ṭeʿamim*. Jerusalem, 1941.

Ibn Gaon, Shem Ṭov ben Abraham. *Keter Shem Ṭov*. Printed in Judah Coriat, ed. *Ma'or va-Shemesh*, fol. 25a–54a. Livorno, 1839. Superior edition, Munich MS 11.

Ibn Gabbai, Meir. *ʿAvodat ha-Qodesh*. Jerusalem, 1973.

———. *Derekh 'Emunah*. Warsaw, 1890. Reprint. Jerusalem, 1967.

———. *Tolaʿat Yaʿaqov*. MS JNUL Heb. octo 3913 (Adrianople, 1547); MS JTSA 1646 (late sixteenth century?); MS JTSA 1553 (late sixteenth century?); *Editio princeps*, Istanbul, 1560; Warsaw ed., 1876. Reprint. Jerusalem, 1967.

Ibn Makhir, Moshe. *Sefer Seder ha-Yom.* Lublin, 1876. Reprint. Jerusalem, 1969.

Ibn Sahula, Meir ben Solomon (attributed). *Be'ur Sodot ha-RaMBaN.* Printed as *Be'ur le-Ferush ha-RaMBaN* in *'Oẓar Mefareshei ha-Torah.* Jerusalem, 1973. (Also see Ibn Shuayb.)

Ibn Shuayb, Joshua. *Be'ur Sodot ha-RaMBaN.* As above.

———. *Derashot.* Krakow, 1596.

Ibn Waqar, Joseph. *Shir ha-Yiḥud u-Ferush le-Shir ha-Yiḥud.* Printed in A. Habermann, ed. *Shirei ha-Yiḥud ve-ha-Kavod,* pp. 99–123. Jerusalem, 1948.

Isaac ben Samuel of Acco. *Sefer Me'irat ʿEinayim.* Edited by Amos Goldreich. Ph.D. dissertation, Hebrew University, 1981.

Isaac the Blind. *Perush le-Midrash Konen.* In J. Dan, ed., *Qabbalat R. 'Asher ben David,* pp. 52–55. Jerusalem, 1979.

Jacob bar Sheshet, *Meshiv Devarim Nekhoḥim.* Edited by G. Vajda. Jerusalem, 1968.

———. *Sefer ha-'Emunah ve-ha-Biṭṭaḥon.* In Ḥ. Cheval, ed. Kitvei RaMBaN. Jerusalem, 1967. Vol. 2: 341–448.

Jacob ben Asher. *'Arbaʿah Ṭurim.* Warsaw, 1860–69. Reprint. 8 vols. New York, n.d.

Jacob ben Jacob ha-Kohen of Soria, *Perush ha-Sefirot.* Printed in G. Scholem, "Qabbalat he-Ḥakham R. Yaaqov he-Ḥasid b. Yaaqov ha-Kohen." *Maddaʿei ha-Yahadut* 2 (1927).

Jacob ha-Levi of Marveges. *She'elot u-Teshuvot min ha-Shamayim.* Edited by R. Margaliot. Jerusalem, 1972.

Jellinek, Adolf, ed. *Beit ha-Midrash.* 6 vols. Leipzig, 1853–78. Reprint. 3 vols. Jerusalem, 1967.

Joseph ibn Shraga. *Sod Qiddush le-Maʿalei Shabbeta'.* Printed in Abraham ben Judah Elmalik, ed. *Liqquṭei Shikheḥah u-Fe'ah,* fol. 39a-b. Ferrara, 1556.

Joseph of Hamadan. *Sefer Ṭaʿamei ha-Miẓvot/* Section 1 [*miẓvot ʿaseh*]. Edited by Menahem Meier. Ph.D. dissertation, Brandeis University, 1974.

———. *Sefer Ṭaʿamei ha-Miẓvot* [including *miẓvot lo' taʿaseh*]. MS JTSA Mic. 1722.

———. *Sefer Tashak: Critical Edition with Text.* Edited by Jeremy Zwelling. Ph.D. thesis. Brandeis University, 1975.

Judah ben Samuel he-Ḥasid. *Sefer Ḥasidim.* Edited by R. Margaliot. 4th ed. Jerusalem, 1970.

———. Edited by J. Wistinetzki, with additions by J. Freimann. Frankfurt am Main, 1924.

Judah ben Yaqar. *Perush ha-Tefillot ve-ha-Berakhot.* Edited by Shmuel Yerushalmi. Second edition, Jerusalem, 1979.

Judah Hadassi. *'Eshkol ha-Kofer.* Defective edition, Gozlow, 1836. Reprint, Jerusalem, 1969.

Judah ha-Levi. *Sefer ha-Kuzari.* Translated by Yehuda Even-Shmuel. Jerusalem, 1972.

Kalkis, Elnatan ben Moshe. *'Even Sappir.* MSS Paris 427 and 428.

Karo, Joseph. *Shulḥan ʿArukh.* 10 Vols. Vilna, 1874/75.

Kol-Bo. Tel-Aviv, n.d.

Labi, Shimon. *Ketem Paz.* Djerba, 1940.

Levi Yiẓḥaq of Berdichev. *Qedushat Levi.* Jerusalem, 1958.

Lifshitz, Jacob Koppel. *Shaʿarei Gan ʿEden.* Korzec, 1803.

Maʿarekhet ha-'Elohut. Mantua, 1558. Reprint. Jerusalem, 1963.

Maḥzor Viṭri. Edited by S. Ish-Hurwitz. Berlin, 1897.

Mekhilta' de-Rabbi Ishmael. Edited by Jacob Lauterbach. 3 vols. Philadelphia, 1933–35.

Mekhilta' de-Rabbi Shimʿon bar Yoḥa'i. Edited by J. N. Epstein and E. Z. Melamed. Jerusalem, 1979.

Menaḥem Azariah of Fano. "Mother of All Life" [Heb., *'Em kol ḥai*]. Excerpted from his *ʿAsarah Ma'amarot.* Translated by M. Krassen in *Kabbalah: A Newsletter of Current Research in Jewish Mysticism* 2:2 (1987): 6–7.

Menaḥem ben Meir Ẓiyyoni. *Sefer Ẓiyyoni.* Reprint, Jerusalem, 1964.

Menaḥem Recanati. *Perush ʿal ha-Tefillot.* MS JTSA 1898 (before 1525).

———. *Perush ʿal ha-Torah.* Jerusalem, 1961.

———. *Sefer Ṭaʿamei ha-Miẓvot.* Przemysl, 1888. Reprint. Brooklyn, n.d.

Midrash Rabbah. 2 vols. Vilna, n.d. Reprint. Jerusalem, 1961.

Midrash Tanḥuma'. Jerusalem, 1965.

Midrash Tanḥuma'. Edited by Solomon Buber. 2 vols. New York, 1946.

Midrash Tehillim. Edited by Solomon Buber. Vilna, 1891. Reprint. Jerusalem, 1966.

Moshe ben Jacob of Kiev. *SHOSHaN Sodot*. [Also transliterated: *Shoshan Sodot*] Partial ed., Koretz, 1784. Complete MS Oxf. Bodl. 1565.

Moshe ben Maimon [RaMBaM]. *The Guide for the Perplexed*. Translated by Shlomo Pines. 2 vols. Chicago, 1963.

———. *Mishneh Torah*. Jerusalem, 1965.

———. *Moreh Nevukhim*. Jerusalem, 1960.

Moshe ben Naḥman [RaMBaN]. *Kitvei RaMBaN*. Edited by Ḥayyim Chavel. 2 vols. Jerusalem, 1967.

———. *Perushei ha-Torah le-R. Mosheh ben Naḥman*. Edited by Ḥayyim Chavel. 2 vols. Jerusalem, 1959–60.

Moshe ben Shem Ṭov de Leon. *'Or Zaruᶜa*. Edited by Alexander Altmann. *Qoveẓ ᶜal Yad*, n.s. 9 (1980): 219–93.

———. *Sefer Maskiot ha-Kesef*. Edited by J. Wijnhoven. M.A. thesis, Brandeis University, 1961.

———. *Sefer ha-Mishqal*. Edited by J. Wijnhoven. Ph.D. dissertation, Brandeis University, 1964. (Earlier corrupt edition: *Ha-Nefesh ha-Ḥakhamah*. Basle, 1608.)

———. *Sefer ha-Rimmon*. MS Brit. Mus. 759; MS Moscow 219; and MS Cambridge Add. 1516.

———. *Sheqel ha-Qodesh*. Edited by A. Greenup. London, 1911.

———. *Sodot*. MS Schocken 14 and MS Vatican 428.

———. *Ẓavva'at Rabbi 'Eliᶜezer*. In *Beit ha-Midrash*, edited by A. Jellinek, 3:131–40. Jerusalem, 1967.

Moshe Jonah of Safed. *Kanfei Yonah*. Defective edition. Koretz, 1786.

Naftali Hirz Treves. *Siddur Mal'ah ha-'Areẓ Deᶜah*. Thiengen, 1560.

Perush ha-Haggadah. Incorrectly attributed to Moshe de Leon. Printed in M. Kasher and S. Ashkenazi, *Haggadah Shelemah*, pp. 121–32. Jerusalem, 1967.

Perush ha-Tefillot. MS Paris, BN 848 (from the circle of Barukh Togarmi?).

Perush le-Sefer ha-Temunah. See *Sefer ha-Temunah*.

Pesiqta' de-Rav Kahana'. Edited by Solomon Buber. Lyck, 1868.

Pesiqta' Rabbati. Edited by M. Ish-Shalom. Vienna, 1880. Reprint. Tel Aviv, 1963.

Pirqei de-R. 'Eliᶜezer. Edited by D. Luria. Warsaw, 1852. Reprint. Jerusalem, 1970.

Saadiah Gaon. *Book of Beliefs and Opinions.* Translated by S. Rosenblatt. New Haven, 1948.

———. *Sefer 'Emunot ve-Deᶜot.* Jerusalem, n.d.

Sefer ha-Bahir. Edited by Reuven Margaliot. Jerusalem, 1951.

———. German Translator and Editor, G. Scholem. [*Das Buch Bahir*] Leipzig, 1923. Reprint, Darmstadt, 1970.

Sefer ha-Minhagim (from the school of Meir b. Barukh of Rothenburg). Edited by I. Elfenbein. New York, 1938.

Sefer ha-Peli'ah. Przemysl, 1883.

Sefer ha-Qanah. Jerusalem, 1973.

Sefer ha-Temunah. Lemberg, 1892.

Sefer Yeẓirah. Warsaw, 1884. Reprint. Jerusalem, 1965.

Sefer ha-Yiḥud (from the circle of Joseph of Hamadan). MS JTSA Mic. 1737.

Sefer ha-Zohar. Edited by R. Margaliot. 3 vols. Jerusalem, 1951.

Siddur Rabbenu Shelomoh mi-Germaiza'. Edited by M. Hershler. Jerusalem, 1971.

Siddur RaSHI. Edited by S. Buber. Berlin, 1911. Reprint. New York, 1959.

Siddur Rav ᶜAmram Ga'on. Edited by D. Goldschmidt. Jerusalem, 1971.

Siddur Rav Saᶜadiah Ga'on. Edited by I. Davidson, S. Assaf, and B. Yoel. Jerusalem, 1941.

Sod ᶜIlan ha-'Aẓilut. Edited by G. Scholem. In *Qoveẓ ᶜal Yad* n.s. 5 (1951): 67–102.

Sod ha-Shem. Printed in *Zohar Ḥadash.* Istanbul, 1740.

Tiqqunei ha-Zohar. Edited by R. Margaliot. Jerusalem, 1951.

Untitled Commentary on the Prayers. MS Paris Hebr. 596.

Wertheimer, A., ed. *Battei Midrashot.* 2 vols. Jerusalem, 1980.

Yalquṭ Re'uveini. 2 vols. Warsaw, 1884. Reprint. Jerusalem, 1962.

Yalquṭ Shimʿoni. 2 vols. Jerusalem, 1960.

Zohar Ḥadash. Edited by R. Margaliot. Jerusalem, 1953.

Secondary Sources and Modern Works

Agnon, S. Y. *Yamim Nora'im.* Tel-Aviv, 1973.

Alon, Gedaliayahu. *Meḥqarim be-Toledot Yisra'el.* Vol. 1. Tel Aviv, 1957.

Alter, Robert. *The Art of Biblical Poetry.* New York, 1985.

Altmann, Alexander. "Moshe Narboni's Epistle on Shiʿur Qomah." In idem, ed. *Jewish Medieval and Renaissance Studies,* pp. 225–88. Cambridge, MA, 1967.

———. "Sefer 'Or Zaruʿa le-R. Moshe de Leon: Mavo', Ṭeksṭ Qriṭi, ve-He'arot." *Qoveẓ ʿal Yad* 9 (1980): 219–93.

———. *Studies in Religious Philosophy and Mysticism.* Ithaca, 1969.

Andreasson, N.A. *The Old Testament Sabbath.* Missoula, 1972.

Ankori, Zvi. *Karaites in Byzantium: The Formative Years, 970–1100.* New York, 1959.

Ariel, David. "Shem Tob ibn Shem Tob's Kabbalistic Critique of Jewish Philosophy in the Commentary on the Sefirot: Study and Text." Ph.D. dissertation, Brandeis University, 1981.

Baer, Yitzḥak. *A History of the Jews in Christian Spain.* 2 vols. Philadelphia, 1961.

Baqal, Meir, ed. *Sefer Pitron ha-Ḥalomot ha-Shalem.* Jerusalem, n.d.

Baron, Salo. *A Social and Religious History of the Jews,* 2nd ed. 18 vols. to date. New York, 1952–83.

Barukh, Y. L., ed. *Sefer ha-Shabbat.* Rev. ed. Tel-Aviv, 1980.

Bension, Ariel. *The Zohar in Moslem and Christian Spain.* London, 1932.

Ben-Shlomo, Joseph. *Torat ha-'Elohut shel R. Mosheh Cordovero.* Jerusalem, 1965.

Berger, Peter. *The Heretical Imperative.* Garden City, NY, 1979.

———. *The Sacred Canopy.* Garden City, NY, 1967.

Biale, David. *Gershom Scholem: History and Counter-History.* Cambridge, MA. 1979.

———. "The Kabbalah in Naḥman Krochmal's Philosophy of History." *Journal of Jewish Studies* 32 (1981): 85–97.

Bialik, H.N. "Gillui ve-Kissui be-Lashon." In *Divrei Sifrut.* Tel-Aviv, 1954.

———. "Halakhah ve-'Aggadah." In ibid.

Blau, Ludwig. "Die erste Ausgabe von Meir ibn Gabbais *Derekh 'Emunah.*" *Zeitschrift fur Hebraische Bibliographie* 10 (1906): 52–58.

Bloom, Harold. *Kabbalah and Criticism.* New York, 1975.

Blumenthal, David. *Understanding Jewish Mysticism,* Vol. 2. New York, 1982.

Bokser, Baruch. "Approaching Sacred Space." *Harvard Theological Review* 78:3–4 (1985).

Bowman, Steven. *The Jews of Byzantium.* University, Alabama, 1985.

———. "Mi Meḥabber Sefer ha-Qanah ve-Sefer ha-Peli'ah?" *Tarbiẓ* 54 (1985): 150–52.

Buber, Martin. *Ecstatic Confessions.* Edited by P. Mendes-Flohr. San Francisco, 1985.

Bynum, Caroline W., Harrell, Stevan, and Richman, Paula, eds. *Gender and Religion: On the Complexity of Symbols.* Boston, 1986.

Campbell, Joseph, ed. *Man and Transformation: Papers from the Eranos Yearbooks.* Princeton, 1972.

Carmi, T., ed. *The Penguin Book of Hebrew Verse.* New York, 1981.

Charlesworth, James, ed. *Old Testament Pseudepigrapha.* 2 vols. Garden City, NY, 1983–85.

Cohen, Arthur A. and Mendes-Flohr, Paul, eds. *Contemporary Jewish Religious Thought.* New York, 1987.

Cohen, Martin S. *The Shiʿur Qomah.* Lanham, MD, 1983.

Cooperman, Bernard Dov, ed. *Jewish Thought in the Sixteenth Century,* Cambridge, MA, 1983.

Dan, Joseph. "The Beginning of the Messianic Myth in 13th Century Kabbalah" [Hebrew]. Hebrew University Institute of Jewish Studies. Jerusalem, 1981.

———, ed. with Kiener, R., translator. *The Early Kabbalah.* New York, 1986.

———. "The Emergence of Mystical Prayer." In idem and Talmadge, F., eds. *AJS Studies in Jewish Mysticism,* pp. 85–120. Cambridge, MA, 1982.

———. *Ḥugei ha-Mequbbalim ha-Ri'shonim.* Jerusalem, 1980.

———. "Samael, Lilith, and the Concept of Evil in Early Kabbalah." *AJS Review* 5 (1980): 17–40.

———. *Torat ha-Sod shel Ḥasidei 'Ashkenaz.* Jerusalem, 1968.

Deikman, Arthur. "Deautomatization and the Mystic Experience." In R. Woods, ed. *Understanding Mysticism,* pp. 240–60. Garden City, NY, 1980.

Deshen, Shlomo and Shokeid, Moshe. *The Predicament of Homecoming.* Ithaca, 1974.

Douglas, Mary. *Natural Symbols.* New York, 1973.

———. *Purity and Danger.* London, 1966.

Eisenstein, J.D. *'Oẓar Dinim u-Minhagim.* New York, 1938.

Eisler, R. *Weltenmantel und Himmelszelt.* Munich, 1910.

Elbogen, Isaac. *Ha-Tefillah be-Yisra'el.* Edited and expanded by Joseph Heinemann. Tel-Aviv, 1972.

Eliade, Mircea. *Images and Symbols.* Kansas City, 1961.

———. *Myths, Dreams, and Mysteries.* New York, 1960.

———. *The Myth of the Eternal Return.* 2nd ed. Princeton, 1965.

———. *Patterns in Comparative Religion.* New York, 1958.

———. *The Sacred and the Profane.* New York, 1959.

———. *The Two and the One.* New York, 1965.

Ellwood, Robert. *Mysticism and Religion.* Englewood Cliffs, NJ, 1980.

Enelow, Hyman. "Midrash Hashkem Quotations in Alnaqua's Menorat ha-Maor." *Hebrew Union College Annual* 4 (1927): 311–43.

Farber, Asi. "Li-Mqorot Torato ha-Qabbalit ha-Mequdemet shel R. Moshe de Leon." *Meḥqerei Yerushalayim be-Maḥshevet Yisra'el* 3 (1984): 67–96.

———. "Qeṭa' Ḥadash me-Haqdamat R. Yosef Giqaṭilia le-Sefer Ginnat 'Egoz." *Meḥqerei Yerushalayim be-Maḥshevet Yisra'el* 1 (1981): 158–76.

Fernandez, James. "The Performance of Ritual Metaphors." In J. David Sapir, ed. *The Social Uses of Metaphor,* pp. 100–31. Philadelphia, 1977.

———. "Persuasions and Performances." In C. Geertz, ed. *Myth, Symbol and Culture,* pp. 39–60. New York, 1971.

Fine, Lawrence. *Safed Spirituality.* New York, 1984.

Finesinger, Sol. "The Custom of Looking at the Fingernails at the Outgoing of the Sabbath." *Hebrew Union College Annual* 12–13 (1937–38): 347–65.

Fingarette, Herbert. *The Self in Transformation.* New York, 1963.

Firth, Raymond. *Symbols: Public and Private.* Ithaca, 1973.

Fishbane, Michael. *Biblical Interpretation in Ancient Israel.* Oxford, 1985.

———. "The Sacred Center." In idem and P. Flohr, ed. *Texts and Responses: Studies Presented to N. N. Glatzer,* pp. 6–27. Leiden, 1975.

———. "The Teacher and the Hermeneutical Task: A Reinterpretation of the Hermeneutical Task." *Journal of the American Academy of Religion* 43 (1975): 709–21.

Fishman, Talya. "Women and Torah Study." *Kabbalah: A Newsletter of Current Research in Jewish Mysticism* 2:2 (1987): 4–6.

Foucault, Michel. *The Order of Things.* New York, 1970.

Frazer, Sir James. *The Golden Bough.* 3rd ed. Volume 3: *Taboos and Perils of the Soul.* New York, 1935.

Freud, Sigmund. *Complete Works.* Edited by J. Strachey. 24 vols. London, 1953–74.

Friedberg, Ch. *Beit ʿEqed Sefarim.* 2nd ed. 4 vols. Tel-Aviv, 1954.

Galili, Ze'ev. "Li-Sh'elat Meḥabber Perush 'Or ha-Ganuz la-Bahir ha-Meyuḥas le-R. Meir bar Shelomo Avi Sahula." *Meḥqerei Yerushalayim be-Maḥshevet Yisra'el* 4 (1985): 83–96.

Gaster, Theodor. *Festivals of the Jewish Year.* New York, 1953.

Geertz, Clifford. *The Interpretation of Cultures.* New York, 1973.

Gennep, Arnold van. *The Rites of Passage.* Translated by M. Vizedom and G. Caffee. Chicago, 1960.

Gilat, Yiẓḥaq. "ʿAl 39 'Avot Mela'khot Shabbat". *Tarbiẓ* 29 (1960): 228–38.

———. "Taʿanit Shabbat." *Tarbiẓ* 52 (1982/83): 1–15.

Ginsburg, Elliot. "The Sabbath in the Kabbalah." *Judaism* 31 (1982): 26–36.

———. *Sod ha-Shabbat (The Mystery of the Sabbath).* [From the *Tolaʿat Yaʿaqov* of R. Meir ibn Gabbai.] Albany, in press.

———. "Ẓelem 'Elohim: Some Thoughts on God and Person in Zoharic Kabbalah." In L. D. Shinn, ed. *In Search of the Divine,* pp. 61–94. New York, 1987.

Ginzberg, Louis. *The Legends of the Jews.* 7 vols. Translated by Henrietta Szold and Paul Radin. Philadelphia, 1968.

Gill, Sam. "Time." In K. Grim, ed. *Abingdon Dictionary of Living Religions,* pp. 759–62. Nashville, 1981.

Goetschal, Roland. *Meir ibn Gabbai: Le Discours de la Kabbale Espagnole.* Leuven, 1981.

Goitein, S.D. "Abraham Maimonides and his Pietist Circle." In A. Altmann, ed. *Jewish Medieval and Renaissance Studies,* pp. 145–64. Cambridge, MA, 1967.

Goldenberg, Robert. "The Broken Axis: Rabbinic Judaism and the Fall of Jerusalem." JAAR 45, Supplement (1977): 869–82.

———. "The Jewish Sabbath in the Roman World." In W. Haase and H. Temporini, eds. *Aufstieg und Niedergang der Romanischen Welt,* II.19.1, pp. 414–47. Berlin, 1979.

———. "Law and Spirit in Talmudic Religion." In A. Green, ed. *Jewish Spirituality* Vol. 1, pp. 232–52. New York, 1986.

Goldreich, Amos, ed., "Sefer Me'irat ᶜEinayim." Ph.D. dissertation, Hebrew University, 1981.

Gottlieb, Efraim. *Meḥqarim be-Sifrut ha-Qabbalah.* Edited by Joseph Hacker. Tel Aviv, 1976.

———. *Ha-Qabbalah be-Khitvei Rabbenu Baḥyya ben 'Asher.* Jerusalem, 1970.

———. *Ha-Qabbalah be-Sof ha-Me'ah ha-Shelosh ᶜEsreh.* Jerusalem, 1969.

Graetz, Heinrich. *History of the Jews.* 6 vols. Translated by Bella Lowy. Philadelphia, 1891–98.

Green, Arthur. "Bride, Spouse, Daughter: Images of the Feminine in Classical Jewish Sources." In Susannah Heschel, ed. *On Being a Jewish Feminist,* pp. 248–260. New York, 1983.

———, ed. *Jewish Spirituality.* Vol. 1. New York, 1986.

———. "Mysticism and Religion: The Case of Judaism." In J. Neusner, ed. *Take Judaism for Example,* pp. 67–91. Chicago, 1983.

———. "Sabbath as Temple: Some Thoughts on Space and Time in Judaism." In S. Fishman and R. Jospe, eds. *Go and Study: Essays and Studies in Honor of A. Jospe,* pp. 287–305. New York, 1982.

———. *Tormented Master: A Life of Rabbi Nahman of Bratslav.* University of Alabama, 1979.

———. "The Zohar: Jewish Mysticism in Medieval Spain." In P. Szarmach, ed. *An Introduction to the Medieval Mystics of Europe.* Albany, 1984.

Greenberg, Moshe. "Sabbath: In the Bible." EJ 14: 558–62.

Gries, Ze'ev. "ʿIzzuv Sifrut ha-Hanhagot ha-ʿIvrit be-Mifneh Me'ah ha-16 u-ve-Me'ah ha-17 u-Mashmaʿuto ha-Historit." *Tarbiz* 56 (1987): 527–81.

Grimes, Ronald. *Beginnings in Ritual Studies.* Washington, D.C., 1982.

Grossman, Avraham. *Ḥakhmei 'Ashkenaz ha-Qadmonim.* Jerusalem, 1981.

Gruenwald, Ithamar. *Apocalyptic and Merkavah Mysticism.* Leiden, 1980.

Guberman, Karen. "The Language of Love in Spanish Kabbalah: An Examination of the 'Iggeret ha-Qodesh." In D. Blumenthal, ed. *Approaches to Judaism in Medieval Times*, pp. 53–105. Chico, 1984.

Guttmann, Julius. *Philosophies of Judaism.* Translated by David W. Silverman. New York, 1964.

Habermann, Avraham. *Shirei ha-Yiḥud ve-ha-Kavod.* Jerusalem, 1948.

Hacker, Joseph. "Lamdutam ha-Ruḥanit shel Yehudei Sefarad be-Sof ha-Me'ah ha-15." *Sefunot* 17 (1983): 21–95.

Harvey, Zev. "Yesodot Qabbaliyyim be-Sefer 'Or ha-Shem le-R. Ḥasdai Crescas." *Meḥqerei Yerushalayim be-Maḥshevet Yisra'el* 2 (1982/83): 75–109.

Heinemann, Isaac. *Ṭaʿamei ha-Miẓvot be-Sifrut Yisra'el.* Vol. 1. 4th ed. Jerusalem, 1959.

Heinemann, Joseph. *Ha-Tefillah bi-Tqufat ha-Tanna'im ve-ha-'Amora'im.* 2nd ed. Jerusalem, 1966.

Heller-Wilensky, Sarah. "Isaac Ibn Latif: Philosopher or Kabbalist?" In A. Altmann, ed. *Jewish Medieval and Renaissance Studies*, pp. 185–223. Cambridge, MA, 1967.

Heschel, Abraham J. "ʿAl ha-Ruaḥ ha-Qodesh bi-Ymei ha-Beinayim." In S. Lieberman, ed. *Sefer ha-Yovel li-Khvod Alexander Marx* [Hebrew Volume], pp. 175–208. New York, 1950.

———. *The Sabbath.* New York, 1951.

Idel, Moshe. "Avraham Abulafia ve-ha-'Appifior." *AJS* Review 7–8 (1982–83): Hebrew Section 1–17.

———. "Demut ha-'Adam me-ʿal ha-Sefirot." *Daʿat* 4 (1980): 41–55.

———. "Ḥomer Qabbali mi-Beit Midrasho shel R. David ben Yehuda he-Ḥasid." *Meḥqerei Yerushalayim be-Maḥshevet Yisra'el* 2 (1983): 169–207.

———. "Infinities of Torah." In Geoffrey Hartman and Sanford Budick, eds. *Midrash and Literature.* New Haven, 1986.

———. "Le-Gilguleha shel Ṭekhniqah Qedumah shel Ḥazon Nevu'i bi-Ymei ha-Beinayyim." *Sinai* 86 (1980): 1–7.

———. *Kabbalah: New Perspectives.* New Haven, in press.

———. "Kitvei R. Avraham Abulafia u-Mishnato." Ph.D. thesis, Hebrew University, 1976.

———. "Magical and Neo-Platonic Interpretations of the Kabbalah." In B. Cooperman, ed. *Jewish Thought in the Sixteenth Century,* pp. 188–242. Cambridge, MA, 1983.

———. "The Magical and Theurgic Significance of Music in Jewish Texts from the Renaissance Period to Hasidism" [Hebrew]. *Yuval* 4 (1982): 33–63.

———. *The Mystical Experience in Abraham Abulafia.* Albany, 1988.

———. "Mysticism." In A. Cohen and P. Mendes-Flohr, eds. *Contemporary Jewish Religious Thought.* New York, 1987.

———. "Perush ᶜEser Sefirot u-Seridim mi-Ketavim shel R. Yosef ha-Ba' mi-Shushan ha-Birah." *ᶜAlei Sefer* 6–7 (1979): 74–84.

———. "Perush Lo' Yaduᶜa le-Sodot ha-RaMBaN." *Daᶜat* 2–3 (1978–79): 120–26.

———. "La prière kabbalistique et les couleurs." In R. Goetschal, ed. *Prière, Mystique et Judaisme,* pp. 107–19. Paris, 1987.

———. "Targumo shel R. David ben Yehuda he-Ḥasid le-Sefer ha-Zohar u-Ferushav la-'Alfa' Beita'." *ᶜAlei Sefer* 8 (1980): 60–72; 9 (1981): 84–98; and 10 (1982): 25–35.

———. "Tefisat ha-Torah be-Sifrut ha-Heikhalot ve-Gilguleha ba-Qabbalah." *Meḥqerei Yerushalayim be-Maḥshevet Yisra'el* 1 (1981): 23–84.

———. "Unio Mystica in Abraham Abulafia." In I. Twersky, ed. *Studies in Medieval Jewish History and Literature,* Vol. 3. Cambridge, MA, in press.

———. " 'We Have No Kabbalistic Tradition on This.' " In I. Twersky, ed. *Rabbi Moses Naḥmanides,* pp. 51–74. Cambridge, MA, 1983.

Idelsohn, I.Z. *Jewish Liturgy and its Development.* New York, 1960.

Jonas, Hans. *The Gnostic Religion.* 2nd ed. Boston, 1963.

Jung, Carl. *The Portable Jung.* Ed. by J. Campbell. New York, 1971.

Karpeles, G. *Geschichte der Judischen Literatur.* Berlin, 1921.

Kasher, Menaḥem. *Ḥummash Torah Shelemah.* Vols. 1- . New York, 1949- .

Katz, Jacob. *Out of the Ghetto.* New York, 1978.

———. *Halakhah ve-Qabbalah.* Rev. ed. Jerusalem, 1985.

Katz, Steven T., ed. *Mysticism and Philosophical Analysis.* New York, 1978.

———, ed. *Mysticism and Religious Traditions.* New York, 1983.

Kiener, Ronald. "Ibn al-ʿArabi and the Qabbalah." *Studies in Mystical Literature* 2 (1982): 26–52.

———. "The Status of Astrology in Early Kabbalah." *Meḥqerei Yerushalayim be-Maḥshevet Yisra'el* 6:3–4 (1987): 1–42, English section.

———, translator. See Dan, Joseph, ed.

Klibansky, R., Saxl, F., and Panofsky, E. *Saturn and Melacholy.* London, 1964.

Kugel, James. "Two Introductions to Midrash." In G. Hartman and S. Budick, eds. *Midrash and Literature,* pp. 77–103. New Haven, 1986.

Laird, D.A. "What Can You Do with Your Nose?" *Scientific Monthly* 4 (1935): 126–30.

Langer, Suzanne. *Philosophy in a New Key.* 3rd ed. Cambridge, MA, 1957.

Lauterbach, Jacob Z. "The Origin and Development of Two Sabbath Ceremonies." *Hebrew Union College Annual* 15 (1940): 367–424.

Lawless, H. and Engen, T. "Association to Odors: Interference, Mnemonics, and Verbal Labelling." *Journal of Experimental Psychology: Human Learning and Memory* 3 (1977): 52–59.

Leach, Edmund. *Culture and Communication.* Cambridge, 1976.

———. "The Symbolic Representation of Time." In W. Lessa and E. Vogt, eds. *A Reader in Comparative Religion,* 3rd ed., pp. 108–16. New York, 1972.

Leibreich, Leon. "An Analysis of U-Ba Le-Ziyyon." *Hebrew Union College Annual* 21 (1948): 175–209.

Levenson, Jon D. *Sinai and Zion.* Minneapolis, 1985.

Lewin, Benjamin. *'Oẓar ha-Ge'onim.* 12 vols. Haifa-Jerusalem, 1928–42.

Lieberman, Ḥayyim. *'Ohel RaḤeL.* Vol. 1. Brooklyn, 1980.

Liebes, Yehuda. "Ha-Mashiaḥ shel ha-Zohar." In *Ha-Raʿyon ha-Meshiḥi be-Yisra'el,* pp. 87–236. Jerusalem, 1982.

———. "Peraqim be-Millon Sefer ha-Zohar." Ph.D. dissertation, Hebrew University, 1976.

Lincoln, Bruce. "Treatment of Hair and Fingernails among the Indo-Europeans." *History of Religions* 16 (1977): 351–62.

Marcus, Ivan. *Piety and Society*. Leiden, 1982.

Marcus, Ralph. *Law in the Apocrypha*. New York, 1927.

Margaliot, Reuven. *Mal'akhei ᶜElyon*. Jerusalem, 1945.

Marmorstein, Arthur. "David ben Jehuda Hasid." *Monatsschrift fuer Geschichte und Wissenschaft des Judentums* 71 (1927): 39–48.

Matt, Daniel, ed. *The Book of Mirrors by R. David ben Yehudah he-Ḥasid*. Chico, 1982.

———. "David ben Yehuda Heḥasid and his *Book of Mirrors*." *Hebrew Union College Annual* 51 (1980): 129–72.

———. ed. and translator. *Zohar: The Book of Enlightenment*. New York, 1983.

Meier, Menaḥem. "A Critical Edition of the Sefer Taᶜamey ha-Mizwoth Attributed to Isaac Ibn Farhi/Section I". Ph.D. dissertation. Brandeis University, 1974.

Mendes-Flohr, Paul and Reinharz, Jehuda. *The Jew in the Modern World*. New York, 1980.

Meyer, Michael. *The Origins of the Modern Jew*. Detroit, 1967.

Moore, G. F. *Judaism*. 2 vols. New York, 1971.

Muẓapi, Ben Ẓion. *ᶜOlamo shel Ẓaddiq*. Jerusalem, 1985/86.

Myerhoff, Barbara. *Number Our Days*. New York, 1978.

Neusner, Jacob. *From Politics to Piety*. 2nd ed. New York, 1979.

———. *A History of the Jews in Babylonia*. 5 vols. Leiden, 1966–70.

———. "Innovation Through Repetition: The Role of Scripture in the Mishnah's Division of Appointed Times." *History of Religions* 21:1 (1981): 48–76.

———. "The Study of Religion as the Study of Tradition: Judaism." *History of Religions* 14 (1974): 191–206.

———. *There We Sat Down*. 2nd ed. New York, 1978.

———. *The Way of Torah*. 3rd ed. Belmont, CA, 1979.

Newsom, Carol. *Songs of the Sabbath Sacrifice: A Critical Edition*. Atlanta, 1985.

Noy, Dov. "Histakkelut ba-Ẓippornayim bi-Shᶜat ha-Havdalah." *Maḥanayim* 85–86 (1963): 166–73.

O'Flaherty, Wendy D. *Women, Androgynes, and Other Beasts.* Chicago, 1980.

Oron, Michal. "Ha-Peli'ah ve-ha-Qanah—Yesodot ha-Qabbalah she-bahem, ᶜEmdatam ha-Datit Ḥevratit ve-Derekh ᶜIẓẓuvam ha-Sifrutit." Ph.D. dissertation, Hebrew University, 1980.

———. "Mihu' Meḥabber Sefer ha-Peli'ah ve-Sefer ha-Qanah?" *Tarbiẓ* 54 (1985): 297–98.

Otto, Rudolf. *The Idea of the Holy.* 2nd ed. London, 1950.

Patai, Raphael. *Hebrew Goddess.* 2nd ed. New York, 1978.

———. *Man and Temple.* 2nd ed. New York, 1967.

Pieper, Josef. *Leisure: The Basis of Culture.* New York, 1952.

Polhemus, T. *Fashion and Anti-Fashion.* London, 1978.

Principe, Walter. "Mysticism: Its Meanings and Varieties." In H. Coward and T. Penelhum, eds. *Mystics and Scholars,* pp. 1–15. Waterloo, Ontario, 1977.

Rosenberg, Shalom. "Ha-Shivah le-Gan ᶜEden." In *Ha-Raᶜyon ha-Meshiḥi be-Yisra'el,* pp. 43–63. Jerusalem, 1982.

Rosenzweig, Franz. *The Star of Redemption.* Translated by W. Hallo. Boston, 1972.

Rubenstein, Richard. *After Auschwitz.* Indianapolis, 1966.

Santayana, George. *Reason in Religion.* New York, 1905.

Schaeffer, Peter. *Synopse zur Hekhalot Literatur.* Tübingen, 1981.

Schechter, Solomon. "Notes on Hebrew MSS in the University Library at Cambridge." *Jewish Quarterly Review* 4 (1892): 245–55.

———. *Studies in Judaism.* Philadelphia, 1908.

Schiffman, Lawrence. *The Halakhah at Qumran.* Leiden, 1975.

———. "Merkavah Speculation at Qumran: The 4Q Serekh Shirot ᶜOlat ha-Shabbat." In J. Reinharz and D. Swetchinski, eds. *Mystics, Philosophers and Politicians,* pp. 15–47. Durham, NC, 1982.

Scholem, Gershom. "Bil'ar, Melekh ha-Shedim." *Maddaᶜei ha-Yahadut* 1 (1925/26): 112–27.

———, ed. *Das Buch Bahir.* Leipzig, 1923. Reprint. Darmstadt, 1970.

———. *Devarim be-Go.* Edited by Avraham Shapira. 2 vols. Tel-Aviv, 1976.

———. "Eine unbekannte mystische Schrifte des Mose de Leon." *Monatsschrift fuer Geschichte und Wissenschaft des Judentums* 71 (1927).

———. "Havdalah de-R. Aqiva." *Tarbiẓ* 50 (1982): 243–81.

———. *Jewish Gnosticism, Merkabah Mysticism and Talmudic Tradition.* New York, 1965.

———. *Kabbalah.* Jerusalem, 1974.

———. "Le-Ḥeqer Qabbalat R. Yiẓḥaq ben Yaaqov ha-Kohen." *Tarbiẓ* 2 (1931): 188–217 and 415–42; 3 (1932): 33–66 and 258–86; 4 (1933): 54–77 and 205–25; 5 (1934): 50–60, 180–98 and 305–23.

———. "Li-Ydiᶜat ha-Qabbalah bi-Sfarad ᶜErev ha-Gerush." *Tarbiẓ* 24 (1954): 167–206.

———. *Major Trends in Jewish Mysticism.* 3rd ed. New York, 1967.

———. "Me-Ḥoqer li-Mqubbal." *Tarbiẓ* 6 (1939): 334–42.

———. *The Messianic Idea in Judaism.* New York, 1971.

———. "Mysticism and Society." *Diogenes* 58 (1967): 1–24.

———. *On the Kabbalah and its Symbolism.* New York, 1965.

———. *Origins of the Kabbalah.* Translated by A. Arkush. Princeton, 1987.

———. "Peraqim be-Toledot Sifrut ha-Qabbalah." *Kiryat Sefer* 4 (1926): 286–327.

———. *Pirqei Yesod be-Havanat ha-Qabbalah u-Semaleha.* Translated by J. Ben-Shlomo. Jerusalem, 1976.

———. *Ha-Qabbalah be-Gerona.* Jerusalem, 1963/64.

———. *Ha-Qabbalah be-Provans.* Jerusalem, 1970.

———. *Ha-Qabbalah shel Sefer ha-Temunah ve-shel 'Avraham 'Abulᶜafiah.* Jerusalem, 1969.

———. "Qabbalot R. Yaaqov ve-R. Yiẓḥaq ha-Kohen." *Maddaᶜei ha-Yahadut* 2 (1926/27): 165–93.

———. *Re'shit ha-Qabbalah.* Jerusalem, 1948.

———. *Re'shit ha-Qabbalah ve-Sefer ha-Bahir.* Jerusalem, 1961/62.

———. *Sabbatai Ṣevi.* Translated by R. J. Z. Werblowsky. Princeton, 1973.

———. "Sefer Ḥemdat Yamim le-Rabbi Shalem Shabbazi." *Kiryat Sefer* 5 (1927/28): 267–72.

———. "Sidrei de-Shimmusha' Rabba'." *Tarbiẓ* 16 (1945): 196–209.

———. "Teᶜudah Ḥadashah le-Toledot Re'shit ha-Qabbalah." In J. Fichman, ed. *Sefer Bialik*, pp. 141–62. Tel Aviv, 1934.

———. *Urpsrung und Anfange der Kabbala*. Berlin, 1962.

———. *Von der mystischen Gestalt der Gottheit*. Zurich, 1962.

———. "Yediᶜot Ḥadashot ᶜal R. Yosef 'Ashkenazi ha-Tana' mi-Ẓefat." *Tarbiẓ* 28 (1958): 58–59 and 201–09.

———. *Zur Kabbala und ihrer Symbolik*. Zurich, 1960.

Sed-Rajna, Gabrielle. "De quelques commentaires kabbalistique sure le rituel dans les manuscrits de le Bibliotheque Nationale de Paris." *Revue des Etudes Juives* 124 (1965): 307–51.

Schutz, Alfred. *The Collected Papers*. Vols. 1–2. The Hague, 1962.

Schweid, Eliezer. "Misṭiqah Yehudit le-fi G. Shalom." *Meḥqerei Yerushalayim be-Maḥshevet Yisra'el*, Supplement to Vol. 2 (1982/83). 88 pages.

———. *Judaism and Mysticism*. Atlanta, 1985.

Septimus, Bernard. *Hispano-Jewish Culture in Transition*. Cambridge, MA, 1982.

———. "Power and Piety in Thirteenth Century Catalonia." In I. Twersky, ed. *Studies in Medieval Jewish History and Literature*, pp. 197–230. Cambridge, MA, 1979.

Shaḥar, Shulamit. "Ha-Catarism ve-Re'shit ha-Qabbalah be-Languedoc." *Tarbiẓ* 40 (1971): 483–507.

———. "The Relationship between Kabbalism and Catharism in the South of France." In Miryam Yardeni, ed. *Les Juifs dans l'histoire de France*, pp. 55–62. Leiden, 1980.

Sharf, Andrew. *The Universe of Shabbetai Donnolo*. Warminster, 1976.

Sharot, Stephen. *Messianism, Mysticism and Magic*. Chapel Hill, 1982.

Sharvit, B. "The Sabbath of the Judean Desert Sect" [Hebrew]. *Beit Miqra'* 21 (1976): 507–16.

Shinn, Larry. *Two Sacred Worlds*. Nashville, 1977.

Shoham, Uri. *Ha-Mashmaᶜut ha-'Aḥeret*. Tel-Aviv, 1982.

Shtall, Avraham. "Qeri'ah Pulḥanit shel Sefer ha-Zohar." *Peᶜamim* 5 (1980): 77–86.

Smith, Jonathan Z. *To Take Place: Toward Theory in Ritual*. Chicago, 1987.

Sperling, Avraham. *Sefer Ṭaᶜamei ha-Minhagim u-Meqorei ha-Dinim.* Lwow, 1895/96. Reprint. Jerusalem, 1972.

Steiner, George. *After Babel: Aspects of Language and Translation.* New York, 1975.

Steinsaltz, Adin. *The Thirteen Petalled Rose.* Translated by Y. Hanegbi. New York, 1980.

Ta-Shma, Israel. "ᶜAl Kammah ᶜInyanei Maḥzor Viṭri." *ᶜAlei Sefer* 11 (1984): 81–89.

———. "Be'erah shel Miriam." *Meḥqerei Yerushalayim be-Maḥshevet Yisra'el* 4 (1985): 251–70.

———. "Heikhan Nitḥabberu Sifrei ha-Qanah ve-ha-Peli'ah?" In *Peraqim be-Toledot ha-Ḥevrah ha-Yehudit bi-Ymei ha-Beinayim u-va-ᶜEt ha-Ḥadashah* [Festchrift for Jacob Katz], pp. 56–63. Jerusalem, 1980.

———. "Tosefet Shabbat." *Tarbiẓ* 52 (1982/83): 309–23.

Talmadge, Frank. "Apples of Gold: The Inner Meaning of Sacred Texts in Medieval Judaism." In Arthur Green, ed. *Jewish Spirituality.* Vol. 1, pp. 313–55. New York, 1986.

Tigay, Jeffrey. "Shabbat." In *'Enẓiqloppediah Miqra'it,* Vol. 7:504–21. Jerusalem, 1981.

Tirosh-Rothschild, Ḥava. "Sefirot as the Essence of God in the Writings of David Messer Leon." *AJS Review* 7–8 (1982–83): 409–25.

Tishby, Isaiah. *Ḥiqrei ha-Qabbalah u-Sheluḥoteha.* Jerusalem, 1982.

———. *Meshiḥiut be-Dor Gerushei Sefarad u-Porṭugal.* Jerusalem, 1985.

———. *Netivei 'Emunah u-Minut.* Ramat-Gan, 1964.

Tishby, Isaiah with Lachover, Fishel. *Mishnat ha-Zohar.* 2 vols. Jerusalem, 1957–61.

Trachtenberg, Joshua. *Jewish Magic and Superstition.* New York, 1939.

Tsevat, Mattityahu. "The Basic Meaning of the Biblical Sabbath." *Zeitschrift Altestamentliche Wissenschaft* 84 (1972): 447–59.

Turner, Victor. "The Center Out There: Pilgrim's Goal." *History of Religions* 12 (1973): 191–230.

———. *Dramas, Fields and Metaphors.* Ithaca, 1974.

———. *The Forest of Symbols.* Ithaca, 1967.

———. *The Ritual Process.* Ithaca, 1969.

Twersky, Isadore, ed. *Rabbi Moses Naḥmanides.* Cambridge, MA, 1983.

———. *Rabad of Posquieres,* rev. ed. Philadelphia, 1980.

Twersky, Isadore and Septimus, Bernard, eds. *Jewish Thought in the Seventeenth Century.* Cambridge, MA, 1987.

Urbach, Ephraim. *Ḥazal: Pirqei 'Emunot ve-De‘ot.* Jerusalem, 1971.

———. *The Sages.* 2 vols. Translated by I. Abrahams. Jerusalem, 1979.

Vajda, Georges. "The Mystical Doctrine of R. ‘Obadyah." *Journal Of Jewish Studies* 6 (1955): 213–25.

———. *Rècherches sur la philosophie et la kabbale dans la pensèe juive du moyen age.* Paris, 1962.

Vaux, Roland de. *Ancient Israel.* New York, 1961.

Verman, Mark. "Sifrei ha-‘Iyyun: The Circle of Contemplation." Ph.D. dissertation, Harvard University, 1984.

Werblowsky, R. J. Zwi. *Joseph Karo, Lawyer and Mystic.* Oxford, 1962.

Wertheimer, Jack. *Unwelcome Strangers: East European Jews in Imperial Germany.* New York, 1987.

Wijnhoven, J. H. A. "Medieval Jewish Mysticism." In *Bibliographic Essays in Medieval Jewish Studies,* pp. 269–332. New York, 1976.

———. "The Zohar and the Proselyte." In M. Fishbane and P. Flohr, eds. *Texts and Responses: Studies Presented to N.N. Glatzer,* pp. 269–332. Leiden, 1975.

Wilhem, Yiẓḥaq. "Sidrei Tiqqunim." In *‘Alei Sefer,* pp. 125–46. Jerusalem, 1948–52.

Winston, David. *Philo of Alexandria.* New York, 1981.

Wolfson, Elliot. "Left Contained in the Right: A Study in Zoharic Hermeneutics." *AJS Review* 11 (1986): 27–52.

———. "By Way of Truth: Aspects of Naḥmanides' Kabbalistic Hermeneutics." *AJS Review* 13, forthcoming.

Woods, Richard, ed. *Understanding Mysticism.* Garden City, NY, 1980.

Yaari, Avraham. "Sefer Pesaḥ la-Shem le-R. Ḥayyim ben Meir ibn Gabbai." *Kiryat Sefer* 9 (1933): 388–93.

Yates, Frances. *The Occult Philosophy.* London, 1979.

Zaehner, R.C. *Zurvan: A Zoroastrian Dilemma.* Oxford, 1955.

Zborowski, M. and Herzog, E. *Life is with People.* New York, 1952.

Zerubavel, Eviatar. *Hidden Rhythms*. Chicago, 1981.

Zimmer, Yiẓḥaq. "Moʿadei Nesi'at Kappayim." *Sinai* 100 (1987): 452–70.

Zinberg, Israel. *A History of Jewish Literature*. 13 vols. Translated by B. Martin. Cleveland and New York, 1972–78.

Zlotnick, Y.L. "Me-'Aggadot ha-Shabbat u-Minhageha." *Sinai* 25 (1950): 75–89.

Index

This index is designed to help locate authors, titles and subjects that appear in the body of the text and in the endnotes. Classical works cited in the endnotes *en passant* have generally been omitted. Detailed information has been provided in certain cases: Biblical, Rabbinic, *Bahir*, and Zoharic references have been annotated; and a sefirotic lexicon, provided. Key Hebrew and technical terms have also been indexed (and their definitions cited) to aid the non-specialist.

Job, Book of, 19:26, p. 193; 28:7, p. 32; 41:19, p. 293

CPSIA information can be obtained at www.ICGtesting.com
Printed in the USA
BVOW031117281212

309010BV00006B/33/A

9 781904 113430